HARVARD ECONOMIC STUDIES

VOLUME XXXVIII

AWARDED THE DAVID A. WELLS PRIZE FOR THE YEAR 1927–28 AND
PUBLISHED FROM THE INCOME OF THE DAVID A. WELLS FUND

THE STUDIES IN THIS SERIES ARE PUBLISHED BY THE DEPARTMENT
OF ECONOMICS OF HARVARD UNIVERSITY, WHICH, HOWEVER,
ASSUMES NO RESPONSIBILITY FOR THE VIEWS EXPRESSED

The Theory of
Monopolistic Competition

A Re-orientation of the Theory of Value

BY

EDWARD HASTINGS CHAMBERLIN

*David A. Wells Professor of Political Economy
in Harvard University*

Eighth Edition

CAMBRIDGE, MASSACHUSETTS

HARVARD UNIVERSITY PRESS

1965

Second printing

DISTRIBUTED IN GREAT BRITAIN BY
OXFORD UNIVERSITY PRESS, LONDON

PRINTED AT THE HARVARD UNIVERSITY PRINTING OFFICE

CAMBRIDGE, MASS., U. S. A.

To

MY MOTHER

PREFACE TO THE EIGHTH EDITION

The eighth (and certainly the final) edition of this book includes three new Appendices: F, The Definition of Selling Costs; G, Numbers and Elasticities; and H, The Origin and Early Development of Monopolistic Competition Theory. The practice of extending the Bibliography with each edition has been dropped. Its projected rate of growth (see Preface to the preceding edition) was such that it was quite out of the question even to consider carrying it further than 1956.

Appendix F on the Definition of Selling Costs is new in print, although former students will recall a long-standing acknowledgment of the need for changes in Chapter VI and discussion over the years of the issues involved in seminars in which they took part.

Appendix G on Numbers and Elasticities is reprinted with permission from *Festkrift til Frederik Zeuthen*, Copenhagen, 1958. It deals with the generally accepted proposition that the larger the number of sellers in a market, the greater is the elasticity of demand for the product of each seller; develops further the conclusion (p. 198, below) that for a differentiated product generalization is not possible, and shows that even for a homogeneous product the proposition is true only under certain special assumptions.

Appendix H on the Origin and Early Development of Monopolistic Competition Theory is reprinted from the *Quarterly Journal of Economics* of November 1961. From its nature it should appear as a "Foreword" to the book, instead of as the last of the Appendices. Above all, it should have been written in 1933 instead of 1961. But unfortunately (to refer to its second paragraph) I had at the earlier time no idea of the "subsequent developments." The article has evoked many letters, but I have been especially gratified to discover how many there were who found in it not merely an interesting bit of "intellectual history" (which might have been written at any time), but a contribution to understanding; and who have commented explicitly on "what a pity" it was that it was not written many years ago.

The new material has been indexed by Miss Karen Polenske, who at the same time has reworked and greatly improved the index as a whole.

E. H. C.

CAMBRIDGE, MASSACHUSETTS
JUNE, 1962

PREFACE TO THE SEVENTH EDITION

The principal change in the seventh edition is the inclusion of a new supplement to the bibliography, embracing the period from May 1948 to May 1956 and reprinted from the *Quarterly Journal of Economics* for November 1956. The last earlier supplement, covering a period of seven years, had added only 234 items, and something of similar magnitude was expected when it was decided to bring the list down to 1956. However, these eight years, even with many omissions for "brevity," yielded 806 titles, or more than the entire period prior to 1948, and brought the total to 1497. (In partial explanation of other omissions, it should be stated that the search was not carried beyond the resources of Harvard University Library, except for reprints received and a few items brought to my attention by others.) In order to find the writings of any particular person in the total bibliography it is now necessary to look in three places, since each supplement has been alphabetized separately in order not to disturb the numbering of the earlier items.

With this seventh edition, I should like to recall the statement in the Preface to the first, that "the book deals, not with a special and narrow problem, but with the whole of value theory." [1] In recent writing I have continued to stress this role of monopolistic competition as a general theory, both with respect to its relevance to the various "applied" fields without exception, and to its "neutrality" on the issues of short- vs. long-run, partial vs. general equilibrium, static vs. dynamic, etc. I do believe that the bibliographical expansion with this edition contains important evidence that some small progress is being made in its recognition as such a theory.

E. H. C.

CAMBRIDGE, MASSACHUSETTS
MAY, 1956

[1] This general character of the theory is developed at length in "Towards a More General Theory of Value," Essay 1 in my book of the same title (New York, Oxford University Press, 1957).

FROM THE

PREFACE TO THE SIXTH EDITION

Corrections and small changes too numerous to mention have been made in the various printings and editions since the first one. The bibliography was added with the second edition, supplemented in the third, and more than doubled in the fourth, the whole being integrated into one list. A further supplement with the sixth edition contains items up to May, 1948.

The greater part, but not all of those added with the fourth edition appeared as "A Supplementary Bibliography on Monopolistic Competition" in the *Quarterly Journal of Economics* for November, 1941, in the preparation of which I had the valuable assistance of Dr. Robert Triffin and financial aid from the Committee on Research in the Social Sciences at Harvard. Those added with the sixth edition appeared in the *Quarterly Journal of Economics* for August, 1948. Beginning with the third edition, a paper on "Monopolistic Competition and the Productivity Theory of Distribution," dating from 1933, has been reprinted as Chapter VIII, through the courtesy of the McGraw-Hill Book Company, publishers of *Explorations in Economics*, in which it first appeared in its present form.

In the fifth edition another chapter was added, entitled "The Difference between Monopolistic and 'Imperfect' Competition," a revision of an article, "Monopolistic or Imperfect Competition?" appearing in the *Quarterly Journal of Economics* for August, 1937.

.   .   .   .

In the sixth edition a further supplement to the bibliography has already been noted, and there have been numerous other small changes. A new analysis of the cost curve of the firm also appears, taking the place of the original Appendix B. The central thesis of the former treatment was the same as that of the present one: that "the problems of proportion and of size cannot ordinarily be separated . . . the most efficient proportion depends upon the size"; a conclusion in itself strikingly out of harmony with prevailing doctrine. But it was maintained in part by means of another commonly accepted proposition: that the assumption of perfect divisibility of factors causes economies of scale to disappear. This latter has been out of harmony for years with my own classroom teaching, and is now expressly repudiated. The present Appendix B deals with this and numerous other matters. It is a reprint (with only slight changes) of an article, "Proportionality, Divisibility and Economies of Scale," in the *Quarterly Journal of Economics* for February, 1948.

E. H. C.

CAMBRIDGE, MASSACHUSETTS
    MAY, 1948

PREFACE TO THE FIRST EDITION

THE title of this book is apt to be misleading, since I have given to the phrase "monopolistic competition" a meaning slightly different from that given it by other writers.[1] Professor Young once suggested "The Theory of Imperfect Competition," and this, although it had to be discarded as inaccurate, comes close to describing the *scope* of the subject. The book deals, not with a special and narrow problem, but with the whole of value theory. Its thesis is that both monopolistic and competitive forces combine in the determination of most prices, and therefore that a hybrid theory affords a more illuminating approach to the study of the price system than does a theory of perfected competition, supplemented by a theory of monopoly. The analytical technique which emerges is distinctive, both from that of the familiar theories of competition and of monopoly, and from any simple compromise between them. A comparison of the conclusions with those of pure competition indicates that economic theory is often remote and unreal, not because the method is wrong, but because the underlying assumptions are not as closely in accord with the facts as they might be.

This study first took form in the two years preceding April 1, 1927, at which date it was submitted as a doctor's thesis in Harvard University.[2] Since that time it has been completely rewritten. Chapter III has appeared, in substantially the same form as now, in the *Quarterly Journal of Economics* for November, 1929.

In the revision the scope of the problem has been more rigidly defined, and the argument throughout has been re-oriented in order to achieve greater unity and logical consistence. Much that was irrelevant to the main conclusions of the theory has been eliminated, gaps have been filled in, and the methods of approach to different phases of the problem have been brought into agree-

---

[1] Professor Pigou, in particular, has used the term to describe what is here regarded as only a portion of the problem, *viz.* oligopoly.

[2] See Appendix H for a more complete account.

ment with each other. Sometimes the conclusions have been slightly altered, but on the whole, the argument as it now appears is merely a more tenable formulation (I hope) of the thesis advanced and filed in Harvard University Library in 1927.

I wish to express my gratitude to Professors F. W. Taussig and J. A. Schumpeter for advice and suggestions; to Professor E. S. Mason and Dr. A. E. Monroe for reading and criticising the manuscript; to Professors W. C. Graustein and W. L. Crum for advice with respect to Appendix A; and to Drs. D. V. Brown and O. H. Taylor for suggestions which were helpful in rewriting Chapter VI. But most of all, I am indebted to the late Professor Allyn A. Young, under whose guidance this study was first written as a doctor's thesis. He encouraged me with a lively interest in the project as it developed, and his kindly and acute criticisms have contributed greatly to such validity and clarity as the theory may have.

E. H. C.

Cambridge, Massachusetts
    October, 1932

CONTENTS

THE THEORY OF MONOPOLISTIC
COMPETITION

CHAPTER I

INTRODUCTION

ECONOMIC literature affords a curious mixture, confusion and separation, of the ideas of competition and monopoly. On the one hand, analysis has revealed the differences between them and has led to the perfection and refinement of a separate body of theory for each. Although the two forces are complexly interwoven, with a variety of design, throughout the price system, the fabric has been undone and refashioned into two, each more simple than the original and bearing to it only a partial resemblance. Furthermore, it has, in the main, been assumed that the price system is like this — that all the phenomena to be explained are *either* competitive *or* monopolistic, and therefore that the expedient of two purified and extreme types of theory is adequate.

On the other hand, the facts of intermixture in real life have subtly worked against that complete theoretical distinction between competition and monopoly which is essential to a clear understanding of either. Because *actual* competition (rarely free of monopoly elements) is supposedly explained by the theory of *pure* competition, familiar results really attributable to monopolistic forces are readily associated with a theory which denies them. This association of the theory of competition with facts which it does not fit has not only led to false conclusions about the facts; it has obscured the theory as well. This is the more serious because the mixture of the two forces is a chemical process and not merely a matter of addition. Slight elements of monopoly have a way of playing unexpected logical tricks, with results quite out of proportion to their seeming importance.

For example, Cournot and Edgeworth, in the problem of "duopoly," or price determination where there are only two competing sellers, arrive at wholly different solutions, although each is attacking, with the precision of mathematical methods, the same problem. Cournot's solution is that price is determinate and will lie between the monopoly price and the "perfectly" competitive price (where the number of sellers is infinite). Edgeworth's is that it is indeterminate, oscillating continually between the two extremes. The differences are explained in part [1] by the fact that competition, supposedly pure except for the fewness of sellers, really contains, in the case as put by Edgeworth, certain other monopoly elements which affect the result.

As another instance, we have the paradoxical reasoning of Professor J. M. Clark, in his analysis of the market: "If all the competitors followed suit instantly the moment any cut was made, each would gain his quota of the resulting increase in output, and no one would gain any larger proportion of his previous business than a monopoly would gain by a similar cut in prices. Thus the competitive cutting of prices would naturally stop exactly where it would if there were no competition." [2] *Perfect* competition, it would seem, gives the same price as perfect monopoly! [3] His conclusion, that it is the "qualified monopoly" enjoyed by each producer which makes the market really competitive after all, and which accordingly permits price reductions, seems only still further to confuse the matter. From a somewhat different point of view, Professor Knight comments that "there does seem to be a certain Hegelian self-contradiction in the idea of theoretically perfect competition after all." [4] These contradictions and paradoxes arise, however, because supposedly perfect competition is really imperfect. The first step in the formulation of a theory of prices must be a clear definition of the two fundamental forces of competition and monopoly, and an examination of each in isolation.

The second step must be a synthesis of the two. This brings us back to the assertion that price theories have followed, in the main, the two extreme channels, without (conscious) recognition of a middle course. Quantitatively, competitive theory has domi-

---

[1] Other factors enter in. The problem is considered at length in Chapter III.

[2] *The Economics of Overhead Costs*, p. 417.

[3] And if we now regard perfect competition as a norm which prices under imperfect competition more or less closely approximate, we reach the startling conclusion that they approximate monopoly prices.

[4] *Risk, Uncertainty and Profit*, p. 193.

nated — indeed, the theory of competition has been so generally accepted as the underlying explanation of the price system that the presumption is in its favor; its inadequacy remains to be proved. Hints at the ubiquity of monopoly elements and at the possibility of an intermediate theory are not entirely lacking, however. Thus Professor Knight remarks that "in view of the fact that practically every business is a partial monopoly, it is remarkable that the theoretical treatment of economics has related so exclusively to complete monopoly and perfect competition,"[1] and Veblen, " . . . it is very doubtful if there are any successful business ventures within the range of modern industries from which the monopoly element is wholly absent."[2] Such fragmentary recognition of the problem is not hard to find.[3] Yet, with the exception of the theory of duopoly, the middle ground between competition and monopoly remains virtually unexplored and the possibilities of applying such a theory relatively little appreciated.[4]

[1] *Ibid.*, p. 193, note. [2] *The Theory of Business Enterprise*, p. 54.

[3] See below, p. 69, note 2, for further citations, referring especially to the idea of a *separate market* for each seller.

[4] Since the above was written, three new writers have championed the cause of an intermediate theory. Professor Sraffa, in an article entitled "The Laws of Returns Under Competitive Conditions" (*Economic Journal*, Vol. XXXVI, [1926]), issues a call "to abandon the path of free competition and turn in the opposite direction, namely, towards monopoly" (p. 542). "We are . . . led to believe," he says, "that when production is in the hands of a large number of concerns entirely independent of one another as regards control, the conclusions proper to competition may be applied even if the market in which the goods are exchanged is not absolutely perfect, for its imperfections are in general constituted by frictions which may simply retard or slightly modify the effects of the active forces of competition, but which the latter ultimately succeed in substantially overcoming. This view appears to be fundamentally inadmissible. Many of the obstacles which break up that unity of the market which is the essential condition of competition are not of the nature of 'frictions,' but are themselves active forces which produce permanent and even cumulative effects. They are frequently, moreover, endowed with sufficient stability to enable them to be made the subject of analysis based on statical assumptions." He proceeds to such an analysis, in which there are striking parallels with some of the ideas presented in subsequent chapters. See also Appendix H, especially pp. 308–311. (At the time when Professor Sraffa's article appeared, the present study, submitted as a doctor's thesis at Harvard University, April 1, 1927, was virtually completed.)

Similarly, Professor Hotelling ("Stability in Competition," *Economic Journal*, Vol. XXXIX, [1929]) criticizes economic theory because it has not generally taken account of "the existence with reference to each seller of groups of buyers who will deal with him instead of with his competitors in spite of a difference in price. . . .

"Pure competition" is taken as a point of departure, the adjective "pure" being chosen deliberately to describe competition unalloyed with monopoly elements. It is a much simpler and less inclusive concept than "perfect" competition, for the latter may be interpreted to involve perfection in many other respects than in the absence of monopoly. It may imply, for instance, an absence of friction in the sense of an ideal fluidity or mobility of factors such that adjustments to changing conditions which actually involve time are accomplished instantaneously in theory. It may imply perfect knowledge of the future and the consequent absence of uncertainty.[1] It may involve such further "perfection" as the particular theorist finds convenient and useful to his problem. Two illustrations will serve to bring out the contrast between pure and perfect competition. The actual price of wheat approximates very inaccurately its normal price, yet the individual wheat farmer possesses not a jot of monopoly power. The market, though a very imperfect one, is purely competitive.[2] On the other hand, monopoly may exist under conditions which are "perfect," or "ideal," in other respects. The static state and perfect competition are wrongly treated as synonymous by J. B. Clark. There is no reason whatever why monopoly of all sorts and degrees should not be present in a state where the conditions as to population, the supply of capital, technology, organization, and wants

Such circles of customers may be said to make every entrepreneur a monopolist within a limited class and region — and there is no monopoly which is not confined to a limited class and region. The difference between the Standard Oil Company in its prime and the little corner grocery is quantitative rather than qualitative. Between the perfect competition and monopoly of theory lie the actual cases" (p. 44). He develops the consequences of such individual markets with particular reference to competition among a small number of entrepreneurs.

Finally, Dr. Zeuthen (*Problems of Monopoly and Economic Warfare*, London, 1930) states the case strongly, perhaps too strongly: "Neither monopoly nor competition are ever absolute, and the theories about them deal only with the outer margins of reality, which is always to be sought between them. A treatment of reality as if it were identical with one of the marginal instances is one-sided and mistaken, whilst the correct indication of the margins alone is insufficient; consequently we ought to study this sphere of reality instead of the purely marginal instances" (p. 62). His book is a notable contribution to the subject.

[1] Professor Knight, *op. cit.*, lays particular stress on this aspect of perfect competition.

[2] It is the long run market which is meant. The market, of course, is not free from manipulation which is a form of partial monopoly control over short periods.

remained unchanged. "Pure" and "perfect" competition must not be identified; and to consider the theory of monopolistic competition vaguely as a theory of "imperfect" competition is to confuse the issues.

Monopoly ordinarily means control over the supply, and therefore over the price. A sole prerequisite to pure competition is indicated — that no one have any degree of such control.[1] This, however, may be analyzed into two phases. In the first place, there must be a large number of buyers and sellers so that the influence of any one or of several in combination is negligible. There is no need that their numbers be infinite (although to treat them for certain purposes as though they were is perfectly legitimate and necessary), but they must be large enough so that, even though any single individual has, in fact, a slight influence upon the price, he does not exercise it because it is not worth his while. If the individual seller produces on the assumption that his entire output can be disposed of at the prevailing or market price, and withholds none of it, there is pure competition so far as numbers are concerned, no matter at what price he actually disposes of it, and how much influence he actually exerts.

Secondly, control over price is completely eliminated only when all producers are producing the identical good and selling it in the identical market. Goods must be perfectly homogeneous, or standardized, for if the product of any one seller is slightly different from those of others, he has a degree of control over the price of his own variety, whereas under pure competition he can have no control over the price of anything. If his product is slightly different from others, it would be a mistake for the producer to proceed on the assumption that he can sell any amount of it at the going price, since buyers might prefer other varieties and take larger amounts of his own only at a price sacrifice or through the persuasion of advertising. (This is the circumstance in which the ordinary business man finds himself, and this is why most markets are not purely competitive.)

Not only goods, but sellers, must be "standardized" under pure

---

[1] I do not mean to assert, as did Cournot, that all of my conclusions are derived from a single hypothesis!

competition. Anything which makes buyers prefer one seller to another, be it personality, reputation, convenient location, or the tone of his shop, differentiates the thing purchased to that degree, for what is bought is really a bundle of utilities, of which these things are a part. The utilities offered by all sellers to all buyers must be identical, otherwise individual sellers have a degree of control over their individual prices.[1] Under such conditions it is evident that buyers and sellers will be paired in "random" fashion in a large number of transactions. It will be entirely a matter of chance from which seller a particular buyer makes his purchase, and purchases over a period of time will be distributed among all according to the law of probability. After all, this is only another way of saying that the product is homogeneous.

The two requirements for pure competition suggest at once the two ways in which monopolistic and competitive elements may be blended. In the first place, there may be one, few, or many selling the identical product in the identical market. Here the common market is shared by all, and such control over price as any one has is a control over the single price at which all must sell. A condition of monopoly shades gradually into one of pure competition as the sellers increase in number. The theory of value for the intermediate ground in this case has been treated, mainly by the mathematical economists, with particular reference to the problem of two sellers, or "duopoly," and we may extend this terminology, adding "oligopoly" for a few sellers.[2] After a consideration of pure competition (Chapter II), this case will be taken up in Chapter III.

In the second place, sellers may be offering identical, slightly different, or very different products. If they are identical, competition is pure (provided also that the number of sellers is very large). With differentiation appears monopoly, and as it proceeds

[1] It might be argued that the utilities purchased would be the same only if the buyers also were "standardized," since they may put the goods to different uses or value them for different reasons. This does not seem to follow. "Utility" means the *capacity* to satisfy a want, and this remains the same regardless of the variety of uses to which individual units of a good may be put.

[2] It came to my attention (in 1936) that the term "oligopoly" was used as early as 1914 by Karl Schlesinger, *Theorie der Geld- und Kreditwirtschaft*, pp. 17, 18, 57. See also "The Origin of Oligopoly," *Economic Journal*, June 1957 (Essay 2 in *Towards a More General Theory of Value*).

further the element of monopoly becomes greater. Where there is any degree of differentiation whatever, each seller has an absolute monopoly of his own product, but is subject to the competition of more or less imperfect substitutes. Since each is a monopolist and yet has competitors, we may speak of them as "competing monopolists," and, with peculiar appropriateness, of the forces at work as those of "monopolistic competition." [1] This case is taken up beginning with Chapter IV.[2]

It is this latter problem which is of especial interest and importance. In all of the fields where individual products have even the slightest element of uniqueness, competition bears but faint resemblance to the pure competition of a highly organized market for a homogeneous product. Consider, for instance, the competitive analysis as applied to the automobile industry. How is one to conceive of demand and supply curves for "automobiles in general" when, owing to variations in quality, design, and type, the prices of individual units range from several hundred to many thousands of dollars? How define the number of units which would be taken from or put upon the market at any particular price? How fit into the analysis a wide variety of costs based mostly upon a correspondingly wide variety of product? These difficulties are great; perhaps they are not insurmountable. The real one is neither of definition nor of interpretation, and cannot be surmounted. Competitive theory does not fit because competition throughout the group is only partial and is highly uneven. The competition between sport roadsters and ten-ton trucks must be virtually zero; and there is probably more justification for drawing up a joint demand schedule for Fords and house room than for Fords and Locomobiles. These are, perhaps, extreme

[1] The term "monopolistic competition" seems a better fit for this second type of problem than for the first, since, where product is differentiated, each seller is truly both a monopolist and a competitor (see below, Chapter IV). It may also be used, however, in a more general sense (as in this book) merely to describe the blending of monopolistic and competitive elements, thus embracing both types of hybrid problems.

[2] The further possibility appears of a combination of the two types of problem: (a) a relatively small number of sellers of (b) a differentiated product. This is considered in its turn, pp. 100 ff. An alternative approach to the whole problem is presented in my article, "Monopolistic Competition Revisited," *Economica*, Nov. 1951, p. 343, and the two approaches compared on pp. 361–362. (Essay 3 in *Towards a More General Theory of Value*, on pp. 67–68.)

cases, but the fact that each producer throughout the group has a market at least partially distinct from those of the others introduces forces, absent under pure competition, which materially alter the result. Prices throughout are adjusted in some measure according to the monopoly principle. Furthermore, advertising and selling outlays are invited by the fact that the market of each seller is limited, whereas the very nature of a purely competitive market precludes a selling problem. The theory of pure competition, in explaining the adjustment of economic forces in such an industry, is a complete misfit.

Because most prices involve monopoly elements, it is monopolistic competition that most people think of in connection with the simple word "competition." In fact, it may almost be said that under pure competition the buyers and sellers do not really compete in the sense in which the word is currently used. One never hears of "competition" in connection with the great markets, and the phrases "price cutting," "underselling," "unfair competition," "meeting competition," "securing a market," etc., are unknown. No wonder the principles of such a market seem so unreal when applied to the "business" world where these terms have meaning. They are based on the supposition that each seller accepts the market price and can dispose of his entire supply without materially affecting it. Thus there is no problem of choosing a price policy, no problem of adapting the product more exactly to the buyers' (real or fancied) wants, no problem of advertising in order to change their wants. The theory of pure competition could hardly be expected to fit facts so far different from its assumptions. But there is no reason why a theory of value cannot be formulated which will fit them — a theory concerning itself specifically with goods which are not homogeneous. This is the purpose of the later chapters of this book. We turn first to the theory of pure competition.

CHAPTER II

VALUE UNDER PURE COMPETITION

"PURE COMPETITION" is descriptive of particular markets, not of the price system generally. This latter is a composite of purely competitive markets and of markets where monopolistic and competitive influences are variously commingled (including *all* monopolies as that term has ordinarily been understood). The monopolistic influence being generally towards prices higher than they would be under pure competition, the idea of a purely competitive *system* is inadmissible; for not only does it ignore the fact that the monopoly influence is felt in varying degree throughout the system, but it sweeps it aside altogether, describing prices as "tending" towards a level which is generally too low. In fact, as will be shown later, if either element is to be omitted from the picture, the assumption of ubiquitous monopoly has much more in its favor.[1] But neither extreme is defensible without going further, for a true picture of the price system involves recognition of its diversity. From this point of view, the theory of pure competition is of interest because it describes a portion of economic activity.

It is considered here only in part for that reason, however. It also serves as a point of departure to the main subject of this study, monopolistic competition, and it is from this point of view especially that certain aspects of it must be set into relief. There is no need to take up the theory in any comprehensive way, for this has been adequately done by others.[2] Only such phases will therefore be considered as are necessary to make the contrast with monopolistic competition. The problem is that of price in a market in which there is competition accompanied by no elements of monopoly whatever.

---

[1] Below, pp. 65–68.

[2] As the theory of "perfect" competition, which involves, among other requirements, this one: that the number of buyers and sellers be large (presumably for a homogeneous product).

1. Equilibrium Distinguished from the Equation of Supply and Demand

I assume demand and supply curves, or schedules, showing the amounts of product which will be demanded and offered respectively at various prices, as tools of analysis familiar to the economic theorist and not requiring further explanation. The question of whether and in what degree they may be interpreted in terms of utility and cost of production, and the nature of such interpretations, does not, in the main, concern us; nor does the distinction between market and normal price. These are, after all, questions of the content of the curves. Given the amounts which those in the market stand ready to buy and to sell at different prices, and given the conditions of pure competition, the price result should be indifferent to the content. Our chief concern is with the price result.

The curves of demand and supply for a product, by their intersection, define the price at which demand and supply will be equated. But they are void of any explanation as to why the price should settle at that point. They show only the amounts of the good which would be taken and offered *if* certain prices were set. In addition to indicating a point at which supply is equal to demand, they indicate many other points at which one is in excess of the other. To say that a certain price will be established *because* it equates supply and demand is to treat this equation as axiomatic. There is no such axiom. Let the question be fairly asked — what will the price be, and why?

Under given conditions of supply and demand, and of competition or monopoly or both, price tends to settle at a point of equilibrium involving a balancing of opposing forces. "Such an equilibrium is *stable*; that is, the price, if displaced a little from it, will tend to return, as a pendulum oscillates about its lowest point." [1] But the equilibrium price is not, in general, the same as the equating price; in fact, it is so only under conditions of pure competi-

---

[1] Marshall, *Principles*, 8th ed., p. 345. In Marshall's text, the statement refers to a competitive market.

tion. A simple instance of divergence between the two will make this point clear, and it is to be found in the case of monopoly. In Fig. 1, with demand and supply curves of *DD'* and *SS'* respectively, the equating price is *BP*. The monopolist, however, sets his price at some higher point, say *AQ*, the figure which will

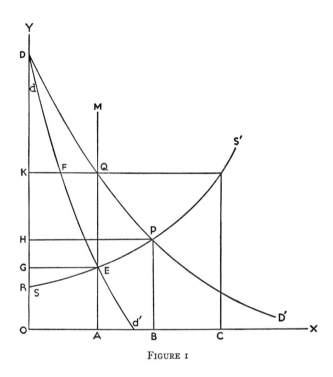

FIGURE 1

maximize his total profit.[1] He is able to maintain it there because, *ex hypothesi*, there is no one to cut under him. Now the curves are not changed by the fact of monopoly,[2] and evidently supply and demand are not equated at this figure, the former being *OC* and the latter *OA*.[3] Yet *AQ* has every right to be called an equilib-

---

[1] I assume absence of the conditions favorable to monopolistic discrimination.

[2] It cannot be said, for instance, that the monopolist's supply curve is *AM*, for this line must mean that the quantity *OA* is thrown on the market regardless of price. It is not. It is conditioned by the price *AQ*, and offered only at that price.

[3] Unless, to be sure, demand and supply are interpreted in the sense of the amount actually bought and sold, in which case they are always identical and the

rium price under the circumstances. Price tends towards it; if it should deviate from this point by the monopolist's miscalculation, or by temporary circumstances, it will tend to return; it represents a balance of opposing forces of loss and gain, which renders the total profit a maximum.

If this does not seem to be a "true" equilibrium, or if it seems to be an equilibrium in some different sense from that of competition, the point may be labored further. DD' is only one of several ways in which the given relationship between demand and price may be expressed. It shows the *average* revenue for each volume of goods sold — the total revenue divided by the number of units. Now let dd' be drawn so as to show the *addition* to total revenue as each successive unit is sold. It may be termed the curve of marginal revenue.[1] It falls more rapidly than the curve of average revenue, DD', because each successive unit, through forcing down the price of the others, adds to total revenue a sum which is smaller than its own price. Thus a unit at A, although selling for the price of AQ, adds only AE to total revenue, since its sale lowers the price slightly on all previous units between O and A. The total revenue from the sale of any volume of goods is given by the appropriate area under this curve of marginal revenue. For the amount OA, it is $ODEA$ ($= OKQA$). Evidently, it will pay the monopolist to increase his output up to OA, for, until that point is reached, each additional unit adds more to his revenue than to his costs. Beyond that, however, he will not go, since the additions to cost would exceed the additions to revenue. He will, therefore, choose the amount OA, and the price per unit will be $ODEA$ divided by OA, or AQ. Equilibrium for the monopolist may be represented by the same graphic device of

law of supply and demand becomes a mere truism. Except in this meaningless sense, monopoly value has nothing whatever to do with the law of supply and demand. The monopolist may choose either (*a*) his price, or (*b*) the amount of the commodity actually exchanged, and these two will bear the relation to each other revealed by the demand curve for his product. Whatever price he chooses, the amount bought and the amount sold will be equal; and whatever the amount he chooses, it will be both bought and sold; but the price and amount will be chosen to maximize his profit, not to equate demand and supply.

[1] Mrs. Robinson mentions a number of others who "discovered" this curve, independently, and at about the same time. Cf. *The Economics of Imperfect Competition*, p. vi. See also below, p. 300.

intersecting lines which is employed for the case of competition. But there is no equating of demand and supply.[1]

The equilibrium of economic forces has been wrongly identified with an equilibrium between demand and supply. The latter is merely a special case of the former. Curves of demand and supply tell nothing, either by themselves or by their intersection, as to what price will be established, until other conditions are known. They are, so to speak, landmarks, but no more. The instance of monopoly has been chosen as a simple and familiar case in order to free the notion of equilibrium from its associations with the intersection of the demand and supply curves. It will be the purpose of this book to show that most prices involve monopoly elements (usually included among the "imperfections" of competition) mingled in various ways with competition, and that the result is very generally equilibrium prices which do not equilibrate supply and demand. It may now be shown why the equilibrium adjustment does take this particular form under conditions of pure competition.

The reason is not that the dominant force in a competitive market is of a different order from that in a monopolistic one. The competitor is in no respect a different sort of person economi-

---

[1] Let us note one more point. The supply curve, SS', is a curve either of average or of marginal costs, depending upon whether the scarcity rents (which, in our illustration, arise as product is increased) are or are not regarded as costs. If they are not so regarded, it represents marginal costs. The total cost of the amount OB, for instance, is $OBPR$, the marginal cost is BP, and the rents are RPH. But if rents are regarded as costs, the curve becomes one of average cost. The total cost, including rent, of the amount OB is $OBPH$, and BP is the average. (A curve of average cost, excluding rent, would begin at R and lie below SS'; a curve of marginal cost including rent would begin at R and lie above SS'. This completes the picture.) Now, to the monopolist, the rents arising from an increased output of his own product are not costs; on the contrary, they are among the sums which he tries to render a maximum. With reference to SS' as drawn, he tries to maximize such areas as $REQK$, not such areas as $GEQK$. To the individual competitor, however, they are costs which are in nowise different from any other outlays, since they are forced upon him by the competition of the others and are not subject to his control. The same curve, SS', is a curve of marginal costs under monopoly, and of average costs under competition. In the light of these considerations, we reach a general conclusion which may be stated as follows: Under monopoly, the equilibrium amount is determined by the intersection of the curves of marginal revenue and of marginal cost; under competition it is determined by the intersection of the curves of average revenue and of average cost. Each is an equilibrium as truly as the other, although only the competitive equilibrium equates demand and supply.

cally from the monopolist.[1] He does not "compete" and cut prices, by contrast with the monopolist who holds them up in order to maximize his profit. He is, presumably, as much bent upon maximizing his profit as is the monopolist, and pursues this end with equal intelligence and foresight. Full appreciation of the identity of monopoly and competition in this respect is essential to an understanding of the nature of a purely competitive market. This identity is revealed, not by comparing two markets, one of which is competitive and the other monopolistic, but by comparing two individuals, one a monopolist and the other a competitor.[2]

2. THE INDIVIDUAL SELLER UNDER PURE COMPETITION

Pure competition has already been defined as involving (1) a relatively large number of buyers and sellers of (2) a perfectly homogeneous product. The first diminishes the influence of any one in the general market situation to negligibility; the second, by identifying completely the product of a single seller with those of his competitors, denies him any measure of control over his own price as distinct from the general market price, which control might exist by reason of buyers' preferences for one variety of good over another. Let the demand and supply curves for such a market be drawn as in Fig. 2a, the equating price being *AP*, so that at that price 10,000,000 units of the good will be exchanged per unit of time. The number of competing sellers we assume to be 1000. The questions to which we now address ourselves are: What is the shape of the demand curve for the product of a *single* seller — that is, as he varies his own offerings, at what price will the different amounts be taken from the market? What is the shape of his own supply curve, as distinct from the general market one? Finally, in the light of these demand and supply curves, what adjustment of his own affairs will maximize his profit? Such individual curves are drawn in Fig. 2b, but we must first

---

[1] Pareto's distinction (*Manuel d'Economie Politique*, pp. 163 ff.) between acting like a monopolist and acting like a competitor is misleading and does not get to the root of the matter.

[2] I. e., a seller in a purely competitive market.

remark the necessity for a change in the scale of the figure. Evidently, the adjustments with respect to a single individual cannot be shown in Fig. 2a, for, there being 1000 sellers, the supply in the hands of each is approximately 1/1000 of OA, which becomes microscopic when laid off along the base line. Fig. 2b, therefore, is drawn to a horizontal scale 1000 times greater, such that oa (Fig. 2b) equals 10,000 units, or 1/1000 of OA (Fig. 2a); the vertical scale remains the same.

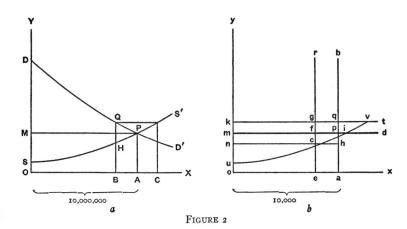

FIGURE 2

The demand curve for the product of any individual seller is a horizontal line at the height of the ruling market price. It is kt if this price is BQ; it is md if the price is AP. It is horizontal for the reason that adjustments of supply within the range shown in Fig. 2b and controlled by any single individual will cause variations in price so small that they may be neglected. Speaking more precisely, the removal from the market of the entire 10,000 units, or their addition to it, would alter the price by an amount equal to the rise or fall in DD' between the point A and a point to the left or right distant from A by 1/1000 of OA (Fig. 2a). This evidently disappears in the graphic presentation, just as it disappears in the calculations of the seller.[1] The horizontality of kt

---

[1] From another point of view, kt or md may be regarded as segments of the curve DD' (Fig. 2a), plotted to the scale of Fig. 2b, the curve falling from D to P over a distance of 1000 oa.

and of *md* reveals in a striking way the absence of any control over price by the individual competitor. He may dispose of any amount he pleases at the ruling market price.

This demand line for the product of any individual seller is a curve both of average and of marginal revenue. Evidently, since it is horizontal, this must be so. A confusion may be caused by the fact that the curve of marginal revenue, if drawn in Fig. 2*a*, would lie below that of average revenue. In Fig. 1, for instance, when the price (average revenue) is *AQ*, marginal revenue is *AE*. It might seem, therefore, that, although horizontal, the line of marginal revenue in Fig. 2*b* should be correspondingly lower than that of average revenue. It is not lower, however, for the reason that, whereas in Fig. 1 (and in Fig. 2*a*) marginal revenue is smaller than average revenue by the loss in price suffered on all units from *O* to *A*, in Fig. 2*b* it is reduced by the loss in price on only 10,000 units, which, when transferred to Fig. 2*a*, are all located at one point, say at *B*. In other words, if the average revenue (price) is virtually constant over a range of 10,000 units, the marginal revenue must be also, and at the same figure.

Various conditions may obtain as to the individual's supply curve. He may have more or less than 10,000 units to offer,[1] and he may offer them all at the same price or at different prices. The curves *nhb*, *ncr*, *uv*, *mtr*, *mpb*, *kgr*, and *kqb* indicate the many possibilities. The first two sellers offer their entire supplies of 10,000 and 8000 units respectively at the price of *BH* (= *ah*). They are within the margin. The third offers his at various prices. The fourth and fifth are marginal sellers, and the last two are extra-marginal. The individual curves are many in number and may be diverse in shape. When added for each price, they give the smooth, even curve, *SS'*, of Fig. 2*a*.

These individual demand and supply curves are the counterparts of those for a monopolized commodity. They are the ones in the light of which the individual seller adjusts his output, presumably with the goal of making his profit a maximum. It may now be shown that the price which equates supply and demand establishes itself under pure competition *because it is the only one*

---

[1] 10,000 units is simply the average.

which is consistent with maximum profits for every seller in the market.

Let us suppose the price to rest momentarily at BQ, the amount of the product offered for sale being only OB. The demand curve, as it appears to each individual seller, is then kt. Each will maximize his profit (the excess over his supply price) by offering the amount indicated by the intersection of his own supply curve with kt, and the total of these amounts is OC (Fig. 2a). The profits indicated in each case (interpreting the supply curves as cost curves) are, in the same order as before, $nhqk$, $ncgk$, uvk, $mfgk$, $mpqk$, o, and o. (The last two are only barely persuaded to offer their goods by the prevailing price, and secure no profit above their minimum supply price.) The continued sale of only OB units at the price BQ is impossible because the maximizing of the profits of each and hence of all competitors at this figure requires the sale of the larger amount OC. It is the attempt of each to maximize his profits which, in fact, lowers the price. His own increased offerings are sold at a price sacrifice which is negligible by itself and to him, yet combined with others it becomes considerable. The demand line kt is lowered and a general revision of calculations takes place. Some of the sellers are forced to drop out, others to reduce their offerings. Each again offers his optimum supply relative to the new demand line and the supply curve for his own product, but if the maximizing of their profits still requires sales in excess of those possible at the ruling price, the demand line must continue to fall. When it is md, the total amount required to render the profits of all a maximum is OA, and since exactly this amount will be purchased, there is no further tendency to change. Price lines lower than md could not stand, for the amounts offered would be reduced, and the price at which these amounts could be disposed of at maximum profit to the sellers would again be higher than AP. The price of AP will be maintained because it is the only one which is consistent with maximum profits for every seller.[1] In all of these adjustments the competitor does exactly

[1] The movement towards equilibrium may be described as well by an analogous argument representing the buyers as maximizing their gains. This is omitted. for the sake of brevity. It may be noted that the action of sellers alone (or of buyers alone) is quite sufficient.

what the monopolist does — he seeks to render his profit a maximum with reference to the demand and supply curves for *his own product.* Competitive equilibrium is not only consistent with unqualified maximum profits for everyone; it involves them as a necessary condition.

The starting point in defining economic equilibrium under monopoly or competition or any combination of the two must be the assumption that every individual seeks, without qualification or delusion, to maximize his economic gain. Although, with given demand and supply curves, the maximizing of profit seems to lead to one result and "competition" to another, this arises not from any difference in the nature of the two forces, but solely from the fact that the curves when representing monopoly conditions pertain to a single seller, whereas, when representing competitive conditions, they embrace a group of sellers. By breaking up the competitive curves into as many parts as there are sellers, the competitive solution is revealed as a thing in nowise different from the monopoly one: in either case the profits of the single seller are maximized. Thus, in order to define the point of equilibrium under pure competition, it is necessary to examine the demand and supply conditions for the individual, as well as for the group. The full significance of this refinement will appear only when monopoly elements are added to the picture.

3. Cost Curves and the Scale of Production

When the problem is one of "normal," or "long run," conditions, cost curves take the place of supply curves,[1] and consideration of the cost conditions for the individual producer leads to an important conclusion as to the scale of production under pure competition. His curve of average cost per unit is simply the curve of "internal" economies, or of the economies of large-scale production, represented by cc' in Fig. 3*b*. (Let the curve mm' be ignored for the moment.) The concept of economies of large-scale production is such a familiar one that the shape of the curve should require no extended elucidation at this point.[2] Unit costs

---

[1] Hence the change in notation (Figs. 3*a*, 3*b*, 3*c*) from SS' to CC'.

[2] It is further considered in Appendix B.

are high for a small volume of output; they decrease as output increases until the most efficient scale of production is achieved, and then rise again as the organization of the producing unit becomes over-complex and cumbrous.

The cost curve for an individual producer must always have these general characteristics,[1] no matter what the commodity (or service), since there must always be a scale of production which is more efficient than any other and on either side of which costs will

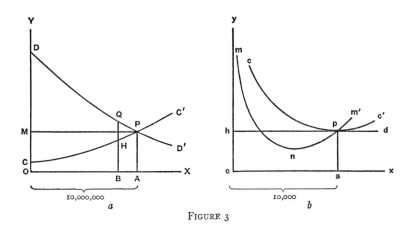

FIGURE 3

be higher. The location of the minimum point and the slope at various stages of the curve will vary widely from industry to industry and somewhat from one producing unit to another within a purely competitive industry.

Let this curve be regarded, for the moment, as describing the conditions of cost for the *marginal* producer when the general market, as pictured in Fig. 3*a*, is in equilibrium. The demand line is *hd*, as already explained. The only output which will not result in actual loss is the one of *oa*, or 10,000 units, where the cost per unit, *ap*, is a minimum and equal to the price. Here profits are

---

[1] Both the long-run and short-run cost curves of the firm are U-shaped, although for quite different reasons. Cf. Appendix B. Here, and elsewhere, it is usually the long-run curve which is in mind; but the analysis is easily adapted to short-run problems by an appropriate interpretation of the content of the U-shaped curve.

just sufficient to cover the minimum necessary to attract capital and business ability into the field, which sum is always included within the cost curve; and this is the result expected under pure competition.

The curve for the intramarginal producers will evidently have the same minimum point, if their rents are included as costs, and they must be so included. Although rents may be surpluses from certain points of view, or for certain purposes, or subject to certain interpretations, they are to the individual producer no different from any other money expense. They do not arise as a surplus from his own operations; they are a cost rigidly imposed upon him by the competition of his rivals for the use of the rent-yielding property. They figure in the same way as do the wages of labor and the interest of capital in his computations as to the most advantageous proportion between the factors and as to the most advantageous scale of operations.[1]

But the most efficient scale of production is not necessarily uniform for everyone. The minimum point of the curve, although at the same distance from the x axis for each producer, may be variously distant from the y axis. Qualitative differences in the factors employed will account for this. As one instance, more costly factors, such as superior land or business ability, will be utilized more intensively,—more of the other factors will be combined with them, — and the result may be a larger-sized producing unit.[2] Again, individual entrepreneurs may differ in their methods, and what is most effective for one is not necessarily most effective for another.

The general shape of cc' (Fig. 3b) is independent of the shape of CC' (Fig. 3a) for the same reason that the horizontality of the demand line hd is not affected by the slope of DD' for the general market. Variations by a single individual of his scale of production will have a negligible effect upon the total output of the product and hence upon cost tendencies for the product as a whole.

---

[1] Cf. below, Appendix B.

[2] It might seem that such considerations would similarly lead to a lower minimum point, but this would be impossible, since the extra gains yielded would constitute a rent which, when attributed to the appropriate factor and capitalized, would raise the curve again.

This is true when costs rise with larger output, due to the scarcity of certain factors of production, as in Fig. 3*a*; it is equally true when they fall, due to "external" economies, or when they are constant, due to the absence of both of these causes or to their cancellation one against the other. Agricultural rent is not affected by one farmer's cultivating his land more intensively; nor are "external" economies appreciably influenced by variations in output within the individual business unit. To put the matter in another way, the individual producer's demand for the factors of production necessary to the commodity is such a small part of the total demand for them that alterations in his scale of production do not affect the cost to him of the elements entering into his product. This being true, variations in the unit cost of his product are due solely to the effectiveness with which he combines and organizes the factors of production within his establishment. It may be asked why, if *cc'* descends in Fig. 3*b*, *CC'* does not do likewise in Fig. 3*a*, at least at the extreme left. Strictly speaking, it does, for very small total outputs requiring only one or a few producers. But as soon as the total output is large enough to require more than a few establishments, there will be no obstacles to the adjustment of each one to conditions of maximum internal efficiency, and the cost curve *CC'*, drawn always with reference to the most efficient conditions of production for each indicated output, must recognize this fact. It is governed by forces applying to the industry or product as a whole, and, whether rising, falling, or horizontal, is the locus of the *minima* for the curves of individual establishments as total output (not output per firm) varies.

Although the shapes of *cc'* and of *CC'* are unrelated, the *position* of the former depends upon the total output, whose average cost (including rent) is indicated for different volumes by the latter. Thus, if the conditions are those of increasing cost (as in Fig. 3*a*), the minimum point of *cc'* will be higher as total output increases, being always equal to the unit cost [1] for the particular volume as indicated by *CC'*. Analogously, under conditions of diminishing cost ("increasing returns") due to external economies, the minimum point of *cc'* will be continually lower as the total output

---

[1] Average, if rent is included; marginal, if rent is excluded.

expands. If costs are constant, its position will evidently remain the same, regardless of the total output. The demand line, likewise, is higher or lower depending upon the price in the general market, as already explained.

The curve *mm'* is a curve of marginal costs for the individual producer, derived directly from the curve of average costs, *cc'*. It indicates the addition to total costs on account of each added unit of product. It reaches its minimum earlier than does the curve of average costs, turns upwards again, and intersects the curve of average costs at the minimum point for the latter. The reason for this is simple. Evidently, as more is produced, average

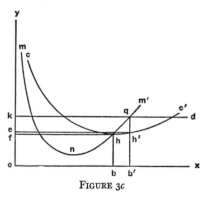

FIGURE 3*c*

costs fall so long as the addition to the total cost is less than the previous average, and rise when the converse is true. The total cost for any volume of product will be indicated by the area under the curve of marginal costs. For the output, *oa*, for instance, it is *oapnm* (= *oaph*). Thus, under equilibrium conditions, the seller,

in adjusting his output to *oa*, not only renders his average cost per unit a minimum, but also equates marginal cost with marginal revenue.[1]

The movement towards equilibrium from a position of maladjustment may be described, and will serve to make clearer the nature of the equilibrium adjustment. If the price were *BQ*, the demand lines for the products of individual sellers would be at this height, and the cost curves, *cc'* and *mm'*, would be lower, as in Fig. 3*c*. If there were fewer sellers and all were adjusted most effectively to this smaller output, the minimum point on the cost curve of each would exactly equal *BH*.[2] Each would

---

[1] Cf. above, pp. 19, 20, where it is argued that the individual competitor does exactly what the monopolist does.

[2] As already stated, these curves, as well as *CC'*, are always drawn on the assumption that the resources used are most effectively adapted to each particular output. If, when output is *OB* (Fig. 3*a*), all resources are not perfectly organized to pro-

adjust his output to ob', corresponding to the intersection of his curve of marginal costs, mm', with his curve of marginal revenue, kd, in order to realize extra profits of $eh'qk$ ($= ob'qk - ob'qnm$). These extra profits would attract others to the field, output would expand, and demand lines would fall and cost curves rise in Fig. 3c, corresponding to the fall in price and rise in cost with larger output as shown in Fig. 3a. The movement would continue until the demand line was tangent to the cost curve, cc', at it lowest point, which adjustment would be achieved at the equilibrium price of AP (Fig. 3a). If, instead of BQ, the original price were lower than AP, all individual supply curves would lie *above* the demand lines, and readjustment would take place by the exit of producers until the supply curves had fallen and the demand lines risen to the point of tangency.[1] The final equilibrium adjustment under pure competition involves not only (1) the equation of supply and demand and (2) maximum profits for each competitor, but also (3) realization of the most efficient scale of production in each establishment.

NOTE ON DEVIATIONS FROM EQUILIBRIUM [2]

A WORD may be said concerning the nature of fluctuations, or deviations, from equilibrium under pure competition. In particular, the misconception that they are in any way related to elements of monopoly must be avoided. Let the distinction between pure and perfect competition be recalled. Purity requires only the absence of monopoly, which is realized when there are many buyers and sellers of the *same* (perfectly standardized) product. Perfection is concerned with other matters as well: mobility of resources, perfect knowledge, etc.[3] It is not to our purpose to list the requirements for perfect competition, but simply to point out that its perfection is a different thing from its purity, meaning by the latter its freedom from monopoly elements.

duce this amount (as they would very likely not be in the case of maladjustment), the minimum point of the curves such as cc' will not be exactly BH. But these refinements are unnecessary to our present purpose.

[1] The readjustment could be shown in another way, corresponding to the earlie example (p. 19), where, at the price BQ, the actual offerings, instead of increasing from OB to OA, decreased from the larger amount called forth by the price BQ, to OA.

[2] For a further discussion of this question, see my article, "An Experimental Imperfect Market," *Journal of Political Economy*, Vol. LVI (1948), p. 95. (Essay 11 in *Towards a More General Theory of Value*.)

[3] Cf. above, p. 6.

It follows that the idea of perfection may be applied to monopoly and to monopolistic competition, as well as to competition. In the case of the monopolist, for instance, there may or may not be a mobility of resources which will enable him to adjust his output quickly to the optimum amount, and to employ his resources most effectively with reference to that output. Likewise, he may or may not have that perfect knowledge of demand and of his own costs which will enable him to hit at once upon his best price. The same considerations hold in a monopolistically competitive group. Monopoly elements change the definition of the equilibrium, but not the facility with which it is achieved. Given the same demand and supply conditions, the equilibrium adjustment is one thing under monopoly, another under pure competition, and another for a group under monopolistic competition. But the exactitude with which actual prices approximate the equilibrium adjustment in any case will depend upon something else — upon the "perfection" with which the economic forces involved work out their results.   Full consideration of what is or should be included within this notion of perfection would lead us too far astray from our main theme, the relations between monopoly and competition.

If a purely competitive market is also perfect, deviations from equilibrium cannot, strictly speaking, occur even momentarily.   The general proof that no price other than the equilibrium one could maintain itself must then be regarded as a proof that no such price could appear even for an instant. There would be neither movement towards an equilibrium nor oscillations about it. The equilibrium price would not be "worked out" by the play of supply and demand; it would coexist with the market through the realization of stability at a single stroke the moment the market came into existence.

Another view would permit, in a perfectly competitive market, deviations which were provisional, to be replaced finally by a stable adjustment to which they would be realigned. In an auction, for instance, a bid is only a tentative price, automatically cancelled the moment a higher bid is made. The existence of a chain of futile bids is in no way inconsistent with the ultimate achievement of a single final price. Edgeworth has described the general theory of competition in such terms, regarding the market as a system of contracts which are constantly remade, a "final settlement" not being reached "until the market has hit upon a set of agreements which cannot be varied with advantage to all the re-contracting parties." [1] Thus, although there may be temporary variations, the market is finally "perfected" by re-contracts until a single determinate figure results. Between the posi-

---

[1] *Papers Relating to Political Economy*, Vol. II, p. 314. See also his *Mathematical Psychics*.

tion that deviations cannot exist at all, and the position that they can exist only to be finally eliminated, there can be little but verbal difference. Either describes satisfactorily the adjustment of economic forces in a perfectly (and purely) competitive market.

The facts of real life remain, however; movements towards and fluctuations about equilibrium characteristically leave a trail of actual prices behind, which may not be revised, but which are final. Markets are, in fact, more or less imperfect. How is this chain of actual prices related to the equilibrium price, and how does the amount sold under fluctuating prices compare with the equilibrium amount? The simple conclusion that actual results will "tend" towards equilibrium is hardly warranted.

Price fluctuations render the volume of sales normally greater than the equilibrium amount which is indicated by the demand and supply curves. For, at all prices higher than the equilibrium one, supposedly excluded sellers have a chance to dispose of their goods and there is no reason why some of them should not do so. Similarly, supposedly excluded buyers may be included when fluctuations carry the price below equilibrium. Since no pair of normally included buyers and sellers can by any circumstance be left out, the total amount exchanged must be greater than that which would equate demand and supply. A diagram will help to make the argument clear. Let the equilibrium price be BP (Fig. 4), and suppose that the actual prices range from AP' to CP''. The sellers from B to C might conclude bargains at prices ranging from BP to AP' with any buyers from O to B, say those represented by OF. Similarly, buyers BC may be paired with sellers OF at prices ranging from BP to CP''. Buyers and sellers from F to B may then be paired and the total volume of sales is OC. This represents the maximum; OB is the minimum; and the actual volume will lie somewhere between these two limits.[1] From this it follows that the average

---

[1] This conclusion implicitly involves the (Marshallian) interpretation of the demand curve, namely not only that OB units will be taken at the price BP, but that OA units will be taken at AP' plus AB units at BP (the total amount paid for OB thus exceeding the area $OBPE$) and so on. The fact that a demand curve cannot be interpreted in this way has been pointed out, and is a fundamental objection to the concept of "consumers' surplus." (Cf. A. A. Young in Ely, *Outlines of Economics*, 5th revised ed., p. 180.) In general, if buyers are willing to take OB units, *all* of them at the price BP, they will be willing to take somewhat less than OB if they have paid more than BP (say AP') for a part of them. It might seem, then, that fluctuations would reduce the volume of sales, instead of increasing it, as we have said. But the fluctuations are below as well as above BP, and a contrary argument holds for this case. If OB units would be taken, the price for all being BP, *more* than OB units would be taken if a part of them were obtained for less than BP (say CP''). The two forces would roughly offset each other. It would seem, therefore, that only minor qualification, if any, is needed on this score, to the conclusions reached above. (Similar considerations would apply to the supply curve also.)

price *BP* at which this amount (greater than *OB*, less than *OC*) is actually disposed of is normally greater than what it would be if the same amount were sold in a perfect market, for, the amount being larger than *OB*, the demand curve *DD'* indicates the single price at which it would be sold.[1] Finally, the amount *OB*, were it sold at fluctuating prices, would, for similar reasons, bring a higher average figure than *BP*.

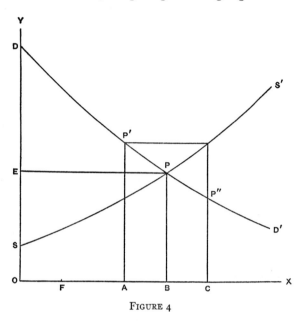

FIGURE 4

A further observation may be made with regard to the part played by speculative activity in helping or hindering the achievement of the equilibrium price. It is sometimes represented that when the price is too high speculators will sell or refrain from buying, thereby causing it to fall, and vice versa. Actions based on the anticipation of future prices are thus viewed as instrumental to achieving more promptly and to maintaining equilibrium conditions.[2]

---

[1] *BP* is the average price, of course, only if sales at higher and at lower prices are equally numerous, and this would be true for the general case. The demand curve might seem to indicate a volume of sales larger below *BP* than above it, but the difficulty of finding sellers, indicated by the supply curve, must not be forgotten. Similarly, the increased offerings when prices are higher than *BP* are offset by the difficulty of finding buyers. The average would be divergent from *BP* only if one side to the bargainings were "stronger" or better informed than the other, and, in general, there is no presumption in favor of either.

[2] Cf. Marshall's description of a corn market, *Principles*, 8th ed., p. 332.

Although speculation *may* actually stabilize prices, the writer is at a loss to find any *a priori* reason why it should do so, or why it should lead to the ultimate establishment of the equilibrium price. The speculator's concern is to make money out of the *movements* of prices. The argument that speculation stabilizes is based on the tacit assumption that the only movements which interest him are those in the direction of the equilibrium price. The speculator is supposed, for instance, to refrain from selling and to buy when the price is below the equilibrium figure. This will tend to send it up or to stop its descent. When the equilibrium figure is reached, he will sell again and check the rise. But, if the price is rising, why should he sell at that particular point? Why should he not rather buy more, or at least refrain from selling, and by so doing give added impetus to the movement? In other words, why should he neglect the opportunities for profits in movements away from the equilibrium price?

Indeed, it seems more likely that speculation would cause more and greater fluctuations. The very presence in the market of large numbers of traders whose purchases and sales ultimately cancel out brings capricious shifts in demand and supply as all flock one way and then the other. Every movement must be accentuated by the attempts of speculators to take advantage of it. As the movement slows down or stops, anxiety to realize on their profits and to lay the basis for new ones may stop it completely and turn it the other way, whereupon it will gain momentum again by the very actions of the speculators themselves.[1] Of course, if everyone knew what the equilibrium price was, there would be no deviations from it whatever, and this with only the original "legitimate" dealers in the market. More perfect knowledge will stabilize prices, but not more speculators.

If it is true that speculation increases fluctuations, this may be linked with the previous conclusion as to the effect of fluctuations on prices. Speculation makes prices higher than they otherwise would be.

[1] No account is taken here of such additional factors as the actions of "pools," and the tactics whereby professional speculators make prices move.

CHAPTER III

DUOPOLY AND OLIGOPOLY [1]

1. STATEMENT OF THE PROBLEM

THIS chapter treats the case intermediate between monopoly and competition, where the number of sellers in a market is greater than one, yet not great enough to render negligible the influence of any one upon the market price.

The solutions which have been offered to the problem are widely divergent, in contrast with the fairly general agreement to be found as to the results of "perfect" competition and of monopoly. It has been held that competition between two sellers will result in a monopoly price, a competitive price, a determinate price intermediate between them, an indeterminate price intermediate between them, a perpetually oscillating price, and no price at all because the problem is impossible. How is such a variety of answers to be accounted for? It is due in part to errors in reasoning. But it is due in much larger part to the actual complexity of an apparently simple hypothesis. I shall, therefore, proceed by considering in turn the various sub-problems into which the central one may be broken. Particular writers will be identified, wherever possible, with the assumptions appropriate to their conclusions.[2]

Either buyers or sellers, or both, may be few in number. We limit ourselves to the problem of a relatively small number of sellers dealing with a large group of buyers — an extension of the ordinary theory of monopoly to include several sellers, but not so many as to render negligible the contribution of each to the total supply.[3] The essential principles are discovered by the specific

[1] See also Essay 2, "The Origin of Oligopoly," in *Towards a More General Theory of Value*.

[2] Mathematical solutions are in all cases translated into non-mathematical terms. They are, however, for the most part, placed in Appendix A.

[3] Although the problem of value where buyers are few and sellers are many (as in an unorganized labor market) is not within the scope of this book, light is frequently shed upon it by analogy. In so far as fewness of sellers gives prices higher than purely competitive ones, there is at least a presumption that fewness of buyers would have the converse effect (the laborers getting the worst of it).

problem of two sellers, or "duopoly." Since it is our purpose to center attention upon the particular kind of monopoly elements embodied in defect of numbers, competition is assumed to be pure in all other respects; in particular, the product traded in is perfectly standardized, and all buyers and sellers are in full communication with each other, so as to constitute really one market.

One of the conditions of the problem must be the complete independence of the two sellers, for obviously, if they combine, there is monopoly. This independence must, however, be interpreted with care, for, in the nature of the case, when there are only two or a few sellers, their *fortunes* are not independent. There can be no actual, or tacit, agreement — that is all. Each is forced by the situation itself to take into account the policy of his rival in determining his own, and this cannot be construed as a "tacit agreement" between the two.

This is true, no matter how complex the manner in which his competitor's policies figure in the determination of his own. A certain move, say a price cut, may be advantageous to one seller in view of his rival's *present* policy, i. e., assuming it not to change. But if his rival is certain to make a counter move, there is no reason to assume that he will not; and for the first seller to recognize the fact that his rival's policy is not a datum, but is determined in part by his own, cannot be construed as a negation of independence. It is simply to consider the indirect consequences of his own acts — the effect on himself of his own policy, mediated by that of his competitor. Of course, he may or may not take them into account, but he is equally independent in either case.

If a seller determines upon his policy under the assumption that his rivals are unaffected by what he does, we may say that he takes into account only the direct influence which he has upon the price. Since the problem of duopoly has usually been conceived of in this way, we shall examine first the results under such an assumption. Following this, it will be argued that the only solution fully consistent with the central hypothesis that each seller seeks his maximum profit is one in which he does take into account the effect of his policy upon his rivals (and hence upon himself again). In this latter case, we may say that he considers his *total* influence upon the price, indirect as well as direct.

One more distinction must be made before the preliminaries are finished. His rival's policy may remain fixed with respect either to the amount he offers or to the price at which he offers it. The solution will be different in the two cases, as we shall see.

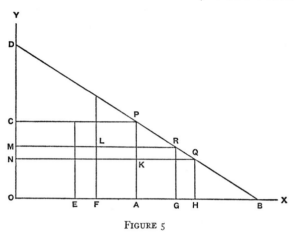

FIGURE 5

2. MUTUAL DEPENDENCE IGNORED: EACH SELLER ASSUMES HIS RIVAL'S SUPPLY CONSTANT

In the first place, let us suppose each seller to determine upon the supply which is most profitable for himself in the light of his rival's present offering, and assuming it not to change. It was in this way that Cournot conceived of the problem, and the exposition here given is a particular application of his theory in non-mathematical terms.[1] Let us assume, with Cournot, two mineral springs, exploited by their two owners without expenses of production, and both contributing to the same market. Let us assume further, for simplicity of exposition, that the demand curve for the mineral water is a straight line, *DB* in Fig. 5, and that $OA = AB$ = the daily output of each spring, the price being

---

[1] *Recherches sur les Principes Mathématiques de la Théorie des Richesses,* Chap. VII. The mathematical statement is given in Appendix A.

exactly zero when the total possible output is put upon the market. If the two producers were to combine, they would supply between them the amount OA at a price AP, their joint profit, $OAPC$, being a maximum at that point. But, since they are independent, if either one alone is selling this amount (his entire output) and enjoying these monopoly profits, the best encroachment that his rival can make is to offer AH, rendering the total supply OH and the price HQ (the rectangular area, $AHQK$, being the largest which can be inscribed in the triangle ABP). Producer I now finds his profits reduced to $OAKN$, and can increase them by diminishing his output to $\frac{1}{2}$ $(OB - AH)$. The process will continue, producer I being forced gradually by the moves of his rival to reduce his output, producer II being able slowly to increase his until each is contributing equally to the total. In these adjustments, each producer will always find his maximum profit by making his supply equal to $\frac{1}{2}$ (OB minus the supply of the other).[1]

The total output will be

$$OB \left(1 - \tfrac{1}{2} + \tfrac{1}{4} - \tfrac{1}{8} + \tfrac{1}{16} - \tfrac{1}{32} \dots\right) = \tfrac{2}{3} OB \ (= OG).$$

The output of producer I will be

$$OB \left(1 - \tfrac{1}{2} - \tfrac{1}{8} - \tfrac{1}{32} \dots\right) = \tfrac{1}{3} OB \ (= \tfrac{1}{2} OG).$$

The output of producer II will be

$$OB \left(\tfrac{1}{4} + \tfrac{1}{16} + \tfrac{1}{64} \dots\right) = \tfrac{1}{3} OB \ (= \tfrac{1}{2} OG).$$

The successive terms of each series indicate the successive adjustments, as they have been described. The final equilibrium will be the same, however, no matter from what point the movements begin. It will also be the same if, instead of the wide movements here described, the two producers increase their outputs gradually and at the same time, from $\frac{1}{2}$ OA each, or if they move in any other conceivable way, so long as the essential conditions of the problem are kept, that each tries to maximize his profit independently of the other, and neglecting his influence upon the other. It is evident from inspection of Fig. 5 that, if either pro-

---

[1] It is evident how the assumption of a straight demand line and of a price of zero for the entire supply simplifies the non-mathematical elucidation of the problem.

ducer is offering OF $(= \frac{1}{3} OB)$, the best his rival can do is to offer $\frac{1}{2} (OB - OF)$, which is FG and equal to OF, securing profits of $FGRL$. Since the other is in the same position, stable equilibrium has been reached at this point.[1]

It may be shown similarly that if there were three producers the total supply would be $\frac{3}{4} OB$, each supplying $\frac{1}{3}$ of this amount; and so on for larger numbers. If there were 100 producers the supply would be $\frac{100}{101} OB$, and if the number were very large, it would be virtually OB, the price being virtually zero (in general, the purely competitive price — zero under present assumptions). The addition of cost curves to the problem will not change the essential conclusion, which is that as the number of sellers increases from one to infinity the price is continually lowered from what it would be under monopoly conditions to what it would be under purely competitive conditions, and that, for any number of sellers, it is perfectly determinate. The equilibrium price, for any given number of sellers, would be closer to the purely competitive price under diminishing cost than under constant cost, and closer under constant cost than under increasing cost. The conclusion is not contingent (in this case) upon the restricted possible output of the sellers: it would be the same if either alone could supply OB or more.

3. Mutual Dependence Ignored: Each Seller Assumes his Rival's Price Constant

Secondly, let us suppose each seller to assume his rival's price (instead of his supply) unchanged. The nature of the difference between the two types of adjustment may be appreciated by a simple example. In Fig. 5, if one producer continues to offer OA, his rival can make no encroachment upon this amount; the most he can do is to force him to sell it at a lower price, by himself offering AH. If, however, the first producer continues to charge a price of AP, the other can, by slightly lowering his own price,

---

[1] This illustration was worked out independently of a similar one by Wicksell, "Mathematische Nationalökonomie" (a review of Bowley's *Mathematical Groundwork*), *Archiv für Sozialwissenschaft und Sozialpolitik*, Vol. 58, Heft 2 (1927), pp. 252–281.

himself dispose of the quantity *OA* (his entire output), and leave the first virtually without customers. The difference between the two types of adjustment may be summarized in this way: if one seller holds his supply fixed, it is his price which is encroached upon; if he holds his price fixed, it is his sales which are encroached upon, by the movements of the other. In the first case, as we have seen, the initial move of his rival is to offer the amount *AH* at the price *HQ*; in the second, it is to offer his entire output, *OA* (= *AB*), at a price fractionally less than *AP*.

It may be objected at this point that, if the two products are identical and if the two producers are competing in a perfect market, there cannot be two prices in existence at the same time, and that therefore this type of competition must be ruled out for the case of a perfectly standardized product.[1] The differences may,

[1] At one stage in the development of the subject, I was disposed to insist rigidly upon this interpretation, but finally relinquished it after discussion with friends, as over-fastidious. The conclusion to which such a position leads may be quickly indicated. Supposing that the maximum possible output of each seller is *OA* = *AB*, as before, let each put his initial supply price at *AP*. The total sales, *OA*, will be shared equally, since there is no reason for buyers to prefer one over the other, and their

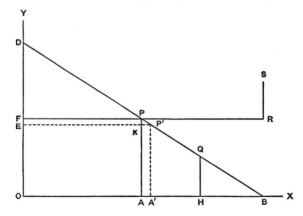

joint profits will be a maximum. Now let either one lower his supply price to *A'P'*. The supply "curve" becomes the broken lines *EKPRS*, and price remains at *AP*, since the one offering a lower price can supply only *OA* out of a total demand of *O '* at that figure. The actual price for both being *AP*, sales will be divided between them, as before, no benefits whatever accruing to the one whose supply price is lower. It is to the interest of his rival to hold his own supply price at *AP*; for at that point his profits are ½ *OAPF*, whereas, if he were to follow suit and set *A'P'*, they would be only ½ *OA'P'E*, which is smaller. If he were to lower his supply price to

however, be regarded as provisional, and consistent with a possible final settlement in which they would be resolved into a single figure; and we shall so regard them.

If each competitor assumes that his rival's price will not be changed, he can, by setting his own only slightly lower, command the market, and dispose of his entire output, increasing his profits virtually in proportion to the increase in his sales. His rival, making the same assumption, will cut still lower, and the downward movement will continue until their entire joint output is disposed of, i. e., until the price is exactly zero in the present instance. This is the first of several possible solutions where prices are adjusted (and where indirect influence is ignored).

It is from this point of view that Cournot's theory was first the subject of attack. Thus Bertrand refuted him by arguing that there would be no limit to the fall in price (he assumed, evidently, that there was no limit to the supply), since each producer could always double his output by underbidding the other.[1] Marshall argued, with especial reference to the case of increasing return, that ". . . if the field of sale of each of the rivals were unlimited, and the commodity which they produced obeyed the law of Increasing Return then the position of equilibrium attained when each produced on the same scale would be unstable. For if any one of the rivals got an advantage, and increased his scale of production, he would thereby gain a further advantage, and soon drive all his rivals out of the field. Cournot's argument does not introduce the limitations necessary to prevent this result."[2] Although what is meant by one of the rivals securing an "advantage" is not certain, it seems most likely that Marshall had in mind price concessions as the means whereby Cournot's equilibrium would be destroyed. Pareto, in his earlier work, pointed out that the results of competition where there were two sellers

---

less than $A'P'$, the price would still be $A'P'$ (his rival's supply price) and his profits would again be $\frac{1}{2} OA'P'E$. Price is therefore determinate at AP. If the sellers were more than two, it would be indeterminate over a range which is wider the greater their number. The details of this strange outcome are hardly worth presentation.

[1] *Journal des Savants* (1883), p. 503.

[2] *Principles*, 1st ed., p. 485, note; 2nd ed., p. 457, note. In the second edition the last sentence of the quotation is changed to: "Cournot ignores the practical limitations which prevent this result from being reached in real life."

would be exactly the same as if there were many, since either would lower his price until all of his supply was sold.[1] He adds that there would be a lower limit if the total supply were fixed.

In truth, this conclusion seems hardly a refutation of Cournot, unless the converse be also granted, that it is in turn refuted by Cournot. The two complement, rather than oppose, each other, each flowing from a particular assumption — one that the seller who for the moment is passive will hold his supply fixed, the

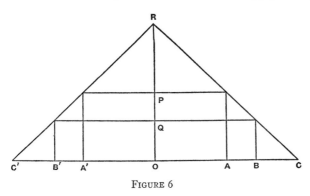

FIGURE 6

other that he will hold his price fixed. No presumption in favor of either the one or the other seems to be created by the general hypothesis that each seeks to maximize his profit.

A second possible solution when it is prices which are adjusted is suggested by Edgeworth.[2] It is that "there will be an indeterminate tract through which the index of value will oscillate, or rather will vibrate irregularly for an indefinite length of time," [3] since, when it has reached the lower limit just described, either seller can, with profit, raise it again. He employs a peculiar construction, reproduced as Fig. 6, which shows the entire market divided evenly between the two sellers. *RC* and *RC'* are the two demand lines for their products, and *OB* and *OB'* the maximum possible output of each. *OP* is the price which would be set if

---

[1] *Cours d'Economie Politique* (1896), p. 68. In his later writings, he develops a more general statement of the theory, which is taken up in Appendix A.

[2] "La Teoria Pura del Monopolio," *Giornale degli Economisti*, Vol. XV (1897). A translation into English appears in his *Papers Relating to Political Economy*, Vol. I, p. 111.　　　　　　　　　　　　[3] *Ibid.*, p. 118.

they combined and *OQ* is the price which will dispose of the entire output, *2OB*, or *B'B*. Now producer I, dealing with half of the buyers, will set a price of *OP*, since this makes his profit a maximum. It will then be to the advantage of II, rather than to set the same price and sell the amount *OA'* (sharing the whole market with his rival), to set a price slightly less than *OP*, secure a part of I's customers, and sell his entire output. Producer I, upon seeing his customers deserting him, will lower his price, and the process will continue until *OQ* is reached.

Thus far, the argument is in accord with that just presented as the outcome of competitive bidding. But, according to Edgeworth, such a price is not stable. "At this point it might seem that equilibrium would have been reached. Certainly it is not the interest of either monopolist to lower the price still further. But it is the interest of each to raise it. At the price *OQ* set by one of the monopolists he is able to serve only *N* customers (say the first *N* on a queue) out of the total number *2N*. The remaining *N* will be glad to be served at any price (short of *OR*). The other monopolist may therefore serve this remainder at the price most advantageous to himself, namely *OP*. He need not fear the competition of his rival, since that rival has already done his worst by putting his whole supply on the market. The best that the rival can now do in his own interest is to follow the example set him and raise his price to *OP*. And so we return to the position from which we started and are ready to begin a new cycle." [1] It is pointed out that oscillation will really take place between *OP* and a point somewhat above *OQ*, since, before the price *OQ* is reached, it will be to the advantage of one of the sellers to raise his price again to *OP* rather than to continue the underbidding. In terms of my own earlier construction (Fig. 5), this reasoning would represent price as oscillating continually between *AP* and a point somewhat below $\frac{1}{2}$ *AP* such that the gains of any seller from offering a still lower price and selling his entire output (*OA*) would be less than those of raising his price to *AP* and selling a portion of it to what remained of the market after his rival had sold *OA* at the lower price.

---

[1] *Ibid.*, pp. 119, 120. Inconsequential changes in notation have been made.

Edgeworth develops his argument for the case of identical commodities, but holds that it applies also for goods which are more or less imperfect substitutes for each other. "The extent of indeterminateness diminishes with the diminution of the degree of correlation between the articles" until, in the limiting case of no correlation, the price for each would be *OP*.[1]

It must first be remarked that this solution of duopoly, although presented by Edgeworth as a part of his general theory of competition, is really quite inconsistent with it. A determinate equilibrium is defined in his *Mathematical Psychics* (p. 19), and the definition is explicitly carried into the article which we are considering. With regard to duopoly, he says, "there will never be reached that determinate position of equilibrium which is characteristic of perfect competition defined by the condition that no individual in any group, whether of buyers or sellers, can make a new contract with individuals in other groups, such that *all* the re-contracting parties should be better off than they were under the preceding system of contracts." [2] This is not true. Such a point of equilibrium is *OQ*, which is perfectly stable by this definition because any buyer or group of buyers, being worse off by re-contracting with one of the sellers at a higher price, would prefer the existing arrangement and refuse to change. To be sure, the same resources being monopolized, the price would be *OP*, for there would be no second seller to re-contract with a part of the buyers (in other words, to bid down the price) in the first place. But two sellers are quite sufficient to give a single "final settlement," or a determinate equilibrium at *OQ*, the same point at which such a settlement would take place if their numbers were very large.[3] This conforms to our first solution for

---

[1] *Ibid.*, p. 121. The theory is also developed for articles which are complementary, but this is beyond the scope of our problem.

[2] *Ibid.*, p. 118. (Italics mine.) For the reader unfamiliar with Edgeworth, it may be explained that a "contract" represents a provisional price which may always be changed (by a "re-contract") if the buyer is offered a lower price by some other seller or if the seller is offered a higher price by some other buyer. No such "re-contract" would take place, of course, unless it were to the advantage of both buyer and seller. The process, though not the terminology, is exactly that more generally known as competitive price bidding, which, under pure competition, destroys all (provisional) prices divergent from the equilibrium, or final, one.

[3] This sufficiency of two sellers, *when there is price bidding*, to give "competitive" results, coupled with the fact that the movement towards a competitive equilibrium

the case where it is prices which are adjusted, and to the argument of Bertrand, Marshall and Pareto given in that connection.[1]

There is oscillation in Edgeworth's solution of duopoly, not because the sellers are few, but because the process is not, as in his general theory, that of contract, or competitive bidding. Price is lowered by this process, but it is raised by the sellers' arbitrarily setting higher prices again and letting the buyers willy-nilly take the consequences.[2] The power of any one seller to do this must be recognized. But its extent is exaggerated by Edgeworth. The wide oscillation which he describes takes place, not because there are only two sellers, but because the conditions of their competition are shifted. In order for the price to descend, their individual markets are completely merged into one, each drawing customers

---

is generally thought of in these terms (of price bidding), probably accounts in part for the scanty attention given to the problems of duopoly and of monopolistic competition generally.

[1] The nature of Edgeworth's error may be better understood, perhaps, by recasting the argument into the more familiar terms of Marshallian demand and supply schedules, or curves. The area on the "contract curve" (cf. *Mathematical Psychics*) within which price is indeterminate corresponds to the area within which there may be "bargaining" when buyers and sellers are few and demand and supply schedules consequently discontinuous. Its limits are, on the one side, the marginal demand price and the first extra-marginal supply price, and on the other, the marginal supply price and the first extra-marginal demand price. As the number of buyers becomes greater, the demand curve becomes more nearly continuous, and the marginal demand price and the first extra-marginal demand price tend to coincide. Similarly, as the number of sellers increases, the marginal supply price and the first extra-marginal supply price tend to coincide. If buyers and sellers are *both* few in number, the limits set by their competition, within which bargaining takes place, may be far apart. Price is indeterminate here in the Edgeworthian sense that a "final settlement" might take place anywhere within these limits — there is "an indefinite number of final settlements." But there is no perpetual oscillation. Now, increase in numbers of either buyers or sellers, but not necessarily of both, narrows this area to a point, and gives a single "final settlement," or a determinate equilibrium price, since a continuous demand schedule and a discontinuous supply schedule (or vice versa) have a single point of intersection. In the example of duopoly, the demand schedule being continuous, a single "final settlement" would take place at *OQ*, and this is the determinate equilibrium price, if prices are made by free contract or competitive bidding, and if each seller assumes the price of his rival to be unaffected by his own policy.

[2] The upward movement is incompatible with the theory of contract, or competitive bidding, because a new "contract" must always be agreeable to all parties. An *upward* movement of prices occurs under competitive bidding only if the movement starts *below* the equilibrium point. An example of this would be an auction sale. Here prices move upward (never downward), each new price being agreeable both to the new bidder and to the seller.

freely from the other by a slight reduction in price. But in order for it to rise again, their markets are completely separated, one seller supplying his customers at OQ (Fig. 6), and the other his at OP, these latter being apparently held apart while the sales at OQ are taking place. Oscillation between the same limits can be demonstrated for an indefinitely large number of sellers [1] if, after the price has been carried to its lowest point by competition, the market is split into parts so that each seller becomes a monopolist dealing with a portion of the buyers in isolation. If there were ten sellers, ten diagrams corresponding to the right (or left) half of Fig. 6 could be drawn, one for each. The conditions of the problem being the same as before, and the price for all having been reduced to OQ, it would pay anyone to raise his price to OP. Similarly, it would pay the second and the third and *all* of them to go back to OP, whereupon someone would cut and the oscillation would continue indefinitely.[2] The same could be said if there were a thousand sellers.

Regardless of numbers, price can rise to OP (under present assumptions of price adjustments with indifference to indirect influence) only if each seller deals with his proportionate share of the buyers in isolation, in which case the price is stable at that point with no cause for a downward movement. If buyers are not isolated, but are merged into one market, the upper limit to price is set by the point to which one seller can raise it by his own action when his rival or rivals are disposing of their entire outputs, the price being always *uniform for all.*

[1] In fact, Edgeworth presents his proof as applying to "two or more" monopolists (*loc. cit.*, p. 116), but it is hardly to be supposed that he would apply it to very many, for his general theory is that "contract with more or less perfect competition is less or more indeterminate" (*Mathematical Psychics*, p. 20).

[2] Mr. Kahn has criticised this argument, pointing out that, although it would pay the first firm to raise its price to the monopoly figure, as soon as one or two others had raised their prices to slightly under this the output of the first firm would be reduced to zero, "and price cutting restores the status quo before the great majority of the firms have a chance of moving. The *amplitude* of the oscillations is unaltered, but they affect a gradually diminishing proportion of the industry as the number of sellers is increased" (letter to the writer). This is true enough if we suppose (what probably corresponds to real life) that most of the sellers are inclined to do nothing until the lead is taken by someone else. But if we regard them as all equally alert we must conclude that there would be no lagging behind. "It would pay *anyone* to raise his price" (above), i. e., it would pay *everyone.*

Uniformity of price must again be interpreted with a shade of leniency, although with only a shade. What has already been said [1] about the result when *absolute* perfection of the market is insisted upon may now be recalled. In this case, a higher price set by one seller would carry the price of the other with it exactly, and the amount sold, whatever the price, would always be evenly divided between the two, the buyers having no reason to prefer one over the other. Neither would be able, by holding his price slightly under the other, to dispose of more than his rival. Either would therefore raise his price at once to the monopoly figure, and would be able to keep it there (*even without the consent of the other*), securing one-half of the maximum joint profits.

If, however, slight differences in price are allowed, we may imagine one seller raising his price from the lower limit to which it has been reduced by competitive undercutting, the other being carried along closely behind him by the competition of buyers, but always enjoying the slight differential which enables him to sell his entire output. Under these circumstances, it would pay either producer, let us say producer I, to raise his price to $\frac{1}{2} AP$ (Fig. 5), but no higher, enjoying profits of $AHQK$, and leaving to producer II profits of (slightly less than) $OAKN$. Producer II has no incentive to give additional impetus to the upward movement, since for him now to raise his price above $\frac{1}{2} AP$ would be to permit his rival to sell his entire output and reduce his own profits not only to less than $OAKN$, their present amount, but to less than $AHQK$, which is one-half of this. A downward movement will set in, however, producer I cutting under his rival, who has been forced by the market to raise his price to (slightly less than) $\frac{1}{2} AP$.[2] The lower limit to this downward movement is $\frac{1}{4} AP$,

[2] This downward movement is required by the hypothesis that each assumes the price of the other fixed, unless we interpret this as referring to the *supply price*, as distinguished from the *price*, taking the position that, in this case, the supply price of producer II might remain at zero, although his price were forced up to (slightly less than) $\frac{1}{2} AP$ by the competition of buyers. In this case, the figure of $\frac{1}{2} AP$, established by producer I, would represent a stable equilibrium, since there is no reason for producer II to alter his supply price of zero, the competition of buyers securing for him the price of $\frac{1}{2} AP$ anyway, and since for producer I to lower his supply price of $\frac{1}{2} AP$ would give him no advantage over his rival, whose supply price remains

since at this point the profits to anyone from selling his entire output at less than that figure would be smaller than those from raising his price and selling half of it at HQ. There is oscillation, then, between $\frac{1}{2} AP$ and $\frac{1}{4} AP$. In the case of three sellers dividing evenly the total output of OB, the movement would take place between $\frac{1}{3} AP$ and $\frac{1}{6} AP$, and so on for larger numbers. In addition to its greater faithfulness to the assumption that all buyers and sellers are in the same market, this solution has the merit (which Edgeworth's has not) that it approaches the purely competitive result with increase in numbers.

It must be remarked that, although the result where each seller assumes his rival's *supply* constant (the hypothesis of Cournot) is independent of the maximum possible output of each, being the same even if one alone could supply OB or more, it is not so independent where each assumes his rival's *price* constant. In this latter case, if either alone could supply OB or more, the other would at once eliminate himself completely, were he to set any price higher than zero. The price would therefore be stable at the purely competitive level (zero in our illustration).[1] This consideration is of great importance where the supply of each seller, instead of being absolutely fixed, is elastic and related to cost. Here a higher price set by one seller would have the effect of removing him from the market at the lower price and of inviting his rival or rivals to increase their outputs. Such a possibility would lower the point to which a single seller could with profit raise the price, and for a relatively small number of sellers would reduce it virtually to the purely competitive level.

Professor Pigou accepts the conclusion of Edgeworth that the quantity of resources devoted to production under duopoly is

---

always at zero. The annoying question of which seller takes the initiative would however, remain unanswered.

[1] Regardless of the total number of sellers in the market, it is necessary for this result that there be at least two, *each* of which could supply the entire market alone. If there were only one, although the *others* could not raise their prices, this one could. The point is important where one large seller dominates a market, permitting a few smaller competitors with limited outputs to participate in it. Cf. Gaston Leduc, *La Théorie des Prix de Monopole*, pp. 257 ff. M. Leduc considers Cournot as refuted by others, and gives as "l'hypothèse la plus générale" for duopoly that of unlimited supply on the part of both sellers.

indeterminate, remarking that it "is now accepted by mathematical economists."[1] His limits of indeterminateness are not those of Edgeworth, however, ranging in terms of aggregate resources invested "from nothing at the one extreme up to the sum of the investment that would maximize *A*'s monopoly revenue in the absence of *B* and the investment that would maximize *B*'s monopoly revenue in the absence of *A*."[2] In Edgeworth's example (Fig. 6), this would make price range from *OR* to *OQ*, and in my own (Fig. 5) from *OD* to zero.

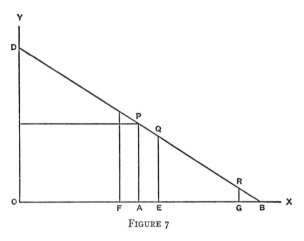

FIGURE 7

The upper limit to price (the lower limit to resources) is, perhaps, hardly to be taken seriously, since it is evident that the price could never under any circumstances exceed that which would maximize the sellers' joint profit. It is to the lower price limit that interest attaches. The curves being straight lines, it is held to be higher (i. e., the investment of resources smaller) than under simple competition. This is not necessarily true, as is revealed by the application just made (at the end of the previous paragraph) of the reasoning to Figs. 5 and 6. But let us take a case where it would be true. In Fig. 7, let the demand curve be *DB*, as before, and let producer I have a maximum possible output of *OF*, and producer II of *OE*, the two added being equal to *OB*. The

[1] *Economics of Welfare*, 3rd ed. (1929), p. 267.
[2] *Ibid.*, p. 268.

first would, in the absence of the other, offer his entire output, OF; the second would, in the absence of the first, offer OA. Their sum is OG. I confess inability to see why any significance should attach to this sum, and consequently to the price GR. The only justification which Professor Pigou gives for it is that "it cannot, in general, pay either to invest more than it would pay him to invest if the other seller were investing nothing." Yet if producer I has set his price at RG, it will pay producer II to cut under him and sell his entire output of OE, which is more

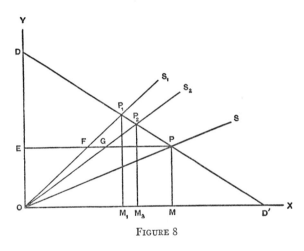

FIGURE 8

than he would offer if producer I were not in the market. Unless the process of competitive bidding (until no further advantage can be gained by anyone) is ruled out, price will descend lower than RG. And if it is ruled out, the lower limit is reached at a higher point, as already explained. Indeed, Professor Pigou's own statement, running in terms of the investment profitable to one producer in the light of what the other is investing, recalls Cournot rather than Edgeworth, and would indicate a determinate solution at a considerably higher point.

If rising cost curves are assumed, as in Fig. 8, it is true that the lower limit to price *as defined by Pigou* is higher than the price under simple competition. In Fig. 8, let DD' be the demand curve for the market in which both are competing, OS_1 the supply curve for producer **I**, OS_2 the supply curve for producer **II**, and OS the supply curve for both together, so drawn that $EP = EF + EG$, and so on. According to the definition, the lower limit to price here is that at which the amount $\frac{1}{2} OM_1 + \frac{1}{2} OM_2$ would be sold, and is inevitably higher than the purely competitive figure. It is even higher than that for which the amount OM_2, which would be offered under simple competition if the smaller source were eliminated, would be sold, as Pigou demonstrates. But, again, it is not evident why it is the lower limit.

Although apparently based upon Edgeworth, Professor Pigou's explanation of indeterminateness is lacking in Edgeworth's statement of the problem, and introduces a factor not yet touched upon. It is that "the quantity [of resources] employed by each depends on his judgement of the policy which the other will pursue, and this judgement may be anything according to the mood of each and his expectation of success from a policy of bluff. As in a game of chess, each player's move is related to his reading of the psychology of his opponent and his guess as to that opponent's reply." [1] This uncertainty is a factor of the utmost importance in the final answer to the problem, but its consideration is best deferred until a later point when all the factors about which there may be uncertainty have been assembled.

4. Mutual Dependence Recognized

I pass now to a new phase of the problem. None of the solutions yet given conforms perfectly to the hypothesis that each seller acts so as to render his profit a maximum. In order to do this, he will take account of his *total* influence upon the price, indirect as well as direct. When a move by one seller evidently forces the other to make a counter move, he is very stupidly refusing to look further than his nose if he proceeds on the assumption that it will not.[2] As already argued, the assumption of independence cannot

[1] *Ibid.*, p. 268.

[2] Cf. Professor Irving Fisher, "Cournot and Mathematical Economics," *Quarterly Journal of Economics*, Vol. XII (1898), p. 126: "... As a matter of fact, no business man assumes either that his rival's output or price will remain constant any more than a chess player assumes that his opponent will not interfere with his effort to capture a knight. On the contrary, his whole thought is to forecast what move the

be construed as requiring the sellers to compete as though their fortunes were independent, for this is to belie the very problem of oligopoly itself. It can refer only to independence of action—the absence of agreement or of "tacit" agreement. For one competitor to take into account the alterations of policy which he forces upon the other is simply for him to consider the indirect consequences of his own acts. Let each seller, then, in seeking to maximize his profit, reflect well, and look to the total consequences of his move. He must consider not merely what his competitor is doing now, but also what he will be forced to do in the light of the change which he himself is contemplating.[1]

We shall suppose them first to adjust amounts, and afterwards, prices.

Let producer I begin by supplying OA (Fig. 5), as earlier, and the best that producer II can do is, again, to supply AH. The first will now reduce his supply to $OE = AH$, and the total amount OA will bring the monopoly price AP.[2] He will set this supply because the *ultimate* consequences of his following through the other chain of adjustments are less advantageous to himself than to share equally with his rival the output OA. The price AP is perfectly stable, under our assumptions, for either seller would, by departing from it, bring disaster upon *himself* as well as upon his rival.

rival will make in response to one of his own." Cf. also Wicksell, *Archiv für Sozialwissenschaft*, Vol. LVIII (1927), p. 272: "Dann wäre es ja sinnlos, wenn der eine Monopolist seinen Preis in der Erwartung herabsetzte, dasz der andere den seinen beibehalten werde." It is strange that Wicksell is led by this consideration to favor Cournot as against Edgeworth, whereas, when "amount" is substituted for "price" in the quotation, it is equally applicable against Cournot. This suggestion has been made by Mr. Kahn.

[1] Professor H. L. Moore, *Quarterly Journal of Economics*, Vol. XX (1906), p. 219, note, defines Cournot's "error" as assuming one producer to order his output without regard to the effect of his act upon the conduct of his competitors, whereas this assumption is held to be justified only (*a*) when the influence of the product of any one producer upon the price per unit of the total output is negligible, and (*b*) when the output of any one producer is negligible as compared to the total output. If this indicates that (since (*a*) and (*b*) are not true) a reversal of the assumption should give the correct solution, it is the one now presented.

[2] This solution is suggested by A. A. Young in his review of Bowley's "Mathematical Groundwork of Economics," *Journal of the American Statistical Association*, Vol. XX (1925), p. 134. Cf. also Professor Schumpeter, *Economic Journal*, Vol. XXXVIII (1928), p. 369, note 1, where he concludes that the solution of duopoly is determinate, being either this one or Cournot's.

If the sellers are three or more, the results are the same, so long as each of them looks to his ultimate interest. There is no gradual descent to a purely competitive price with increase of numbers, as in Cournot's solution. The break comes when the individual's influence upon the price becomes so small that he neglects it, and here again the distinction must be made between direct and indirect influence. Neglect of the latter will lower the price only to the figure given by Cournot's solution, and this conforms to the competitive level only if the number of sellers is infinite — or, let us say, very large. However, as soon as the sellers begin to neglect their direct influence upon the price, it will fall at once to the competitive level — zero in our illustration — regardless of their numbers. Thus, under duopoly, the price being AP, if each seller supposed himself to have no influence upon it he would at once offer his entire output and it would fall to zero. Mathematically, the neglect of either type of influence would be justified only if the number of sellers were infinite. Practically, it might take place when they were relatively few, especially since the demand curve is known only in a vague and uncertain way.

The result is the same when the sellers adjust their prices instead of their supplies. Supposing the price to rest temporarily at AP, if either one were to cut below it he would, by the incursions made upon his rival's sales, force him at once to follow suit. To the argument that if he did not cut his rival would, the answer is that his rival would not for the same reason that he does not. If each seeks his maximum profit rationally and intelligently, he will realize that when there are only two or a few sellers his own move has a considerable effect upon his competitors, and that this makes it idle to suppose that they will accept without retaliation the losses he forces upon them. Since the result of a cut by any one is inevitably to decrease his own profits, no one will cut, and, although the sellers are entirely independent, the equilibrium result is the same as though there were a monopolistic agreement between them.

As in the case where amounts are adjusted, the break towards purely competitive levels comes when the number of sellers is so large that each is led to neglect his influence upon the price. Neglect of either indirect or direct influence gives, by the theory of contract, or competitive bidding, the same result as if there were pure competition, so long as there are at least two sellers, or, by recognition of the full power of each, oscillation at a somewhat higher level, as shown above. It must again be emphasized, however, that *this result does not flow from the assumption that each seeks independently to maximize his profit.* On the contrary, this latter leads to the conclusion of a monopoly price for any fairly small number of sellers. No one will cut from the monopoly figure because he would force others to follow him, and thereby work his own undoing. As their numbers increase, it is impossible to say at just what point this consideration ceases to be a factor. If there were 100 sellers, a cut by any one which doubled his sales would, if his gains were taken equally from each of his competitors, reduce the sales of each of them by only $\frac{1}{99}$, and this might be so small as not to force them, *because* of the cut, to do anything which they would not do without it. At whatever point this becomes true, the barrier to the downward movement of price from the point which will maximize the joint profits of all is removed. No one seller will look upon himself as *causing* the dislodgment, since he secures his gains with comparatively little disturbance to any of his rivals. Under these circumstances there is no reason for him to withhold a shading of his price which is to his advantage, and which has no repercussions. Nor is there any reason for the others not to do likewise, and the price becomes the purely competitive one.[1]

---

[1] Professor J. M. Clark argues (*Economics of Overhead Costs* [1923], p. 417) that "if all the competitors followed suit instantly the moment any cut was made, each would gain his quota of the resulting increase in output, and no one would gain any larger proportion of his previous business than a monopoly would gain by a similar cut in prices. Thus the competitive cutting of prices would naturally stop exactly where it would if there were no competition." This agrees with my own conclusion when competitors are relatively few in number; but, as has just been shown, *it does not apply when their numbers are large.* The results of perfect competition and of monopoly are not identical. Likewise, the conclusion that "the retarded action of the market which permits different prices to prevail at the same time is not really an 'imperfection,' as theoretical economics has been inclined to regard it," but " . . . an essential requirement, without which it [the market] could not produce its characteristic effects," is not a valid criticism of theoretically perfect competition. Large numbers are a sufficient requirement for the market to produce competitive results, without retarded action or any other type of imperfection. The reason that it fre-

All of the above has been reasoned on the assumption that the response of each seller to a move by his rival is instantaneous. If one cuts, the others are supposed to cut at once, leaving him no interval in which to enjoy the larger profits he anticipated. Indeed, there being no interval, the very conception of one reducing his price below the rest may well be dropped. The prices of all move together, and from this it follows at once that the equilibrium price will be the monopoly one.[1] The same conclusion is reached if the idea of "re-contract" is introduced, for this insures that, although the provisional contracts may diverge, final ones do not. There is no incentive to make a new provisional contract (with a larger number of buyers at a slightly lower price), which is advantageous, if the very act of making it puts into motion forces which must destroy it and substitute one less advantageous than the original one. Such is the case unless the number of sellers is very large. In fact, "re-contract" is another way of expressing the absence of friction. The results are the same whether the friction is never permitted or whether it is permitted and then removed.

The results are different, however, if friction is permitted and is not removed.[2] If an interval, no matter how long, elapses between price adjustments (and if every sale is final), the one who cuts his price will enjoy an advantage during that interval which will be a factor in his decision as to price policy. This phase of the matter may be summed up by the general statement that the *ultimate* consequences of his price cut (through his indirect influence upon price) are a factor of more or of less significance to the seller, depending on whether the time lag is short or long *relative* to the

quently does not produce such results is that numbers are small, and that even the compounding of "imperfections" does not suffice.

[1] Prices also move together, and with the same result, when there is a generally recognized price leader — a dominant competitor to whose prices all others adapt themselves, recognizing that therein lies their greatest ultimate gain. In this event, it makes no difference how many competitors there are or what percentage of the total each produces; the price established is identical with that which would be set if there were no competition at all. The price leader, knowing that the others will follow him, has as much control as the group acting in unison.

[2] I am speaking, of course, of the case where the number of sellers is not large enough to render the effect of each negligible. The argument now to be given has no applicability where the number of sellers is very large.

period he expects to continue selling. If he is in business permanently, the temporary gains of a price cut are of negligible importance. He will give full weight to the indirect, or ultimate, consequences of his acts, and make no move which will force future sales at a lower figure.[1] On the other hand, if he is in the market only temporarily, bent on disposing of a certain amount of product, the ultimate consequences do not enter into his calculations at all. If he can effect a sale of his goods at a slight sacrifice from the prevailing price, he has no more to sell, and cares nothing for the figure at which subsequent sales are made. Midway between these two extremes lie cases where immediate gains must be balanced against ultimate losses, direct and indirect influence upon price being given such weight as is appropriate.

5. THE EFFECT OF UNCERTAINTY

There remains to take account of the factor of uncertainty on the part of one seller as to what the other is going to do. This factor has been deferred until last in order not to throw a haze prematurely over the working of the various forces *about which* there may be uncertainty. We have seen that the solutions varied all the way from the equilibrium price defined by monopolistic agreement to the one defined by conditions of pure competition, depending upon the various assumptions which one seller might make as to the conduct of his rival. If, now, he does not know what assumption to make, the conclusions must be that the price may be anything between these limits, depending upon the one which chance, shrewdness, or desperation leads him to choose, and depending also upon whether his rival chooses the same one. Such uncertainty cannot be asserted, however, without establishing a reason for it. What basis is there, then, for doubt on the part of one seller as to what his competitor will do?

The first element of uncertainty lies within the limits of the problem as stated with reference only to the direct influence of each seller upon price. If each assumes his rival's present policy

[1] If he is a speculator, both buying and selling, he may do just the opposite: sell at a price sacrifice, hoping to start a selling movement which will carry prices still lower and enable him to buy back for a profit what he has sold.

to continue, unaffected by his own, he still has no way of knowing whether this fixity of policy will express itself with regard to his rival's supply or his price.[1] The general answer here must therefore be a price ranging anywhere from Cournot's solution to the purely competitive figure. If, on the contrary, he is certain that his rival's policy *is* affected by his own, there is no indeterminateness on this score, for it makes no difference then whether it is his price or his supply which is affected — the result when *total* influence upon price is taken into account is always the monopoly figure.

A second possible element of uncertainty has regard to the degree of intelligence and far-sightedness of the competitors. It is true that, for relatively small numbers, if *each one* could see the ultimate consequences of his price cut there would be no downward movement of price from the monopoly figure. But even though some can thus pursue their interests coolly, there may be others so eager for economic gain that they see nothing but the immediate profits from cutting under their rivals. Any one seller may be perfectly aware of his own indirect influence upon the price, but uncertain as to how many of his competitors are aware of theirs. He will then be in doubt as to the effectiveness of his own foresight in maintaining the price, and therefore in doubt as to whether he should lower or maintain it.

A third element of uncertainty arises when numbers are such as to leave doubt in the mind of any one as to the extent of the incursions which his move will make upon the sales of the others. (Let the previous element of uncertainty be laid aside and kept distinct by the assumption here that each and every seller is aware of his own indirect influence and aware that the others are aware of theirs.) Uncertainty and hence indeterminateness are now present, not when numbers are small, but when they are fairly large yet not large enough to make the conditions those of pure competition. If numbers are fairly small, any one seller can be *certain* that his incursions upon the others by a price cut will be

---

[1] Perhaps this is the interpretation to be given to Pareto's insistence that the problem is "too determinate" rather than "indeterminate." *Manuel d'Economie Politique* (1909), pp. 595 ff.

large enough to cause them to follow suit; and therefore no one will cut. If they are very large, he can be certain that his incursions will be such a negligible factor to each other seller that no one will "follow suit" (i. e., cut *because* he did); and therefore everyone will cut. But in between there is a range of doubt. At what point exactly do the effects of a price cut upon others become "negligible"? It is undeniable that they are not so when numbers are small and that they become so when numbers are very large. Between these limits the result is unpredictable.

A fourth element of uncertainty appears in the case where there is "friction" in the working of the market. It arises with regard to the length of the time lag. (The question of the relative certainty of the final result has already been considered.) The "immediate" effects of a price cut (i. e., those enjoyed before the rival also cuts) are not realized immediately in point of time, but with a delay the length of which is uncertain, depending upon the rapidity with which knowledge of the cut spreads and buyers are brought to alter established relationships. This creates uncertainty as to the result of a price cut by one seller, even though his rival were sure to maintain his price; but especially important is the added uncertainty as to (*a*) *how soon* pressure will actually be brought to bear upon the other, by the reduction in his sales, to follow suit, and (*b*) the degree to which he will anticipate it. This leaves each competitor in doubt, not as to what his rival will do, but as to when he will do it, which suffices, however, to make him uncertain as to what to do in the first place. Under these circumstances, no assumption as to the intelligence which the sellers apply to the pursuit of their maximum gain, short of omniscience, would render the outcome determinate.

6. Summary

The most important conclusions of this chapter may now be summarized:

1. Oligopoly is not one problem, but several. The solution varies, depending upon the conditions assumed. Putting to one side the factor of uncertainty, it is (with minor exceptions) de-

terminate for each set of assumptions made. (Cf., however, 5, below.)

2. If sellers have regard to their *total* influence upon price, the price will be the monopoly one. Independence of the producers and the pursuit of their self-interest are not sufficient to lower it. Only if the number is large enough to render negligible the effect of an adjustment by any one upon each of the others is the equilibrium price the purely competitive one. If the market is imperfect, however, true self-interest requires the neglect of indirect influence to a degree depending upon the degree of imperfection.

3. If sellers neglect their indirect influence upon price, each determining upon his policy as though his competitors were uninfluenced by what he did, the results vary, depending upon further circumstances. If each assumes his competitors' supplies to be unchanged, the equilibrium price is continually lower than the monopoly one as the sellers are more numerous, descending to the purely competitive level only when their numbers are infinite. If each assumes his competitors' prices unchanged, and if competitive bidding, or "re-contract," continues until no further price change can be made without disadvantage to someone, the equilibrium price is the purely competitive one for only two sellers, and, of course, for any greater number. If the full power of the seller to alter his price, even to the disadvantage of the buyer, is recognized, however, price will oscillate over an area which becomes narrower and approaches more closely the purely competitive figure as the number of sellers becomes larger.

4. If sellers neglect both their indirect and their direct influence upon price, the outcome will be the purely competitive price, *regardless of numbers*.

5. Uncertainty, where present, as to (*a*) whether other competitors will hold their amounts or their prices constant, (*b*) whether they are far-sighted, (*c*) the extent of the possible incursions upon their markets, and (*d*), in the case of a time lag, its length, renders the outcome indeterminate for the particular reasons indicated in each case.[1]

---

[1] Since this chapter appeared as an article in the *Quarterly Journal of Economics*, I have been in correspondence with Mr. R. F. Kahn of Cambridge, England, whose

dissertation entitled "The Economics of the Short Period," virtually completed at that time, contains a section on duopoly. The similarities between our two studies are remarkable, both as to general method of attack and as to many specific points of theory. Mr. Kahn makes the distinction between holding amounts or prices constant, and then recognizes a third case including "all the complex possibilities that emerge when the business man realizes that neither the outputs nor the prices of his competitors will remain constant if he alters his own price." (Cf. above, pp. 46 ff.) In relation to this latter case his conclusions diverge somewhat from my own, but since I have seen only his provisional draft, I do not feel at liberty to discuss them. Two specific points of similarity are especially interesting. (1) Mr. Kahn recognizes the time lag as a factor in the solution, observing that "the policy of a firm . . . depends on the extent of the time lag and the relation between its desire for immediate profits and its desire for profits in the more distant future." (Cf. above, pp. 50, 51.) (2) He distinguishes between the indeterminateness of Pigou and that of Edgeworth. In this connection it is amusing that the quotation from Pigou (above, p. 46) occurs in identical form, with even the same additions and omissions.

Dr. F. Zeuthen, in his *Problems of Monopoly and Economic Warfare* (London, 1930), devotes a chapter to "Monopolistic Competition." His mode of attack is novel (and tricky until one becomes accustomed to it) in that the usual demand curves are replaced by "coëfficients of extension," represented graphically by angles. Under the assumption of "the highest degree of mobility, so that only a slight reduction of price by one competitor will immediately give him all the sales in so far as his capacity allows it," only two solutions appear, those of Edgeworth and of Cournot. The possibility is discussed (p. 28) of the monopoly result if each producer "always reckons with having half the sale," but it is dismissed on the ground that "this presupposes . . . that they are bound together tacitly or expressly. . . ." Dr. Zeuthen discusses at length the case where the product is differentiated. (Cf. below, p. 102, note 2.)

A recent study on a related subject is *Partial Monopoly and Price Leadership*, by A. J. Nichol (published by the author, 1930).

Paul Braess ("Kritisches zur Monopol- und Duopoltheorie," *Archiv für Sozialwissenschaft und Sozialpolitik*, Vol. 65, Heft 3 [1931], pp. 525–538) concludes that the normal case of duopoly must end in a kartell in order for the price to be really stable. Otherwise it could be stable only if the structure of the demands were known by both sellers from the first.

A. E. Monroe (*Value and Income* [1931], pp. 24–28) shows that the determination of price between the monopolistic and competitive extremes may be influenced by the number of units of the commodity in the possession of each seller. Although the argument is presented without reference to the number of sellers (in the illustration there are many), I believe that it is valid only for small numbers, since, as has been shown in Chapter II, the entire output of a commodity must be sold in any event if there are many competitors. (Cf., however, below, pp. 102 ff.)

CHAPTER IV

THE DIFFERENTIATION OF THE PRODUCT

1. The Meaning of Differentiation

The interplay of monopolistic and competitive forces now to be considered is of a different sort from that described in the previous chapter. It arises from what we shall call the differentiation of the product. This chapter introduces the subject by explaining what differentiation means, and how and in what relationship it involves both monopoly and competition.

A general class of product is differentiated if any significant basis exists for distinguishing the goods (or services) of one seller from those of another. Such a basis may be real or fancied, so long as it is of any importance whatever to buyers, and leads to a preference for one variety of the product over another. Where such differentiation exists, even though it be slight, buyers will be paired with sellers, not by chance and at random (as under pure competition), but according to their preferences.

Differentiation may be based upon certain characteristics of the product itself, such as exclusive patented features; trade-marks; trade names; peculiarities of the package or container, if any; or singularity in quality, design, color, or style. It may also exist with respect to the conditions surrounding its sale. In retail trade, to take only one instance, these conditions include such factors as the convenience of the seller's location, the general tone or character of his establishment, his way of doing business, his reputation for fair dealing, courtesy, efficiency, and all the personal links which attach his customers either to himself or to those employed by him. In so far as these and other intangible factors vary from seller to seller, the "product" in each case is different, for buyers take them into account, more or less, and may be regarded as purchasing them along with the commodity itself. When these two aspects of differentiation are held in mind, it is evident that virtually all products are differentiated, at least slightly, and that over a wide range of economic activity differentiation is of considerable importance.

In explanation of the adjustment of economic forces over this field, economic theory has offered (*a*) a theory of competition, and (*b*) a theory of monopoly. If the product is fairly individual, as the services of an electric street railway, or if it has the legal stamp of a patent or a copyright, it is usually regarded as a monopoly. On the other hand, if it stands out less clearly from other "products" in a general class, it is grouped with them and regarded as part of an industry or field of economic activity which is essentially competitive. Thus, although patents are usually classed as monopolies, trade-marks are more often looked upon as conferring a lesser degree of individuality to a product, and hence as quite compatible with competition (sometimes even as requisite to it). By this dispensation, the value of patented goods is explained in terms of the monopolist's maximizing his total profit within the market which he controls, whereas that of trade-marked goods is described in terms of an equilibrium between demand and supply over a much wider field. All value problems are relegated to one category or the other according to their predominant element; the partial check exerted by the other is ignored.

This procedure has led to a manner of thinking which goes even further and denies the very existence of the supposedly minor element. Monopoly and competition are very generally regarded, not simply as antithetical, but as mutually exclusive. To demonstrate competition is to prove the absence of monopoly, and vice versa. Indeed, to many the very phrase "monopolistic competition" will seem self-contradictory — a juggling of words. This conception is most unfortunate. Neither force excludes the other, and more often than not both are requisite to an intelligible account of prices.

2. Patents and Trade-Marks

The general case for a theory which recognizes both elements concurrently may be presented by inquiring into a particular problem: does any basis really exist for distinguishing between

patents and trade-marks? Patents (and copyrights) are ordinarily
considered as monopolies. They are granted under the authority
vested in Congress by the United States Constitution to secure
"for limited times, to authors and inventors, exclusive rights to
their respective writings and discoveries." The privilege granted
is *exclusive* — the inventor has the sole right to manufacture and
sell his invention for seventeen years. The monopoly nature of
this privilege is generally recognized both in the literature of patents and in that of general economics.[1] To be sure, the issue is
usually not sharply drawn, but one gains the impression that here
are instances where the principles of monopoly value are true
without qualification.

On the other hand, the competitive element has been pointed
out, and it has even been claimed that patents are, in their
essence, competitive rather than monopolistic. Vaughn argues
that "Patented products may be in competition both with patented and unpatented goods. In fact, the patent law is conducive
to competition in that it stimulates individual initiative and private enterprise."[2] Seager points out that "a large number of
them [patents] are for the protection of rival processes and serve
to stimulate rather than to diminish competition among those
employing the different methods."[3] The Committee on Patents
in the House of Representatives reported in 1912 that before the
era of trusts and combinations in restraint of trade "the monopoly granted by the patent law, limited as it was, in time tended
to stimulate competition. It incited inventors to new effort, and
capitalists and business men were encouraged to develop inventions. Under these conditions a patent, while granting a monopoly in a specific article, had rarely a tendency to monopolize
any branch of the trade, because few inventions were so fundamental in character as to give the owner of the patent a monopoly in any branch of the trade, and every great financial

---

[1] A few references are chosen at random: Elfreth, *Patents, Copyrights and Trade-
Marks*, p. 33; Prindle, *Patents as a Factor in Manufacturing*, p. 16; Mill, *Principles* of
Political Economy, Book V, Chap. X, Sec. 4; Ely, *Outlines of Economics*, 5th ed.,
p. 561; Garver and Hansen, *Principles of Economics*, p. 258.

[2] *The Economics of Our Patent System*, p. 26.

[3] *Principles of Economics* (1917), p. 414.

success arising from an individual patent was sure to result in rival inventions." [1] The report goes on to demonstrate the competition normally present if patents are separately held, in the following words: "Capital seeking to control industry through the medium of patents proceeds to buy up all important patents pertaining to the particular field. The effect of this is to shut out competition that would be inevitable if the various patents were separately and adversely held." [2] Evidently, when they are so held, the fact that they are monopolies does not preclude their being in competition with each other. Every patented article is subject to the competition of more or less imperfect substitutes.

It is the same with copyrights. Copyrighted books, periodicals, pictures, dramatic compositions, are monopolies; yet they must meet the competition of similar productions, both copyrighted and not. The individual's control over the price of his own production is held within fairly narrow limits by the abundance and variety of substitutes. Each copyrighted production is monopolized by the holder of the copyright; yet it is also subject to the competition which is present over a wider field.

Let us turn to trade-marks. Their monopolistic nature has not been entirely ignored. Says Johnson, "Somewhat analogous to the profits arising from a patent are the profits arising from the use of a trade-mark or from the 'good-will' of a concern." These returns "fall under the general head of monopoly profits." [3] The tone of hesitancy should, however, be noted, for it is characteristic. These profits are not *the same* as those arising from a patent; they are only "somewhat analogous." Ely classifies trade-marks as "general welfare monopolies," [4] and, although "it may be questioned whether they ought to be placed here," [5] he argues that they should be. "They give the use or monopoly of a certain sign or mark to distinguish one's own productions. . . . Of course, another person may build up another class of goods, and may establish value for another trade-mark." He therefore concludes that

---

[1] House Report No. 1161, 62nd Congress, 2nd Session, pp. 2, 3. (Cited in Vaughn, *op. cit.*, p. 27.)

[2] *Ibid.*, p. 5.

[3] *Introduction to Economics*, pp. 246–247.

[4] *Monopolies and Trusts*, p. 43.   [5] P. 48.

"it is a monopoly only in a certain line, marking off the goods of one manufacturer." Veblen speaks of monopolies "resting on custom and prestige" as "frequently sold under the name of goodwill, trade-marks, brands, etc." [1]   Knight puts "in the same category of monopoly. . . the use of trade-marks, trade names, advertising slogans, etc., and we may include the services of professional men with established reputations (whatever their real foundation)." [2] The list might be extended further.

On the other hand, trade-marks and brands are commonly regarded in the business world as a means of enabling one seller to compete more effectively with another — as congruous with and even necessary to competition. The view is implicitly sanctioned in economic literature by a common failure to take any cognizance of trade-marks whatever. They are simply taken for granted as a part of the essentially competitive régime. Frequently patents and copyrights alone are mentioned as monopolies; the implication is that trade-marks are not. A positive stand is taken by the late Professor Young in Ely, *Outlines of Economics*, where the elaborate classification found in Ely, *Monopolies and Trusts*, is reproduced with the significant change that trade-marks are omitted. "Trade-marks, like patents, are monopolies in the strictly legal sense that no one else may use them. But, unlike patents, they do not lead to a monopoly in the economic sense of giving exclusive control of one sort of business." By means of a trade-mark a successful business man "may be able to lift himself a little above the 'dead level' of competition . . . he is able to obtain what might be called a quasi-monopoly. But because his power to control the price of his product is in general much more limited than that of the true monopolist, and because competition limits and conditions his activities in other ways, his business is more properly called competitive than monopolistic." [3] Against this position it may be urged, first, that single patents, as has been shown, do not ordinarily give exclusive control of one sort of business and do not confer a monopoly in this sense of the term; and secondly, that, even granting that patents do give *more* control,

---

[1] *The Theory of Business Enterprise*, p. 55.
[2] *Risk, Uncertainty and Profit*, p. 185.   [3] 5th ed., pp. 562, 563.

this is simply a matter of degree, reducible to relative elasticity of demand. Both patents and trade-marks may be conceived of as monopoly elements of the goods to which they are attached; the competitive elements in both cases are the similarities between these goods and others. To neglect either the monopoly element in trade-marks or the competitive element in patents by calling the first competitive and the second monopolistic is to push to opposite extremes and to represent as *wholly* different two things which are, in fact, essentially alike.

An uncompromising position as to the competitive nature of trade-marks is found in Rogers, *Goodwill, Trade-Marks and Unfair Trading.* "These things [patents and copyrights] are monopolies created by law.... A trade-mark is quite a different thing. There is no element of monopoly involved at all.... A trade-mark precludes the idea of monopoly. It is a means of distinguishing one product from another; it follows therefore that there must be others to distinguish from. If there are others there is no monopoly, and if there is a monopoly there is no need for any distinguishing." [1] Here explicitly is the dialectic behind the attitude widely prevalent in economic and legal thinking, to which reference has already been made, that monopoly and competition must be regarded as alternatives. Evidently, it applies equally well to patents, for, to paraphrase the argument, no matter how completely the patented article may be different from others, there are always others, and therefore no monopoly. Monopoly becomes, by this reasoning, a possibility only if there is but one good in existence. What is the difficulty? Assuredly, two things may be alike in some respects and different in others. To center attention upon either their likeness or their unlikeness is, in either case, to give only half of the picture. Thus, if a trade-mark distinguishes, that is, marks off one product as different from another, it gives the seller of that product a monopoly, from which we might argue, following Rogers, that there is no competition. Indeed, Rogers himself falls into the trap and refutes his own argument a few pages further on, where, speaking of a buyer's assumed preference for "Quaker Oats," he says, "It is a habit

[1] Pp. 50–52.

pure and simple, and it is a *brand* habit, a *trade-mark* habit that we and others like us have, and that habit is worth something to the producer of the goods to whose use we have become habituated. It *eliminates competition*, for to us there is nothing 'just as good.'" [1] If trade-marks "preclude monopoly" and "eliminate competition," one may well ask the nature of the remainder.

Are there any bases, after all, for distinguishing between patents and trade-marks? Each makes a product unique in certain respects; this is its monopolistic aspect. Each leaves room for other commodities almost but not quite like it; this is its competitive aspect. The differences between them are only in degree, and it is doubtful if a significant distinction may be made even on this score. It would ordinarily be supposed that the degree of monopoly was greater in the case of patents. Yet the huge prestige value of such names as "Ivory," "Kodak," "Uneeda," "Coca-Cola," and "Old Dutch Cleanser," to cite only a few, is sufficient at least to make one sceptical. It would be impossible to compute satisfactorily for comparison the value of the monopoly rights granted by the United States Government in the form of patents and copyrights, and the value of those existing in the form of trade-marks, trade names, and good-will. The insuperable difficulty would be the definition (for purposes of deduction from total profits) of "competitive" returns, and of profits attributable to other monopoly elements. Allowance would also have to be made for the difference in duration of patents and trade-marks, for the enhanced value of patents in many cases by combination, and for other factors. But merely to suggest such a comparison is to raise serious doubts as to whether the monopoly element in patents is even quantitatively as important as that in trade-marks.

Let us apply the reasoning to the second phase of differentiation mentioned above,—that with respect to the conditions surrounding a product's sale. An example is the element of location in retail trade. The availability of a commodity at one location rather than at another being of consequence to purchasers, we may regard these goods as differentiated spatially and may apply the term "spatial monopoly" to that control over supply which

---

[1] *Ibid.*, p. 56. (Italics mine.)

is a seller's by virtue of his location. A retail trader has complete and absolute control over the supply of his "product" when this is taken to include the advantages, to buyers, of his particular location. Other things being equal, those who find his place of business most convenient to their homes, their habitual shopping tours, their goings and comings from business or from any other pursuit, will trade with him in preference to accepting more or less imperfect substitutes in the form of identical goods at more distant places; just as, in the case of trade-marked articles and of goods qualitatively differentiated, buyers are led to prefer one variety over another by differences in their personal tastes, needs, or incomes.

In this field of "products" differentiated by the circumstances surrounding their sale, we may say, as in the case of patents and trade-marks, that both monopolistic and competitive elements are present. The field is commonly regarded as competitive, yet it differs only in degree from others which would at once be classed as monopolistic. In retail trade, each "product" is rendered unique by the individuality of the establishment in which it is sold, including its location (as well as by trade-marks, qualitative differences, etc.); this is its monopolistic aspect. Each is subject to the competition of other "products" sold under different circumstances and at other locations; this is its competitive aspect. Here, as elsewhere in the field of differentiated products, both monopoly and competition are always present.

Speaking more generally, if we regard monopoly as the antithesis of competition, its extreme limit is reached only in the case of control of the supply of all economic goods, which might be called a case of pure monopoly in the sense that all competition of substitutes is excluded by definition. At the other extreme is pure competition, where, large classes of goods being perfectly standardized, every seller faces a competition of substitutes for his own product which is perfect. Between the two extremes there are all gradations, but both elements are always present, and must always be recognized. To discard either competition or monopoly is to falsify the result, and in a measure which may be far out of proportion to the apparent importance of the neglected factor.

Hence the theory of pure competition falls short as an explanation of prices when the product is (even slightly) differentiated. By eliminating monopoly elements (i. e., by regarding the product as homogeneous) it ignores the upward force which they exert, and indicates an equilibrium price which is below the true norm.[1] The analogy of component forces, although not exact, is helpful. Actual prices no more approximate purely competitive prices than the actual course of a twin-screw steamship approximates the course which would be followed if only one propeller were in operation. Pure competition and pure monopoly are extremes, just as the two courses of the ship, when propelled by either screw separately, are extremes. Actual prices tend towards neither, but towards a middle position determined with reference to the relative strength of the two forces in the individual case. A purely competitive price is not a normal price; and except for those few cases in the price system where competition is actually pure, there is no tendency for it to be established.

It might seem that the theory of monopoly would offend equally in the opposite sense by excluding the competitive elements. This would be true, however, only in the case of *pure* monopoly, as defined above — control of the supply of all economic goods by the same person or agency. The theory of monopoly has never been interpreted in this way. It applies to particular goods, and as such always admits competition between the product concerned and others. Indeed, we may go so far as to say that the theory *seems* fully to meet the essential requirement of giving due recognition to both elements, and the interesting possibility is at once suggested of turning the tables and describing economic society as perfectly monopolistic instead of as (almost) perfectly competitive. Subsequent chapters will carry the refutation of this view. Meanwhile the issues are clarified by displaying the large element of truth it contains. Let us see upon what grounds it may *not* be refuted.

[1] The full explanation of this will appear in subsequent chapters.

3. THE ECONOMIC ORDER AS PERFECTLY MONOPOLISTIC

The essence of monopoly is control over supply.[1] May not the entire field of differentiated product therefore be described in terms of perfect monopolies, one for each seller?

The first objection which may be made is that substitutes exist for many products which are, in fact, virtually the same product; whence it would appear that the element of monopoly, instead of being absolute and perfect, is almost non-existent.

Now, of course, the owner of a trade-mark does not possess a monopoly or any degree of monopoly over the broader field in which this mark is in competition with others. A monopoly of "Lucky Strikes" does not constitute a monopoly of cigarettes, for there is no degree of control whatever over the supply of other substitute brands. But if, in order to possess a perfect monopoly, control must extend to substitutes, the only perfect monopoly conceivable would be one embracing the supply of everything, since all things are more or less imperfect substitutes for each other. There is no reason to stop with the supply of cigarettes any more than with the supply of cigarettes within a certain quality or price range (which would be narrower) or with that of tobacco in all forms (which would be broader). The term "monopoly" is meaningless without reference to the thing monopolized. A monopoly of diamonds is not a monopoly of precious stones, nor, to go still further, of jewelry. Differentiation implies gradations, and it is compatible with *perfect* monopoly of one product that control stop short of some more general class of which this product is a part, and within which there is competition.

Although the idea has never been developed into a hybrid

[1] An able defense of a broader definition of monopoly to include all cases of scarcity appears in Dobb, *Capitalist Enterprise and Social Progress*, pp. 105 ff., together with references to prove that such a definition has "the sanction of usage." To the writer this seems misleading and dangerous. Mr. Dobb distinguishes three kinds of monopoly (scarcity) — natural, institutional, and deliberate, the latter referring to control of the supply by one person or group of persons. Clearly the third type must be distinguished from the other two, and even though qualifying adjectives are employed, the distinction is weakened and confused analysis invited by broadening the definition to include all cases of "restriction," or scarcity. The Greek derivation of the word ($\mu \acute{o} \nu o s$, alone $+ \pi \omega \lambda \epsilon \hat{\iota} \nu$, to sell), as well as the *preponderance* of economic usage, is definitely against such extension.

theory of value, it represents, so far, no departure from currently accepted doctrine. Two writers only need be cited. According to Taussig, "Copyrights and patents supply the simplest cases of absolute monopoly by law." [1] Yet he is explicit that "the holder of such a monopoly must reckon with the competition of more or less available substitutes, and thus is compelled to abate his prices and enlarge his supplies more than he would otherwise do." [2] Ely points out that "the use of substitutes is consistent with monopoly, and we nearly always have them. For almost anything we can think of, there is some sort of a substitute more or less perfect, and the use of substitutes furnishes one of the limits to the power of the monopolist. In the consideration of monopoly we have to ask, what are the substitutes, and how effective are they?" [3]

To the conception of economic society as perfectly monopolistic it may be objected, secondly, that, if differentiation is slight, even perfect control over *supply* may give a control over *price* which is negligible or non-existent. This is the ground upon which Professor Young, choosing between alternatives, preferred to call trade-marks competitive rather than monopolistic. [4] Seager also makes control over price an important element in his definition of monopoly. [5] Now a monopolist's control over price may be limited for either of two reasons: first, because his control over the supply is only partial, or secondly, because the demand for his product is highly elastic. If control over the supply is not complete, clearly the monopoly is not perfect, and control over price is only partial. But a highly elastic demand is a limitation of another sort. A monopolist's control over price is never complete in the sense that he can set it without regard for the conditions of demand for his product. It is to his advantage that the demand be inelastic, to be sure, but it is not in accord with general usage to measure the perfection of his monopoly by the degree of its elasticity.

The demand for a good may be so elastic that the seller's best price is little different from that of others selling products almost

[1] *Principles of Economics*, 3rd ed. revised, Vol. II, p. 114.
[2] *Ibid.*, Vol. I, p. 209.   [3] *Monopolies and Trusts*, p. 35.
[4] Above, p. 60.   [5] *Principles of Economics*, p. 213.

identical. It may be lower instead of higher, or it may conform to a commonly accepted price for the general class of goods. But the fact that all the producers set the same price does not indicate absence of monopoly, for, as will be shown later, this price will be higher than it would be if the commodity were perfectly homogeneous and sold under conditions of pure competition. Of course, prices might be higher yet if, instead of a monopoly of each different brand, there existed a monopoly of the entire class of product. The more substitutes controlled by any one seller, the higher he can put his price. But that is another matter. As long as the substitutes are to any degree imperfect, he still has a monopoly of his own product and control over its price within the limits imposed upon any monopolist — those of the demand.[1]

Thirdly, it may be objected that distinctive features often give profits which are not excessive, unreasonable, or above the "competitive level." This is, of course, true, but it has no bearing on the question. Most patents come to nothing; but they are not for this reason competitive. They are worthless monopolies — things nobody wants. Many copyrighted books are unsuccessful, and others, although sold at prices higher than they would be under pure competition, are sold in such small volume that the profits are nominal or wholly absent. It is quite possible for the preferences of buyers to be distributed with rough uniformity among

---

[1] There is an apparent difficulty in the case where, the differences between products being very slight, the seller might be unable to dispose of anything at all above the generally accepted price for that type of goods, the demand schedule for his product being perfectly elastic — the horizontal line which has been identified with pure competition. Buyers might prefer his goods at the same price, whereas they would go *en masse* to his competitors if there were the slightest difference.

The difficulty would not appear if the monetary unit were infinitely divisible. For if buyers had a preference for one product over another at the same price, it would require at least a slight divergence in price to eliminate it. The amount of this divergence would vary with individual buyers, and hence, if there were many of them, the demand schedule for each product would be continuous and tipped slightly from the horizontal. Actually, however, let it be granted that, at the next price above the one asked, sales may fall to zero. Monopoly is not thereby eliminated, for profits may be high through a large volume of sales as well as through a high price. Where this is the case, extra profits must be attributed to differentiation, for if the product were perfectly homogeneous, buyers would have no basis whatever for choice and would trade with different sellers at random, giving them each approximately the same volume of sales. Any excess of actual profits over what they would be under pure competition must be regarded as due to monopoly.

the products of a number of competing sellers, so that all have about the same profits. Monopoly necessarily involves neither a price higher than that of similar articles nor profits higher than the ordinary rate.

In summary, wherever products are differentiated, the theory of monopoly *seems* adequately to describe their prices. Competition is not eliminated from the explanation; it is fully taken into account by the recognition that substitutes affect the elasticity of demand for each monopolist's product.

4. MONOPOLISTIC COMPETITION [1]

It may now be asked in what respect monopolistic competition differs from this. Is it anything more than a new name, designed to soften a much wider application of the theory of monopoly than has heretofore been made? And if it is more, wherein lies the deficiency of the theory of monopoly, which has just been defended as adequate?

The answers to these questions are fully developed in the chapters to follow. Monopolistic competition is evidently a different thing from either *pure* monopoly or *pure* competition. As for monopoly, *as ordinarily conceived and defined,* monopolistic competition embraces it and takes it as a starting point. It is possible to do this where it would not be possible to take competition as a starting point, for the reason which has just been set forth at such length: that the theory of monopoly at least recognizes both elements in the problem, whereas the theory of competition, by regarding monopoly elements as "imperfections," eliminates them.

The theory of monopoly, although the opening wedge, is very soon discovered to be inadequate. The reason is that it deals with the isolated monopolist, the demand curve for whose product is given. Although such a theory may be useful in cases where substitutes are fairly remote, in general the competitive interrelationships of groups of sellers preclude taking the demand schedule for the product of any one of them as given. It depends upon the nature and prices of the substitutes with which it is in close com-

---

[1] In the matter of terminology, cf. above, p. 9, note 1.

petition. Within any group of closely related products (such as that ordinarily included in one imperfectly competitive market) the demand and cost conditions (and hence the price) of any one are defined only if the demand and cost conditions with respect to the others are taken as given. Partial solutions of this sort, yielded by the theory of monopoly, contribute nothing towards a solution of the whole problem, for each rests upon assumptions with respect to the others.[1] Monopolistic competition, then, concerns itself not only with the problem of an *individual* equilibrium (the ordinary theory of monopoly), but also with that of a *group* equilibrium (the adjustment of economic forces within a group of competing monopolists, ordinarily regarded merely as a group of competitors). In this it differs both from the theory of competition and from the theory of monopoly.

The matter may be put in another way. It has already been observed that, when products are differentiated, buyers are given a basis for preference, and will therefore be paired with sellers, not in random fashion (as under pure competition), but according to these preferences. Under pure competition, the market of each seller is perfectly merged with those of his rivals; now it is to be recognized that each is in some measure isolated, so that the whole is not a single large market of many sellers, but a network of related markets, one for each seller. The theory brings into the foreground the monopoly elements arising from ubiquitous partial independence. These elements have received but fragmentary recognition in economic literature, and never have they been allowed as a part of the general explanation of prices, except under the heading of "imperfections" in a theory which specifically excludes them.[2] It is now proposed to give due weight to whatever

---

[1] Algebraically speaking, simultaneous equations are not solved by expressing each variable in terms of the others.

[2] Several instances of fragmentary mention given to the idea of a separate market for each seller may be cited. Fisher points out (*Elementary Principles of Economics*, p. 323) that "the slight undercutting of prices by one grocer will not ruin the trade of another in another part of the same town for the reason that the two are not absolutely in the same market. Each has a sphere which the other can only partially reach, not only because of distance, but also because each has his own 'custom,' i. e., the patronage of people who, from habit or from other reasons, would not change grocers merely because of a slight difference in price." Marshall (*Principles*, 8th ed., p. 458; also Mathematical Appendix, note xiv) speaks of "industries in

degree of isolation exists by focusing attention on the market of the individual seller. A study of "competition" from this point of view gives results which are out of harmony with accepted competitive theory.

which each firm is likely to be confined more or less to its own particular market," but seems to regard this as entirely a short time phenomenon. The particular demand curve of the producer's own special market, he thinks, "will generally be very steep," probably on this account. No doubt it will be less elastic for a short period than for a long period, but, the differentiation of product remaining, it will never become horizontal, as under pure competition. The following passage is found in Dobb, *Capitalist Enterprise and Social Progress*, p. 88: "In any fairly-established line of business . . . each firm will probably possess a 'private market' of its own, composed of a fairly regular clientele which in various ways it has attached to itself." The accompanying brief discussion as to the effect on prices is in the vein of Chapter V, below.

J. M. Clark, in explaining his conception of a qualified monopoly as necessary to competition, says that "to a limited extent, each producer has his own individual market, connected more or less closely with those of his competitors, so that discrepancies are limited in amount and in duration, becoming narrower and briefer in proportion to the standardized character of the goods." (*Economics of Overhead Costs*, p. 418.) But he develops the idea no further, and thinks of competition as taking place in one large market. A. B. Wolfe points out the fallacy of treating retail merchants in different cities as if they were in the same market, and finds that even in the same city there are "distinct, though not absolutely independent, markets, defined by location and by class of custom." ("Competitive Costs and the Rent of Business Ability," *Quarterly Journal of Economics*, Vol. XXXIX [1924], p. 50.) But he never reaches the logical conclusion of the argument — a "distinct, though not absolutely independent," market for each seller. To him, "each town or locality constitutes a market," though with many qualifications and adequate recognition of its imperfections. F. H. Knight ("Cost of Production and Price over Long and Short Periods," *Journal of Political Economy*, Vol. XXIX, at p. 332, reprinted in the *Ethics of Competition and Other Essays*, see p. 213) states clearly the case for applying the theory of monopoly rather than that of competition to the "partial monopoly" resulting from differentiated products. Actually, however, he has shown no inclination to modify his fundamental position that "economic theory" is simply the theory of perfect competition. See my comment, *American Economic Review*, Vol. XXXVI (1946), no. 2 (Proceedings), p. 93. (See also Essay 15, "The Chicago School," in *Towards a More General Theory of Value*.)

CHAPTER V

PRODUCT DIFFERENTIATION AND
THE THEORY OF VALUE

1. Introduction

UNDER pure competition, the individual seller's market being completely merged with the general one, he can sell as much as he pleases at the going price. Under monopolistic competition, however, his market being separate to a degree from those of his rivals, his sales are limited and defined by three new factors: (1) his price, (2) the nature of his product, and (3) his advertising outlays.

The divergence of the demand curve for his product from the horizontal imposes upon the seller a price problem, absent under pure competition, which is the same as that ordinarily associated with the monopolist. Depending upon the elasticity of the curve and upon its position relative to the cost curve for his product, profits may be increased, perhaps by raising the price and selling less, perhaps by lowering it and selling more. That figure will be sought which will render the total profit a maximum.

The adjustment of his product is likewise a new problem imposed upon the seller by the fact of differentiation. The volume of his sales depends in part upon the manner in which his product differs from that of his competitors. Here the broad sense in which the word "product" is used must constantly be held in mind.[1] Its "variation" may refer to an alteration in the quality of the product itself — technical changes, a new design, or better materials; it may mean a new package or container; it may mean more prompt or courteous service, a different way of doing business, or perhaps a different location. In some cases an alteration is specific and definite — the adoption of a new design, for instance. In others, as a change in the quality of service, it may be gradual, perhaps unconscious. Under pure competition a pro-

---

[1] To this end, it will frequently be inclosed in quotation marks.

ducer may, of course, shift from one field of activity to another, but his volume of sales never depends, as under monopolistic competition, upon the product or the variety of product he chooses, for he is always a part of a market in which many others are producing the identical good.[1] Just as his sales may, under pure competition, be varied over a wide range without alteration in his price, so they may be as large or as small as he pleases without the necessity of altering his product. Where the possibility of differentiation exists, however, sales depend upon the skill with which the good is distinguished from others and made to appeal to a particular group of buyers. The "product" may be improved, deteriorated, or merely changed, and with or without a readjustment of price. To it, as well as to the price, the conventional assumption of profit maximization will ordinarily be applied.[2]

Thirdly, the seller may influence the volume of his sales by making expenditures, of which advertising may be taken as typical, which are directed specifically to that purpose. Such expenditures increase both the demand for his product, and his costs; and their amount will be adjusted, as are prices and "products," so as to render the profits of the enterprise a maximum. This third factor is likewise peculiar to monopolistic competition, since advertising would be without purpose under conditions of pure competition, where any producer can sell as much as he pleases without it. But it does not necessarily make its appearance with the monopoly elements already introduced. It will be argued later that gains from this source are possible because of (a) imperfect knowledge on the part of buyers as to the means whereby wants may be most effectively satisfied, and (b) the possibility of altering wants by advertising or selling appeal. It will be helpful to proceed slowly, postponing this range of considerations until after the consequences of differentiation *per se* have been traced. For the present, then, advertising as a competitive activity is put

---

[1] To put the matter in another way, slight differences are not inconsistent with pure competition, provided that *for each variety* there be a large number of producers competing in a single market.

[2] For an extended discussion of product variation, see my article, "The Product as an Economic Variable," *Quarterly Journal of Economics*, Vol. LXVII (1953), p. 1. (Essay 6 in *Towards a More General Theory of Value*.)

to one side, and attention confined to the two variables of price and "product." This may be done by proceeding explicitly on the assumption of given wants and perfect knowledge concerning the means available for satisfying them.

Where both prices and "products" may be varied, complete equilibrium must involve stability with respect to both. The notion of a "product equilibrium" needs explanation, and its importance may not at once be apparent. The theory of value, concerning itself with the price adjustment for a given product, has passed it by completely, and it seems to have occurred to no one [1] that the inverse problem might be put of the product adjustment for a given price. Price adjustments are, in fact, but one phase, and often a relatively unimportant phase, of the whole competitive process. More and more is price competition evaded by turning the buyer's attention towards a trade-mark, or by competing on the basis of quality or service (or by advertising, excluded for the present). The fact of such competition should at least be brought into the open by including the "product" as a variable in the problem.

For a complete picture, indeed, each element of the "product" should be regarded as a separate variable. What, for instance, is the adjustment with regard to location when price and the *other* aspects of the "product" are given? Quality, service, etc., might be isolated in the same way.[2] Some indication of the peculiarities to which such analysis might lead is given in Appendix C, where an attempt is made to isolate the factor of location. Aside from this, however, variation of the "product" is considered only in its most general aspects.

The markets for goods which are substitutes for each other being closely interrelated, the position and elasticity of the demand curve for the product of any one seller depend in large part

---

[1] With the single exception of Hotelling, "Stability in Competition," *Economic Journal*, Vol. XXXIX (1929).

[2] It may be remarked at this point that there seems to be no reason why competition which is compounded with monopoly elements should necessarily tend to improve the "product" in these or other respects. The result will depend upon circumstances. Just as a seller may, under monopolistic competition, gain by raising his price and selling less as well as by lowering his price and selling more, so he may gain by deteriorating his product as well as by improving it.

upon the availability of competing "products" and the prices which are asked for them. The equilibrium adjustment for him, therefore, cannot be defined without reference to the more general situation of which he is a part. However, it is not inconsistent with recognition of this interdependence that the conditions with respect to his competitors which define his own market be held constant while his own adjustment is considered in isolation. A complex system may be better understood by breaking it into its parts, and the problem of individual equilibrium will serve as a helpful introduction to the more complicated one of the adjustments over a wider field.

Aside from this purpose, which may be regarded as entirely expositional, a solution of the equilibrium adjustment for the individual enterprise has other justification in that it is often directly applicable to the facts. Theory may well disregard the interdependence between markets wherever business men do, in fact, ignore it. This is true (1) in a multitude of cases where the effects of a change inaugurated by any one seller are spread over such a large number of competitors that they are negligible for each. It is also true (2) when there are *no* very direct substitutes for the product, so that the increase in its sales brought about, say, by a lowering of its price, is not predominantly at the expense of any closely competing product or group of products, but rather at the expense of goods of all kinds. Here we have the implicit assumption of "isolation" underlying the traditional theory of monopoly; indeed the phase of the problem here considered may be regarded merely as an extension of the theory of monopoly to include the adjustment of "product" as well as of price. In sum, the theory of individual equilibrium is significant (1) in itself, and (2) as an introduction to the problem of equilibrium over the wider field embracing what is usually regarded vaguely as an "imperfectly competitive" market.

2. Individual Equilibrium

Assuming given conditions with respect to all substitutes, both as to their nature and as to their prices, let us describe the adjustment of price and of "product" which will render a maximum the profits of the individual seller to whom our attention is given. The seller may, in fact, adjust both together, or either one separately, depending upon circumstances. If his price is set by custom or imposed upon him by trade practice or (if a retailer) by the manufacturer, he is free to vary only his "product." On the other hand, if his product is set by its very nature or by a previous decision, then the only variable in fact is his price. If both may be varied, the equilibrium adjustment must involve both. Our

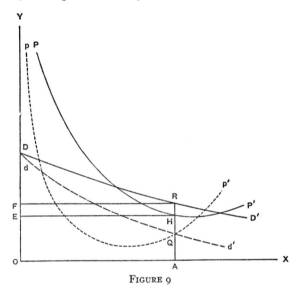

FIGURE 9

method will be to consider each in turn and finally to combine them. Again, each isolated problem may have its own value, as suggested above, or may be regarded as a step towards the final solution where the parts are reunited.

First, let the "product" be held constant, attention being turned to the price adjustment. In Fig. 9, *DD'* is the demand curve, rigidly defined by the fixity of *all* products and of *all other* prices; *PP'* is the curve of cost of production. It will be recalled that the latter traces the economies of large-scale production, descending to a minimum point and then rising again.[1] (Let the

---

[1] See above, p. 20; also Appendix B. The notation of *PP'* refers to the fact that the costs included are those of production only. It is open to the objection that

dotted lines be ignored for the moment.) The position of the curves relative to each other will depend upon the position assumed for the fixed elements in the problem. *DD′* must either intersect *PP′* in two places, as in Fig. 9, or be tangent to it, as in Fig. 10. (It could not lie at all points below the cost curve, else the good would not be produced at all.) It is bound to cut across *PP′* in the manner indicated, i. e., lying below it at either ex-

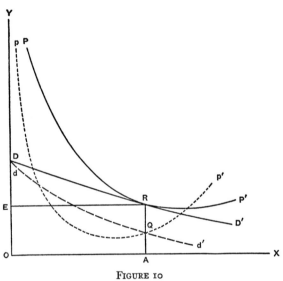

FIGURE 10

tremity, by the nature of the two curves. It lies below it to the left because, whereas the demand will characteristically become zero at a finite price, and a fairly low one on account of substitutes, the necessity of covering overhead or supplementary costs (including the minimum profit of the entrepreneur), no matter how small the production, defines the cost curve as meeting the *y* axis at infinity. *DD′* lies below *PP′* again to the right because the demand curve must fall gradually to zero (granting that the good may conceivably become so abundant as to be a free good), whereas the cost curve can never fall to zero, but must

"*P*" can no longer be employed, as is usual, to designate the price. However, it is believed that the innovation will justify itself when it becomes necessary at a later stage to distinguish between cost of production and cost of selling.

turn upwards again after the most efficient scale of production has been reached.

Now, supposing the conditions of demand and of cost as given, the price determined upon will evidently be AR, the profit area, $EHRF$, being a maximum. (The cost curve, PP', includes at all points the *minimum* profit necessary to secure the entrepreneur's services; therefore his *total* profit will be a maximum if the excess HR over this per unit, multiplied by the number of units, OA, is a maximum.) The amount sold is OA. If DD' is tangent to PP' as in Fig. 10, there is only one price which will not involve actual loss, and it is AR, for the output OA.[1] Equilibrium here involves no profits above the necessary minimum; yet, since these are covered, the adjustment is perfectly stable and profits are as truly maximized as in Fig. 9, where an excess exists.

The point of maximum profit may also be defined with reference to curves of marginal costs and of marginal revenue. The nature of these curves has already been explained.[2] They are derived from the curves of average costs and of average revenue (price), and are indicated by the dotted lines pp' and dd', respectively. As production increases up to their point of intersection at Q, profits are continually increased, since each additional unit adds more to revenue than to costs. Beyond Q, the converse is true, and total profits will accordingly be a maximum when output is adjusted to OA. The price per unit at which this amount will be sold is not AQ, however, but AR, as revealed by the demand curve DD' (the curve of average revenue).

It may now be seen that the effect of monopoly elements on the individual's adjustment (barring the possibility of advertising, to be considered later) is characteristically to render his price higher and his scale of production smaller than under pure competition. This is the result of the sloping demand curve, as compared with the perfectly horizontal one of pure competition. No matter in

---

[1] The demand and cost curves may be so shaped that they are tangent at several points or for a considerable distance. Similarly, in Fig. 9, a slight "wave" in either curve might give two or several solutions. Clearly, there are manifold possibilities for indeterminate solutions on this score. The theory, here and later, however, will be developed only for curves which are smooth and "regular" in shape.

[2] See above, p. 14.

what position the demand curve is drawn, its negative slope will define maximum profits at a point further to the left than if it were horizontal, as under pure competition. This means, in general, higher production costs and higher prices.[1] The matter will be developed further as the argument proceeds.

Secondly, let the price be held constant while the "product" adjustment is examined. The entrepreneur may be regarded as accepting a price generally prevalent, one established by tradition or trade practice, or one determined upon by an earlier decision, and to which his customers have become habituated. He now chooses his "product" — or whatever phases of it are subject to variation. If he is setting out initially upon his venture, he is free to choose all phases of the product, even such more or less permanent attributes of it as his place of doing business, if he is a retailer, or his trade-mark, if he is a manufacturer. Later, the field of choice is more limited, yet rarely is it diminished to nothing. In retailing, service and other circumstances surrounding the sale are always subject to change; in manufacturing, technical and qualitative variations, either in the product or in its container, if it has one, are always possible. Some products are in their very essence incapable of becoming set. The publication of a newspaper, or of a magazine, for instance, involves a continual choice as to what shall be offered to its readers. In this particular case, it may be remarked that our assumptions are further realized in that price does not vary while such decisions are being made.

A peculiarity of "product" variation is that, unlike variation in price, it may and ordinarily does involve changes in the cost of production curve. Qualitative changes in the product alter the cost of producing it. They also, of course, alter the demand for it. The problem becomes that of selecting the "product" whose cost and whose market allow the largest total profit, price being given.

Another peculiarity is that "product" variations are very often qualitative, rather than quantitative, and in this case can-

---

[1] One qualification must be made. If the demand curve is extremely elastic *and also lies at a considerable distance above the cost curve*, the most profitable scale of production may equal or exceed the most efficient scale. (The price, however, would always exceed the competitive price.) The importance of this possibility can best be judged after discussion of the group problem including diversity, further on.

not be measured along an axis and displayed in a single diagram.[1] Resort must be had, instead, to the somewhat clumsy expedient of imagining a series of diagrams, one for each variety of "product." In Fig. 11, let *OE* be the fixed price. For simplicity, only two varieties of product, which we shall call "A" and "B," are illustrated, superimposed, in the same graph. The cost curve for product "A" is *AA'* and the amount demanded (at the fixed

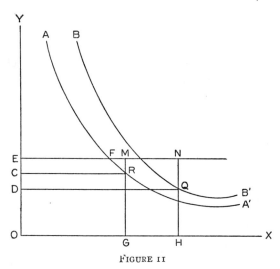

FIGURE 11

price *OE*) is *OG*. Total profits are *CRME* and total cost *OGRC*. For product "B" the cost curve is *BB'* and the amount demanded is *OH*. Total profits are *DQNE*, total costs *OHQD*. It must be remembered that the line *EN* is not a demand line, indicating indefinitely large demand at the price *OE*. For each variety of product the amount demanded is limited, and is defined by the fixed conditions with respect to the nature and price of substitute "products" and the price of this one. It is not possible, then, to move back and forth along the cost curve, say along *AA'*, in order to find the best supply to put upon the market; rather, the movement is from one curve to another, as "product" changes, the

---

[1] The problem of measurement is discussed more fully in "The Product as an Economic Variable," *op. cit.*, esp. p. 8. Also, recalling that location is an aspect of the "product," see Appendix C.

amount which can be sold being rigidly defined for each case. Comparing the two possibilities illustrated, it is evident that "B" is to be preferred to "A." By making similar comparisons between the costs and demands for all possible varieties, the seller may choose the one which seems to him most advantageous.

It must be remarked that the "product" selected is not necessarily that whose cost of production is the lowest (AA' is lower than BB', yet the latter affords a greater profit); nor is it necessarily the one the demand for which is greatest, for cost of production must be taken into account. Furthermore, the output bears no relation to the most efficient scale of production, revealed by the lowest point on the curve of cost of production.

Evidently, as different conditions are assumed with regard to the fixed elements in the problem, the demand varies, and the positions of the curves and of the price line change. Possibilities of extra profit are more and more restricted as competitive pressure is greater. Better, cheaper (or more extensively advertised) substitutes mean perhaps a lower price line, perhaps a higher cost curve through the necessity for improving the "product," perhaps a recession in demand, or perhaps all three together. If the demand were only EF for product "A," and if no better "product" choice were possible, minimum costs would only just be covered; if it were less, production would have to cease. Similarly, if the cost curve were higher, or the price line lower, profit opportunities would be more restricted, and if the former lay above the latter, for every possible variety, production at a profit would be impossible.

The adjustments of both price and "product" have now been considered in isolation, and it remains to combine them in order to describe the general case where the seller is free to vary both. This is a simple matter of addition. If constructions such as Figs. 9 and 10 are drawn for every possible variety of "product," that combination of "product" and price may easily be chosen which offers the largest total profit of all. Or if constructions such as Fig. 11 were drawn for all possible combinations of "product" and price, the optimum combination of the two would again be revealed. The clumsiness of representing "product" **variation** graphically makes it impossible to summarize the whole adjustment in a single diagram. However, either Fig. 9 or Fig. 10 may be regarded as embodying such a summary, if drawn with reference to the optimum "product." By definition, no better choice in this respect would then be possible, and it is evident from the figure that the price of AR could not be improved upon.

3. GROUP EQUILIBRIUM

Let us turn now to what we may call the group problem, or the adjustment of prices and "products" of a number of producers whose goods are fairly close substitutes. The group contemplated initially is one which has *ordinarily* been regarded as composing one imperfectly competitive market: a number of automobile manufacturers, of producers of pots and pans, of magazine publishers, or of retail shoe dealers.[1] From our point of view, each producer within the group is a monopolist, yet his market is interwoven with those of his competitors, and he is no longer to be isolated from them. The question now to be asked is: what characterizes the system of relationships into which the group tends to fall as a result of their influence one upon another? The conclusions reached will be especially illuminating when considered alongside of those yielded by the theory of pure competition, ordinarily applied to the same phenomena.

One difficulty encountered in describing the group equilibrium is that the widest variations may exist in all respects between the different component firms. Each "product" has distinctive features and is adapted to the tastes and needs of those who buy it. Qualitative differences lead to wide divergences in the curves of cost of production, and buyers' preferences account for a corresponding variety of demand curves, both as to shape (elasticity) and as to position (distance from the x and y axes). The result is heterogeneity of prices, and variation over a wide range in outputs (scales of production) and in profits. Many such variations are, of course, temporary, and are constantly in process of being eliminated. Our main concern, however, is with those which

[1] On the essential elasticity of the group concept, however, see pp. 102–4; 196–202.

persist over a long period of time. To a very considerable extent the scheme of prices is the result of conditions unique to each product and to its maiket — it defies comprehensive description as a "group" problem, even when monopolistic forces are given their full value in the explanation.

The matter may be put in another way by saying that the "imperfection" of competition is not uniform. It is not as though a few elements of friction, such as imperfect knowledge, or partial indifference to economic gain, spread an even haze over the whole; nor as though immobility of resources gave a general tendency for "normal" results to be retarded in working themselves out. These factors would apply with equal force in all portions of the field, at least over periods long enough for chance short time irregularities to be ironed out. But the differentiation of the product is not, so to speak, "uniformly spaced"; it is not distributed homogeneously among all of the products which are grouped together. Each has its own individuality, and the size of its market depends on the strength of the preference for it over other varieties. Again, if high average profits lead new competitors to invade the general field, the markets of different established producers cannot be wrested from them with equal facility. Some will be forced to yield ground, but not enough to reduce their profits below the minimum necessary to keep them in business. Others may be cut to the minimum, and still others may be forced to drop out because only a small demand exists or can be created for their particular variety of product. Others, protected by a strong prejudice in favor of theirs, may be virtually unaffected by an invasion of the general field — their monopoly profits are beyond the reach of competition.

These variations will give no real difficulty in the end. Exposition of the group theory is facilitated, however, by ignoring them for the present. We therefore proceed under the heroic assumption that both demand and cost curves for all the "products" are uniform throughout the group. We shall return later [1] to a recognition of their diversity, and to the manner in which allowance for it is to be made. Meanwhile, it may be remarked that diversity

[1] P. 110.

of "product" is not entirely eliminated under our assumption. It is required only that consumers' preferences be evenly distributed among the different varieties, and that differences between them be not such as to give rise to differences in cost. This might be approximately true where very similar products were differentiated by trade-marks. It is also approximately realized in the fairly even geographical distribution of small retail establishments in the outlying districts of a city.[1]

Another complication in the group problem arises in connection with the number of competitors included within the group and the manner in which their markets "overlap." If numbers are few, complexities similar to those described in Chapter III become important. This complication may be adequately recognized by considering first the case where numbers are very large, then the case where they are small. Specifically, we assume *for the present* that any adjustment of price or of "product" by a single producer spreads its influence over so many of his competitors that the impact felt by any one is negligible and does not lead him to any readjustment of his own situation. A price cut, for instance, which increases the sales of him who made it, draws inappreciable amounts from the markets of each of his many competitors, achieving a considerable result for the one who cut, but without making incursions upon the market of any single competitor sufficient to cause him to do anything he would not have done anyway.

As in the case of individual equilibrium, we shall first focus attention upon the price adjustment by assuming "products" stable; then reverse the process; and finally combine the two results.

Let the demand and cost curves for the "product" of *each* of the competing monopolists in the group be DD' and PP' respectively (Fig. 12). Each seller will at once set his price at AR, since his profits, $GHRE$, at that point are a maximum. In spite of the extra profit which all are enjoying, there is no reason for any one to reduce his price below this figure, since the business gained would not make up for the price sacrifice. The extra profit will,

---

[1] The concentration of population (at the time of making purchases) in the center would make it untrue there. Cf. Appendix C.

however, attract new competitors into the field, with a resulting shift in the demand curves and possibly in the cost curves. The demand curve for the "product" of each seller will be moved to the left, since the total purchases must now be distributed among a larger number of sellers. The cost curve we shall assume for the moment to be unaffected. With each shift in the demand curve will come a price readjustment so as to leave the area correspond-

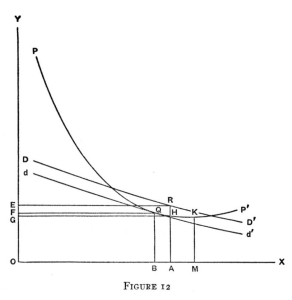

FIGURE 12

ing to *GHRE* a maximum, the process continuing until the demand curve for each "product" is tangent to its cost curve, and the area of surplus profit is wiped out. The price is now *BQ*, and the ultimate demand curve, *dd'*. The same final adjustment would have been reached if the original demand curve had lain to the left of and below *dd'*, through an exodus of firms caused by the general realization of losses, and the movement of the demand curve to the right and upwards as the total sales were shared by a smaller number of competitors, until it settled in the position of *dd'*. Here is a position of equilibrium. Price equals cost of production and any seller will lose by either raising or lowering it; it is therefore stable. There will be no further flow of resources into or out of the field, since profits are just adequate to maintain the amount then invested.

Let us now return to the question of the cost curves in the adjustment. As new resources flow into the field, these curves may be raised (by an increase in the price of the productive factors employed); they may be lowered (by improvements in the organization of the group as a whole — "external economies"); or they may remain the same (owing to the absence of both of these tendencies or to their cancellation one against the other). These three possibilities correspond respectively to the familiar increasing, decreasing, and constant cost of competitive theory. In the simple illustration just given no allowance was made for a shift in the curves; in other words, the assumption was implicitly made that conditions of constant cost obtained for the group as a whole. This assumption will be continued throughout, and for two reasons: (1) the theory in this form is widely applicable to the facts, and (2) where it is not applicable, its extension to cover cases of increasing and decreasing cost for the group is easily made.

First, as to its applicability. It has already been explained (see above, p. 22) why variations in output by a single producer will, if he is one of many producers, have a negligible effect upon the total output for all and hence upon cost tendencies for the product as a whole. Similarly, whenever the quantity of resources employed in one field of production is small relative to their quantity employed generally, an increase or decrease in output within this one field will have a negligible effect upon the prices of the productive factors employed and hence upon costs. An increase in the manufacture of scissors will not appreciably affect the price of steel. Nor will an increased output of rubber boots raise the price of rubber. What conditions obtain in any particular case is, of course, a question of fact. It is only meant to point out that tendencies towards increasing (or decreasing) cost with respect to particular kinds of resources or factors of production are transmitted to finished products almost always with diminished force and often with a force which is negligible.[1] To this must be added

[1] The extent to which they are transmitted depends partly on the breadth of the class of finished product considered (the cost tendency for lumber would be trans-

the fact that the resources themselves may be obtainable at fairly constant cost. If increased supplies of cement, sand, and gravel are readily available, expansion of the building industry will be possible at constant costs so far as these materials are a factor. In sum, it is likely that many fields of production are subject to conditions of approximately constant cost so far as the prices of the resources involved are concerned.

Do improvements in the organization of resources with larger output — "external economies" — result generally in a tendency to diminishing cost? The answer is yes, where they are appreciable. But it must be realized that such economies include only those made possible by the expansion of this particular field, exclusive of (*a*) those arising from the expansion of smaller fields (the individual establishments) within it — "internal economies" — and (*b*) those arising from the expansion of larger fields of which it is a part — the largest of which would be industry generally. The former are excluded because they may be realized to the full, independently of the output of the group (see above, p. 22); the latter, for a similar reason, because, since the group in question is small relative to larger fields of which it is a part, its expansion or contraction has a negligible effect upon economies in this larger field.[1] To illustrate, an expansion of the retail grocery trade does not enable the individual grocer to approximate any more closely the most effective conditions of production within his own shop; neither does it contribute appreciably to such economies as are made possible by a large volume of retailing generally. In the

mitted to furniture more than it would be to chairs), and partly on the number of uses to which the particular resource is put (the cost tendency for wheat would be transmitted to flour to a greater extent than that for lumber would be to furniture, since most wheat becomes flour, whereas lumber is put to many important uses other than furniture).

[1] Cf. Sraffa, "The Laws of Returns Under Competitive Conditions," *Economic Journal*, Vol. XXXVI, especially pp. 538–541. The literature on cost and supply curves has expanded rapidly in recent years. A bibliography is to be found in an article by Dr. Morgenstern, "Offene Probleme der Kosten- und Ertragstheorie," *Zeitschrift für Nationalökonomie*, Band II, Heft 4 (March, 1931), to which may be added: Harrod, "Notes on Supply," *Economic Journal*, Vol. XL (1930), and "The Law of Decreasing Costs," *Economic Journal*, Vol. XLI (1931); Viner, "Cost Curves and Supply Curves," *Zeitschrift für Nationalökonomie*, Band III, Heft 1 (1931); and Schneider, "Zur Interpretation von Kostenkurven," *Archiv für Sozialwissenschaft*, Band LXV, Heft 2, (1931) and "Kostentheoretisches zum Monopolproblem," *Zeitschrift für Nationalökonomie*, Band III, Heft 2 (1932).

group problem, then, the only economies which may be admitted as lowering the cost curves with increase of output are those which are due to the expansion of the group itself. Whether such economies exist in any particular case is, again, a matter of fact. Wherever they do not or where they are of only negligible importance, the result is a tendency to constant cost for the group.

The theory as developed for the case of constant cost may also be applicable if there are opposing tendencies of increasing and decreasing cost which approximately offset each other. Thus, expansion of the automobile industry may lead to (1) higher costs because of increased demand for materials, and (2) lower costs because of improved organization within the industry, the two roughly balancing each other and giving a net result of constant cost.

Secondly, the theory is not developed to include the cases of increasing and decreasing cost for the group because to do so in detail is not necessary. Where increasing costs obtain, the curves of all producers will rise as the resources employed in the field are increased, and fall as they are diminished, equilibrium being reached at a higher or at a lower point as the case may be. (Rents will be affected as in purely competitive theory, and are here to be included within the cost curves of the individual producers.) Similarly, in the case of decreasing cost the curves of all producers will fall as resources are increased and rise as they are diminished, the equilibrium being correspondingly lower or higher. These observations need not be repeated at every stage of the argument. Regardless of the cost tendency for the group, the equilibrium is always defined in the same manner with respect to the individual curves, and the divergences from the norms of purely competitive theory are always of the same sort. Our interest lies primarily in these matters, and they are most clearly revealed in the simple case of constant cost, to which attention will be confined from this point on.

Before introducing further complications, we may note some general conclusions as to monopolistic competition which follow from the first very simple putting of the case. In the first place, we see the necessity for distinguishing carefully between competitive prices and competitive profits. If there were no monopoly elements, prices would correspond to the cost of production under the most efficient conditions, MK in the figure. The demand curve for the product of any single producer would be a horizontal line, and would be lowered by competition until it was tangent to PP' at K. The monopoly elements inevitably carry it higher, although the profits made by the individual producer are no greater, costs being exactly covered in both cases. Competition, in so far as it consists of a movement of resources into the group, reduces profits to the competitive level, but leaves prices higher to a degree dependent upon the strength of the monopoly elements. Competitive profits, then, never mean competitive prices under monopolistic competition, for the demand curve is never tangent to the cost curve at its lowest point.

In the second place, the price is inevitably higher and the scale of production inevitably smaller [1] under monopolistic competition than under pure competition. It might be argued that a price reduction on the part of one seller, although it would increase his sales only within limits, would conceivably increase them to OM, and that successive moves on the part of all would establish the price MK. But this is impossible. It is true that for the position of DD' shown in Fig. 13 a reduction, if made, would in fact give the price of MK and the most efficient scale of production, OM. But such a reduction would not be made, for any seller could increase his profits by raising his price to AR, where $FHRE$ is a maximum; and equilibrium will be reached, as described earlier, when DD' has moved to the left until it is tangent to PP', the price at this point being higher than MK and the scale of production smaller than OM.

A third conclusion is that general uniformity of price proves nothing as to the freedom of competition from monopoly elements. The general explanation of such tendency towards a uniform price as exists in actuality is that the demand curve for the product of each seller is of about the same elasticity, so that each finds his maximum profit at the same point. In the field of retailing, for instance, if the market of each seller is a random sample

[1] See, however, a qualification in note 1, page 78.

of the whole population, prices in an entire area will be fairly uniform, and grouped about a modal, or most prevalent, price according to the law of probability. Of course, such freedom of
movement as exists among buyers contributes to this result, for
the more elastic the demand schedules, the more closely will price
deviations be grouped about the mode.[1] But apart from such
freedom of movement (the elasticity of demand), they will also be
grouped more closely about the mode as each sample is more

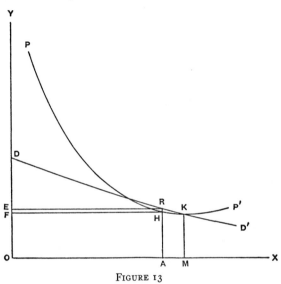

FIGURE 13

nearly the same in composition as the whole. If each dealer's
market were made up of exactly the same proportion of rich and
poor, and of those of different tastes and preferences, prices would
everywhere be the same, even though a wall separated the province of each seller, isolating his market completely from those of
his competitors. General uniformity of prices, therefore, proves
nothing as to the purity of competition, or, we might say, as to
the relative proportions of monopoly and competition in the
admixture.

Let us return to the main thread of the argument. The nature
of the equilibrium adjustment pictured in Fig. 12 will be better

---

[1] I. e., the standard deviation will approach more closely to zero.

understood if another route by which it may be reached is described. The maladjustment which was corrected in the movement towards this equilibrium was one of an unduly small number
of firms, which gave to each one a larger market and the possibility of profits above the minimum level. It was corrected by an
influx of new firms until markets were diminished and the extra
profits eliminated. Let us now suppose the number of firms to be
that corresponding to the equilibrium adjustment and to remain
unchanged while a ruling price higher than the equilibrium one is
corrected. Graphic representation of this situation requires the
introduction of a new type of demand curve.

The curve DD', as heretofore drawn, describes the market for
the "product" of any one seller, *all* "products" and *all other*
prices being given. It shows the increase in sales which he could
realize by cutting his price, *provided* others did not also cut theirs;
and conversely, it shows the falling off in sales which would attend
an increase in price, *provided* other prices did not also increase.
Another curve may now be drawn which shows the demand for
the product of any one seller at various prices on the assumption
that his competitors' prices are always identical with his. Evidently
this latter curve will be much less elastic than the former, since
the concurrent movement of all prices eliminates incursions by one
seller, through a price cut, upon the markets of others. Such a
curve will, in fact, be a fractional part of the demand curve for the
general class of product, and will be of the same elasticity. If
there were 100 sellers, it will show a demand at each price which
will be exactly 1/100 of the total demand at that price (since we
have assumed all markets to be of equal size). Let DD' in Fig. 14
be such a curve, and let the price asked by all producers be, for
the moment, BQ. The sales of each are OB, and the profits of each
(in excess of the minimum contained within the cost curve) are
$FHQE$. Now let dd' be drawn through Q, showing the increased
sales which any one producer may enjoy by lowering his price,
provided the others hold their fast at BQ.[1] Evidently, profits

[1] It may seem that anyone reducing his price from BQ would enjoy all the additional demand at the lower price for the entire market, i.e., 100 times that shown by
DD' in Fig. 14; and that this fact alone would, by the reasoning developed in connection with pure competition, make the curve dd' virtually horizontal. This is not

may be increased for any individual seller by moving to the right along dd'; and he may do this without fear of ultimately reducing his gains through forcing others to follow him[1] because his competitors are so numerous that the market of each of them is inappreciably affected by his move. (Each loses only 1/99 of the total gained by the one who cuts his price.) The same incentive of larger profits which prompts one seller to reduce his price leads

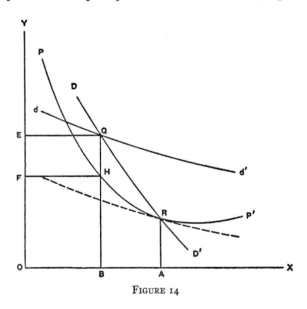

FIGURE 14

the others to do likewise. The curve dd', then, explains why each seller is led to reduce his price; the curve DD' shows his actual sales as the *general* downward movement takes place. The former curve "slides" downwards along the latter as prices are lowered,

---

the case, however. The increased demand when all lower their prices, indicated by the so-called demand curve for the general market, contains its due proportion of those who prefer each variety of the product, and the lower price offer by one producer will attract only a portion of them. In fact, the very concept of a demand curve for the general market of a differentiated product is open to the objection that people do not demand the product "in general," but particular varieties of it, so that the amount which any buyer will take depends not only upon the price but upon the variety which is offered him.

[1] Cf. above, pp. 46 ff.

and the movement comes to a stop at the price of AR.[1] Evidently it will pay no one to cut beyond that point, for his costs of producing the larger output would exceed the price at which it could be sold.

The position of DD' depends upon the number of sellers in the field. It lies further to the left as there are more of them, since the

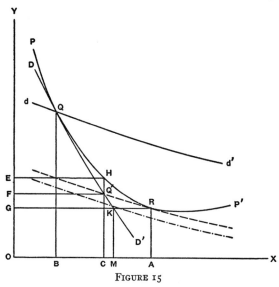

FIGURE 15

share of each in the total is then smaller; and further to the right as there are fewer of them, since the share of each in the total is then larger. It was drawn through R, the point of tangency of dd' with PP', in the example just given, since the number of sellers was assumed to be that consistent with the final equilibrium adjustment. Let us now suppose that, at prices in the neighborhood of BQ, temporarily prevailing, additional sellers are attracted by the high profits, and intrench themselves in the field before the price-cutting corrective takes place. Such an inflow of resources may conceivably continue until DD' is pushed leftwards to a position of tangency with PP', as in Fig. 15, the price being BQ and the output per firm OB. Here cost exactly equals price, be-

[1] At any particular stage of this movement the *position* of dd' depends on the uniform price which momentarily obtains for all sellers. Its *elasticity* is represented as roughly unchanged throughout the movement because there seems to be no way of telling *a priori* how it would be affected by higher or lower *general* prices, and some reason to think that it would be affected very little.

cause the uneconomical scale at which each is producing has raised costs to meet it. The situation is unstable, however, because of the possibility of increased profits, represented for any producer by the demand curve dd', drawn through Q. That each, and hence all, will cut prices is evident from dd'; and that each, and hence all, are involved in ever increasing losses as the process continues is evident from DD', which shows the sales of each as the prices of all are lowered. When the price has fallen to CQ', for instance, the sales of each are OC, and his losses $FQ'HE$. An escape is offered to anyone by further cuts, however, as is indicated by the dotted line passing through Q'. Any seller, by cutting to AR, will avoid losses and exactly cover his costs. It might seem that equilibrium has been reached at this point, since dd' is now tangent to PP', as required. However, the number of sellers is so great that when all cut to AR, as they must, the sales of each are not OA, but OM, as indicated by DD', and losses are larger than ever. Equilibrium can be achieved only by the elimination of firms.

Before this takes place, however, price cutting may continue still further. Although, for positions of dd' lower than the dotted line, it is no longer possible to escape losses of some magnitude, it is still possible to reduce them. Evidently, if dd' is only slightly lower than the dotted line passing through R, this will be true. Soon, however, a lower limit will be reached, represented by the dot-dash line, where departure by any one from the adjustment for all on DD' will no longer diminish his losses, and here the movement will stop.

The curve dd' having reached any position below that of tangency, there is no escape from general losses until the number of firms is reduced. As this takes place, DD' will move to the right, and the movement must continue until it passes through R—in other words, until the output of each producer when all are charging the same price is OA. Equilibrium, then, is defined by two conditions: (a) dd' must be tangent to PP', and (b) DD' must intersect both dd' and PP' at the point of tangency.

We may regard the elasticity of dd' as a rough index of buyers' preferences for the "product" of one seller over that of another.

The equilibrium adjustment becomes, then, a sort of ideal. With fewer establishments, larger scales of production, and lower prices it would always be true that buyers would be willing to pay more than it would cost to give them a greater diversity of product;[1] and conversely, with more producers and smaller scales of production, the higher prices they would pay would be more than such gains were worth. In Fig. 14 this is evident from drawing a curve of the elasticity of dd' through a point on PP' to the right of R for the first case, and to the left of R for the second case. In either case there would be a gain in the surplus, over cost, of what buyers are willing to pay, by an adjustment towards R, for dd' would lie above PP' in that direction.

We pass to consideration of the second variable, the "product." The meaning of product variation has already been described, and the difficulties in its quantitative representation must be recalled. In order to retain the precision of statement which is possible only if the markets of all the competing sellers are alike, we must imagine, consistent with continued differences between the "products" of all sellers, possibilities of product variation which are uniform for all, so that the adjustments of *each* may be represented by a single graph, as in the price analysis. This is not so difficult as it sounds. A concrete instance is that of spatial differentiation in retailing, where each seller offers a "product," adapted by convenience of location to those buyers who are nearest to him geographically; yet the possibilities of a change in location are open to each, and an inflow or outflow of resources in the general field will decrease or increase the average distance between stores, and hence the size of the market enjoyed by each. Again, differentiation with regard to location often remains unchanged while "products" are altered by competition based upon service, or upon other qualitative factors. Still another instance, in the manufacturing field, is that of a number of products continually distinguished by trade-marks while qualitative changes are made in them.

[1] In retailing, this greater "diversity" would, in part, take the form of the location of stores at smaller intervals, thus giving to buyers greater convenience. The necessity of interpreting the terminology to fit the different aspects of product differentiation must be constantly borne in mind.

Product variation is isolated by the device, already explained, of holding the price for all the "products" constant. Let it be *OE* in Fig. 16, which will display the adjustments of any one seller; and let a horizontal line, *EZ*, be drawn at this height. As already pointed out, it does not indicate indefinite demand at this price, but will serve as a line along which the demands for each

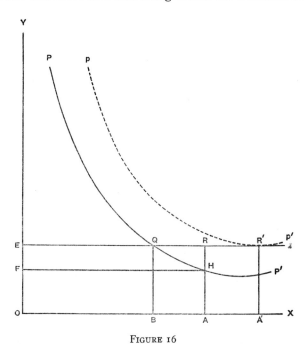

FIGURE 16

variation of the "product" may be measured. Curves of cost of production for different variations in the "product" of any seller may now be drawn, as in the earlier case of "product" variation where it was sought to define the individual equilibrium, and that variation offering the largest total profits will be chosen by each seller, as before. Let *PP'* represent the cost of production for such an optimum variation of the "product." The demand for it we will suppose to be *OA*. The total cost of producing this volume is *OAHF*, and the total profit (above the minimum included under *PP'*) is *FHRE*. The elimination of this profit, which is essential to an equilibrium adjustment, may take place in either or all of several ways. Since, by definition, this is the optimum variation for each seller, there will be no further "product adjustment." The extra profit will, however, attract new competitors to the field, and reduce the sales of each until they reach *OB*, where, cost being equal to price, there will be no further movement. Similarly, if the number of competitors were so great that the market of each was reduced below *OB*, losses would drive them from the field until those remaining had markets equal to *OB*, and were again meeting their costs.

In addition to the flow of resources into and out of the field, something analogous to price cutting may take place among those who occupy it at any one time. If any seller can increase his profits by improving his "product" (analogous to lowering his price), while the products of his competitors remain unaltered, he will do so. Such an improvement would increase demand along *EZ* and also increase costs, shifting *PP'* upwards and to the right. A new and larger profit area would result for the new "product." But when, with the same objective, his competitors made the same move, the increase in sales enjoyed by each would be only his proportionate share of the total increase for the general class of product on account of its general improvement (analogous to the increase in demand for a given class of product when all producers lower their prices). Higher costs remain, however (just as lower prices remain after everyone has cut his price), and the profit of each has been reduced by the general movement. The process may now be repeated, and will, in fact (as under price cutting), continue so long as it is possible for any seller to increase his gains in this way. What is the position of *PP'* when the limit has been reached? Evidently, it cannot be higher than the dotted curve, *pp'*, in Fig. 16, for if it were, the product could not be produced at all. It may, in fact, be lower; for it must not be forgotten that *EZ* is not a demand line (indicating indefinite demand at the price of *OE*), and that the mere fact that the cost curve descends below it does not indicate that greater profits are possible by an adjustment of output to achieve minimum costs. The demand for any one variation of the "product" is definitely limited; it cannot (under the present hypothesis) be increased by a price reduction, and its increase by improvement of the "product" involves altered cost conditions. There is no reason to suppose (especially when the cost curve for each has risen to a position only slightly below that of pp') that further improvement of the "product" of any one seller, which would shift his cost curve to the position of pp', would result in a demand for it of OA'.[1] The difficulties of representing graphically the variation of "product" render hazardous any attempt to define with precision the exact point of equilibrium. It would seem that the most that can be said is that it will be characterized by (1) the equation of cost and price, and (2) the impossibility of a "product" adjustment by anyone which would increase his profits. It will involve either the intersection of the price line with the curve of cost of production, or its tangency to it.

If "product" and price are both variable, however, it is easily shown that the cost curve must cut below the horizontal line drawn at the height of the equilibrium price. This may be seen at once in Fig. 16, by imagining a sloping demand curve drawn through the point R'. Such a curve would evidently lie above pp' immediately to the left of R', since it would have a negative slope as it passed through R', whereas pp' has a slope of zero. Profits could be increased by raising the price slightly and reducing the sales. (Cf. Fig. 13, page 89, where profits of zero at the price of MK are increased to $FHRE$ by raising the price to AR, thereby reducing sales from OM to OA.) An influx of new competitors would then push the demand curve for the product of each to the left until equilibrium was reached when it was tangent to pp'. The conclusion is that, although when price is *actually* fixed (as by custom, or, for the retailer, by the manufacturer) the improvement of "product" *may* be carried to the point where the most efficient conditions of production are realized, when it is not actually fixed (but only assumed so for logical purposes of isolation) it will not be carried that far. When the seller is free to vary

---

[1] However, if this proposed variation of the "product" were *arbitrarily assumed*, together with a fixed price of OE, the ingress or egress of firms would establish an output per firm of OA'.

either "product" or price or both, his adjustments will not stop until all possibilities of increasing his profit are exhausted. The impossibility of production under the most efficient conditions is settled once and for all by the shape of the demand curve.

When both "product" and price are variable, an equilibrium adjustment will be reached for both which is a combination of that for each in isolation. Under given conditions with regard to the "products" and prices of his competitors, each seller will choose that combination of price and "product" for himself which will maximize his profit. For each variety of "product" possible to him there will be a price which will render his profit a maximum *relative* to that "product." From these relative maxima he will choose the largest of all. Readjustments will be necessary as his competitors do the same thing, until finally a point is reached, as for each variable in isolation, where no one can better his position by a further move. At the same time, resources will flow into the field in order to reduce profits which are higher than the competitive minimum, or out of it in order to raise them to this minimum, so that the number of producers finally occupying the field will be such as to leave the costs of each exactly covered and no more.

A graphic summary of this comprehensive equilibrium is attempted in Fig. 17, although, in fact, because of the difficulties of reducing "product" variation to graphic terms, it shows little more than the price equilibrium of Fig. 12. PP' must be regarded as the cost curve for the optimum "product" and dd' as the demand curve for it. (Let the dotted line pp' be ignored for the moment.) The equilibrium price is AR, for, R being the point at which dd' and PP' are tangent to each other, it is evident that either a higher or a lower price would give unit costs in excess of price. Since, by definition, the "product" is the optimum one, either a better or a poorer "product" would likewise leave unit costs, for the amount which could be sold, in excess of the price OE. A better "product" would, by raising the cost curve, move its intersection with EZ further to the right than it would move the demand (measured along EZ). A poorer "product" would similarly, by lowering the cost curve, move its intersection with

EZ to the left by a shorter distance than it would decrease the demand (measured along *EZ*). The total output in the field under these conditions of equilibrium will be *OA* multiplied by the number of producers.

The conclusion seems to be warranted that just as, for a given "product," price is inevitably higher under monopolistic than under pure competition, so, for a given price, "product" is inevi-

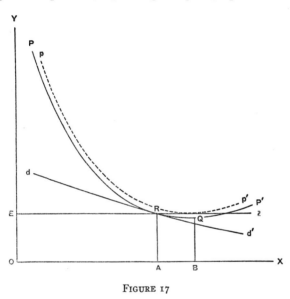

FIGURE 17

tably somewhat inferior. After all, these two propositions are but two aspects of a single one. If a seller could, by the larger scale of production which is characteristic of pure as compared with monopolistic competition, give the same "product" for less money, he could, similarly, give a better "product" for the same money. This is illustrated in Fig. 17. If competition were pure, *dd'* would be horizontal, and competitive pressure would lower it to the point of tangency with *PP'* at *Q*, where the price would be *BQ*, lower than *AR*. But if the price were now held constant at *AR*, and any seller could dispose of any amount he pleased at that price (as under pure competition), each would expand his output to approximately *OB*, and the extra profits there being realized would be reduced, not by a fall in price, which is impossible by hypothesis, but by general improvement of the "product" with consequent rise in cost curves to the position of the dotted line pp', whose minimum point equals AR. It follows that the impossibility of selling all he pleases at the going price creates a tendency not only towards higher prices, but also towards inferior product. Against these forces must, of course, be offset the gain through increased variety and freedom of choice.

4. The Small Group: Oligopoly plus Product Differentiation

Having now considered the problems of individual equilibrium, and of equilibrium within a group large enough to render each member of it a negligible influence upon the others, we pass to what might be regarded as the intermediate case — that of a group of relatively few sellers, perhaps only two. The nature of the problem and the chief forces at work have already been set forth in Chapter III, with this difference, that in the earlier case the product was standardized and in this case it is not. In Chapter III there was only one element of monopoly — the fewness of sellers. In the group problem just considered there was likewise only one, the differentiation of the product. Both are now to be combined — the sellers are relatively few in number, and each enjoys a market which is to a degree protected from those of the others. The result is a composite of the results of the two types of monopoly elements in isolation.

Returning to Fig. 14, let us interpret it as before, supposing it, however, to apply to each of a relatively small number of sellers. If each sought to maximize his profit with regard for his full influence, direct and indirect, upon the situation (see Chapter III), the price BQ, yielding the maximum total profits to all, would be set. This corresponds to AP in Fig. 5 (page 32). To be sure, any individual could, by reducing his price from this point, secure the larger profits indicated by the demand curve dd', *provided* the others did not follow suit. But since their own losses by his action would be considerable, the proviso does not hold. Each would, therefore, hold his price at *BQ* because the *ultimate* consequences of his doing anything else would be less advantageous.

If sellers neglect their indirect influence upon the price, each assuming the others to be unaffected by his own actions, it will be lower than *BQ*. If they assume their rivals' *prices* fixed, it will fall to *AR* by their competitive bidding, and (for only two or a very few sellers) perhaps oscillate between intermediate points as described earlier. If they assume their rivals' *amounts* fixed, it will settle at a determinate point between *BQ* and *AR*, which point is lower as their numbers are greater, coinciding with *AR* if their numbers are very large (as in the group problem already considered), and always defined by the condition that no seller can increase or decrease his supply with profit, the supplies of the others remaining constant. It must be noticed that the extreme limit, *AR*, below which price can never descend is higher than that for a standardized product, the latter coinciding with the lowest point of the cost curve *PP'*. The reason for this has already been explained.

The neglect of indirect influence which would lead to these results would be accounted for, as before, by the absence of any permanent or long-time interest in the market, by short-sightedness even where such an interest existed, or by uncertainty as to the response of competitors (which latter would make it uncertain whether indirect influence would be regarded, not necessarily lead to disregard of it). As to the last of these, the same elements of uncertainty are present here as under the simpler hypothesis of a standardized product (see above, page 51). Each seller may be in doubt as to his rival's policy, and therefore as to his own, because he does not know (*a*) whether, if his rival's present policy continues, it will continue with respect to his price or with respect to his output, (*b*) how intelligent and far-seeing his rival is, and (*c*) how large would be the incursions made upon him by his own price cut. This last factor is augmented by a new unknown — the extent of buyers' preferences for his own product over others, expressed by the shape of the demand curves for the individual "products."

Under the assumption of perfect knowledge which we have

made in order to exclude advertising, competitive adjustments would take place instantly, so that no question of a time lag in the functioning of the market could arise. If one seller cut his price, all buyers would know it at once, and there would be no delay in their taking advantage of it. These assumptions may be laid aside for a moment, however, to point out that knowledge of the lower price may reach buyers slowly and that their response to it may also develop slowly as established buying habits are broken. Where this is the case, the distinction made between immediate and ultimate results is obscured and new elements of uncertainty are introduced.

The conclusion as to where price would settle under conditions of relatively few sellers and a differentiated product can be given for any individual case only in terms of the relative importance of the various elements enumerated. It cannot normally lie outside the limits of BQ and AR, and it may rest at either extreme or between them, depending upon circumstances.[1] These limits approach each other, and the range of possible variation diminishes as the markets of the individual products are more distinct, i. e., as the slope of dd' approaches that of DD'.[2]

Since all uncertainties with respect to indirect as against direct influence disappear when the number in the group is very large, the question may well be raised at this point as to what meaning is to be given to the concept of a "large group." Even though, by the recognition of monopoly elements, the error is avoided of looking upon all sellers of any broad class of goods as being in the same market, and of explaining their prices by the theory of pure competition, it is easy to fall into another — that of regarding them uncritically as composing a large group, so that the conclusions presented for such a case in the present chapter are valid. Almost any general class of product divides itself into subclasses. A price cut by one automobile manufacturer, for instance, affects

[1] Further consequences of its lying above AR, the minimum point, will be set forth shortly.

[2] Dr. Zeuthen (cf. above, p. 54, note) has ingeniously elaborated a series of possible solutions for two sellers on the basis of various assumptions as to the possibility of capturing (*a*) each other's customers, and (*b*) new customers, and as to whether or not the gain is permanent.

especially the sales of those other manufacturers whose product is in approximately the same price class, and probably causes much less disturbance outside of these bounds. Similarly, most kinds of retail goods fall into certain quality or price classes, and these into subclasses, appealing to different groups of consumers according to their incomes or tastes. Evidently, a group may be large or small, depending upon the degree of generality given to the classification, but even if it is large, if subgroups exist, this fact cannot be disregarded. That a group is large does not necessarily mean that the market of every seller in it overlaps the markets of *all* the others in such a way that his gains from a price cut are derived evenly from the whole field, which condition is necessary for the conclusion with regard to a large group that the price necessarily falls to its minimum point, AR. More characteristically, any individual seller is in *close* competition with no more than a few out of the group, and he may seek to avoid price competition for the very reason given as applying to small numbers — that his cut will force those in *closest* competition with him to follow suit.

Similar considerations may hold, even though the larger grouping does not fall readily into distinct subdivisions. Retail establishments scattered throughout an urban area are an instance of what might be called a "chain" linking of markets. Gasoline filling stations are another. In either of these cases the market of each seller is most closely linked (having regard only to the spatial factor) to the one nearest him, and the degree of connection lessens quickly with distance until it becomes zero. Under such circumstances subgroups cannot be distinguished. Were an area to be marked off arbitrarily, stores at its border would compete with those on the border of the adjoining area more than with those in other portions of the area in which they were placed. Classes of custom are often indistinct, and shade into each other in a similar way. Again, the various types of differentiation may cut across each other. As an instance of this, markets which overlap spatially do not in other respects, and vice versa. The result is then a network of markets so intricately interwoven that, even though it is certainly not one, it defies subdivision which stops short of the individual seller. Where this is the case, considerations relative to small numbers hold even though the "group" be large, since each seller is in close competition with only a few others. The price may settle anywhere between AR and BQ.

Two new possibilities are suggested by the chain relationship. A cut by one seller may lead to a smaller reduction by the one next to him and soon dissipate itself without spreading far. Or, under other circumstances, it might force those nearest him to meet it in full, this in turn forcing others, and so on indefinitely (as blocks in a row will tumble if the first one is started). In this latter case, *through the chain relationships*, a single seller may bring about a general movement, though he be but a negligibly small part of the whole group. Here, even though numbers are large, consideration of indirect influence enters in, with the results already traced in this connection where numbers are small.

The general conclusion must be that the considerations relevant to competition between small numbers are much more generally applicable than might at first be supposed. Certainly, over a wide range of economic activity, the price not only *must*, on account of a differentiated product, be higher than the purely competitive level by at least an amount corresponding to what has been called "a sort of ideal"; [1] it *may* rest at any higher point up to a figure which would maximize the joint profits of those whose markets are related. The extent to which such high prices are prevalent in the economic system is disguised by the fact that they are quite consistent with profits no higher than the ordinary competitive level, as will now be shown.

5. Equilibrium with Excess Capacity [2]

Let us suppose the extreme case, where price rests at its upper limit, BQ in Fig. 14, this point being found the most advantageous by each of the sellers, as already explained. This does not mean that the profits $FHQE$, temporarily enjoyed, will persist, provided the general field may be entered by competitors. The establishment of new enterprises will soon divide the business available

[1] Above, p. 94.
[2] On the "doctrine of excess capacity," see also "Mr. Harrod's Recantation," Essay 14 in *Towards a More General Theory of Value*, and further references there to Mr. Harrod's and other writing.

at that figure among a larger number of sellers, pushing DD' to the left until its position is as pictured in Fig. 15, where, at the price BQ, cost equals price and extra profits are eliminated, the sales of each being OB. Such an adjustment is perfectly stable. There will be no further flow of resources into or out of the field, and it is not to the interest of anyone to raise or lower his price. If the price were intermediate between AR and BQ cost would be equated to price by a similar, but smaller, increase in the investment of resources over the "ideal" amount.

Before commenting further on this result — here ascribed to the fact that each seller is in close competition with only a relatively small number of others — let us give it its full importance by noting other circumstances which lead to the same outcome. Price cutting may be absent for many other reasons than that of the general recognition that competitors will follow suit, which arises from small numbers. In the first place, business men may set their prices with reference to costs rather than to demand, aiming at ordinary rather than at maximum profits, and more or less taking it for granted that they will continue to enjoy about their usual share of the total business.[1] They take whatever business comes their way, and expect others to do likewise — to live and let live. In this case, since the prices of all move roughly together, buyers have nothing to gain by trading with one merchant rather than with another, and the curve dd' is of no significance. The price may be anything between AR and BQ, depending upon the number of sellers occupying the field. It might at first be AR; but then suppose that new resources entered the field, perhaps through miscalculation or simply through the persistent efforts of others to find a place for themselves in business. The demand curve, DD', would be pushed to the left, and at the price AR costs would not be covered. Lower prices would only make matters worse; business men generally would find a higher "margin" necessary in order to make both ends meet; they would therefore

[1] This "full cost" principle is presented by Hall and Hitch ("Price Theory and Business Behavior," *Oxford Economic Papers*, No. 2, 1939) as a criticism of "current doctrine" including specifically (pp. 29-30) my own analysis. It was evidently overlooked that the principle in question has always been an integral part of Monopolistic Competition theory. For further discussion, see my article, " 'Full Cost' and Monopolistic Competition," *Economic Journal*, Vol. LXII (1952), p. 318. (Essay 13 in *Towards a More General Theory of Value*.)

increase it, and prices would again equal costs of production. **It is a case where an increased supply means higher instead of lower prices.**[1] The limit to this process is BQ, and once enough business men are established in the field to bring about this price, it is perfectly stable, for a figure either higher or lower would give an excess of cost over selling price. Any lower figure, down to AR, would also be stable (the number of sellers being correspondingly less), for the price always just covers costs and adapts itself to the number of establishments whose costs must be covered. The mere possibility of more sellers making a living in the field when prices are below BQ, however, gives a strong tendency for the maximum equilibrium price to be set.

The outcome described involves no combination — not even a tacit agreement — among the sellers. It is the result of each seeking independently his "ordinary" profit. The idea of conspiring (even "tacitly") with his rivals may not enter the head of the man who takes it as a matter of course that he deals with his own customers and charges enough to make a good profit. But it is fortified in actuality by formal or tacit agreements, open price associations, trade association activities in building up an *esprit de corps*, "price maintenance," the imposition of uniform prices on dealers by manufacturers, and excessive differentiation of product in the attempt to turn attention away from price. Business or professional "ethics" are another factor. It has long been considered unethical in the professions to compete on the basis of price. There is therefore no reason whatever why the supply of doctors and lawyers cannot multiply with economic impunity until high prices corresponding to BQ are reached. In so far as business men succeed in making it "unethical" over wider fields to offer lower prices, they protect, over short periods, to be sure,

---

[1] Compare Cairnes's explanation of retail prices, *Political Economy*, pp. 115–116. He refers to "the excessive amount of capital which, from one cause or another, has found its way into the business of mere distribution. The inevitable consequence is that the capital thus in excess, taking it as an aggregate, turns slowly — more slowly than it need turn consistently with the due discharge of its functions; and that those who have embarked in retail business *are compelled, in order to obtain average profits on their capital, to charge higher prices* for their goods than would be necessary if the total amount of capital in the trade were less." (The italics are mine.) Cf. also Wicksell, *Lectures on Political Economy*, Vol. I, p. 88.

their profits, but over longer periods, their numbers, since when prices do not fall costs rise, the two being equated by the development of excess productive capacity.

Another deterrent to price cutting is the inference by the consumer that the product is of inferior quality because its price is lower. Although, strictly speaking, excluded by our present hypothesis of perfect knowledge, this factor is of such importance that it must be mentioned parenthetically at this point. In so far as the consumer, conscious of his inexpertness of judgment, blindly links quality with price, the ordinary law of demand is reversed — the amount demanded diminishes with a lower price and, conversely, increases with a higher one.[1] In addition to this factor, the price cutter may suffer an undesirable change in the nature of his clientele, for price is often an important factor in setting the "tone" of an establishment.

Furthermore, price cuts may be disguised or hidden, with the idea of reducing the likelihood of competitors' following suit. Thus one prominent gasoline retailing concern in New England regularly displayed the same price per gallon as its competitors, and as regularly sold for two cents less by the device of passing out cou-

---

[1] In *Printer's Ink*, September 21, 1916, p. 17, appears an interview with W. A. Baker, sales manager of the American Electric Heater Co., in which he tells the experience of a Cleveland department store in selling two brands of electric irons, one at $3.75, the other at $5. The cheaper iron was guaranteed and recommended by the store, its lower price was emphasized, and every attempt was made to sell it rather than the $5 one. Sales of the latter, however, were 50 per cent above those of the cheaper product. Excerpts from Mr. Baker's conclusions are: "The public is not half as anxious for cut prices as the average dealer thinks it is. . . . It is more than an equal chance that the customer does not know what a good article *should* cost, and that the average customer will pay nearly any price which is quoted to him as reasonable."

In an article in *System*, September, 1912, p. 227, entitled "What Makes Men Buy," C. D. Murphy classifies buying motives under five heads, one of which is money gain or money saving. He concludes that "over-emphasis of this money motive, however, may result in a loss of prestige and patronage where prospects want utility — quality rather than cheapness."

Professor Taussig sums up the case effectively in his remarks on "price maintenance" (*American Economic Review Supplement*, March, 1916, Proceedings of the 28th Annual Meeting of the American Economic Association, pp. 172–173): "If articles thus lauded [through 'quality' advertising] are offered at cut prices, if they are knocking about in quantities on the counters of cheap shops at less than the announced price, if they are used as 'leaders' to seduce the bargain hunters, — their prestige is endangered. . . . In the long run, the lower price, so far from enlisting purchasers, is as likely to repel them."

pon books free to every customer. To post openly the price reduction might have brought retaliation. As another instance, a garage offers over-night parking for 50 cents, the usual price, but throws in a gallon of gasoline for good measure. All extra considerations of this sort, premiums, coupons, or what not, may be regarded as hidden price cuts. The effect is to give to the secret price-cutter an increase in business somewhat less than that indi-

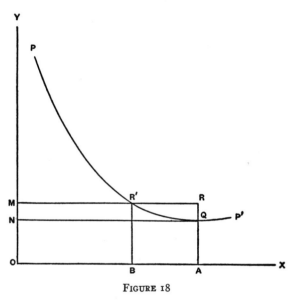

FIGURE 18

cated by *dd'* (Fig. 14 or 15), yet more secure because of the reduced possibility of others following him, and thereby to hold prices artificially high.

Finally, prices may not be free to move at all. They may be set by custom or tradition. A particular price may have come generally to be associated with a product so that it cannot be changed without disaster. With the increasing importance given today to brands and trade-marks, prices are more and more imposed upon the retailer by the manufacturer, either by specific agreement, by persuasion, or by suggestion. Not only prices, but percentages of mark-up, become crystallized by trade practice. In such cases, the supply and scale of production adjust themselves to the price.

The price could not be lower than AQ (Fig. 18), or no one would handle the good. It is very apt to be higher, especially when set by the manufacturer, for a liberal margin to the dealer is usually more important than a low price to the consumer. Suppose it to be AR. The total which consumers purchase at this price will be divided among the retailers in the field. If their numbers are such that each has sales of OA, each will make excess profits of $NQRM$. The result will be more sellers and higher unit costs until the reduced volume of each lowers profits to the minimum level, the price remaining always the same, and the scale of production being finally OB.[1]

The common result of this assemblage of factors is excess productive capacity, for which there is no automatic corrective. Such excess capacity may develop, of course, under pure competition, owing to miscalculation on the part of producers, or to sudden fluctuations in demand or cost conditions. But it is the peculiarity of monopolistic competition that it may develop over long periods *with impunity*, prices always covering costs, and may, in fact, become permanent and normal through a failure of price competition to function. The surplus capacity is never cast off, and the result is high prices and waste. The theory affords an explanation of such wastes in the economic system — wastes which are usually referred to as "wastes of competition." In fact, they could never occur under pure competition, and it is for this reason that the theory of pure competition is and must be silent about them, introducing them, if at all, as "qualifications," rather than as parts of the theory. They are wastes of monopoly — of the monopoly elements in monopolistic competition.[2]

---

[1] Compare the observation of Mill: "Retail price, the price paid by the actual consumer, seems to feel very slowly and imperfectly the effect of competition; and when competition does exist, it often, instead of lowering prices, merely divides the gains of the high price among a greater number of dealers. Hence it is that, of the price paid by the consumer, so large a proportion is absorbed by the gains of retailers. . . ." *Principles*, Book II, Chap. IV, Sec. 3.

[2] J. M. Clark, *op. cit.*, pp. 437–439, 464–467, concludes, similarly, that excess capacity is a general characteristic of industry. He is concerned, for the most part, however, with the phenomena of the business cycle as, for instance, the creation of plant capacity to take care of the "peak" demand — capacity which is therefore redundant at times when the demand is less than this.

6. The Diversity of Conditions Surrounding
Each Producer

The development of the "group" theory has, so far, employed the device of assuming the market of each seller to be of the same size and elasticity, and the cost conditions of each to be identical.[1] Actually, of course, they differ widely. The demand curves for particular products vary both in location with reference to the x and y axes, and in elasticity, depending upon the vagaries of consumers' preferences, the quality of the product, the number and degree of perfection of available substitutes, the class of customers to which appeal is made, and upon many other factors. Similarly, the cost curves vary, both as to location and as to shape, for the simple reason that the products themselves are different. Finally, the two curves vary in their position relative to each other. This diversity must now be explicitly recognized and related to the conclusions established under the simpler hypothesis of uniformity.

Let us at first ignore the last-named factor, — variation in the positions of the curves relative to each other, — assuming that adjustment to a position of tangency always takes place as described above.[2] Our attention, then, is centered upon diversity within any group (a) as to the location of the curves with reference to the x and y axes, and (b) as to their shape.

(a) Differences between the various products in the group as to quality, size, physical characteristics, etc., lead to wide variations in the level at which the adjustments take place. To picture the situation adequately, a separate figure should be drawn for each product, or perhaps for each subgroup of products falling within the same price or quality class. A group of producers would then be represented by a group of diagrams of various sizes. The forces of competition already traced would assure that demand curves were tangent to cost curves throughout, and profits would nowhere be higher than the competitive level; yet prices and scales of production would vary, corresponding to the range of quality, size, etc., of the product. No modification of theory is necessary

---

[1] See above, pp. 81, 82.   [2] Pp. 83, 84.

ın order to allow for this phase of the problem — there is needed only an interpretation of the earlier diagrams as short-cuts of exposition. Let the figure as drawn always be exact for some particular producer. It may then be taken as *illustrative* of what is true for everyone within the group at levels appropriate to each.

(*b*) The question of shape is likewise a problem only of exposition. Where demand curves are less elastic the point of tangency will be correspondingly higher, and vice versa. Similarly, variations in the slope of the cost curve at different points will affect the point at which the demand curve is tangent to it. The *general* shape of the curves is as already described,[1] however, and the form of the adjustment in each individual case is the same. It suffices to consider a single pair of curves as *illustrative* of the group, recognizing that, on account of diversity, both as to location and as to shape, a corresponding diversity of prices, costs, and outputs (but not, so far, of profits) obtains throughout.

We come now to the last-named factor — variation in the position of the curves relative to each other. It has been argued, under the assumption of uniform curves, that, where profits are above the competitive level, multiplication of producers will reduce them, so that, although monopoly prices remain, profits are competitive and uniform for every one.[2] The argument rested upon the implicit assumption that the production of substitutes within the general field and any portion of it was sufficiently possible to bring about this result. However, in so far as substitutes of such a degree of effectiveness may not be produced, the conclusions are different—demand curves will lie to the right of the point of tangency with cost curves, and profits will be correspondingly higher. This is the explanation of *all* monopoly profits, of whatever sort.[3] A few types may be considered in order to show the relation of such profits to the general theory.

Patents, copyrights, trade-marks, etc., afford the first example. Although exceptionally high returns may be reduced by the

---

[1] Pp. 75 ff.   [2] See above, pp. 83, 84.

[3] Not only that there are no competitors producing the identical product and sharing the demand typified by a certain curve, but also (and more important) that there are no competitors effectively offering similar products in such a way as to push the curve back to the point of tangency with the cost curve.

appearance of competing products, the possibilities are often limited. Individual patents and trade-marks preëmpt portions of the general field, either because effective substitutes cannot be produced or because established consumers' preferences are strong. Competition, in so far as it enters the field at all, pushes the demand curves to the left in uneven degree, leaving monopoly profits scattered throughout the field.

Peculiarities of any individual establishment which cannot be duplicated (such as the personality of the proprietor, for instance) lead to profits which fall into the same category; likewise reputation, skill, and special ability, in the professions. All of these find their explanation as monopoly returns. The skillful physician does not sell his services in the identical market with the ordinary one, for their services are not interchangeable and do not sell for the same price (as do the products of better and poorer wheat lands). To be sure, one man may, because of superior physical strength or rapidity, be enabled to produce more per unit of time than another. The competitive theory of rent explains differences in income in so far as they arise from such a source. But further differences are accounted for only by the theory of monopoly. Impediments to others producing the *same* thing in the *same* market hold the demand curve for the individual's product or service far to the right, with resulting larger profits attributable to the element of uniqueness in question. In the case of professional services, the result is, characteristically, higher prices; in that of a patented or trade-marked product, it is more often larger sales. In both instances, however, the explanation is the same—limitations on the effectiveness of substitutes to diminish profits within certain portions of the field.

Urban rents are a third example of the same type of income. If entrance to every portion of a retail field were unimpeded, there would be no differences in the rents paid throughout. The impediment of land scarcity where customers are most numerous and opportunities for profit therefore greatest gives larger returns at some locations than at others — returns which cannot be reduced by other sellers moving in to share them. Competition from a distance is not without effect, but the markets afforded by different locations are sufficiently distinct to leave wide variations in rents. The rents of the locations giving superior markets are properly regarded as monopoly returns, and their theoretical explanation is quite different from that of agricultural rents. This subject is further developed in Appendix D.

To sum up this phase of the matter, our statement of the group problem must be modified by recognizing that the demand curves are not adjusted uniformly to a position tangent to the cost curves. In so far as profits are higher than the general competitive level in the field as a whole or in any portion of it, new competitors will, *if possible*, invade the field and reduce them. If this were always possible, as hitherto assumed, the curves would always be tangent and monopoly profits would be eliminated. In fact it is only partially possible. As a result, some (or all) of the curves may lie at various distances to the right of the point of tangency, leaving monopoly profits scattered throughout the group — and throughout the price system.[1]

Our theory has now taken into account that which pure competition omits — the special forces at work within the market of each seller. The existence of factors affecting each *variety* of the product can no more be ignored in the theory of value than can the existence of special forces affecting each general *class* of products. To ignore these latter would be to accept as a complete explanation of prices a theory explaining only the general price level. Absurd as this would be, it is only different in degree from stopping short with general classes of products and neglecting all the variety of economic forces at work within these classes. To smooth and perfect competition in this way not only gives a *general* bias to the results; it also levels down and removes at one sweep a whole class of differential elements which forms an essential part of the price structure.

7. PURE AND MONOPOLISTIC COMPETITION COMPARED

In the development of the theory of pure competition, it was shown that the equilibrium price is that one which equates demand and supply *for the reason that this is the only price consistent*

---

[1] It is interesting to contrast this result with Schumpeter's conception of monopoly as wholly dynamic. See Essay 10 and pp. 62–64 in *Towards a More General Theory of Value.*

with maximum profits for each producer.[1]   Comparison between monopolistic and pure competition is facilitated by restating the central thesis of this chapter in terms of this earlier argument. Where monopoly elements are present, the equilibrium price is *for this same reason*, inevitably higher than the one indicated by the intersection of the competitive demand and cost curves.

Let DD' and PP' (Fig. 19*a*) be the demand and cost curves, respectively, for a good sold under conditions of pure competi-

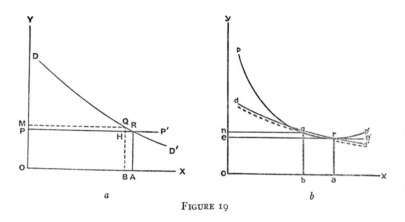

a b

FIGURE 19

tion.[2] There are many buyers and sellers and the good is perfectly homogeneous. The equilibrium price is AR. In Fig. 19*b* the conditions with respect to the individual producer are shown, and (as in the similar pair of figures in Chapter II, page 21) the horizontal scale is that of Fig. 19*a* divided by the number of sellers. (If there are fifty sellers, *oa* is 1/50 of *OA*.) The vertical scale is the same in the two figures. The demand and cost curves for the product of the individual producer are, respectively, *ee'* and *pp'*. He adjusts his output to *oa*, his most efficient scale of production, and the price, *ar*, exactly covers his costs. His profits are a maximum, for any other adjustment would reduce them below the necessary minimum included in the cost curve.

---

[1] Above, pp. 19, 20
[2] Conditions of constant cost alone are taken up. The argument would be analogous for increasing and for decreasing costs.

Now let the product be differentiated, and let us suppose the differentiation to be of such nature that the curves of cost of production are not materially affected. Let us assume, further, that the demand curve for the general market, DD', is unaltered by the fact of differentiation.[1] The demand curve for the goods of any one producer does not remain unaltered, however. The fact of differentiation tips it slightly, so that it may be represented by the solid line dd' (Fig. 19b), passing through r. Reactions already traced in detail may now be quickly summarized. Each producer's profits will be increased by raising his price, and this rise will attract new competitors to the field. The curve dd' will be moved to the left to the position of the dotted line, and prices for all will settle at bq, where this line is tangent to the curve of cost of production, pp'.[2] The output of each is ob, and to obtain the total for all, this must be multiplied by the number of sellers. Turning now to Fig. 19a, it is seen that this total must be OB, the amount which will be purchased at the price of BQ. This amount, although produced by a larger number of establishments than would be present under purely competitive conditions, is smaller (by BA) than the competitive output, the reason being that each is producing on a reduced scale. The total cost of this volume is not $OBHP$, as the competitive cost curve indicates, but $OBQM$, which is greater. Although the equilibrium price is higher under monopolistic competition than under pure competition, the result is not, therefore (as might be expected), a discrepancy between cost and price.

Although higher than the intersection of the demand and cost curves, the price of BQ in Fig. 19a is perfectly stable. As was the case in the theory of pure competition, the reason must be sought in the conditions pertaining to the individual sellers. It is that BQ is the only price consistent with maximum profits for them. The necessity for distinguishing carefully between the equilibrium price and the purely competitive price is again

[1] It would, in general, lie further to the right if wants were more exactly satisfied with a differentiated product.

[2] Possibilities of the price rising higher than this (compare above, pp. 101ff.) are omitted for the sake of brevity. Their explanation would be analogous. Also, diversity of conditions is ignored in this simple comparison.

brought to the fore. The two are always divergent when the product is differentiated. Indeed, in this case, the answer to the price problem is not to be had from the purely competitive assumptions or graphic representations. It is impossible to tell from Fig. 19*a* what the price will be, for the point Q is derived from Fig. 19*b*, pertaining to the individual seller.

It might seem that this difficulty would be obviated by drawing the curve of costs above the competitive cost curve and parallel to it, representing the costs which must be covered under the conditions of monopolistic competition, instead of under the conditions of pure competition. Such a cost curve would pass through Q, and, in the case of constant cost, would be horizontal, being an extension of MQ in Fig. 19*a*. But such a curve is not a cost curve, for it does not show the cost at which different amounts of the good can be produced; it can play no part in determining the price BQ. It can be drawn only *after* BQ has been defined by the demand and cost curves of the individual products, and, being the locus of these individual equilibria for different total volumes of product, it is as much a curve of demand as of cost. It is defined by the equilibrium price, and can contribute nothing to the explanation of it. This cannot be said of a true cost curve — either PP' or pp'.

The question is squarely presented of whether competitive theory should be applied at all where monopoly elements are present. We may grant that economic principles work out only in the rough, and that the *actual* price may be neither AR nor BQ; nevertheless, it tends towards or approximates BQ, not AR. The price problem for a differentiated product cannot be forced into the mould of competitive demand and cost curves without introducing into the conclusions definite errors — the price is always too low, the cost of production is too low, the scale of production is too large, and the number of producers is too small. Furthermore, two added phases of competition, those of product variation and of selling outlays, are omitted altogether.

CHAPTER VI

SELLING COSTS *VS.* PRODUCTION COSTS [1]

AT THE beginning of the previous chapter three factors were described which limited and defined the market for the product of any particular seller under monopolistic competition: (1) his price, (2) the nature of his product, and (3) his selling outlays. In order to simplify the exposition, the last of these was then eliminated temporarily by the assumption that the buyers had (a) given wants and (b) perfect knowledge concerning the means available for satisfying them. Attention was confined to the adjustments of price and product alone. Consequently, the outlays included in the cost curves up to this point have been solely those of producing goods to meet a demand, not those of creating or increasing a demand. The theory must now be completed by recognition of the fact that demands are changed by advertising and that an important part of the calculations of business men concerns the most profitable adjustment of expenditures directed to this purpose.

Selling costs are defined as costs incurred in order to alter the position or shape of the demand curve for a product. Later on an attempt will be made to draw a fine line between such costs and costs of production. For the moment, we need only suggest examples. Advertising of all varieties, salesmen's salaries and the expenses of sales departments, margins granted to dealers (retail and wholesale) in order to increase their efforts in favor of particular goods, window displays, demonstrations of new goods, etc., are all costs of this type. Under the assumption that wants are given (i. e., "held constant"), and that buyers have perfect knowledge, none of these would be of any avail. But with the removal of these assumptions, they become a powerful force acting upon sales volumes and hence upon prices and profits.

[1] See also below, Appendix G.

1. How Selling Costs Affect the Demand

Let us take advertising as typical of these expenditures and in-quire how its results are brought about. The explanation may be related to the two factors of (*a*) imperfect knowledge, and (*b*) the possibility of altering people's wants by advertising or selling appeal.

It is imperfect knowledge with particular reference to the buy-ers which is important for the problem of advertising.[1] This has various aspects. Buyers often do not know or are but dimly aware of the *existence* of sellers other than those with whom they habitually trade or of goods other than those they habitually con-sume; they are ill-informed of comparative prices for the same thing sold by different merchants; they are ignorant of the quali-ties of goods, in themselves, compared with other goods, and com-pared with the prices asked. Advertising increases a seller's mar-ket by spreading information (or misinformation) on the basis of which buyers' choices as to the means of satisfying their wants are altered. This is equivalent, of course, to a change either in the shape or in the location of the demand curves for their products.[2]

The shape of the curve will be affected primarily when it is a question of price competition. A seller will be successful in in-creasing his sales at a lower price in proportion as the knowledge of his offer reaches a larger number of possible buyers. By spreading this knowledge, advertising makes the demand for his product more elastic — at the lower price it increases, not only by the limited amount possible if no one but regular and a few casual purchasers knew of it, but by a larger amount depending upon the size of the advertising outlay and the skill with which it is applied. Imperfect knowledge (of prices) makes the demand curves for products less elastic; advertising, through offsetting it, makes them more so. It offers greater opportunities for price competi-

---

[1] The business man's imperfect knowledge of the future which has been connected with the risk theory of profits, for instance, is not a part of our problem.

[2] At this point we are concerned only with the direct effect upon the advertiser's market. The effects of advertising within a group of sellers or throughout the eco-nomic system are taken up in the following chapter.

tion, but at an added cost which must be covered by the price.

The location of the curve will be affected primarily when competition takes place on the basis of the product itself. The effect of advertising is to shift to the right the demand curve for the advertised product by spreading knowledge of its existence, by describing it, and by suggesting the utilities it will provide the purchaser. Certainly new products and new varieties of old products would have virtually no market at all without selling outlays of this sort. Similarly, the markets for older, better established products could be increased but slowly and within narrow limits if nothing were expended for selling — that is, if the producers merely sat and waited for orders to come in. In the face of aggressive sales methods employed by their newer, more active competitors, they would be worsted at once, in spite of the excellence of their product. Quality competition, like price competition, is stimulated by the possibility of informing a large number of potential buyers, through advertising, of quality changes or of existing attributes of a product of which they were not aware. If the information is truthful, wants are more effectively satisfied; if not, they are less effectively satisfied. In either case, the satisfaction of *existing* wants is sought with different information at the disposal of the buyer, as to the means whereby it may be done. An altered system of demand curves is the result, with the effect upon elasticity unpredictable.

Advertising affects demands, in the second place, by altering the wants themselves. The distinction between this and altering the channel through which existing wants are satisfied, although obscured in practical application by the fact that the two are often mingled, seems to be clear analytically. An advertisement which merely displays the *name* of a particular trade-mark or manufacturer may convey no information; yet if this name is made more familiar to buyers they are led to ask for it in preference to unadvertised, unfamiliar brands. Similarly, selling methods which play upon the buyer's susceptibilities, which use against him laws of psychology with which he is unfamiliar and therefore against which he cannot defend himself, which frighten or flatter or disarm him — all of these have nothing to do with his knowledge.

They are not informative; they are manipulative. They create a new scheme of wants by rearranging his motives.[1] As a result, demand for the advertised product is increased, that for other products is correspondingly diminished.

Selling costs do not always affect the consumer directly, and our description needs amplification to include the complexities introduced by the chain of dealers intervening between him and the manufacturer. The retailer is concerned only with the demand of the ultimate consumer, and his selling costs represent the attempt to expand his own market for the products in which he trades. The manufacturer, however, must divide his efforts between the consumer and the dealer, often devoting most or all of them to the latter. It would be disastrous for him to create a consumer's demand and trust this to be communicated to him automatically through the intervening middlemen. Unless he or the wholesaler establishes connections with the retailer by persuading him to stock the goods, consumers will not find them when they have been led by his advertising to make inquiry. The expenditure is then wasted, for the impulse to buy is either dissipated or diverted to another variety of the product.

The manufacturer's connections with retailer and wholesaler do not come of themselves. To be sure, if a dealer finds his customers repeatedly demanding a certain product, and experiences difficulty in selling them something else "just as good" which he has in stock, he may make the effort to find out where and how the goods can be obtained. But this rarely happens. The manufacturer who left intermediate relations to take care of themselves in this way would find only a small fraction of the demand filtering through to him. It is clearly to his interests to make it easy,

---

[1] Cf. the following: "The buyer's brain is the board upon which the game is played. The faculties of the brain are the men. The salesman moves or guides these faculties as he would chess men or checkers on a board. In order to understand the ground upon which your battle must be fought, and the mental elements which you must combat, persuade, move, push or attract, you must understand the various faculties of the mind." (W. W. Atkinson, *The Psychology of Salesmanship*, p. 70.) "In undertaking to psychologize about the conduct of the buyer, let it be understood that we purpose to catalogue the sensations, ideas and feelings animating him and to discover the springs of his action . . . we seek merely to give a complete description and explanation of the buyer's conduct, and explain how to manipulate it." (H. D. Kitson, *The Mind of the Buyer*, p. 8.)

not difficult, for the retailer and the jobber to secure his goods. Dealers must be sought out, informed, and persuaded, not only to carry the goods in stock, but to exert sales effort in their behalf.

For so-called "convenience" goods,[1] requiring a maximum number of retail outlets, the jobber's salesman performs an indispensable service for the manufacturer. He has a first-hand knowledge of the territory and without him many dealers would be missed. The cost merely of getting in touch with these dealers is a cost of securing the demands which they control.

Further costs must be incurred in order to persuade jobber, wholesaler, and retailer to carry the goods in stock. They are all besieged with propositions and must choose. The dealer cannot stock everything, and, just as the consumer tries to apportion his income so as to get the most satisfaction out of it, so he tries to discriminate in tying up his capital and disposing of his facilities, in order to secure a maximum profit. He must undertake the risk of reselling the goods at a remunerative price. An advertising campaign to the consumer or the promise of one is a powerful argument with the retailer; active sales efforts with the retailer are a help in winning over the jobber. Both must be convinced that the product is going to succeed, and this may require all the technique of skillful appeal so necessary with the consumer. The margin of profit is an important consideration. It must be at least as high as that on similar products, perhaps a little higher.

The dealer must also be persuaded to make an effort to sell the goods. The retailer, by reason of his direct contact and his personal influence, occupies a strategic position in directing the consumer's demand far superior to that of the manufacturer through his advertising. In considerable measure he controls the trade of his market or territory. The same may be said for the jobber and wholesaler. Without special inducement any of these may sell a particular brand only when it is insisted upon, choosing to divert the rest of the demand to others upon which he receives a higher margin of profit or which he considers superior. This is known as

---

[1] See the interesting classification of goods into "convenience," "shopping," and "specialty" goods, by Professor M. T. Copeland, "Consumers' Buying Motives," *Harvard Business Review*, Vol. II (1924), p. 139.

"substitution." He may give preference to other brands only when none is specified, or when his opinion is requested. At the other extreme, he may, whenever possible, "substitute" in favor of the brand in question. Aside from the question of "substitution," dealers may expend on the product any amount of sales effort from the very minimum of indifference to the maximum of skillful and aggressive salesmanship. The manufacturer must be as attentive to winning their favor as to winning that of consumers through direct advertising. Especially must the price of the product be high enough to reward adequately, even generously, all those who control the distributive outlets. A large slice of these "margins" must be regarded as the cost of securing a demand (cost of selling) rather than as the cost of satisfying it (cost of production). Often the granting of a little higher margin is the most effective kind of advertising.

For some types of goods the desired control over prices and merchandising policies can best be secured by granting "exclusive agencies," either to jobbers or to retailers. This practice is widespread in the "specialty" field — automobiles, tires, phonographs, men's clothing and shoes, jewelry, tractors and farm machinery, pianos, vacuum cleaners, high grade candy, etc. The manufacturer grants a monopoly of his product to one dealer in a city, or perhaps to several in different districts of a large city. This protects the dealer completely from the competition of others who would cut his price, and assures him that all sales efforts he makes in the district will redound to his own benefit instead of being shared with others. The price is fixed by the manufacturer and covers a liberal commission to the agent for his sales efforts.

Another method of securing the desired aggressiveness and control is the operation by the manufacturer himself of his own distributive outlets. Sales agencies or branches establish the connections with retailers in each district and perform roughly the functions of the jobber. When this extends to retailing, chains of stores, stocking typically only the manufacturer's products, constitute an elaborate organization which assures him of a market by the effective device of preëmpting one and closing it to competitors. This integration in marketing has also developed from the opposite direction, retailers extending their activities into the manufacturing field, often through securing others to manufacture for them and to brand the goods to order. All of these types of integration erect barriers in the way of competitors securing distribution except by integrating themselves. The result is much duplication of distributive machinery, and higher margins of profit which attract more people into the field and bring still more waste, always subtly concealed by the fact that the average profit per business man or per business unit is held down by the increase in numbers. In the last analysis, these costs, borne by the consumer, must be counted as selling costs — costs of *altering* his demands, rather than as production costs — costs of satisfying them.

2. SELLING COSTS DISTINGUISHED FROM PRODUCTION COSTS

Let us now draw more sharply the distinction between these two types of costs. Cost of production includes all expenses which must be met in order to provide the commodity or service, transport it to the buyer, and put it into his hands ready to satisfy his wants. Cost of selling includes all outlays made in order to secure a demand, or a market, for the product. The former costs create utilities in order that demands may be satisfied; the latter create and shift the demands themselves. A simple criterion is this: of all the costs incurred in the manufacture and sale of a given product, those which alter the demand curve for it are selling costs, and those which do not are costs of production.

Cost of production is not the same as manufacturer's price, nor is cost of selling the same as the difference between this and the final retail price. Many costs incurred after a commodity leaves the factory are costs of production — those for transportation, handling, storing, and delivering, all of which add utilities to the good, i. e., make it more capable of satisfying wants.[1] Likewise,

---

[1] G. B. Dibblee, having insisted upon the importance of distinguishing selling from production costs, falls into error at this point. "One, and the larger, part of the cost of selling may be approximately obtained by finding the difference between the

there are included in the manufacturer's price to the wholesaler charges to cover the expenses of building up his "connections" and securing outlets, as well as similar charges of other producers who have sold him raw materials and supplies, and whose selling expenses he has recouped. The two types of costs are interlaced throughout the price system, so that at no point, such as at the completion of manufacture, can one be said to end and the other to begin.

The entire cost of a good to the consumer may, however, be analyzed into its two parts by a successive consideration of the outlays of everyone who has had anything to do with producing or selling it, from the retailer or salesman back to its obscure origin. Many costs will at once fall wholly into one category or the other. Selling costs of this type are: advertising in its many forms, salaries of salesmen and the expenses of sales departments and sales agencies (except where these agencies actually handle the goods), window displays, and displays and demonstrations of all kinds. In other cases an outlay covers both, and the total must be divided according to the degree to which it pertains to one function or to the other. A large part of the expenses of those engaged in the "distribution" of products are of this sort, and most profits are a composite income. To the extent that the business man concerns himself with the efficient conduct of his plant, the minimum profits he requires are a cost of production; to the extent that he devotes his time and energies to building up his "connections," they are costs of selling.

One or two types of costs *apparently* increase demand, but are really costs of production. Transportation is an example, since nothing could be sold if the goods were not conveyed to market. This outlay might be thought of as one made to secure a demand, the demand being zero *at the factory*. This view, however, is seen to be false if we suppose the consumer to order the goods directly from the manufacturer and to pay the freight himself, as in the case of a mail order establishment. The demand is not zero at the

first wholesale price of the completely finished article, and the final retail price at which it passes into the hands of the consumer." (*The Laws of Supply and Demand,* p. 53.) He goes on to explain that the remainder is made up of the cost to the manufacturer of building up his "connection."

factory — it exists at a price equal to the price delivered minus the transportation cost. This is always true, whether the buyer pays the transportation charges directly or whether he pays them indirectly in the price of the article. In either case, the demand was always present, both at the market and at the factory. The fact that it might not have been satisfied had the cost not been incurred does not mean that the cost created the demand. This could be said equally well of the material and labor which have gone into the product — and of production costs generally.

Another puzzling case is that of site rent. The rent paid by a department store seems to be paid in order to secure the larger volume of business which a location in the shopping district affords, and therefore to be the same sort of expenditure as advertising, which is incurred for a like purpose. Yet any expenditure directed towards meeting a demand more accurately, such as an outlay to improve quality, will, if it succeeds, increase sales. In paying for a location, the merchant is simply meeting demand more exactly by providing more convenience.[1] He is adapting his goods to the demand, and in no way trying to change it. On the other hand, the merchant located in the outskirts who advertises urging people to come to him because he is "out of the high rent district" is adapting, not himself, but his customers. He is giving them less, not more, convenience, and trying to divert their attention from it. We arrive at another way of stating the distinction between the two kinds of costs: those made to adapt the product to the demand are costs of production; those made to adapt the demand to the product are costs of selling.

3. The Significance of the Distinction

The distinction between the two types of costs is as fundamental for value theory as the distinction between supply and demand, and indeed arises necessarily from it. Costs of selling increase the demand for the product on which they are expended;

---

[1] This should be qualified in so far as the site affords peculiar opportunities for effective advertising, in the form of window displays which will be seen by large numbers, etc.

costs of production increase the supply. It would seem that there could be no more simple and obvious mistake than to combine them, yet economic theory has done exactly this, counting all the entrepreneur's outlays as his "costs of production." Perhaps it would be more exact not to say that they have been combined (since they have never been distinguished), but that selling costs have been completely ignored. The demand is always taken as something which already exists, and such costs as are incurred are for the production of goods to meet it. Of course it is recognized that wants may change, and that this involves a change in the demand curves; but the problem of dealing theoretically with expenditures which make them change seems never even to have been conceived of, let alone answered.[1]

The explanation lies partly in the failure to synthesize monopolistic and competitive theory. Selling costs are very naturally passed over in competitive theory, since they are at odds with the

---

[1] Selling costs are distinguished from production costs by Dibblee (*op. cit.*) and the importance of the distinction insisted upon. Professor Knight refers to them, only to conclude that they are no different from other costs. "In so far as they [changes in wants] result from a deliberate expenditure of resources, they become as all other economic operations. . . . In fact, as we have previously observed, the advertising, puffing, or salesmanship necessary to create a demand for a commodity is causally indistinguishable from a utility inherent in the commodity itself." (*Risk, Uncertainty and Profit*, p. 339.) Marshall, in his treatment of large-scale production, remarks that in the case of specialties "the sales of each business are limited, more or less according to circumstances, to the particular market which it has *slowly and expensively acquired*; and though the production itself might be economically increased very fast, the sale could not." (*Principles*, 8th ed., p. 287. Italics mine.) But for him also, "cost of production" embraces all the business man's outlays. Davenport (*Economics of Enterprise*, pp. 133 ff.), defining production, competitively viewed, as mere acquisition, includes advertising, along with all other outlays which bring a gain, as productive. Cf. also Ely, *Outlines*, 5th revised ed., p. 113. Among writers on business economics, A. W. Shaw (*An Approach to Business Problems*, Chapter XV) has illustrated an increase in demand on account of advertising by moving the demand schedule to the right; but it is the demand schedule for a general class of product which is moved, and he at once encounters difficulties because the effect on the merchant who advertises cannot be shown in the general diagram, and because of the different prices at which the differentiated product sells. No attempt is made to deal with the costs of moving the curve.

Since this and the following chapter were written an article has appeared by Dorothea Braithwaite ("The Economic Effects of Advertisement," *Economic Journal*, Vol. XXXVIII [1928], p. 16), who distinguishes between production and selling costs, divides the latter into "true" selling costs and advertising costs, and discusses the effects of the latter upon the national dividend and economic welfare. Cf. also Harrod, "The Law of Decreasing Costs," *Economic Journal*, Vol. XLI, p. 566.

assumption of pure competition; they seem, likewise, to have no place in monopolistic theory, since there is apparently no one upon whom the monopolist, in possession of the entire market, could encroach. The explanation lies also in the fact that economic theory has not yet adapted itself to changes which have taken place in recent years. The tremendous possibilities of making profits by demand creation have been more and more appreciated, technical methods of exploiting them have been perfected, and selling has come to the fore as a business activity coördinate with production. Indeed, the typical business man of today is probably more concerned with the former than with the latter. Meanwhile theoretical economics continues to regard him as a producer only, and as enjoying a demand which is already there and which has cost nothing. The theory of pure competition tacitly assumes that all costs are incurred in order to increase the supply of goods and that these goods are sold with neither effort nor expense. It is by neglecting selling costs that it most obviously falls short of explaining the facts of economic life.

In the explanation of why selling expenditures are inconsistent with the assumption of pure competition both of its requirements — a standardized product and a large number of competitors — play their part. Product being standardized, there is no basis for distinguishing one seller's goods from those of another. No one, therefore, could take business from his competitors by advertising; on the contrary, his goods being indistinguishable from theirs, he would be forced to increase or diminish their sales *pari passu* with his own. Now, the number of competitors being large, any one is a correspondingly small factor in the whole situation. An advertising expenditure very large to him would have a very small effect on the total demand, and his own increase would be a negligibly small fraction of this. Wherever conditions of pure competition obtain, this reasoning is clearly supported in fact. A single wheat farmer or a single orange grower does not advertise to increase the consumption of his product. Advertising takes place here, if at all, only by coöperation between all producers, which coöperation gives conditions of monopolistic competition, the whole body of sellers acting as one in competing for their market with sellers of other goods.[1] Another way of putting the case is to say that under pure competition, since the market for any one seller is infinitely large, his advertising would be to no purpose, for he can sell all he wants to without it.[2]

In applying purely competitive theory beyond its proper province, the disposition of selling costs is a perplexing problem. To make the theory consistent with itself, they should be excluded. Yet this is open to two objections. In the first place, it leads to the conclusion that prices tend to approximate cost of production with no allowance for selling, which they clearly do not, since costs of selling must also be covered if the entrepreneur is to remain in business. In the second place, it leads to the conclusion that prices tend to approximate costs under the most efficient scale of production, since the absence of difficulties in selling sweeps away all obstacles to the achievement of this scale. Thus purely competitive theory gives a norm which is *two steps* below that defined by monopolistic competition: the costs of selling are omitted, and costs of production are understated.

On the other hand (if purely competitive theory is to be applied generally), consistency with itself might be sacrificed to consistency with the facts, selling costs being included in the cost curve, along with costs of production. In favor of this disposition of them, it might be argued (1) that all costs are alike in that they form an aggregate which must be met if the entrepreneur is to remain in business, and (2) that, although costs of selling produce demand rather than goods, they produce it for one individual by taking it away from others, thereby leaving the total demand, which is the significant force in determining price, the same. One is led naturally enough to this second conclusion if he is thinking in terms of pure competition. But a theory which does not permit of advertising could hardly be relied upon to describe its results. The truth is that an advertisement is not limited in its effects to

[1] The California Fruit Growers' Exchange, not being all-inclusive, found it necessary to brand their product in order that the benefits should accrue to the members of the Exchange, so far as possible, instead of to citrus fruit growers generally.

[2] Cf. Pigou, *Economics of Welfare*, 3rd ed., p. 198, note: "Under simple competition, there is no purpose in this advertisement, because, *ex hypothesi*, the market will take, at the market price, as much as any one small seller wants to sell."

those consuming other varieties of the same general class of goods. It is not even true that there is less resistance to be broken down by addressing the advertising appeal to consumers using other varieties of the same general class of product. Often, the consumer who is well satisfied with the brand he is using is not easily persuaded to discard it and to experiment on something new. It may be easier to sell a Chevrolet or a Ford to someone who has never owned an automobile than to someone who has owned one of another make. Furthermore, new uses for a product may be suggested which will induce greater consumption generally, and, by skillful suggestion, draw a large share of the increase to the advertised variety. The best policy will depend upon the nature of the "potential" market. It is, indeed, conceivable that the advertiser's market should be increased entirely at the expense of his nearest competitors. But it is much more likely that the increase will be only partly or not at all at their expense. It is even a familiar result that sellers are *benefited* by the advertising of their closest rivals. These considerations deprive the second argument of most of its force.

Let us return, then, to the first. True, selling as well as production costs must, in the long run, be covered if a producer is to remain in business. Both must be included in the cost curve, and both are so included in the following chapter, where our theory is given further expansion in order to take account of selling outlays. The reason why this may not be done under the theory of pure competition is that no criterion exists as to the amount of selling costs which should be included (that is, no criterion except the manifest one indicating that it should be zero). The theory affords a clear-cut answer to the question of how far any individual producer and how far all together will carry their outlays for *production.* But how far will any one of them and how far will all together carry their expenditures for *selling?* Selling costs being extraneous to the theory of pure competition, the latter affords no technique for answering these questions. The next chapter attempts to answer them by relating them to conditions of monopolistic competition.

CHAPTER VII

SELLING COSTS AND THE THEORY OF VALUE

1. The Curve of Selling Costs

ADVERTISING[1] "increases the demand" for the product, that is, it enables the seller, at whatever price he decides upon, to dispose of more than he could without it. Graphically, this means a shift of the demand curve for his product upwards and to the right. At each price more of the commodity can be sold; for each amount the marginal demand price (the price at which this amount will just be taken from the market) is higher.[2]

The magnitude of the result depends upon the amount expended, and the question at once arises of whether advertising outlays are subject to increasing, constant, or diminishing returns. As the outlay increases, is the increase in sales more than proportional, proportional, or less than proportional to the increase in advertising expenditure? Evidently, the putting of such a problem involves holding the price constant throughout the variations in selling outlays. Sales are a function of both price and advertising, and the nature of their variation with the latter can be discovered only by holding the former constant. Graphically, this means that, although advertising increases the demand at *all* prices (the whole curve being shifted to the right), its effects can be measured quantitatively only by selecting one price and measuring the increase in demand at that price. It might seem that, if advertising did not have the same proportionate effect at all prices (if a certain expenditure did not increase the amount demanded by the same fraction, say one-tenth, at all points on the demand curve), it would be a matter of some consequence which price were chosen for the problem at hand. A certain outlay might, for in-

---

[1] In this chapter "advertising" will often be used as synonymous with selling costs generally.

[2] If the advertisement refers specifically to a particular price, only a portion of the curve may be affected.

stance, yield increasing returns at one price and diminishing returns at another. The element of truth in this contention may, however, be taken into account without further complicating the procedure. Suppose it to be discovered that, for one particular price, increased advertising expenditure yields for a while increasing returns and thereafter decreasing returns indefinitely. There is every reason to suppose that the same stages will be gone through for any other price on the demand curve for the product, although the rate of increase or decrease and the point at which diminishing returns set in may vary for different prices. Our present problem, to repeat, is the behavior of the return at any given price, and for this purpose it seems to be a matter of indifference what price is chosen. Let it be remembered, finally, that we are, for the present, concerned with variations in sales volume, not in money receipts, nor in profits.

Selling costs, like production costs, are finally analyzable into outlays for the several economic factors, say land, labor, and capital, which factors may evidently be combined for selling purposes, as well as for production purposes, in different proportions. In expending an appropriation for magazine advertising, for instance, more may be spent for the expert services of advertising writers or artists, and less for magazine space, or vice versa. In window display, space (land) may be varied through deepening the windows; and the outlays for salaries of technical experts, for materials, and for equipment may be varied over a wide range. If samples are to be distributed, they may be larger or smaller, or they may be distributed with all degrees of efficiency, depending upon how much is spent on the labor of planning and executing the campaign. The most efficient combination of factors will always be sought for any given total expenditure, and the general laws governing its determination will be the same for the sales organization as for the production organization.[1] Every (divisible) factor will normally be used within the stage of diminishing returns for that factor; that is, under conditions such that increased outlay for it alone (the others remaining constant) would

---

[1] Cf. Carver, *Distribution of Wealth*, Chap. II; F. M. Taylor, *Principles of Economics*, 9th ed., Chaps. IX–XI; Knight, *Risk, Uncertainty and Profit*, Chap. IV.

give an increase in sales less than proportionate to the increased expenditure. Within this stage, the more expensive factors will be economized more than those less expensive, and, the relative prices of the factors being given, there will be one combination which represents the most effective employment of a given total expenditure. To discover this combination will be the goal of the business man's calculations, so far as proportionality is concerned.

The most effective combination is not an absolute thing. It varies, in the first place, as the nature of the product and of its potential market dictates the form of the advertising required. Thus the small retail merchant may be restricted to window display, an attractive disposition of his wares within his shop, and the exertion of personal sales effort on those who cross his threshold. A large department store will use a different type of window display, and exact different methods from its sales force. It will also employ new media on a large scale, such as newspaper space and the device of special bargain sales. Again, certain household products need demonstration, which is perhaps best provided through house-to-house canvassing. Manufactured goods for which a "national market" may be created usually require magazine advertising and an elaborate organization of distributing agencies and salesmen. The technical requirements of each of these and other avenues of sales expenditure dictate in large measure the kind and proportion of factors utilized.

The most effective combination of factors varies, secondly, with the magnitude of the total expenditure. This is true in part because the nature of the advertising medium or media to be used depends in a measure on the amount to be spent, that is, on the size of the potential market. We have seen that the small retail trader is more restricted than the large department store. Similarly, the small manufacturer who cannot hope to achieve national distribution must use the sales methods and media adapted to the geographical area or social stratum which he hopes to exploit. It is true, again, because even the same general type of selling effort changes qualitatively with the scale upon which it is carried on. Thus the larger the volume of newspaper or magazine advertising, the more will it pay to employ the most skilled advertisement writers. Again, store display on a small scale and on a large scale employs different facilities and therefore different combinations of economic factors. In sum, the choice of the medium or combination of media and of the proportion of economic factors to be used depends upon the nature of the product and of its market, and upon the magnitude of the total expenditure. As we turn now to the question of whether increased *total* outlay (as distinguished from increased outlay for particular factors) will yield increasing or diminishing returns, and to the question of how far total expenditure will be carried, it must be held in mind that a given outlay is always assumed to be most effectively utilized in these respects.

The net results of increased advertising expenditure are a composite of several tendencies which must be considered separately. In the first place, results are frequently cumulative through repetition, and in so far as this is true, additional expenditure yields increasing returns. The commonplace among advertising men that a small expenditure is wasted is explained by the psychological laws of habit. Existing propensities with regard to spending one's income cannot be broken down by a single assault. They have been fortified by repetition, and can be overcome only by repeated suggestions of an alternative. In this respect the art of the advertiser is akin to that of the hypnotist. Control of the buyer's consciousness must be gained, and while it is being gained additional expenditure yields increasing returns.

Another factor leading to increasing returns is improvement in the organization of the expenditure as its total amount is increased. The economies of large-scale operations apply to the selling organization as well as to production: the employment of more resources means greater specialization in their use. This familiar idea does not need elaboration. It applies to all phases of selling activity — to the administrative staff, to advertisement writers and artists, to salesmen, to ordinary laborers.[1] Not

[1] In addition to these "internal" economies which are realized in the individual firm, "external" economies, such as the development of agencies whose function it is to place most effectively the advertising of their clients, are realized as selling activity in general is extended. These can and must be neglected in constructing a curve of selling costs for the individual firm, however, since the effect upon them of

only may the division of labor be carried further with a given set of factors, but new and more effective factors may be chosen. The distinction is largely one of point of view. The employment of an advertising expert, impossible for the small firm, may be regarded as an extension of the division of labor for the large firm, since one man specializes in a function which is performed, along with many others, by the proprietor of the smaller enterprise. Or it may be regarded as the introduction by the larger firm of a new and different factor, since the expert is different qualitatively from his counterpart in the smaller firm. Among the more effective factors whose use is made possible by larger outlays are more effective media. We have already seen that the medium used is conditioned in part by the amount expended. The most effective media may be those whose use requires a large outlay. As expenditure increases, then, a shift may take place to continually more effective media, so that a tendency to increasing returns is imparted to the cost curve. The most effective choice of media may involve the use of several in combination, as when samples of a new food product are distributed in conjunction with the use of newspaper space and the exertion of sales pressure by retail grocers. In other instances the increasing returns due to repetition may be realized or intensified by the use of several media.

In opposition to these forces, there are others towards diminishing returns, which, although perhaps submerged in the early stages, gather strength with larger outlays and sooner or later dominate the result.

In the first place, buyers are not equally accessible: some have greater potential needs for the commodity than others; and some are more susceptible to advertising and to selling appeal than are others. Desires for the commodity are not everywhere awakened with uniform ease; the "sales resistance" to be broken down varies widely for different buyers and for different groups of buyers. Under these circumstances, the richest potential mar-

---

variations in the selling expenditure of any one firm (expenditures of other firms remaining the same) is negligible if there are many firms.

kets — those lying nearest at hand and those offering the least resistance — will be exploited first, and selling costs per unit will rise as efforts are directed towards successively poorer ones. This is subject, of course, to the qualification already considered, that the exploitation of the best markets (i. e., the use of the best media) may be conditioned upon a fairly large total outlay, and that up to this point increasing returns may be obtained. Beyond this point, diminishing returns are inevitable, for the remaining potential markets offer smaller possibilities than those already undertaken.

Secondly, diminishing returns are encountered in the more intensive exploitation of any given market, or group of buyers. Let us look at the case of the single individual. He may be persuaded to consume a larger amount of any commodity only by reducing correspondingly his consumption of other things.[1] If the satisfactions afforded by the good itself are not such that physiological or psychological factors set an early limit to increase in his consumption of it, at least the sacrifice of other continually more important wants will increase his resistance as more selling effort is expended upon him. In general (perhaps again after an initial stage of increasing returns), it will cost more to persuade him to consume each successive unit. This being true for the individual, it is true by addition for any group of individuals regarded as a market, and it is true for any single advertising medium, since this is simply a means through which a particular group of buyers is reached.

Diminishing returns, then, are encountered for two reasons: first, because, in general, the best potential markets are exploited first, additional expenditures yielding ever smaller results as successively poorer markets are taken up; and, secondly, because added selling effort applied to any one market (i. e., to any one group of potential buyers) can succeed only by inducing the sacrifice of continually more important alternative wants. If these forces are placed alongside of those leading to increasing returns, it will be evident at once that the latter ultimately give way be-

---

[1] Leisure included, i. e., he may work longer hours, sacrificing leisure in order to enjoy more goods.

fore the former. Increasing returns from repetition and from improved organization sooner or later come to an end, whereas the resistances accounting for diminishing returns are ever increasing in strength as sales outlays are extended. The curve of (average) selling cost per unit of product, being a composite of all of these forces, will evidently fall as returns are increasing, reach a minimum, and then rise again under diminishing returns. The curve

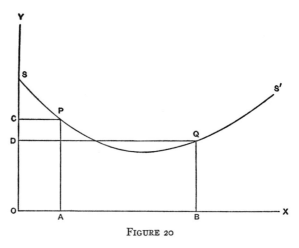

FIGURE 20

SS' in Fig. 20 illustrates the movement graphically. Costs of selling only are considered (costs of production being omitted); units of product are measured along the horizontal axis, and costs along the vertical axis. Thus *AP* is the average cost of selling the quantity *OA* (the total cost being *OAPC*), and *BQ* is the average cost of selling *OB* (the total cost being *OBQD*). The position of the curve and the exact point at which it turns upward will depend upon the nature of the "product," upon its price, and upon the competing substitutes which limit its market. The curve for any product can, of course, be drawn only on the assumption that all of these other factors remain constant while selling outlays only, and for this product only, are varied. Evidently, the curve will be differently defined for each set of conditions with regard to these other factors. As the product itself is improved (or made more salable in any way, say by the clever choice of a name) the resistance to its sale will be reduced; the curve of selling costs will be lowered throughout, and its minimum point will, perhaps, be lowered somewhat to the right. Conversely, as the quality of the product is deteriorated, the curve will be raised, and its minimum point will lie further to the left, since diminishing returns in its sale will be encountered sooner. In general, as its price is lowered, the curve of selling costs will be lowered, and conversely. As substitutes encroach more and more upon its market through increase in their number, improvement in their quality, reduction in their prices, or increase in their advertising outlays, the curve of selling costs for this product will be raised and curled backward, for diminishing returns will be encountered sooner and the minimum point will be moved to the left. The shape of the curve is not a given thing under which an equilibrium of economic forces is worked out, but is a part of the problem of equilibrium itself. Even assuming given conditions, so that the curve is rigorously defined, there can be no conclusion with regard to how far selling outlays will be carried until the cost of production is also taken into account. The next step, then, is to combine the curves of selling cost and of production cost.

This is a simple process of addition.[1] In Fig. 21, let PP' be the curve of cost of production per unit, as heretofore defined and employed. Now to the cost of producing each particular amount let the cost of selling the same amount be added, so that the cost of producing and selling will be given by the curve CC'. Cost of selling alone will be given by the distance between the two curves PP' and CC'. Thus, for the quantity OA, the production cost per unit is AM, the selling cost per unit is MQ, and the combined cost [2] per unit is AQ. The total cost of production for all units is $OAME$; of selling, $EMQF$; and of both, $OAQF$. Evidently, the minimum combined unit cost of producing and selling will not,

---

[1] The alternative procedure has been developed by Henry Smith and others of *subtracting* selling costs from price. It is discussed in Essay 8, "Advertising Costs and Equilibrium," in *Towards a More General Theory of Value*, where further references to the literature will be found. See also T. H. Silcock, Bibliography No. 1356.

[2] The notation "CC" for this curve refers to *combined* cost, as "PP'" refers to *production* cost. (A better term might be *total* cost, were it not so easily confused with "total" in another sense of comprising all units.) CC' may also be regarded as designating *cost*, since this is the only curve which may be legitimately referred to, without qualifying adjective, as a cost curve, comprising, as it does, *all* costs.

in general, coincide with the minimum for either producing or selling alone. In Fig. 21, the minimum combined cost is BR, corresponding to the output OB; the minimum production cost is DH, corresponding to the most efficient scale of production, OD; and selling costs per unit are a minimum at GL.[1]

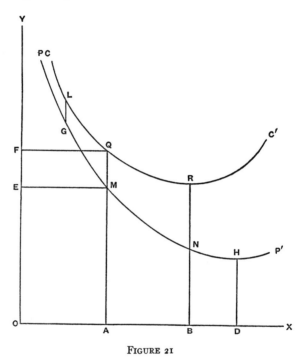

FIGURE 21

A curve of (combined) marginal costs, MM', may now be added, and this is done in Fig. 22 (p. 142). It indicates the addition to total cost on account of each successive unit and bears a simple relation to the curve CC'. For any indicated amount of product, the area enclosed under the curve MM' must be equal to the rectangle inscribed under CC'. For the quantity OD, the area $ODTM$ is equal to $ODQS$, for evidently the sum of the costs added by each successive unit will equal the total cost, as will also

[1] It is possible that the minimum cost of selling, and hence the minimum combined costs, will lie to the right of D.   Cf. below, p. 161.

the average multiplied by the number of units. For the quantity *OD*, then, *DT* is the marginal combined cost of producing and selling, and *DQ* the unit, or average, combined cost of producing and selling. The curve of marginal cost must cross the curve of average cost at *L*, the minimum point for the latter, since, as output increases, average costs fall only so long as the cost added by another unit is less than the average, and rise as soon as the cost added by another unit is greater than the average. Curves of marginal cost of production alone and of selling alone would be derived in exactly the same way and bear the same relation to their respective curves of average cost. Added, they would give the curve of combined marginal cost, *MM'*. They are not indicated in the figure.

The curve of selling costs has been defined without reference to the period of time and to the distinction between short-time and long-time results. This has been done deliberately, for the interaction of monopolistic and competitive forces is present in both short-time and long-time market situations. The curve of selling costs, like the curve of production costs, must include such outlays and results as are relevant to the period of time taken into account by the business man when he decides upon his policies, and must be interpreted with reference to such a period. A merchant who is conducting a bargain sale will determine upon his price and advertising policy primarily with regard to that sale, whereas one who is determining upon his advertising budget for the year has regard to adjusting the organization of his business to longer-run, perhaps to "normal," conditions. The two problems are not independent, of course. Those who are attracted by the bargain sale may become permanent customers, thus increasing future sales; on the other hand, future sales may be diminished — the longer-time market "spoiled" — by persuading those who would buy anyway to concentrate their purchases during the sale. Again, in some kinds of business, the long-time market may be made up in large part of a series of short-time bargain sales. A maze of intricate problems is suggested by considerations such as these, the elaboration of which would go far beyond this introductory attempt to indicate the general effect of monopoly elements in the economic system. Although much of the technique here developed may be applied to such problems, what is held in mind primarily in the analysis to follow is the long-time, or "normal," problem. The curves are best interpreted as indicating rates of expenditure per unit of time, say per year; so that BR, for example, on the curve CC' (Fig. 21) indicates the cost per unit of producing and selling (at a given price) OB units annually.

2. Individual Equilibrium

Following the method of Chapter V, let us consider first the problem of individual equilibrium, and afterwards that of group equilibrium. The first will deal with the most advantageous adjustment for the individual producer under given and unchanging conditions with regard to the prices, products, and selling policies of all competitors. It will ignore the actual interdependence between the markets for goods which are substitutes for each other — the fact that a price cut or an increase in advertising outlay by one seller gains customers from his rivals alters the demand curves for their products, and hence leads to changes in the general adjustment. The second problem, on the other hand, will concern itself with precisely these interrelationships within groups of products which are fairly close substitutes for each other. It will also consider movements of resources into and out of such groups as profits are generally high or low within the group.

Assuming, then, substitutes whose nature and prices are given, and the selling outlays for which do not change,[1] let us turn to our individual producer. He seeks to maximize his profit and to this end adjusts his product, price, and selling outlays. In the general case, he is free to adjust all three, and may do so simultaneously. Frequently, however, one or two of the factors may be set by external circumstances, custom, or his own previous decision, and he may concern himself only with finding the best

[1] It should be noted that the *markets* for the substitutes — the demand curves for each of them, and hence their sales volumes — are not taken as given. They must necessarily be influenced by the adjustments of the seller whose policies are being examined.

adjustment for those which remain. These "partial" problems may, with advantage, be considered first. The method of procedure will be to examine the adjustment of each of the three variables in turn, the other two being, in each case, held constant; and then, finally, to permit two or all three of them to vary at once. Each of the solutions has an intrinsic importance through its direct applicability to economic situations with which its assumptions are in accord. Aside from this, each has its value also as an aid to the understanding of the total problem through isolating a part of it.

Let us first regard product and price as given. We assume that the product changes neither in itself nor in the circumstances surrounding its sale; the price, let us say, is set by a previous decision or by custom, is imposed by the manufacturer, or has come to be tacitly accepted by business men. The question is, how far, under these conditions, will advertising expenditure be carried? In Fig. 22, let the curve of cost of production be PP', and let the combined curve of (average) cost of production and selling *at the given price* be CC'. (MM' is ignored for the moment.) This price may conceivably be higher than, lower than, or equal to the minimum combined cost, AL. Let us take first the case where it is higher, say OF, and draw FZ parallel to the base line.[1] For any output of product where the combined cost curve CC' lies below this horizontal line, the profit per unit is the distance between the two, and the total profit which the entrepreneur attempts to make a maximum will be this difference multiplied by the output. The most profitable output is seen to be OB, for which the total profit area, $ENRF$, is larger than any other rectangular area which can be drawn, in the manner indicated, between CC' and the horizontal line FZ. For this amount, the total selling cost is $HGNE$, and the total cost of production is $OBGH$. The entrepreneur "chooses" this amount, not directly, but through adjusting his selling expenditure. In the light of the market conditions

---

[1] It should be noted that this is not a horizontal demand line such as has been drawn above (p. 17) in connection with pure competition, indicating that an unlimited amount would be demanded at the price OF. Under present conditions the amount demanded will vary with advertising expenditure; for instance, it is OB when the total advertising expenditure is $HGNE$.

surrounding his product, he determines upon the sum of *HGNE*
for advertising, since any appropriation larger or smaller than
this would be less profitable.[1]

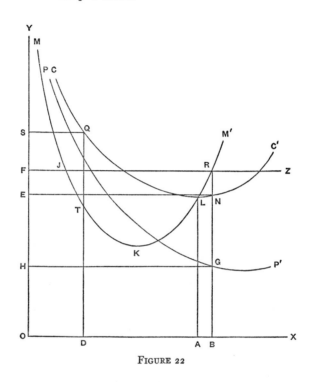

FIGURE 22

The point of maximum profit may also be defined with reference to marginal costs. *MM'* is the curve of (combined) marginal
costs; its nature and its relation to the cost curve *CC'* have already been described.[2] The most profitable output will be indicated by the intersection of this curve with the line *FZ* at *R*, that
is, it will be such that marginal cost equals the selling price. It is
OB, of course, as before, and total profits are *OBRF* − *OBRKM*
(= *ENRF*). As output increases from zero up to the first point of
intersection of *MM'* and *FZ* at *J*, losses are increasing, the added

[1] As in Chapter V, solutions are presented only for curves which are smooth and
"regular" in shape.

[2] Above, p. 138.

cost of each new unit being greater than its selling price. Beyond *J* losses diminish until they disappear, and profits grow to their maximum at *R*; the reason being that between *J* and *R* the added cost of each new unit is less than its selling price. Beyond *R*, profits again diminish.

If we suppose the price with reference to which *CC'* is drawn to be exactly equal to the minimum combined cost of producing and selling, *AL*, selling expenses would be incurred which were just sufficient to dispose of the quantity *OA*. With this price and output surplus profits are eliminated, but there remains that minimum amount necessary to insure production, which is always included within the cost curve. If the price were lower than *AL*, losses would be incurred and production would not normally be continued (provided, of course, that no alteration of price or "product" were possible which would give new curves eliminating the loss).

Secondly, let us suppose product and selling outlays to be given, and turn our attention to the price adjustment. The assumption of a given product is continued from the case just considered, but the supposition of a fixed price, which allowed variations in selling outlays to be examined in isolation, is abandoned. Selling outlays are now held constant in order that the adjustment of price may, in turn, be studied separately. Economic situations are often found where they do not vary, and where the assumptions are fairly in accord with the facts. Selling expenditures may be determined by a previous decision as to the annual budget, by habit or inertia on the part of the individual entrepreneur, or by generally accepted trade practice. There are trades and industries where expenditures for the maintenance of "connections" and for advertising become fairly set — a certain annual outlay and certain methods of expending it come to be regarded as "normal." The amount is not accidental — in fact, it is the sum which long experience has revealed as the most advantageous or as normally required for the marketing of the product. To this type of case the theory may be applied directly; yet, even where selling expenditures are not, in fact, constant, to assume them so again serves the purpose of breaking a complicated whole into its parts for isolated study.

Selling expenditures being taken as fixed, the curve of selling cost per unit of product will have an elasticity of unity, indicating the distribution of this fixed total over all the various possible outputs. It may be seen at once that when this curve is added to the curve of production cost, the resulting curve of *combined* cost has

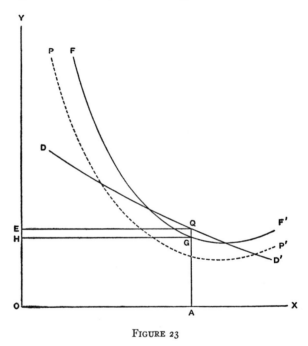

FIGURE 23

the same general shape as the latter: it descends to a minimum point and then rises again. The minimum point of the combined cost curve, however, lies further to the right than that of the cost of production curve. This is of considerable importance, as will be shown later on.

The product and selling outlay being set, the entrepreneur's attention is given to choosing the most advantageous price. A demand curve for his product may be drawn, as *DD'* (Fig. 23), indicating the amounts which will be demanded at various prices. The position and slope of this curve will depend, as already pointed out, partly on the strength of the monopoly elements in the general field, i. e., on the number of competitors and the degree of perfection of the substitutes which they offer. It will depend also on the nature of the "product" and the amount of the selling outlay. Since all of these things have been taken as given, the curve is defined. FF' is the curve of combined producing and selling costs.[1] The price will be such as to yield the maximum profit, say AQ, volume of sales being OA, total profits $HGQE$, and the total combined costs $OAGH$. This differs from the familiar solution of the simple problem of monopoly value only in that the cost curve FF' includes selling costs of a given amount, which are an important factor in defining the position of the demand curve.

Depending on the conditions assumed with regard to the factors held constant, the demand curve would, of course, be variously defined. It might lie further to the right or to the left of its position in Fig. 23; the optimum price would accordingly be higher or lower, and the profit area larger or smaller. If it were tangent to the cost curve FF', the perpendicular dropped from the point of tangency would indicate the price, and there would be no profits at all above the minimum amount included within the cost curve. Production would continue, however, for necessary costs would be covered. If it lay still further to the left, necessary costs would not be covered, and production would not normally be continued.

The third possible variable is the "product," and, in order to focus attention on this phase of the problem, selling outlay and price must be taken as given. We now regard the entrepreneur as having already decided upon his price and selling policy, or as taking it for granted that he will charge the going price and spend a "normal" amount for advertising. Such an assumption may correspond to the facts in particular cases, or may be regarded, again, as a logical step in building up a complete explanation of the whole problem. "Product" variation has already been de-

---

[1] The contrast between this curve and the combined cost curve previously discussed (Figs. 21 and 22, for example) must be held in mind. The earlier curve showed the cost of producing and selling each amount of product, the price being given. If the indicated expenditure was made, the corresponding amount was sold. The present curve simply distributes fixed selling costs (hence the notation FF') over different volumes of product, asserting nothing as to the amount actually sold. This latter depends upon the price, as indicated by the demand curve.

scribed and analyzed in connection with the simpler case where selling costs were omitted.[1] The introduction of fixed selling expenses, since it does not change the general shape of the cost curve, does not change the nature of the earlier analysis, which need not be reproduced in detail. The cost curve (Fig. 11, p. 79), which in the earlier case included merely costs of production, must now be interpreted as a combined cost curve including also the fixed selling outlay (as in the case of price variation just considered). This curve will, in general, be different for each variety of "product," and for each the amount demanded will be defined by the fixed elements in the case (product, price, and selling outlay for this good and for all those competing with it). Of all the "product" possibilities, that one will be chosen which yields the maximum profit.

Just as, in the earlier illustration, the product selected is not necessarily the one whose cost of production is the lowest, so here it is not necessarily the one whose curve of combined cost is the lowest, nor the one the demand for which is greatest. The output, again, bears no relation either to the most effective scale of production or to the most effective scale of producing and selling.

As different assumptions are made with regard to the fixed elements in the problem, the cost curve, price line, and amount demanded will be altered correspondingly. Better, cheaper, or more extensively advertised substitutes will restrict the possibility of profit by lowering the price line, by diminishing the amount demanded, or by raising the cost curve through the necessity of choosing a product of better quality, or perhaps in all three ways. Evidently, in order for production to go on at all, competitive conditions with respect to these factors must not be such as to leave no product choice possible at which the necessary costs, including minimum profits, can be met. It must not be forgotten, however, that although such a product choice may be impossible for a particular assumption with respect to price and selling outlay, it may be possible for another.

The analysis of each variable — product, price, and selling outlay — in isolation is now completed. It has been repeatedly

---

[1] Above, pp. 78–80.

asserted that each of these simplified cases may have its direct application, but that it must also be regarded as a first step in the explanation of cases where two or all three factors are free to vary at the same time. The explanation of such cases is merely a matter of putting together the parts. Suppose, for instance, that product and price are both free to vary, selling outlays alone being held constant. Instead of a fixed amount demanded, as *OG* for product *A* in Fig. 11 (page 79), we now have a demand curve showing the amounts demanded at various prices. For each "product" there will be a price at which total profits are a maximum, and that combination of product and price will be chosen which offers the largest total profit of all.

Suppose, as a second instance, that product is set, and price and selling outlay are free to vary. A construction similar to Fig. 22 for each possible price would show the most advantageous selling outlay for that price, and one of this series would be the best of all, thus revealing both optimum price and optimum selling outlay. The same result is reached by reversing the order in which the two variables are taken up. A series of constructions similar to Fig. 23 would show the most advantageous price for every possible selling outlay. One of these would be the best of all and would indicate, again, both optimum selling outlay and optimum price.[1]

Finally, when product, price, and selling expenses are all three subject to variation, the solution may be reached by an extension of the same method. Let the procedure of the last case, giving the most advantageous price and selling outlay for a given "product," be repeated for all possible "products," and that one chosen which affords the largest profit of all. Or let the procedure for the discovery of the best combination of product and price be repeated for all possible selling outlays. It matters not in what order the parts are assembled. Together they compose and illustrate the very general proposition that (all circumstances with regard to competing substitutes being given) the entrepreneur will select that combination of product, price, and selling expenditure for which his total profits are a maximum.

[1] An alternative method of representation would be a three-dimensional diagram.

A graphic summary of the characteristics of this optimum adjustment, except for the variations in "product," is possible, and is presented in Fig. 24. We have seen [1] that there may or may not be extra profits above the necessary minimum, and the case is chosen for illustration where there are not. The figure must be

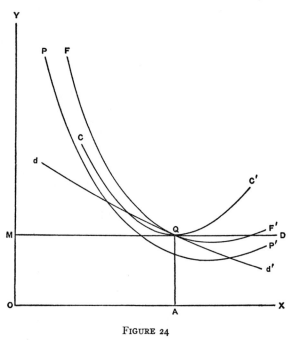

FIGURE 24

regarded as pertaining to the "product" which is most advantageous in relation to the whole solution. *PP'* is the curve of cost of production, and *CC'* the curve of combined cost of producing and selling on the assumption that the price is constant at *OM*. The output is *OA* since this amount is indicated by the point of tangency of *CC'* with the price line *MD*. *FF'* is the curve of combined cost of producing and selling on the assumption that selling costs are constant, and *dd'* is the demand curve showing the variations of demand with price when selling costs are held at the figure which defines *FF'*. These two curves are likewise tangent to each

[1] Above, pp. 141–143.

other at Q. Examination of the figure will reveal the impossibility of any variation in selling expenditure or in price without incurring a loss. An increase or decrease in selling expenditures, the price remaining the same, would involve a loss because CC' lies above MD on either side of Q; and an increase or decrease in the price, selling expenditures remaining the same, would involve a loss because FF' lies above dd' on either side of Q. And since the curves have been drawn with reference to the best selection of "product," no change is possible in this respect. A similar representation might be constructed for the case where there were profits above the minimum included in the cost curve, in which case variation from the optimum solution would involve a diminution in profits instead of a loss.

3. GROUP EQUILIBRIUM

Let us now turn to the group problem. The diversity of conditions as between producers has already been described in Chapter V.[1] To summarize briefly, individual products possess distinctive features and vary widely among themselves in size and quality. The result is a variety of curves of cost of production within the group. These same factors combined with the diversity, as between various markets, of buyers' incomes and tastes, and the vagaries of their preferences, lead to a similar variety of demand curves; and now, we may add, of curves of selling costs. A given selling expenditure, planned and executed with given skill, may achieve results varying with the product to which it is applied, both because products are different and because the potential market to which appeal is made is different. Similarly, whatever the increase in sales, it may be drawn unevenly from the markets of other members of the group or from those outside of the group.

A method of dealing with these difficulties has likewise been developed in Chapter V. We proceed first by ignoring them, making the drastic assumption that demand curves, production cost curves, and selling cost curves are uniform for all the products in the group; their actual diversity will be taken into ac-

---

[1] Above, pp. 81, 82.

count at a later point. Meanwhile let us not exaggerate the drastic nature of this assumption. Markets are often fairly uniform in composition, consumers' preferences fairly evenly distributed, differences between products such as to give rise to no marked differences in cost, and selling methods stable and unsensational. Where these things are true, our assumptions are sufficiently realistic to make the results of some direct applicability.

The question of the number included within the group and of the manner in which their markets overlap is again important. If numbers are small, complexities arise analogous to those described in Chapter III. Each seller may contemplate the fact that, his rivals being few, his own advertising will make such incursions into their markets that they will be forced *by his action* to protect themselves and follow suit. Since this would redound to his disadvantage, he may decide from the first against a policy which, immediately speaking, would be profitable. For the present we leave this difficulty to one side, assuming that the incursions made by his advertising into the markets of others are spread in such a way as to make them inappreciable in any individual case. None of his rivals would then be led by his actions to do anything which he would not have done anyway, and the complexities of "indirect influence" are disposed of. It will be seen, for reasons to be presented at once, that, where advertising is concerned, this condition may hold even though the number in the group be fairly small.

The competing monopolists whom we now group together may, as we have already seen, adjust either their prices, their "products," or their selling outlays, or any of these in combination. As in the problem of individual equilibrium, let us consider each of the three variables in turn. First, let prices and products be given for all sellers, the competition for markets being carried on solely by means of advertising. As in previous cases, the nature of the equilibrium adjustment may be revealed by assuming conditions divergent from it and describing the corrective movement. Let us suppose, then, that the number of sellers and the distribution of markets have been worked out under the conditions of Chapter V. Introduce, now, the possibility of increasing sales by advertising. How is the adjustment which would have taken place under simpler conditions altered?

The distribution of the results of advertising between the members of the group on the one hand, and those outside of it on the other, must be described before its effects within the group itself may be understood. The inclination is strong to pass over this phase of the problem, and to regard the results of advertising as confined to the group, since the common interpretation of the problem in terms of the theory of pure competition would indicate this result. If, according to the demand curve for automobiles, 100,000 units will be taken from the market at a price of $1000, it seems to follow directly that what one producer within the group sells the others do not sell. The argument, however, overlooks two things: (1) that for any one variety of automobile others are but *imperfect* substitutes, and (2) that there are many other substitutes besides automobiles. The increased market of any one producer is derived not alone from the markets of the closest substitutes for his product, but from the markets of *all* substitutes (i. e., from the markets of all other products). To the extent, then, that advertising leads people to buy automobiles instead of house room or train fares, the total sold at a price of $1000, subsequent to the advertising, will be more than 100,000 units. Just as the amount sold by any single producer depends not only on his price, but also on his selling outlays, so the total amount sold by any group of producers depends, in part, on their total advertising outlays. These do not entirely cancel out within the group.

We may, with advantage, compare the effect when one seller advertises to the effect when one seller cuts his price. In the latter case, he may secure his increased market in large part by taking business away from his competitors. But he is bound to attract, as well, others who are induced to buy for the first time or to buy more only because of the lower price. Otherwise, the demand curve would always be a perpendicular line. Similarly, when he advertises, he may gain partly at the expense of his immediate competitors, but he is bound also to attract a "new" increment of demand. When all or most sellers advertise, the sales of the general class of product increase much more, of course, and in a manner quite comparable to the increase in sales when all cut their prices.

To be sure, the distribution of the results of advertising depends in large measure on the nature of the appeal. If an automobile manufacturer, for instance, directs his appeal specifically to those who are already "in the market," seeking to persuade them to buy his product instead of a competing one, most of its effect may be dissipated in this way. Even in this extreme case, however, he can hardly fail to have some influence towards creating "new" demand. If all or most manufacturers are engaged in this kind of narrow competition, their efforts, although perhaps mostly cancelling out, can hardly fail also to call attention to the general class of product and to increase its sale. On the other hand, advertisements are more and more framed in other terms than these; sales pressure is exerted to the end of opening up "new" markets instead of intensifying the struggle for the old. This is for the reason that people are frequently unaware of the satisfactions to be had from a new direction of expenditure, and, when informed, are readily converted to it; whereas, if they are already familiar with the general type of good, they may not so easily change from one brand or variety of it to another. When the appeal is framed in this way to draw from new sources, the result will be achieved in larger measure — the increase in demand for the general class of product on account of advertising is bound to be considerable.

We turn to the effects *within the group* of advertising by one of its members. Evidently the advertiser will make some depredations upon his immediate competitors. There will be a readjustment in his favor of the sales total of the group. But what of the "new" sales added to this total from without? It is, in general, impossible for the advertiser to direct all of this new demand to himself; he attracts it in his direction, but a part of it is dropped to his competitors on the way. When the automobile manufacturer describes the satisfactions to be had from motoring and suggests the purchase of his car in order to realize them, most of those influenced may investigate his product first, but few will buy without looking at others, and many will end by purchasing elsewhere. Thus the products of his rivals are advertised as well as his own. In fact, the expansion of his market from "new" sources involves two phases: first, winning the customer to a new general mode of expenditure; and, secondly, winning him specifically to his own variety of it. Upon the relative ease with which each of these is accomplished depends the extent to which his advertising benefits his competitors. But the tendency to create demand for their products as well as for his own is always present.

The advertiser, then, both adds to and subtracts from the markets of his immediate competitors. It is difficult to generalize as to the net outcome. It would seem that, when differentiation within the group was very slight, customers would be more easily won from his rivals, there being a less substantial basis for preferring one variety to another. Yet, for the same reason, "new" demand, even though created by a single advertiser, would be shared more largely with others in the group. Would this "new" demand, however, be a considerable factor if product were not greatly differentiated? The answer is not certain. It might seem that the mere fact of a more homogeneous product would result in the sales effort of each competitor being more naturally directed against the markets of his immediate rivals, thus giving a net result adverse to them. This would be true especially if the number of competitors were large, for then the potential market of each (i. e., the actual markets of the others) would be large relative to his own. But on the other hand, his rivals will reason in the same way; and this very intensification of the struggle within the group may divert attention to the more stable and lasting results to be had by directing sales efforts elsewhere. Bread is a product not greatly differentiated, yet competing baking companies tell the public to "eat more bread." Apparently no general conclusion as to the effect within the group of advertising by a single seller can be reached on the basis of the degree of differentiation. Where products are very different, it would not be expected that the sale of one would be increased by the advertising of another. Yet it is reported that the advertising for carpet sweepers, when the market for them was first being created, had the effect of increasing the sale of even such remote substitutes as brooms and floor mops, through arousing a general interest in house cleaning.[1] After all, whether a seller's more immediate competitors gain or lose as a result of his advertising must depend upon the peculiarities of each individual case.

If we now suppose advertising to be general among the sellers whom we have grouped together, each will be fortified against the invasions of his rivals. He will retain, through his own advertising, customers he would have lost without it; he will lose others to his competitors; he will gain still others from them. Recalling our assumption of a similarity of conditions throughout the group, the conclusion must be that the sales of *all* producers are increased through the incursions of the group upon the markets of those outside of it, and much more than if only one or a few advertised. What, now, if sellers in *other* groups advertise? In the analysis to follow, we shall not go beyond the adjustments within the single group. It will be evident that a method similar to that applied as between the individuals in one group could be extended to systems of interdependent groups and even to the all-inclusive problem of the whole economic system.

In Fig. 25, let PP' be the curve of cost of production for each individual producer, OM his price, and OA his volume of business. The total volume of business done by all will then be OA multiplied by the number of sellers. Profits, it will be seen, have been reduced to the minimum (included within the curve PP') necessary in order to attract and maintain capital and business ability. CC' is the curve of combined cost of producing and selling at the price $OM = AR$ for any one producer. In subsequent analysis, it will always be drawn on the general assumption that the selling outlays of all others except the single one who advertises are held constant; in the specific case at hand, they are held constant at zero — the other producers do not advertise at all.[2]

---

[1] "Markets which Come without Calling," *Printer's Ink*, November 16, 1911, p. 52. Other examples are given. The advertising for safety razors increased the sale of other razors through leading people to shave at home, and that for phonographs increased the sale of pianos.

[2] It is for this reason that the curve does not extend to the left of A, since, in the absence of advertising generally, any one firm can dispose of the amount OA without incurring any selling expenses. As soon as advertising becomes general, however, the amount which any one producer can sell without it is reduced by the sales efforts of

From the figure, it is evident that it will pay him to make total selling outlays of *FHDE*, increasing his sales from *OA* to *OB*, decreasing his unit costs of production from *AR* to *BH*, and introducing extra profits of *EDQM*. The various possible effects of this manoeuvre by a single producer, on the markets of his competitors have already been traced — they may be decreased, left the

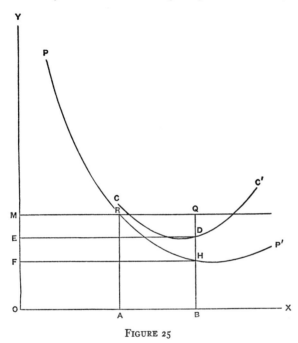

FIGURE 25

same, or increased. The markets of competitors will be decreased if the incursions made upon them directly exceed their gains through the increased consumption of the general class of product. They will be unaffected if these two approximately cancel each other, and they will be increased if the increase in consump-

the others, and the curve must be extended further to the left, as in previous constructions. In spite of a possible initial stage of increasing returns, the curve does not begin at a higher point for the reason that selling costs are averaged, not over the units beyond *A* for whose sale outlays are necessary, but over all the units sold, *including* the units from *O* to *A*, whose selling costs are zero. Thus, although the cost of selling the first unit after *A* might be very high, the curve *CC'*, showing the *average* costs, divides it by the quantity (*OA* + *1*).

tion of the general class of product exceeds the increase in consumption of the variety advertised.   If their markets are decreased, the incentive to advertise, already present for everyone just as for the one on whom we have focused attention, is heightened by the losses which would be incurred without it. If they are increased, the incentive to advertise is weakened by the gains which would be enjoyed without it. Such gains could always be increased for any seller by outlays of his own, however, and so the incentive is always present for everyone. This being true, let us inquire into the result when advertising becomes general.

The curve *CC'* is so defined that the profits *EDQM* are possible only for one seller, and on the assumption that he alone advertises. It explains why each and every seller in the group is led to make such outlays. To the extent that each adds to his market by subtracting from the markets of others in the group, however, there is shifting without net change: when all advertise, the sales of each firm remain constant at *OA*. Let us first inquire as to the outcome in the extreme and limiting case where *all* selling efforts cancel out in this manner within the group.

Let us carry selling outlays for each producer forward to a certain sum, and note the results. Let the total expenditure of each be *MREK* in Fig. 26, where *PP'* is reproduced from Fig. 25 and *FF'* is constructed so as to add to *PP'* this total selling outlay regardless of volume. Thus *NDQM* = *MREK* = any other rectangle similarly drawn between *PP'* and *FF'*.[1] The distinction between *FF'* (Fig. 26) and *CC'* (Fig. 25) must be carefully noted. The latter shows by its distance from the base line the cost *to one firm* of producing and selling different volumes *on the assumption that the selling outlays of the others remain constant* (as originally drawn, since no one was advertising as yet, they remained constant at zero); the former shows by its distance from the base line the combined cost of producing and selling different volumes of product *on the assumption that all producers in the group carry their selling outlays to a given total amount.* The area *MREK* represents not only the total advertising outlay of each seller, but also the exact amount of his losses so long as the number of sellers in the

[1] Mathematically, $x(y_f - y_p) = k$.

field remains undiminished, total cost for each being *OAEK* and total revenue *OARM*. Let us suppose their numbers to remain undiminished for a time. There is yet a possibility of escaping these losses through further advertising.

Let the curve *CC'* of combined costs of producing and selling for any one producer, on the assumption that the selling costs of the

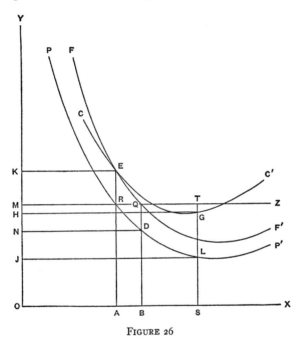

FIGURE 26

others remain constant, be drawn again with reference to the new condition that all other producers are making the total selling outlays (of *MREK*) indicated by the curve *FF'*. It will pass through *E*, since the expenditure of *MREK* is now necessary in order to sell the amount *OA*; and it must lie below *FF'* to the left of *E* and above it to the right of *E*, since expenditures smaller than those of his rivals will be sufficient to sell quantities less than *OA* and expenditures larger than those of his rivals will be necessary to sell more than *OA*. It may or may not dip below the horizontal price line *MZ*. If it does not, losses, although they may be reduced by further advertising, cannot be converted into profits. If it does, as in Fig. 26, profits of *HGTM* may be realized by making selling expenditures of *JLGH*. Output would become *OS*, cost of production per unit *SL*, selling cost per unit *LG*, and profit per unit *GT*. But as others do the same thing, the only result is to move *FF'*, and with it *CC'*, further to the right and upwards.

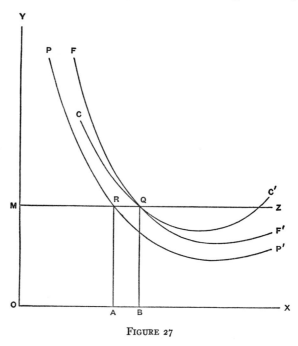

FIGURE 27

Further selling outlays will cease when the individual producer can no longer better his position by moving to the right along *CC'*.[1]

This result is not stable, however; in fact, the above must really be regarded as a digression from the main thread of the argument.

[1] The condition necessary for this is not that *CC'* be tangent to *MZ*. This would mean that the individual producer could wipe out his losses and earn the necessary minimum profits by moving to the point of tangency. In fact, so long as he could reduce his losses at all by increasing selling outlays, he would do so. The movement would stop when *CC'* had moved upwards and curled backwards so that the optimum point on it coincided with the point of intersection of *CC'* and *FF'*.

Our producer is now incurring losses, typified by *MREK* (Fig. 26), but actually much larger because *FF'* now lies further upwards and to the right. For these losses there is no permanent escape save through the exodus of some of the sellers, with the surrender of their markets to those remaining.[1] Let us suppose selling outlays to remain for a time as represented by *FF'*, and examine the outcome as sellers drop out, discouraged by their losses, of which *MREK* is representative. As the adjustment takes place, the markets of those remaining are enlarged, and combined costs of producing and selling fall along the curve *FF'*. Soon costs will again equal price, and losses will be eliminated when enough have quit the field to increase the output of those remaining to *OB*. The equilibrium between cost and price is, however, only temporary. *CC'* may be drawn again, as in Fig. 27, passing through *Q* this time, since the number of sellers has been reduced. It indicates the profits available to any producer through fresh selling expenditures. When these expenditures become general, however, the expected profits are turned into losses, as before, by the movement of *FF'* still further to the right. The losses are again eliminated by the exodus of firms, and the round of adjustments is repeated. As selling expenses increase and the elimination of firms in the competition proceeds, *FF'* and *CC'* move together to the right, intersecting always on the price line *MZ*. The movement will stop and equilibrium will be reached when *CC'* has become tangent to *MZ*, which condition of tangency takes place of necessity at its point of intersection with *FF'*. This result is illustrated in Fig. 28. Here, with an output of *OA*, cost equals price; there is therefore no tendency for resources to enter or leave the field. The balance will not be upset by further advertising because further outlays by anyone from this point would give rising (average) costs and consequent losses, independently of whether others followed or not.

That such a point will be reached sooner or later is evident

---

[1] The tendency by which producers are forced out of business through advertising competition is wholly comparable to that through which they are forced out of business by price competition. (Cf. above, p. 84.) In both cases, cost exceeds price; in the latter case the excess is brought about by the fall of price below cost, in the former by the rise of cost above price.

from the nature of the forces involved. As the selling expenditures of all producers are increased, the intensification of the struggle will make it more and more difficult for each to enlarge his market. For this reason, the selling outlay per unit (indicated by the difference between CC' and PP') is continually greater beyond Q as Q moves to the right. On the other hand, unit cost of

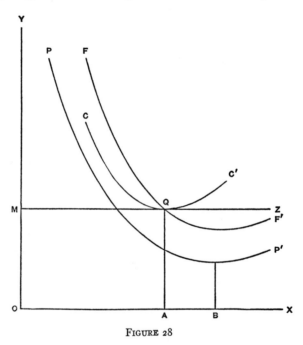

FIGURE 28

production (indicated by PP') falls less rapidly with expanding output (i. e., with the movement of Q to the right), and finally begins even to increase. Both of these forces are working to increase the combined cost of producing and selling beyond Q, in other words, to rotate CC' about Q as Q moves to the right, until the position of tangency to MZ is reached. There is still another and more ultimate influence working towards the same result. It is evident that, since PP', the curve of cost of production, drops to a minimum and then rises again, FF', lying above it, must do the same thing. As selling outlays of all products in the group increase, FF', moving away from PP', finally must become tangent to the price line MZ. As it moves in this way, it rotates about Q^1, its moving point of intersection with MZ, until the position of tangency is reached. But CC' also rotates about Q and necessarily lies above FF' to the right of Q. If the final tangency of FF' to MZ is inevitable, the tangency of CC' to MZ is so, *a fortiori*, CC' being pushed into this position, as it were, by the movement of FF'. (Since equilibrium is defined by the tangency of CC', as already set forth, the movement would never proceed beyond that point — the tangency of FF' to MZ would never actually be achieved.)

It is of interest to note in passing that the scale of production may be either larger or smaller than the scale OB (Fig. 28), which would be established under pure competition. It has definite limits, however. It is identified with the minimum for the curve CC', which is inevitably to the left of the minimum for FF', as has been shown. From the nature of FF',[2] its minimum must always lie to the right of B, the minimum for PP'. Thus, the requirement that the minimum for CC' lie to the left of the minimum for FF' does not preclude the possibility that it might lie to the right of B, instead of to the left of it, as in Fig. 28. The result would depend upon the slope of the curves, and particularly on the magnitude of the angle between CC' and FF' at Q.

The adjustment to equilibrium has taken place in the illustration, as so far developed, by the reduction of the number of sellers with consequent increase in sales volume of each of those remaining. This was made necessary by the assumption that the total sales of the general class of product were unaffected by the selling outlays, their net effect being simply to cancel out within the field under consideration. Modification of the argument under the more realistic assumption that total sales of the general class of product are increased by the advertising is not difficult. Let us return to Fig. 26, where the first losses incurred by the general increase of selling outlays are illustrated by $MREK$. These

---

[1] Evidently, FF' intersects MZ twice. It is always the intersection to the left which is meant.

[2] Cf. above, p. 156.

losses, it will be remembered, were reduced by an exodus of firms until the markets of those remaining were increased from OA to OB. Now let the same expenditure increase the total sales of the group, so that they are, for each producer, somewhat greater than OA. If they are greater than OA and less than OB, fewer sellers will have to leave the field in order to complete the adjustment of cost to price. If equal to OB, the number of sellers need not change at all, for with this output selling costs will be covered. If greater than OB, there will be extra profits, and new producers will be attracted until the markets of each are reduced again. In the same way, as selling outlays are extended further, costs will be kept equal to selling price, and the individual firm in the final adjustment will have the same characteristics as already described (Fig. 28). It will not be identical in the two cases, however, for the slope of CC' is affected by the new conditions. According to these, the selling outlays of the individual producer may attract custom not only from his immediate rivals (those within the group), but from more remote sources as well. Increased expenditures, thus playing over a wider range, bring greater results; in other words, the selling cost per unit will fall more rapidly as output increases than heretofore. Graphically, this means that the minimum point of CC' will lie further to the right than under the old conditions. It follows at once that the resulting scale of production will be larger than under the earlier, more restricted, solution. There is nothing here, however, to alter the conclusion that it may be either larger or smaller than under pure competition.

We pass now to the second phase of the group problem. We have assumed competition carried on solely by means of advertising, prices and "products" remaining unchanged. Let us now hold selling outlays and "products" fixed, and turn our attention to that part of the whole competitive process which is on the basis of price. The analysis, it will be remembered, may be regarded in a twofold light. It is the examination of one part of a complex whole in isolation. It is also applicable directly to economic situations where an approach to the conditions assumed is found. The scope of advertising and selling activities may be narrowly prescribed by trade practice or by professional ethics; or the annual selling outlay may become fairly set through custom or inertia. If, in addition, the "product" is fairly well defined, the conditions are met.[1]

The effect of fixed selling expenses upon the cost curves has already been considered,[2] and we may at once draw (Fig. 29) a curve of cost of production, PP', and above it a curve of combined cost of producing and selling, FF', for the individual producer.

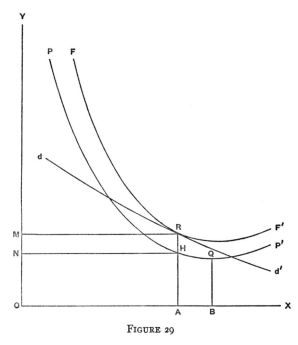

FIGURE 29

The position of these curves remains unchanged throughout the analysis. In this respect, the nature of the curve of combined cost especially must be firmly fixed in mind. It does *not* show the variations of sales volume with selling expenses — the outlay necessary to produce and sell each amount of goods. The ordi-

---

[1] The position that selling outlays are proximately set for each firm may be regarded as taken implicitly by the accepted mode of analysis in terms of (competitive) cost curves for industries as a whole or for broad classes of products. Only on the basis of such an assumption (never expressed), or of the assumption that there were no selling costs at all, could "competitive" cost curves and demand curves be drawn.

[2] Above, p. 156.

nate at any point indicates the unit cost of producing the corresponding volume of goods, plus its proportionate share of the fixed selling costs. The volume of sales is not here dependent upon selling outlays (nor upon "product"), but upon price. It is shown by the demand curve, dd', the nature of which will be recalled from previous analysis.

The problem of price competition which is now presented may be disposed of summarily, since it differs in no essential respect from that considered in Chapter V under the more simplified conditions involving the complete absence of selling costs; provided only that the curve of cost of production, PP', in the earlier analysis give place to the curve of combined cost, FF', here presented. Analytically, the two cases are identical. They both involve the basic assumption that selling costs (and "products") are held constant while prices are allowed to vary. In Chapter V the selling costs are held constant at zero, so that FF' (Fig. 29) and PP' coincide. In the present case they are held constant at a figure in excess of zero, so that FF' and PP' diverge and the necessary costs to be covered are revealed by the former. As prices are varied and as resources enter and leave the general field, the demand curve dd' now plays about FF' in the same manner as it formerly played about PP' (which may be regarded as FF' in the special case where selling costs are constant at zero). With this difference only in mind, the entire analysis of the group problem as it appears in Chapter V is now relevant. The two types of demand curves [1] should be drawn, and the same variety of solutions presents itself, depending upon whether the sellers are few or many in number.

Only the "general" solution for large numbers will be repeated at this point, in order to show how the earlier analysis may, without alteration in form, be complemented by the inclusion of sell-

[1] Pp. 90, 91, and Fig. 14. It may now be seen that the two types of curves of selling cost, FF' and CC', in the present chapter (pp. 156 ff.) are analogous to these two types of demand curves. CC' measures the costs incurred by one producer as he increases his sales, the expenditures of the others remaining constant, just as dd' shows the price reduction of one producer as he increases his sales, the prices of the others remaining constant. FF' shows the increase in costs as all expand their selling outlays (it does not show the increase in sales), and DD' shows the result when all have cut their prices.

ing costs. The outcome is an equilibrium where dd', interpreted as the demand curve for one seller on the assumption that the prices of the others are constant, is tangent to FF'. This is illustrated in Fig. 29, where the output is OA and the price AR; the unit cost of production, AH, plus the unit cost of selling, HR, gives a combined unit cost equal to the price. The total production cost for all units is $OAHN$; total selling cost $NHRM$; and the total combined cost, $OARM$, equals total revenue, leaving no extra profit above that necessary to attract and maintain capital and business ability.

It is easily shown that no other adjustment than this one could stand. If the number of firms were smaller, so that dd' for the individual firm lay to the right and above its equilibrium position, there would be possibilities for extra profits. Temporarily, the optimum price for the representative producer would be somewhat higher, and his output would be larger. The extra profits would attract new sellers, however, and the demand curve for the product of the individual firm would move to the left as the total output in the field was redistributed. The movement would continue until the extra profits were entirely squeezed out, dd' being tangent to FF', as in Fig. 29. If the demand curve lay temporarily to the left and below its equilibrium position, the opposite set of corrective adjustments would take place. Losses would be incurred, producers would leave the field, and the curve would move to the right and upwards until it was again tangent to FF'.

Some much debated questions as to the effect of advertising upon prices and upon the economies of large-scale production may now be given an answer. It has been alleged, on the one hand, that advertising is a waste — and that it makes prices higher because of the additional cost which must be met; on the other hand, that it is justified because it widens markets, promotes large-scale production, and thus lowers costs and prices.

Let us first compare the results of monopolistic competition (which includes advertising) with those of pure competition. It has been observed earlier,[1] in that part of the argument where selling expenses were isolated, that the scale of production may be

[1] P. 161.

either larger or smaller than under pure competition. The same conclusion holds (as it must if the whole theory is sound) where the price adjustment is isolated. We have seen that FF' reaches its minimum to the right of B. If dd' were very elastic (it would have to be virtually horizontal), it might conceivably be tangent to FF' at a point to the right of B, in which case the scale of production would be larger under monopolistic competition than under pure competition. Such extreme elasticity must be very unusual, however, and, although the general conclusion is that the scale of production *may* be either larger or smaller than under pure competition, it seems much more likely to be smaller. As to prices, they are inevitably higher, for under pure competition the individual firm is producing most effectively and without selling costs an output of OB at the price BQ (Fig. 29), and the curve of combined cost never descends as low as this. In fact, it may be said that under monopolistic competition prices are two steps higher than under pure competition. They are higher, first because selling costs must be added, and secondly, because the demand curve is tipped from the horizontal, thus moving the point of tangency with FF' to the left and upwards from the minimum point on the curve.

The conclusions are different, however, when comparison is made, not with pure competition, but with conditions as they would be without advertising. It is now seen that although, similarly, the scale of production *may* be either larger or smaller with selling outlays than without them, it is much more likely to be larger. If the slope[1] of the demand curve dd' is unaffected by the selling outlays, its point of tangency with FF' is bound to lie to the right of its point of tangency with PP' (since for any possible output the slope of FF' is steeper than that of PP'). If the slope of the demand curve is diminished, the point of tangency would, *a fortiori*, lie still further to the right, and the scale of production would be still larger. It is only if selling outlays, by attaching buyers more firmly to particular "products," made demand curves steeper, that a possibility would exist of the point

---

[1] Always taken at equilibrium. Many difficulties appear in comparing the slopes and elasticities of one curve with those of another which are not gone into here.

of tangency with FF' lying to the left of the point of tangency with PP'. This certainly happens in some, perhaps in many, isolated instances. But preferences which can be made can be unmade, and it seems very unlikely that this could be a general result. Prices (although inevitably higher than under pure competition), may be either higher or lower than they would be without advertising. If the slope (at equilibrium) of the demand curves remains approximately the same, the price will be higher, for the point of tangency with FF' will then lie above the point of tangency with PP'. But if the selling costs are not great, so that FF' does not lie far above PP', and if, as a result of the advertising, the slope of the demand curves is very much diminished, the point of tangency with FF' may lie below that with PP', and price will be lower. Theory can give no more definite answer than this, because there is no more definite answer to be given. The effect of advertising in any particular case depends upon the facts of the case.

We pass, thirdly, to the variations of "product"; price and advertising outlay being constant. The nature of the problem is sufficiently clear from earlier statements,[1] and it may be disposed of even more summarily than was the preceding case of price competition. The conclusions are, again, identical with those reached earlier where there were no selling costs, except that the curve of cost of production, PP', in the earlier analysis must be replaced by the curve of combined producing and selling costs, FF'. In Fig. 30, let OM be the fixed price, PP' the cost of production curve for any one variation of an individual product, and FF' the curve of combined producing and (fixed) selling costs. The size of the individual producer's market depends upon the total demand for the general class of product and the number of firms who share in it. It will be recalled that, graphically, each variation in product means, in general, an alteration, both in the cost curves PP' and FF' [2] and in the amount of the product demanded. The vagaries of this type of competition and the limited

---

[1] Cf. above, pp. 78–80.

[2] They would, however, always remain the same distance apart, since selling costs are constant.

possibilities of subjecting it to analysis and to quantitative statement have already been set forth. In so far as an equilibrium can
be defined, however, "products" must "settle down," subject to
the condition that all extra profits are eliminated. This means an
output of OA ($= MR$) determined by the intersection of the curve
of combined cost, FF', with the price line, MZ. If the market of

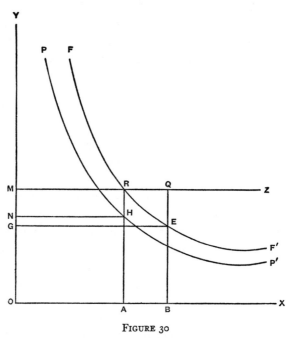

FIGURE 30

the individual firm were larger, say OB, the extra profits, $GEQM$,
would attract new competitors and it would be reduced. If it
were smaller than OA, losses would reduce the number of sellers
until the maladjustment was corrected. Under the same condition as previously, it is possible that FF' should be tangent to
MZ, the scale of production conforming to the point of tangency.[1]
This reveals, again, the possibility of a scale of production greater
than for the same product under pure competition, since the mini-

[1] The condition is that price is *actually* immovable. If it is only assumed so for
purposes of isolation, the sloping demand curve reveals at once that FF' could not be
tangent to MZ.

mum for *FF'* may lie to the right of the minimum for *PP'*. The general conclusion is, again, that it may be either larger or smaller, although the chances seem much greater that it will be smaller.

There remains the synthesis of the three cases just examined in isolation. What characterizes the group equilibrium when competitors are on the alert to vary any or all of the three factors — prices, "products," or selling outlays — which affect their markets? Evidently the adjustment must be the optimum one with respect to all of the variables, and this is simply a matter of addition, after the manner which has already been indicated in connection with the individual problem, where the case chosen for illustration involved no profits above the necessary minimum.[1] Under present assumptions this will be true for every producer in the group. The individual firm will always seek to adjust such of the factors as are, in fact, variable (price may be set by custom; or "product," by its very nature, may be rigidly defined) so as to maximize its profits. If this adjustment for the individual firm is yielding profits above those necessary to maintain capital and business ability in the field, the result will be more firms and contracted markets for each. Demand curves will be lower and lying further to the left, products may be altered and improved in quality, and curves of selling costs will be higher and curling upward more sharply. All of these forces reduce profits, and the movement will continue until they are entirely eliminated and the equilibrium adjustment of Fig. 24 (page 148) is achieved for each firm. If the necessary profits are not being earned, correction will take place in the opposite direction by a reduction in the number of firms and enlargement of the market of each. Demand curves will be higher and lying further to the right, products will be deteriorated, and curves of selling costs will be lower and curling upward less sharply. Only when each firm is adjusted as represented in Fig. 24 (drawn with reference, it must be recalled, to the optimum "product" adjustment for each) will it be impossible for any one to improve his situation by a variation of some sort. The manner in which any deviation from this adjustment would involve a loss has been explained above.

[1] Above, p. 147.

4. The Small Group and Selling Costs

We turn now to questions which are raised by the competition of small numbers. In so far as this affects the adjustment of price or of "product," the matter has already been considered in Chapter V.[1] It remains only to examine its relation to selling costs. To return to Fig. 25, the output of each seller being OA, if numbers are large, no one is deterred from making the selling outlays which would increase his profits to $EDQM$, by the consideration that his move might cause others to advertise and thus convert his momentary profits into losses of $MREK$ (Fig. 26). If he is one of many, he knows that his own move is a negligible factor in the whole situation and that, whatever he does, the policies of the others will be the same. As a result everyone will advertise and the movement will continue until, with or without the elimination of firms, the equilibrium pictured in Fig. 28 is reached. If numbers are small, however, the effect of a move by any one seller is concentrated in larger measure upon the market of each of his rivals, and hence it may be a factor in their deciding upon policies which they would not otherwise have adopted. Let us suppose that each one recognizes this. If no one is advertising, no one may begin, each realizing that his own aggressive policy would affect so adversely each of his competitors that they would be forced to advertise in order to protect themselves, and that in the end all would lose. The argument is analogous to that presented above [2] relative to price competition, and leads to a similar conclusion — that, where numbers are small, competition by means of advertising may be cut short even though the possibility exists for any one producer to increase his profits on condition that the selling outlays of the others do not change.

Of course, even where such indirect influence exists, if sellers ignore it advertising outlays will be made, with results the same as those already described for large numbers. They would be led to ignore it, as in the case of price competition, either by the absence of any permanent or long-time interest in the market, by short-sightedness even where such an interest existed, or by the

---

[1] Pp. 100–104. Selling costs must, of course, now be added to the cost curve.
[2] Pp. 46 ff.

further and very important factor of uncertainty on the part of any one seller both as to the extent to which his rivals' markets would be affected and as to whether his rivals' policies would be governed by the same far-sightedness as his own. To these must be added further elements of uncertainty arising from the fact that (and especially in the case of advertising) the distinction between immediate and ultimate results is a vague one at best. In summary, whenever the conditions are such that advertising by any one seller would make considerable incursions into the market of any one of his competitors, the amount of his selling expenditure is, in general, indeterminate between the limits of zero and a sum determined after the manner in which selling outlays are defined in Fig. 28.

5. Selling Costs and Excess Capacity

It was shown in Chapter V [1] that whenever price competition fails to function, whether because each seller is in close competition with only a few others or for any other reason, the result is not merely higher prices, but also excess capacity as a permanent and normal characteristic of the equilibrium adjustment. The argument may be briefly reviewed in relation to the present hypothesis, which includes selling costs. Let us turn to Fig. 29 (page 163). The demand curve dd', there drawn, represents the demand at various prices for the product of any one seller on the assumption that the prices of his rivals (as well as the selling outlays both of himself and of his rivals) remain constant while the price adjustments are made. It corresponds to dd' in Fig. 15 (page 92), where selling outlays are omitted. We must now imagine, in Fig. 29, a curve corresponding to DD' in Fig. 15, representing the demand at various prices for the product of any one seller on the assumption that the prices of his rivals change with his own. It will be steeper than dd' and its point of tangency with FF' will therefore be to the left of and higher than R. The scale of production will be smaller than OA, and the number of producers larger than under the conditions as pictured in Fig. 29.

[1] Pp. 104 ff.

If we may assume that DD' in Fig. 29 is of the same elasticity as DD' in Fig. 15 (i. e., that its elasticity is unaffected by the advertising), then it is evident from the position of FF' relative to PP' that the scale of production will be larger than it was without advertising. Whether the number of producers will be larger or smaller will depend upon the extent to which the selling outlays have increased the demand for the general class of product. Wherever price competition functions imperfectly, then, it seems likely that advertising diminishes the discrepancy between the actual and the most efficient scale of production. But total costs and prices are higher. Selling costs per unit are greater than the decrease in production costs. The resources expended to achieve this result are therefore greater than those saved by achieving it. And, of course, the balance of excess capacity remains.

6. The Diversity of Conditions Surrounding Each Producer

The difficulties presented by the diversity of conditions surrounding each producer and defining his market are largely expositional. In so far as the demand curves, production cost curves, and selling cost curves of different producers vary in location and in shape, a separate figure should be drawn for each. The analysis presented under the assumption that they are all alike should be considered as *illustrative* of what happens for each producer at levels appropriate to his own product and to his own market.[1] There will be a wide variety of prices, production costs, selling costs, and outputs; but so long as the production of substitutes is sufficiently possible, there will be no profits above the competitive level, for the multiplication of producers will reduce them.

The way in which monopoly profits arise when the field in general or parts of it are sufficiently protected from incursion has been described at length in Chapter V. Demand curves will lie to the right of the point of tangency with cost curves, which now include both production and (fixed) selling costs, and monopoly profits will appear in the interval between them. Another way

---

[1] Cf. above, pp. 110 ff.

of describing the same result is to say that the curve of selling costs which is drawn on the assumption that the outlays of other producers remain constant will dip under the price line, as CC' dips under MZ in Fig. 25 (page 155), allowing permanently the monopoly profits of $EDQM$. The reason is that the competitive forces which raise the curve and curl it backwards are absent.

The possibilities of monopoly profits are increased by the presence of advertising. Wherever a particular field is protected from incursion, a demand for the product may be created or an existing demand augmented and monopoly profits obtained which are far greater than those possible under our earlier assumption (Chapter V). Here is an important field for business ability little recognized in competitive theory for the reason that the demand curve is usually regarded as a datum. The business man finds scope for his ability in seeking to raise the demand curve for his product as well as in seeking to lower its cost curve. Of course the demands which can be created for rival products set a limit to the process, but we are here considering the case where this limit is sufficiently removed to allow for profits above the minimum level. In case rival products can establish themselves, all profits will be reduced, as described above, to this level. Finally, the minimum level itself is affected by the hazards introduced into business through the possibility of shifting demands by advertising appeal.

7. CONCLUSION

At the close of Chapter V a comparison was made between pure and monopolistic competition, and the conclusion drawn that "the price problem for a differentiated product cannot be forced into the mould of competitive demand and cost curves without introducing into the conclusions definite errors — the price is always too low, the cost of production is too low, the scale of production is too large, and the number of producers is too small." [1] In that comparison selling costs were ignored. They must now be taken into account, and the result is a condemnation of the theory of pure competition which no longer runs in terms

[1] Cf. above, p. 116.

of mere errors in degree. Wherever selling costs are incurred, —
and they are incurred in some measure for almost all commodities,
— to cast the price problem in terms of "competitive" demand
and cost curves is not merely inaccurate; it is impossible. To
assume such curves and to explain prices in terms of them is to
go through an exercise which has nothing to do with the problem.

The root of the difficulty (and a direct index of how remote is
the theory of pure competition from the facts) is that under conditions of pure competition there would be no selling costs. In
constructing demand and cost curves for the products of a group
of competing producers, such costs should therefore be omitted.
Without them, however, the demand curve is not the actual one
which plays a part in determining the price; it is a fictitious and
irrelevant one which includes only a fraction of the demand —
that part which would exist if no selling expenditures were made.
Without them, likewise, the cost curve is not the actual one which
should include all the costs to be met; it is a fictitious and irrelevant one which includes only a part of them — the production
costs. The price indicated by the intersection of these two curves
is of no interest.

The only alternative to omitting the selling costs is to include
them and blink the inconsistency. But here one is checked by
the impossibility of determining how much to include, for the
amount of selling costs cannot be defined without a theory which
recognizes the monopoly elements responsible for them. Furthermore, as has been pointed out at the close of Chapter V, it is
equally impossible to know, without a theory of monopolistic
competition, what *production* costs should be included, since we
may not, as under pure competition, draw the cost curve under
the assumption that the resources used are always most effectively utilized. The analysis of monopolistic competition, then,
is fundamental, and must be carried out as a preliminary to drawing the *supposedly* competitive demand and cost curves now
considered. But if this is so, the problem has already been solved
before these curves are drawn. The "competitive" curves do
not constitute even an intermediate step in the analysis. There
is therefore no point to drawing them at all; and, above all, it is

false to represent them as *determining* the price indicated by their intersection.

Still further objections may be made to such curves. They can be drawn only under the assumption either that the qualitative differences between the varieties of product are such that they do not lead to differences in cost or price, or that the differences in cost or price on this account are reduced by some mathematical device, say by averaging, to a common figure. This difficulty alone is enough to make one despair of using such curves in economic analysis. But there is an added complication in interpreting the cost curve. The curve of selling costs which is superimposed on the curve of production costs must be a rectangular hyperbola distributing over different volumes of product the fixed total of selling costs which defines the demand curve. It is *not* a curve showing the costs of producing and selling different volumes of product. No single demand curve would be valid for this latter type of cost curve, for the position of the demand curve shifts with each alteration in total selling expenditure. In summary, the "competitive" cost curve which includes selling costs is inconsistent with itself, it is useless, it is misleading, and it is of very limited meaning. It has been set up for such detailed criticism because, if one seeks to defend the traditional method of applying "competitive" reasonings to differentiated products, it seems to be the only alternative to the true competitive cost curve which omits selling costs altogether.

Certain *quantitative* comparisons between the results of monopolistic and pure competition are possible by referring to any of the figures which represent the equilibrium adjustment under monopolistic competition, say Fig. 24 (page 148). The summary at the close of Chapter V, quoted at the beginning of this section, must be reëxamined in the light of selling costs. The conclusions with respect to price and cost are valid, and, indeed, are reënforced. Although, with advertising in the picture, it is theoretically possible that production costs should be at their minimum, it is highly unlikely, and, in any case, selling costs must be added. We may say, then, that in general the theory of pure competition understates both price and cost, first by understating production costs, and, secondly, by omitting selling costs altogether. The conclusion that pure competition represents the scale of production as too large is no longer certain, but is highly probable. If true, the number of producers is represented as too small *for any given demand.* Because the presence of selling costs in the economic system increases some demands and decreases others, no further general conclusion as to the number of producers is possible.

It is the *qualitative* comparison with pure competition which is the most significant, however. Competitive theory is unreal in large part because it fails truly to represent the forces at work in the economic system.

The theory of monopolistic competition has not been carried in this study beyond its beginnings. The theory of value has been considered only in its most general terms, and the theory of distribution has been ignored altogether.[1] Furthermore, no applications to particular economic problems have been attempted or even suggested. Economic thinking has been completely dominated by the idea of an equilibrium defined by the equation of supply and demand in competitive theory. A reworking of its various fields of interest in terms of monopolistic competition is in order.

---

[1] Incomplete studies seem to indicate the conclusion that the productivity theory of distribution loses much of its validity when monopolistic elements, and particularly selling costs, are recognized.

CHAPTER VIII

MONOPOLISTIC COMPETITION AND THE PRODUCTIVITY THEORY OF DISTRIBUTION [1]

WITHOUT raising controversial questions about the productivity theory itself, let it be accepted, for purposes of this argument, as valid under the conditions of pure competition to which it has always (until recently) been implicitly or explicitly related. Its central tenet, that factors of production are paid according to their "marginal productivity," is subject to a variety of interpretations.[2] For our purposes, three possible meanings seem to be important. "Marginal productivity" may refer (*a*) to the physical product, (*b*) to the value of the physical product, or (*c*) to the revenue; which is added, in any case, by the presence of the marginal unit of a factor.

As to the first, it is conceivable that, even in an economic system characterized by a high degree of division of labor, factors of production might be paid literally in their physical product. Farm workers, restaurant employees, and domestic servants are laborers who receive at least a part of their wages in the product which they have helped to produce; and there might be mentioned also the case of a large distilling company which recently paid its stockholders a dividend in whisky. Ordinarily, however, income receivers consume little or none of the product of the enterprise with which they are associated, and it can be marketed so much more effectively by the enterprise itself than by individuals that it would obviously be absurd (and often impossible, as in the case of services) to pay incomes in product and place the burden of exchange upon the income receivers. For this reason, although "marginal product" has ordinarily

---

[1] A revision of a paper read at a meeting of the American Economic Association in Philadelphia, December, 1933, summarized in part in the *American Economic Review*, Vol. XXIV (1934), sup., p. 23. Reprinted with permission from *Explorations in Economics*, New York, McGraw-Hill Book Co., 1936.

[2] Cf. Machlup, "On the Meaning of the Marginal Product," *Explorations in Economics*, p. 250.

meant physical product, the proposition that factors are paid according to their "marginal productivity" has meant that they are paid, not the product itself, but the money obtained from its sale. Thus the second meaning of "marginal productivity," referring to the value of the physical product, merely recognizes the fact of exchange: it is the equivalent of the physical product in money terms, the physical product multiplied by its selling price. It is this meaning which will be adhered to throughout this chapter.

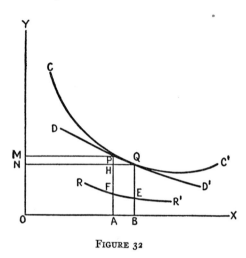

FIGURE 32

The marginal revenue product (or marginal value product, as it has usually been called), on the other hand, is, in general, quite dissociated from the physical product or its money equivalent. It refers to the added *revenue* — the total revenue (price per unit multiplied by the number of units) when the last unit of the factor is used less the total revenue when it is not used. In Fig. 32, if the amount of product is increased from *OA* to *OB* by the addition of another laborer, the value of the marginal product is *ABQH*; the marginal revenue product is *OBQN-OAPM* (or *ABQH-NHPM*). The marginal revenue product may be defined most neatly by the use of the marginal revenue curve. It is the marginal physical product multiplied by the marginal revenue.[1] If *RR'* in Fig. 32 is the marginal revenue curve, it is *ABEF.*

Now it is evident that the entrepreneur is always and everywhere, whether under pure or under monopolistic competition, interested only in the marginal revenue products of the factors he employs. But under pure competition, since he can change his output without appreciable effect upon the price, this will always be identical with the value of the marginal product. In other words, under pure competition, the demand curve for the product of an individual producer being a horizontal line, his marginal revenue curve coincides with it. Marginal revenue is

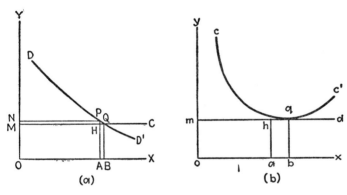

FIGURE 33

always equal to selling price. Hence marginal product and marginal revenue product *to the individual competitor* are always identical. Thus it is that, interested only in a factor's marginal revenue product, the entrepreneur arrives nevertheless at paying it its marginal product.

This is shown graphically in Figs. 33*a* and 33*b*. Figure 33*b* is the familiar diagram showing the demand and cost curves (*md* and *cc'*, respectively) for an individual producer under pure competition; Fig. 33*a* shows the demand and cost curves (*DD'* and *MC*, respectively, constant cost being assumed) for the

[1] Strictly speaking, each unit of the marginal product must be multiplied by its own marginal revenue and the sum taken.

product of *all* the producers. The two figures thus show the *same* facts from two different points of view. It is clear from Fig. 33*b* that, as I have argued, the value of the marginal product (*abqh*) is equal to the marginal revenue product (*obqm-oahm*) in the eyes of the individual producer. There is an apparent contradiction to this in Fig. 33*a*, where the value of the marginal product is *ABQH* and the marginal revenue product is less than this, *ABQH-MHPN* (equal to *OBQM-OAPN*). But it must not be forgotten that the marginal revenue product in which the individual seller is interested is his own, not that for the market as a whole. If we assume the elasticity of *DD'* between *P* and *Q* in Fig. 33*a* to be unity, then as an individual seller increases his product by the amount *AB*, he adds nothing to the value of the whole supply, and therefore nothing to the revenue derived by all producers together from its sale. But he adds proportionately to the value of his own (Fig. 33*b*), for the sacrifice in price is spread over a large number of producers whereas the greater volume is enjoyed by himself alone. It is for this reason that price will settle at *BQ* (Fig. 33*a*) instead of at *AP* (or at any other point), where the value of the whole supply may be the same. And it is for this reason that each factor will receive the value of its marginal product under pure competition.

Turning to monopolistic competition, let it first be recalled that the number of variables in the problem has increased. Output is now conditioned only in part by price. It is a function also of the "product" in its various phases, and of selling costs.[1] The relation of product variation to the productivity theory will not be taken up here. It is assumed that variations in the proportions of the factors result in different amounts of the *same* product, not in different *kinds* of product. (We may, if we like, suppose that the optimum "product" has been found and that the decisions to be made have been correspondingly narrowed.) As for selling costs, they will be put aside only for the time being. The problems they raise are complex, and will be indicated briefly later on.

Let us look, then, for the moment, at the price-quantity re-

---

[1] These matters are discussed more fully above, pp. 71 ff.

lationships under monopolistic competition. Because of the sloping demand curve for the product of an individual producer, it appears at once that the marginal revenue product of a factor to him is inevitably smaller than the value of its marginal product. If *DD'* in Fig. 32 is the demand curve for the product of one seller under monopolistic competition, and an additional laborer increases the product from *OA* to *OB*, the value of his marginal product is *ABQH*, and his marginal revenue product is *ABQH* less *NHPM*. Since, in adding labor, the entrepreneur is guided by the latter, rather than by the former, it follows that he will never find it profitable and he will often find it impossible to pay to *any* of the factors the value of their marginal products. It will be impossible if competition has pushed his demand curve to the left until all surplus profit is eliminated, as in Fig. 32. If the demand curve lies further to the right, the surplus profit obtained may or may not be enough to permit each hired factor to be paid its marginal product, but if we assume that entrepreneurs seek to maximize their profits, none of it will be put to this use anyway, and the lot of the other factors is in nowise changed. There is no escaping the conclusion that even a slight element of monopoly necessarily reduces the remuneration of all factors employed in a given firm below the value of their marginal products.[1]

It should be emphasized that the deviations of the distributive shares from their marginal products are always in one direction — the share is always smaller. This fortifies conclusions stressed elsewhere in the general theory of monopolistic competition, that pure competition is an extreme, a limit, rather than a norm.

[1] It should be remarked parenthetically that the cost curve which is relevant to variations in one factor while the others are held constant is not the long-run curve which is usually envisaged in our study, where resources are most effectively organized with reference to each volume of output. Assuming them most effectively organized with reference to the output *OB*, the point *Q* would lie on this latter curve. Since a variation in any one factor from this point without changing the others would, in general, involve conditions of production somewhat less effective than the optimum ones for the resulting outputs, the curve here relevant would lie above the curve defined by the most efficient organization of factors for each output at all points except *Q*, being tangent to it at that point. On the relation between these two sets of cost curves, cf. Appendix B.

Actual prices, distributive shares, and conditions of production generally do not tend toward or oscillate about what they would be under pure competition. Rather, they tend toward norms in the definition of which the monopoly elements must be given full recognition. Except where the conditions are actually those of pure competition, competitive theory is a distortion of reality rather than an approximation to it.

Let it be noted that *all* factors (not merely any one, say, labor) receive less than their marginal products; yet it is evident from the figure that this is consistent with a total paid to them which is exactly equal to the total product valued at its selling price. Only minimum profits are included in the cost curve: there is no excess which might be attributed to "exploitation." [1] This requires looking into. Apparently each factor produces more than it gets, yet there is nothing left over after all have been paid.

The answer lies in the fact that the sum of the incomes computed on the basis of marginal products is greater than the total product. The two will be equal only when the productivity function is a homogeneous function of the first degree, i.e., when a small proportionate change in *all* the factors together will yield a proportionate change in product. This will be true only where both average costs and average revenue (price) remain constant with such a change. In other words, it will be true only under pure competition, where, for small deviations from equilibrium (the minimum point on the cost curve) both demand and cost curves are approximately horizontal. At this point the value of the marginal product and the marginal revenue product are equal, and total payments to the factors in terms of either will exactly equal the total income to be distributed. As the demand curve is tipped more and more from the horizontal, under monopolistic competition, so that its point of tangency with the cost curve lies further and further to the left of this minimum point, the discrepancy between marginal products and marginal revenue products increases. The sum of the latter continues to ex-

[1] Cf. Mrs. Robinson, *The Economics of Imperfect Competition*, pp. 283 ff., for a different view.

haust the total product; the sum of the former grows more and more in excess of it. In the case of firms, the demand curves for whose products lie above the cost curves, there is, of course, a monopoly profit, and this suggests the possibility of increasing the incomes of the *hired* factors to some extent, perhaps even to the value of their marginal products. It is impossible, however, even here, for *all* factors to get their marginal products: hired factors would gain at the expense of the profits share, entrepreneurship receiving now not only less than its marginal product as before, but even less than its marginal revenue product. (Entrepreneurship, or any other factor, may, of course, receive less than its marginal revenue product consistent with getting more than its supply price.) Furthermore, it seems obvious that to pay any particular factor, say labor, more in such firms would be to establish uneven rates of pay for the same work in different enterprises. The remedy is clearly to eliminate the monopoly profits by a price adjustment in favor of the consumer rather than to turn a part of them over to labor.

Evidently the Pigovian definition of exploitation as a wage less than the marginal physical product of labor valued at its selling price [1] is appropriate only to conditions of pure competition, where, if labor receives less than the value of its marginal product, employers are, in fact, pocketing a part of the revenue which the marginal laborer brings in, and where the relation between marginal products and the total product is such that it is possible for labor and all factors to be paid the full value of their marginal products without exceeding the amount to be distributed. It is not appropriate to monopolistic competition, where these conditions do not hold. Here *all* factors are necessarily "exploited" in this sense in order that total payments may be brought within the bounds of the amount available to be paid; it would be impossible for employers to avoid the charge of "exploitation" without going into bankruptcy. Yet Mrs. Robinson adopts such a competitive definition for this field, and even considers how the "exploitation" might be removed, dis-

---

[1] *Economics of Welfare*, p. 549.

covering, naturally enough, that, in general, it could not be, except by setting up conditions of "perfect" competition![1]

I pass now to another phase of the problem. It has been tacitly assumed up to this point that the product added by another laborer in any firm is a net addition to social product, not offset by a lessened product elsewhere in the system. This may well be true. But let us examine briefly at least one case where it is not. There are a number of reasons why prices may rest permanently and normally at some level higher than that to which unrestrained price competition would carry them.[2] This may be true wherever any particular seller is in direct competition with only a few others, a condition which obtains over a large section of industry. It is a possible result, also, wherever there are restraints upon price competition — actual or tacit agreements, business or professional "ethics" which condemn the "price cutter," the imposition of retail prices by the manufacturer or by tradition or custom, and, in general, the expenditure of competitive energy in other directions than that of price competition. If prices are held up by these factors, there can be a larger investment of resources in the general field without diminishing the profits earned by each firm. In so far as it is possible for new firms to set themselves up and secure a part of the business, they will do so, and a condition of general excess capacity may develop disguised by the fact that profits generally are not above the competitive level. Under these circumstances what is the value of the marginal product of any factor of production as more resources are employed? The productivity to society of any factor or of any group of factors composing an enterprise must be considered as the total product it creates less that which its presence prevents others from creating. Let us suppose that three gasoline filling stations are adequately supplying the demands for gasoline at a particular corner at going prices when a fourth company sets itself up in business. What product does the new station add? If the outcome is simply the sharing of the available business by the four at the old prices, as it is very apt to be, it is difficult to see where there has been any appreciable addition at all. The value of the services provided by the newcomer less those no longer provided by the three others is approximately zero. To be sure, there may be some additional convenience to those for whom the new station is more advantageously located. The product then will not be zero, but it will be far less than that indicated by regarding the new firm alone. There is a further complication. Since each firm is suffering a reduced volume of sales, average unit costs are higher. It is quite possible that the profits of the first three firms were sufficient before the fourth entered so that all four can now cover their costs including minimum profits without a price adjustment. It is also possible that, faced with higher costs, they will all find it necessary to raise prices, and possible to do so with little fear of undercutting, since each has a strong interest in avoiding a price so low that he cannot cover costs when enjoying his normal share of the available business.[1] Under these circumstances the appearance of the fourth seller has actually diminished (through higher prices) the output of the group. The physical product of the resources he employs being negative, their value at current prices would likewise be negative. Wherever price competition fails to function effectively, complications such as these arise and must be taken into account in defining the net product added by a new firm or by the marginal unit of any factor which it employs. In such cases it appears that the value of the net social marginal product of a factor may even be negative, and, in any event, that it will be far less than its marginal product to an individual firm. Clearly, the value of its net social marginal product bears no relation whatever to its marginal revenue product to the firm, and hence to its income.

What is perhaps the most damaging impact of monopolistic competition upon the productivity theory is in relation to advertising and selling costs. Such costs, it is now generally admitted, are wholly incompatible with pure competition; the productivity

[1] Cf. p. 106.

theory, on the other hand, is compatible *only* with pure competition. It is not surprising, therefore, that the incomes of factors engaged in selling activity find no explanation whatever under the theory.

Although selling costs, as will be remembered, are directed toward altering demands rather than toward producing goods to satisfy them, they may indirectly affect productivity. As the first result of such outlays, whether by a single firm, a group of firms in an "industry," or all firms, a new system of demand curves comes into being. To be sure, producers, pulling in opposite directions, will, to some extent, neutralize each other's efforts, leaving the demands for their products unaffected, and merely raising their costs by the amount of the advertising outlay.[1] In general, however, some spend large amounts, others less, others nothing at all; the results will vary in effectiveness and are bound to be uneven. Thus, although, on the one hand, selling outlays, by definition, contribute nothing toward the satisfaction of the new set of demands which they have created, on the other hand, they may be the indirect cause of a redistribution of productive resources with a consequent increase or decrease in aggregate product.

In attributing such an indirect productivity to selling costs it is evidently necessary, first of all, to deduct the cost of *producing* the goods in question. This being done, the marginal product of additional outlays for factors engaged in selling would be measured by the value of the added product which they had called forth, less the value of the goods which were no longer produced because demand had been shifted away from them.[2] Assuming constant total money incomes, it begins to look as though the positive and negative elements would cancel out exactly, leaving a net marginal product of zero.

There are other complications, however. For example, advertising may, and certainly does, in general, alter the elasticities

---

[1] These higher costs, of course, mean higher prices, different total amounts spent for the general class of goods in question, and thus, indirectly, different demand curves for other goods.

[2] Among these goods no longer produced, there ought to be included leisure, if the advertising has induced people to sacrifice leisure in order to produce more goods.

of the demand curves. In so far as preferences for particular products are created or strengthened, demands are made less elastic, firms are multiplied, and conditions of production become, in general, less efficient. In so far as information about products, prices, and market conditions is spread more effectively, demands may become more elastic, the number of firms may diminish, and output per firm increase with attendant economies.[1] In defining the marginal productivity of factors applied to selling, it would be necessary to take all such information into account, adding up all the elements in order to arrive at the net product, either positive or negative, valued at market prices (less the cost of production, as distinguished from the cost of selling), for which the selling outlay was responsible. It thus appears that to *conceive* of a marginal product for factors engaged in selling in terms strictly parallel to the definition as derived from the field of production is perfectly possible. The difficulties are all in the discovery and measurement of the elements involved. What is to our purpose, however, is that, even assuming that it *could* be discovered, there would be no connection whatever between such a marginal product and the marginal product to a firm of a factor engaged in altering demands in its favor. To hold that factors employed in selling activity are paid in accord with the value of their marginal products would be a manifest absurdity.

The leading proposition that a sloping demand curve for the individual firm reduces the remuneration of a factor below the value of its marginal product has now (1936) received some measure of general acceptance. In view of the fact that it is so readily demonstrable and that it has not, to my knowledge, been contested by anyone, it seems fair to say that its acceptance is general among those who have turned their attention to the

---

[1] It is this latter influence which is most frequently brought forward by the advertising industry itself in its own defense. Clearly, however, if the social justification of advertising were to be judged on this score, it would be necessary to compare the increment to product obtained indirectly through applying resources toward making demands more elastic with the increment to product obtained by the same resources if they were applied directly to production.

problems of monopolistic and imperfect competition in recent years.[1] Indeed, since Mrs. Robinson has *defined* marginal productivity[2] as what I have here called marginal revenue product, and has been followed by others, the danger now appears that it will be *too* readily accepted. By this I mean that it will be accepted by many without any appreciation of the metamorphosis which has taken place. It was generally held that factors were paid according to their "marginal productivity" under pure competition; it is now held that they are paid according to their "marginal productivity" under monopolistic competition; and so it would appear that the principle involved was at least substantially the same in the two cases — whereas it is evidently not the same at all. True, the rule for monopolistic competition applies also to pure competition, for it is universal.[3] It is universal because, as a moment's reflection reveals, it is little more than a restatement in terms of increments of the axiom from which economic analysis ordinarily proceeds, *viz.*, that producers seek to maximize their profits. But the further rule for competition — that factors are paid according to the value of their marginal products — applies only to competition. As has been shown above, there is no tendency whatever for factors to be paid in this way when monopoly elements are present. Yet, just as value theory has been cast in competitive terms, so with distribution — and the productivity theory of distribution has commonly been taken to mean that the incomes of factors were equal to the values of their marginal products.[4]

---

[1] In addition to Mrs. Robinson, who has done more than anyone else in the analysis of problems of distribution as affected by "imperfect" competition, there may be mentioned: N. Kaldor (*Economica*, Vol. I, new series [August, 1934], p. 337); R. F. Kahn (*Economic Journal*, Vol. XLV [March, 1935], p. 3); Fritz Machlup in *Explorations in Economics*, p. 250); and probably others.

[2] *Op. cit.*, p. 237.

[3] Monopsonistic situations excepted.

[4] Lack of space forbids the inclusion of numerous quotations in support of this interpretation of the "productivity" theory. Marshall, although he states the principle in its more general terms of a net addition to the value of the total product of the firm (*Principles*, pp. 406, 521), seems to do so because he holds that definite units of physical product cannot usually be separated (p. 407). On the issues here discussed, he clearly justifies the competitive formulation (Mathematical Appendix, n. XIV). See also Pigou (*Economics of Welfare*, p. 119) and Hicks (*Theory of Wages*, p 8). Knight's interpretation is doubtful. Although he defends as productive both

It is in order to make clear that when monopoly elements are recognized, such interpretations of marginal productivity in terms of the money equivalent of the physical product are no longer possible, that I have introduced in this connection the term "marginal revenue," which Mrs. Robinson has exploited so ingeniously elsewhere. Certainly the possibility ought to be avoided of carelessly identifying dissimilar concepts by giving them the same name. If the terms "value of marginal product" (for the competitive principle) and "marginal value product" (for the more general principle embracing both pure and monopolistic competition) were strictly adhered to, this would go far toward the desired end. But they will not be strictly adhered to. Inevitably, the "value" drops out of one or the other in the hands of different writers [1] and the abbreviated terms "marginal product" and "marginal productivity" acquire a shifting and unstable meaning. Even if the "value" were always included and put in the right place, the two phrases sound deceptively similar from the fact that they are made up of the identical words in different sequence.

By designating the addition to money income of the firm as a "marginal revenue product" the two concepts receive the necessary sharp contrast. The term "marginal revenue" may be applied as appropriately to a unit of a factor of production as to a unit of product, and has a well-established meaning with reference to the latter which is readily transferred to the former. "Revenue" has the further advantage over "value" in the present connection of being a concept closely associated with the individual firm; it therefore serves to emphasize what may easily be missed — that the principle involved stops short with the

monopolistic restriction of output (*Risk, Uncertainty and Profit*, p. 186) and selling costs (p. 339), the competitive formulation is also clearly stated (p. 107 n.). Illustrations abound in the textbooks. See, for instance, Garver and Hansen, *Principles*, p. 409 (*revised ed.*, p. 384).

[1] Thus we speak of the "marginal productivity" theory of distribution, Marshall uses the term "net product," Mrs. Robinson uses "marginal productivity" to mean marginal value product, etc. Mr. Kahn (*loc. cit.*, p. 3) uses "productivity" in both senses. His "marginal private productivity" is defined as a value product, whereas, in a footnote a few lines further on, he says that "in what follows . . . [social?] 'productivity' is the 'value of product.'"

individual firm. There is asserted merely that the income of any factor tends to equal its marginal contribution to the revenue (may we say the "profits"?) of the firm employing it. Nothing at all about its contribution to any total outside the firm which is of social, as compared with individual, significance: to such aggregates, for instance, as the total product or value of the product available to the economic community. Only by postulating pure competition may the incomes of factors be related at all to such concepts as these. At any rate, so it now appears. Perhaps the next step in the analysis is the formulation of other than purely competitive criteria by which the results of monopolistic competition may be judged.[1]

[1] For a further analysis of monopoly elements in distribution, with particular reference to wages, see my article, "The Monopoly Power of Labor," in *The Impact of the Union*, New York, 1951. (Essay 12 in *Towards a More General Theory of Value*.) Also my booklet, *The Economic Analysis of Labor Union Power*, American Enterprise Association, Washington, D.C., 1958; and "Labor Union Power and the Public Interest" in *The Public Stake in Union Power*, Philip D. Bradley, ed., Charlottesville, Va., 1959.

CHAPTER IX

THE DIFFERENCE BETWEEN MONOPOLISTIC AND "IMPERFECT" COMPETITION [1]

THIS CHAPTER deals critically with some mistaken notions in the general field of monopolistic and "imperfect" competition. The most mistaken notion of all is that the two are merely two different names for the same thing. However, the first part of the chapter recognizes the similarity of technical apparatus used in that portion of the whole subject matter which the two theories exploit in common,[2] and looks briefly into a number of misconceptions, either vaguely current or held by specific writers, as to the nature of this *general type* of theory. The second part has regard to the dissimilarities. Its purpose is to reaffirm the nature of monopolistic competition as a composite of monopoly and competition, calling attention here to a fundamental difference between Mrs. Robinson's conception of the problem and my own, and to some of its consequences.

1. SOME GENERAL MISCONCEPTIONS

Let us proceed first to the misconceptions with respect to the general type of theory. The first of these is that "imperfect" and monopolistic competition are in some special way related to the marginal revenue curve. The association might be described

[1] A revision of an article entitled "Monopolistic or Imperfect Competition?" appearing in the *Quarterly Journal of Economics* for August 1937. The article called forth a reply by Mr. Nicholas Kaldor, disputing the views here advanced, in the same *Journal* for May 1938, and a further defense of them by myself, portions of which are now incorporated into the chapter. The whole matter has since been discussed exhaustively by Dr. Robert Triffin in his *Monopolistic Competition and General Equilibrium Theory*. No attempt is made here to refer in detail to Dr. Triffin's book.

The original article acknowledged the helpful criticisms of several colleagues, especially of Professor Wassily Leontief and Dr. Donald H. Wallace. I should now add thanks to Mr. Kaldor for the criticisms in his reply, which have resulted in a clarification of statement at several points and led to some additions.

[2] Specifically, those parts having to do with price-quantity relationships in the absence of monopsony, discrimination, small numbers, product variation, and selling costs.

as an historical accident. With reference to the marginal revenue curve, Mrs. Robinson states,[1] "This piece of apparatus plays a great part in my work, and my book arose out of the attempt to apply it to various problems. . . ." The applications are indeed ingenious, and Mrs. Robinson has effectively demonstrated the value of this particular bit of technical equipment; but she seems prone to exaggerate its importance. For instance, on page 6 she says, "Whilst many pieces of technical apparatus have no intrinsic merit, and are used merely for convenience, the use of marginal curves for the analysis of monopoly output contains within itself the heart of the whole matter." It is, to be sure, an "intrinsic merit" of the marginal curves that their intersection reveals monopoly *output* more neatly than does the fitting of areas between curves of average cost and average revenue. At the same time, it is an intrinsic demerit that they do not indicate the *price* at all. It is a further intrinsic demerit that they do not readily indicate *profits*, either per unit or in the aggregate. It is certainly because of these shortcomings that we do not find a single one of the eighty-two diagrams in Mrs. Robinson's book in which the marginal revenue curve appears unsupported by the average revenue curve.[2] Furthermore, when we get beyond equilibrium for the single firm in isolation, the marginal curves do not contain "the heart of the whole matter," even for output. This appears in Mrs. Robinson's own description of "competitive equilibrium" (under "imperfect" competition), where we find that full equilibrium "requires a *double* (my italics) condition, that marginal revenue is equal to marginal cost, and that average revenue (or price) is equal to average cost." [3] Instead of containing "the heart of the whole matter," the marginal curves would appear to be quite subordinate. Even for the problem of equilibrium for the single firm, they are merely an alternative technique for reaching the same results as by the use of the average curves. Mrs. Robinson herself points this out when she says, "It is clear that the

---

[1] *The Economics of Imperfect Competition*, p. vi.
[2] Marginal cost curves frequently appear without average cost curves.
[3] P. 94.

marginal method of analysis will produce exactly the same results as the method, used by Marshall, of finding the price at
which the area representing 'monopoly net revenue' is at a maximum, since net revenue is at a maximum when marginal revenue and marginal cost are equal." [1]

With so much of the theory of imperfect competition developed in terms of marginal revenue and marginal cost, it is not
surprising that marginal revenue should be closely associated in
the minds of many with imperfect competition. Thus Mr. Harrod, in his article on "Imperfect Competition and the Trade
Cycle," [2] says that "the leading principle of the theory of imperfect competition is that entrepreneurs tend to equate marginal cost to marginal revenue." Yet it is perfectly obvious
that the equation of marginal revenue and marginal cost is a
general principle for the individual firm under any circumstances whatever, even under the purest of pure competition.
It is, at bottom, only another way of saying that producers seek
to maximize their profits, and contributes nothing to distinguishing "imperfect" competition from pure competition and
monopoly.

A second misconception might be described as an exaggera-
tion or distortion of the relation which imperfect and monopolistic competition bear to "increasing returns." An historical
association between them has arisen only from the fact that the
theory as crystallized in Mrs. Robinson's book seemed to evolve
out of a series of articles by Professor Knight, Mr. Sraffa, Professor Pigou, Mr. Shove, Mr. Harrod, Mrs. Robinson, and
others on the nature of increasing returns and whether or not
they were compatible with competition. But although "imperfect" competition appears, in this instance, to have derived
historically from increasing returns, such was not the case for
monopolistic competition; [3] and the *logical* derivation, in so far
as it exists, seems to be quite the other way round. Both Mrs.
Robinson and myself have clearly defined the problem (for the

[1] P. 54, note 2.   [2] *Review of Economic Statistics*, Vol. 18, p. 84.
[3] Cf. Preface, above, p. xi, second paragraph. The cluster of articles on "increasing returns" appeared in the late twenties and very early thirties.

case of large numbers) with reference to factors affecting the shape of the *demand* curve, and without reference to cost conditions.[1] It is true that equilibrium under this type of theory is usually (though not necessarily) reached within the diminishing cost phase of the (production) cost curve for the individual firm; but when we bear in mind that the cost curve for the firm has the same U-shape, whether under pure or monopolistic competition, it appears at once that "increasing returns" in the vicinity of equilibrium for the firm are the *result* of monopolistic competition and no part of the definition of it.[2] The shape of the cost curve is, of course, a factor in defining equilibrium, but this may be said of any problem in value where there *is* a cost curve. It is the shape of the demand curve which marks the contrast between monopolistic and pure competition.[3]

A third misconception may be disposed of briefly. It is the notion that monopolistic competition is concerned only with situations where the demand and cost curves are tangent, hence where there are no monopoly profits, whereas any situation where there are such profits is to be classed as a monopoly. A moment's reflection will show that this is an artificial distinction. The issue does not really arise in connection with Mrs. Robinson's "imperfect" competition, for the reason that she includes as a cost *all* profits which are being earned when there is no tendency for the number of firms in an "industry" to alter, thereby making the demand and cost curves for *all* individual

---

[1] *Imperfect Competition*, p. 51, and above, pp. 7, 17, 71. Professor Hutt, in his article, "Economic Method and the Concept of Competition" (*Journal of South African Economics*, Vol. 2, p. 3), regards the increasing returns genealogy as having an important bearing upon the "authoritative" character of Mrs. Robinson's writings as compared with my own (p. 4).

[2] "Industry" curves of increasing, constant, and decreasing cost seem all three to be compatible with both pure and monopolistic competition.

[3] With respect to the more general question of *conditions* of "increasing returns" in the cost curve (as distinct from increasing returns at equilibrium), it seems clear that such conditions are neither *necessary* nor *sufficient* for monopolistic competition. They are not necessary because (for example) monopolistic competition is possible with no cost curve whatever, or with any other shape. They are not sufficient because the familiar U-shaped cost curve is compatible with pure competition.

firms tangent by definition.[1] It does arise, however, in connection with monopolistic competition, and the view that the tangency of cost and demand curves is the central principle involved is one which I have encountered many times.[2] It may perhaps be accounted for by the over-prominence given to this solution in my own statement of the theory. All that need be done here is to call attention to passages above, (p. 82 and pp. 110 ff.) where it is made clear that the solution of tangency flows from certain heroic assumptions which are later dropped, and is to be regarded as of only limited direct applicability, being mainly an expositional device, which represents an intermediate stage in the development of the theory.

The essential point to be made is that both with and without tangency of the two curves there is a blending of competition and monopoly. The only essential difference between them is in the matter of profits: with tangency, monopoly profits disappear, but all the other phenomena which arise from the monopoly elements in the situation remain. Among them are monopoly prices and outputs, selling expenditures, and possibly discrimination. Perhaps the matter is most easily cleared up by the realization that the whole theory of monopoly as familiarly conceived is part and parcel of the theory of monopolistic competition, at least as I have sought to describe it.

Parenthetically, there might be mentioned an argument frequently encountered, especially in the field of public utilities and railroads: that a field is competitive if profits are not excessive. Thus it has been held that the railroads need no longer be regulated, since their profits are held in check by the competition of other forms of transportation; and similar propositions have been made with respect to other utilities. The answer is, of

---

[1] *Imperfect Competition*, Chaps. 7 and 9. Mr. Kaldor has rightly called attention to the "merely formal similarity" between Mrs. Robinson's version and my own in this respect. Cf. "Market Imperfection and Excess Capacity," *Economica*, February 1935, p. 34.

The significance of this treatment for the theory of profits will be mentioned further on.

[2] See the remarks on this point by Professor Machlup at the Chicago round table, *American Economic Review*, June 1937, p. 325; and his article "Monopoly and Competition: A Classification," *ibid.*, September 1937.

course, that profits are only one element in the situation; rates, discriminatory practices, service in all its aspects, investment, and other policies may be strikingly influenced by monopoly elements, even though profits are not excessive.

A fourth misconception is that differentiation of product is reducible to a matter of numbers in the market, in the sense that with larger numbers the demand curves for the individual firms would become more and more elastic until conditions of pure competition were reached. This idea I have encountered again and again in discussions; indeed it appears to have an astounding — and disconcerting — vitality. It makes a fleeting appearance in Mrs. Robinson's book, where she considers the possibility that, with greater demand for her homogeneous commodity, new firms would be set up "so to speak, in between the old firms (either geographically or in respect to special qualities which appeal in various degrees to different customers). The difference, from the point of view of buyers, between any one firm and the next would thus be reduced, the customers of each firm would become more indifferent, and the elasticity of demand would be increased . . . successive increases of demand of this type would ultimately *remove market imperfection altogether.* . . ."[1] She goes on to point out, however, that in the real world, advertisement and other devices would be brought into play before this happened, and would break up the market again. With Mrs. Robinson, this flattening out of the demand curves is only one of several possibilities. With Mr. Kaldor[2] the argument is stated in more general terms, although the illustration is again that of new firms coming "in between" the old ones as numbers increase.

Do larger numbers make the demand curves approach more nearly to the horizontal position characteristic of pure competition? — that is the question. Clearly there is no general presumption that they do. For instance, if we think of stores distributed over an area, their number may increase by an expansion of the area, rather than because of a denser population

[1] *Imperfect Competition*, p. 101 (my italics).
[2] *Loc. cit.*, p. 42.

within it. The new firms in this case are not in between the old ones at all, and "products" are no more nearly alike than they were before. In non-geographical problems new firms, selling new varieties of product, are bound to appeal to at least some new buyers, and hence to have always an effect analogous in some degree to the expansion of the area in this geographical example. Moreover, the concept of "in-between products" is not always easy to apply outside of geographical problems. Can gas refrigerators be regarded as "in between" some other two varieties, say electric and natural ice? Are menthol cigarettes "in between" some other two brands? It seems clear that large or small numbers indicate nothing *necessarily* as to the degree of substitutability between the products concerned. This is perhaps most clearly evident from the fundamental proposition that the number of producers in any field depends first of all upon how broadly the field is defined.

But even where the products may easily be thought of as coming "closer together" with a larger number of producers, the result is not necessarily a closer approach to pure competition. If we suppose producers and their customers to be located along a line, the demand curve for the product of any one firm will be a straight line of slope determined by costs of transport or by the valuation per unit of distance put upon the element of convenience.[1] Now if high profits lead to an increase in the number of sellers, so that the curve moves to the left, it will remain of the same *slope* so long as the rate at which buyers value convenience does not change.[2] There appears to be no tendency for the curve to approach the horizontal with larger numbers, unless there is a change in the valuation put upon convenience; and although this latter might possibly be affected

---

[1] Products are here considered homogeneous except for the element of convenience in location.

It is not necessary for the argument that convenience be subjected to a rational calculation. People may buy at the nearest store merely by impulse or chance, without any calculation whatever.

[2] Its elasticity at any particular price would evidently increase as the curve moved to the left, while its elasticity at any particular output would decrease. What would happen to elasticity at the equilibrium point could be known only by introducing cost curves.

by the alteration in numbers, it does not seem clear why it should be. On the other hand, there is a definite relationship in the reverse direction. Changes in the valuation put upon convenience (or, in general, upon *variety* in the product) are bound to affect numbers. A lower valuation would flatten the demand curves and thus reduce the number of sellers; a higher valuation would do the opposite. Evidently an actual increase in numbers may be associated in fact with a strengthening rather than a weakening of the elements of monopoly in any particular situation.[1]

The general conclusion must be that with a differentiated product the "number of producers" ceases to have the definite meaning which it has in relation to any particular (standardized) product, and that broad generalization as to the effect of numbers upon the elasticities of the demand curves for individual producers is no longer possible.[2]

Closely allied with the question of numbers is that of divisibility. If all factors were perfectly divisible, what would happen to monopolistic competition? The answer is very clearly, nothing at all. But it has been maintained by Mr. Kaldor that "where everything is perfectly divisible, and consequently economies of scale completely absent, 'perfect competition' must necessarily establish itself solely as a result of the 'free play of economic forces.' No degree of 'product-differentiation' and no possibility of further and further 'product-variation' will be sufficient to prevent this result, so long as all kinds of 'institutional monopolies' and all kinds of indivisibilities are completely absent." [3] ("Institutional monopolies" play the rôle, in his argument, of preventing the reduction of profits to their minimum. Let us here assume such forces absent.) The supposed transformation of monopolistic into pure competition with perfect

---

[1] Cf. Mrs. Robinson's three types of increase in demand, *Imperfect Competition*, p. 100.

[2] It must not be forgotten that, in increasing numbers, each new producer produces a new product under *monopolistic* competition. There is therefore no increase in the ratio of producers to products as there is under pure competition, and as there is also under Mrs. Robinson's "imperfect" competition. Cf. below, p. 209.   [3] *Loc. cit.*, p. 42.

divisibility comes about (1) because economies of scale disappear, so that the cost curve is a horizontal line, *and* (2) because, as more firms are drawn in by the profits which appear when such a cost curve is combined with a sloping demand curve, the demand curves themselves swing around to the horizontal position, for reasons presented above. But his conclusion fails if *either* of these propositions is false, and the falsity of the second has just been demonstrated. The falsity of the first is established at length in Appendix B.

It may be of interest to note that even if it were accepted that absence of economies of scale followed from perfect divisibility, nevertheless if demand curves did *not* become horizontal, as has been argued in general above, we have an absurd result: the influx of firms would simply continue indefinitely (because there would always be profits under constant costs); and the final outcome would appear to be an infinite number of infinitesimally small firms. Incidentally, it ought to be assumed, I suppose (shades of Ruskin!), that buyers, too, are infinitely divisible. This would remove completely any reasons for a flattening out of the demand curve with infinite divisibility, since sellers would not become more numerous and closer together *relative* to buyers.[1]

On the other hand, even if it were accepted that demand curves *did* become more elastic as the number of firms increased, if cost curves were still U-shaped, there would be no reason to identify group equilibrium with a number of firms sufficiently large to bring about perfectly elastic demand curves.

We may conclude that, since infinite divisibility does nothing to the shape of the cost curves, and the number of firms does nothing for certain to the shape of the demand curves, there is no conversion of monopolistic into pure competition by any of these lines of reasoning.

Fifthly, there are various misconceptions having to do with

---

[1] Fundamentally, there is no more reason to suppose that differences within any broad class of product would be eliminated by the perfect divisibility of factors or by increasing numbers than there is to think that all products in the whole economic system would be reduced to a single homogeneous mass.

"restriction of entry." We may begin with the view that "restriction of entry" is incompatible with perfect competition, and hence necessarily indicates monopoly or "imperfection." Mrs. Robinson has dealt with this matter at length, and I can only record my agreement with her conclusion that restriction of entry into an industry is quite compatible with perfect (and with pure) competition, provided only that conditions within the industry are such as to make the demand curve for the output of an individual firm perfectly elastic.[1] Restriction of entry is likewise compatible, of course, with imperfect and with monopolistic competition; and there can be no doubt that freedom of entry is compatible with perfect (and pure) competition.

The question remains whether "freedom of entry" is compatible with monopolistic competition. There seems to be no doubt that Mrs. Robinson thinks it is, and I have, on occasion, spoken about the matter in a way not fundamentally consistent with the meaning of a differentiated product. Mr. Kaldor has rightly pointed out that the statement that "entrance to the field in general and to every portion of it in particular was unimpeded"[2] implies that "every producer *could*, if he wanted to, produce commodities completely identical to those of any other producer — if he does not, this is merely because he would not find it profitable to do so."[3] Logically, this is what "free entry" in its fullest sense must mean, and it is quite incompatible with a differentiated product. With respect to the *particular product* produced by any individual firm under monopolistic competition, there can be no "freedom of entry" whatever. No one else can produce a product identical with it, although he may be able

---

[1] "What is Perfect Competition?" *Quarterly Journal of Economics*, Vol. 49, pp. 104–111.

[2] The quoted words appear in editions of *Monopolistic Competition* prior to the fifth, on p. 111, as an "implicit assumption" underlying the earlier description of the tangency solution. The issue of "freedom of entry" was never actually raised, however, and the earlier argument is more accurately summarized on p. 113 without mention of the concept: "In so far as profits are higher than the general competitive level in the field as a whole or in any portion of it, new competitors will, if possible, invade the field and reduce them. If this were always possible, as hitherto assumed, the curves would always be tangent. . . ."

[3] *Loc. cit.*, pp. 43–44.

to produce others which are fairly good substitutes for it. Under monopolistic competition, then, there can be freedom of entry only in the sense of a freedom to produce substitutes; and in this sense freedom of entry is universal, since substitutes are entirely a matter of degree.

In order to give the concept meaning, it might be defined as freedom to produce substitutes within an arbitrarily delimited range of goodness, say a range sufficiently good to eliminate profits in excess of the necessary minimum. If, however, we now speak of "industries" in the common sense of the word, it is evident that parts of an industry may be characterized by freedom of entry in this sense, while others are not; "goodwill" is the familiar evidence of such a situation. We may well ask, then, into what is entry free? We could not speak of freedom of entry into an industry, even in the limited sense here defined, unless profits for *all* producers in the industry were reduced to the minimum included in the cost curve, through demand curves being everywhere tangent to cost curves. Even supposing that this were true, there would remain the bothersome fact that some of the profit elimination is achieved, not by substitutes composing the "industry," but by substitutes outside of it; in other words, the results in terms of which freedom of entry *for an industry* are defined, actually involve a degree of freedom to produce substitutes over a much wider range than the "industry" as defined. The upshot of the matter seems to be that the concept is not very useful and is even seriously misleading in connection with monopolistic competition. It is, in reality, a concept usually related to a market for a definite commodity, and the fundamental difficulty is that there is no such commodity under monopolistic competition beyond that produced by an individual firm.[1] In the matter of entry, all that we need to say is that wherever in the economic system there are profit possibilities they will be exploited so far as possible. The enjoyment of large profits by any particular firm is evidently an indi-

---

[1] This difficulty does not appear under "imperfect" competition, where a commodity is identified, not with a firm, but with an "industry," and described as *homogeneous* within the industry. Cf. below, p. 209.

cation that others, by producing close substitutes, may be able to compete some of them away. The results may be very simply described without any concept of freedom or restriction of entry — without even the concept of an "industry": some firms in the system earn no profits in excess of the minimum counted as a cost, others earn more than this, and in various degrees.[1]

Last among the misconceptions must be mentioned Mrs. Robinson's attempt to show that "imperfection" is not to be associated with differentiation of the product. "Professor Chamberlin's attitude to the perfection of the market," she says,[2] "is not quite clear. He seems to associate imperfection simply with differentiation of the product. But . . . physical differentiation is not a *necessary* condition for market imperfection. . . . Nor is differentiation a *sufficient* condition for market imperfection." She argues that differentiation is not *necessary* because "two commodities may be alike in every respect *except the names* of the firms producing them, and yet the market in which they are sold will be imperfect if different buyers have different scales of preference as between the two firms" (Italics mine). Yet at the very place cited by her the names attached to products are specifically mentioned as a phase of differentiation, and it is made clear that the basis of differentiation "may be real or fancied, so long as it is of any importance whatever to buyers, and leads to a preference for

---

[1] It is not meant by this argument to discard completely the concept of an "industry." In many connections, it is obviously useful to delimit a portion of the economic system and study it in some degree of isolation from the rest. And if this can be done, although entry is never "free," it is not wholly without meaning to speak of the *relative* ease with which this particular field may be entered, in the sense of the relative ease with which substitutes for the particular products which compose the "industry" may be produced. One emerges from any attempt to classify industries, however, with a feeling that it is all exceedingly arbitrary. The "common sense" definitions of industries in terms of which practical problems are likely to be studied seem to be based much more upon technological criteria than upon the possibility of market substitution.

[2] *Quarterly Journal of Economics*, Vol. 49, p. 112. Mrs. Robinson's objections to differentiation here are a confirmation that her description of the product within an industry as *homogeneous* (*Imperfect Competition*, p. 17) was not a "slip," but an essential part of her approach to the problem. This complete absence from imperfect competition of what is probably the most fundamental concept in monopolistic competition underlies the striking divergences between them in their interpretation of the economic system, as explained below.

one variety of the product over another."[1] Mrs. Robinson's objection to differentiation as *necessary* turns out to be an instance in support of it.[2] Her argument that it is not *sufficient* consists in showing that, even though products were differentiated, *if* all buyers were alike in respect to preferences and *if* each buyer dealt with only one firm at a time, the market would nevertheless be perfect. This seems to be obviously true. But the conditions are severe, to say the least, and examples would be difficult, if not impossible, to find. Perhaps it is for this reason that

[1] P. 56, above.

[2] In no one of the four references to *Monopolistic Competition* contained in Mrs. Robinson's article has she stated or interpreted correctly what I have said. In the first place, her evident misunderstanding of the distinction between "pure" and "perfect" competition (p. 105) leads her to misapply it and to conclude that it is "misleading" and "pays a verbal tribute to the old confusion." On this matter see the article by Mr. White, "A Review of Monopolistic and Imperfect Competition Theories," *American Economic Review*, December 1936, at pp. 642–643, where he holds that her arguments strengthen rather than weaken the case for such a distinction.

Secondly, there is the misdirected criticism of the differentiation of the product, discussed in the text above.

Thirdly, with respect to numbers, she says (p. 114), "It is sometimes supposed that for competition to be perfect it is necessary that the number of buyers should be large. [Footnote reference to myself, although almost anyone else would have done as well.] But this is the reverse of the truth." My own statement is clearly made with reference to both buyers and sellers, and Mrs. Robinson herself says the same thing elsewhere (*Imperfect Competition*, p. 216). It becomes the "reverse of the truth" in her vain effort to make "perfect competition" compatible with a differentiated product. For this it is necessary that buyers be "exactly alike in respect of their preferences," and we cannot be certain of this, as Mrs. Robinson shows, unless there is only one buyer. For perfect competition *among sellers*, then, we must have monopsony. Mrs. Robinson now has the truth "in reverse" at full speed. For perfect competition *among buyers* we must have only one seller, or monopoly. Are we to conclude that for full perfection the requirement is bilateral monopoly?

Finally, Mrs. Robinson summarizes by saying that there is "not one universal value for the 'large number of firms' which ensures perfect competition" (p. 120), and leads the reader to think, by a footnote reference, that I have suggested 100 as such a "large number." In the particular passage to which she refers (p. 49 above) it seems clear that 100 is taken merely for illustrative purposes, and the statement is explicitly made that, as the number of sellers increases, "it is impossible to say at just what point this consideration [having to do with small numbers] ceases to be a factor," a conclusion which seems quite in accord with her own, although, to be sure, for different reasons. Mrs. Robinson ends by announcing that, although I had said that 100 would be a "large number," two would have been enough in the particular case I was considering (p. 49). No explanation is given, and, having explained at length myself why two would *not* be enough, I remain unmoved by a mere conviction, however intensely felt, that it is not so.

she gives none, but speaks only of product A and product B throughout. If tastes or preferences differ — and they appear to do so very generally — it would seem that differentiation, *as I have defined it*,[1] is also a *sufficient* condition of monopolistic competition.

2. MONOPOLISTIC, DISTINGUISHED FROM IMPERFECT, COMPETITION

Let us turn now to the question of what monopolistic competition *is*, and, in particular, how it is different from imperfect competition. "Monopolistic competition" is a challenge to the traditional viewpoint of economics that competition and monopoly are alternatives and that individual prices are to be explained in terms of either the one or the other. By contrast, it is held that most economic situations are composites of both competition and monopoly, and that, wherever this is the case, a false view is given by neglecting either one of the two forces and regarding the situation as made up entirely (even though "imperfectly") of the other. This seems to be a very simple idea. Indeed if one is not quite set in the way of thinking which involves mutual exclusiveness, it is grasped at once. Its inherent reasonableness was never better expressed than by a student who observed to me after class, "Chapter IV is easy — you don't say anything in it."

My own observation on Chapter IV, however, would be quite different. "The Differentiation of the Product" is by all odds the most difficult subject of all, and the reason is not far to seek. It contains, not a technique, but a way of looking at the economic system; and changing one's economic *Weltanschauung*

---

[1] Including the words "significant," and "so long as it is of any importance whatever to buyers, and leads to a preference . . ." (p. 56, above). Defining it more broadly as any difference whatever, it seems clear that differentiation is necessary, but not sufficient, to monopolistic competition. Without *some* difference, even if only as to location, it would be impossible to distinguish one unit from another and hence to *have* a preference at all. Hence differentiation is necessary. On the other hand, every unit of product (every grain of wheat, for instance) is in some small degree different from every other. *Mere* differentiation in its broadest sense is not sufficient; it must also be of at least some slight consequence to at least some buyers.

is something very different from looking into the economics of the individual firm or adding new tools to one's kit. I shall show in a moment that this concept of a blending of competition and monopoly is quite lacking in Mrs. Robinson's *Imperfect Competition*. The dichotomy appears to be as distinct there as it is in Pigou, Marshall, Taussig, or John Stuart Mill.

The weight of the tradition that monopoly and competition are mutually exclusive alternatives is a heavy one indeed, and one may well despair of gaining really serious recognition for the idea that actual situations are typically a combination of the two — recognition which will go so far as to accept some appropriate theoretical structure in which both elements find their place. Especially is there misunderstanding about the nature of this theoretical structure. Because it uses a monopoly technique and brings into the picture what competitive theory leaves out entirely — the elements of monopoly actually present in any situation — it has been regarded by some with alarm as a swing too far in the direction of monopoly. Combined with the notion that where there is monopoly there is no competition, this easily develops into an accusation that the theory leaves competition out of the picture entirely. Such seems to be the view of Professor J. M. Clark, when he says, "Theorists have often said that typical industrial situations 'contain elements of monopoly'; and recently there has been a tendency to go farther and draw the boundary line so as to classify as monopoly all situations which do not have the characteristics of 'pure' or 'perfect' competition, thus placing virtually all industries in the 'monopoly' classification." Reference is then made to the books of Mrs. Robinson and myself.[1]

Now no one has done anything of the kind. To say that each producer in an industry has a monopoly of his own variety of product is not to say that the industry is monopolized. On the contrary, there may be a very intense competition within the industry, not of the sort described by the theories of pure competition to be sure, but different by virtue of the fact that

[1] NRA Report on the Basing Point System in the Iron and Steel Industry p. 59.

each producer has a monopoly of his own variety of product. Thus every monopolist faces the competition of substitutes, and it becomes clear at once that monopolistic competition embraces the whole theory of monopoly. But it also looks beyond, and considers the interrelations, wherever they exist, between monopolists who are in some appreciable degree of competition with each other. However great the degree of competition, it can be fully recognized by a demand curve (a) appropriately elastic, and (b) appropriately located with reference to the cost curve. It is here that the superiority of approaching the problem through the theory of monopoly rather than through that of competition is at once apparent. The theory of competition, by its very nature, eliminates the monopoly elements completely, thus erasing a part of the picture and giving an account of the economic system which is so false that in most cases it could not even be called an approximation to it. The theory of monopoly eliminates nothing. It brings into the picture monopoly elements hitherto neglected, and, by an extension to include the interrelations of groups of producers, gives full recognition to whatever competition and whatever monopoly may be present in any particular situation.

In the literature of the subject, although the term "monopolistic competition" is very widely used, there is also a strong preference for "imperfect competition." The explanation is not difficult. First may be mentioned a certain spiciness in the phrase itself — if books on etiquette had often been entitled "Perfect Behavior," what more alluring title for a variation on established manners than "Imperfect Behavior"? But probably a much greater factor than this in the wide use of "imperfect competition" is that it involves no more than an explicit recognition that actual competition is imperfect, which anyone would always have admitted anyway. The term is purely negative. Competition and monopoly go their ways without the least overlapping, and interference with one's categories of thought is held at a minimum. Thus "imperfect competition" has undoubtedly contributed and will contribute a great deal to perpetuating competition and monopoly as mutually exclusive categories.[1]

"Imperfect" and monopolistic competition have been commonly linked together as different names for the same thing. Their elements of similarity seem to be adequately [2] appreciated; their dissimilarities hardly recognized. Mr. White presents,[3] in addition to a useful summary of the theories themselves, a discerning analysis of some of the differences in scope and treatment. In adding what appears to me to be a fundamental difference in conception of the problem, I am quite aware that many will not grasp its importance, but will see involved only a question of terminology. I submit, however, that there is no evidence (at least that I have been able to find) that Mrs. Robinson thinks of monopoly (in its ordinary sense) and competition in any other way but as mutually exclusive.[4] This difference in conception between us is in fact the key to an understanding of many other differences in treatment of the problems involved. Among the matters clarified by crediting Mrs. Robinson with the conventional dichotomy might be mentioned: most of the article "What is Perfect Competition?" which takes on new meaning when read with this interpretation in mind — for instance, her discussion of the issue as between "pure" and "perfect" competition, her rejection of "product differentiation," her discussion of the definition of a "commodity"; [5] in *Imperfect Competition*, her separate chapters on

---

[1] Mr. White comments (*loc. cit.*, p. 643): "Not only does this terminology [the triad of perfect competition, imperfect competition, and monopoly] disguise the essential features of the theoretical re-orientation, it actually contradicts the premise that competition and monopoly are mutually compatible rather than mutually exclusive." The explanation is not difficult when it is realized that Mrs. Robinson has no such premise.

[2] Even more than adequately. I have seen references to *Monopolistic Competition* for a treatment of matters discussed only by Mrs. Robinson, and vice versa.

[3] *Loc. cit.*

[4] They are not mutually exclusive, to be sure, according to her definition of a monopoly as an "individual firm": individual firms are quite compatible with competition. The real problem of compatibility arises only when monopoly is defined in its usual sense of control over supply.

[5] Perhaps, also, her oft-expressed feeling that my own treatment is "misleading," "not quite clear," "rather weak," etc.

"Monopoly Equilibrium" and on "Competitive Equilibrium"; her treatment of profits, discussed below; and her analysis of "exploitation," also discussed below. It seems worth while, then, to look into Mrs. Robinson's analysis of the nature of competition and monopoly and of their relations to each other.

On pages 4 and 5 of *Imperfect Competition* she considers the matter of gradations in substitutes. Her presentation of the facts is almost exactly like my own, but the conclusions are strikingly different. The possibility of arranging "actual cases in a series of which pure monopoly would be the limit at one end and pure competition at the other" she finds "tempting," but rejects it as involving insuperable difficulties. The comparison should be made here with the treatment above, pages 63 and 64, where this view is specifically embraced as the cornerstone of the theory. Mrs. Robinson seeks to define a "commodity" in order to define a "monopoly," and finds herself blocked by the possible variations in breadth of the definition. Thus she is turned back from an answer by the very answer itself. Apparently it is never seen that the familiar meaning of monopoly is perfectly satisfactory as soon as it is anchored to *any commodity whatever*, however broadly or narrowly defined, and is wholly consistent with competition between that commodity and others. And so it is to escape from imaginary difficulties that she is led to give the term "monopoly" a definition it has never had before or since, to my knowledge; it is made to refer merely to an individual seller. "Every individual producer has the monopoly of his own output — that is sufficiently obvious — and if a large number of them are selling in a perfect market the state of affairs exists which we are accustomed to describe as perfect competition." [1] The individual seller, then, *even under perfect competition*, is a "monopolist"! In the chapter on "Monopoly Equilibrium," she says, "For the sake of simplicity the individual producer may be referred to as a *monopolist*," [2] including within this chapter a discussion of the equilib-

[1] P. 5.
[2] P. 52.

rium adjustment for the individual firm under *perfect* competition. In Book IV, "The Comparison of Monopoly and Competitive Output," Mrs. Robinson defines "monopoly" in the usual way as the control over output by a single authority, and apologizes for such a definition in her summary on page 9, saying that "This title . . . is sanctioned by custom, and though it is verbally inconsistent with the conception of monopoly *on which this book is based*, it would have been pedantic to avoid the use of it." (Italics mine.) There is no doubt, then, as to the meaning she attaches to the word "monopolist" — an individual seller under any circumstances whatever — and which she describes on page 6 as the "logical definition."[1] Barring her own peculiar definition, there is no monopoly whatever in Mrs. Robinson's conception of imperfect competition. Again, in the final chapter on "A World of Monopolies," she reverts to the conventional definition of monopoly as control over supply, but always with reference to an *industry*, never to the product of a particular firm within an industry.

Mrs. Robinson's analysis, in spite of a limited technical similarity with that of monopolistic competition, misleads in precisely the same way as does the theory of perfect competition — by describing a hybrid situation in terms which omit completely the monopoly side of the picture, together with all its manifold implications. Monopoly, arising as explained above, out of a differentiated product, is omitted by explicitly identifying an "imperfectly competitive" *industry* with a commodity "which may be regarded for practical purposes as *homogeneous* within itself."[2] Among the commodities mentioned explicitly as illustrations of this homogeneity are motor cars, for, she says at

---

[1] In "logic" it might be likened to defining any single part in a play as a monologue, either rail of a railway track as a monorail, or the marriage relations of a polygamist with any particular wife as monogamy.

[2] *Imperfect Competition*, p. 17. (Italics added.) "For practical purposes" evidently refers to the practical purposes of theorizing. Mrs. Robinson is led, logically enough, to this strange position by her refusal to be "*reduced*" (my italics) to regarding the output of each producer as a separate commodity (p. 5). Thus she never refers to an individual firm's *product*, but always to its *output*. Since for her the "industry" produces a *homogeneous* product (albeit in an "imperfect" market), it is not surprising that the concept of monopoly (in the

once, "A demand curve represents a list of prices at which various amounts of a certain commodity will be bought in a market during a given period of time, . . . the number of motor cars bought in England per month . . . may be represented by a demand curve." The gulf between monopolistic and "imperfect" competition may be strikingly appreciated by the coincidence that the *same* illustration of motor cars is used by myself above [1] for the *reverse* purpose of showing the complete inadequacy of any analysis which assumes them to be homogeneous; and thus to establish the necessity of a theory of monopolistic competition which recognizes explicitly their heterogeneity.

It is significant in this connection that, although both Mrs. Robinson and myself employ a "uniformity" assumption — that the demand and cost curves for the individual producers are alike throughout the group —[2], the use to which it is put is strikingly different. With Mrs. Robinson it is never removed, and thus remains a part of the final theory. This is what one would expect if a homogeneous product were sold in an "imperfect" market, since the "imperfections" would be distributed without prejudice amongst the various contributors to the homogeneous total. By contrast, in my own treatment it is an "heroic" assumption adopted only as a temporary expedient to facilitate exposition [3] and finally removed in order to embrace within the theory the "diversity of conditions surrounding each producer," [4] which diversity is a natural concomitant of heterogeneity, with monopoly control by each producer over his own product.

There seems not a shred of evidence that Mrs. Robinson conceives of the individual producer under "imperfect competition" as having in any sense or degree a monopoly as that term has

sense of a control over supply) as related to the individual producer plays no part in her theory — a producer who is not recognized in the theory as having a product, or "commodity," distinct from those of others, has nothing the supply of which he might control.

[1] P. 9.
[2] *Imperfect Competition*, p. 98; and above, p. 82.
[3] Above, p. 82.
[4] Pp. 110, 172.

been used traditionally in economics and as it continues to be used in this book. Mr. Kahn, whose extensive collaboration in the writing of *The Economics of Imperfect Competition* Mrs. Robinson acknowledges in her Foreword, has been categorical in affirming precisely this: "It is to be understood that the phrase *imperfection of competition* does not carry with it any of those implications with which by tradition the word *monopoly* is associated." [1] This statement is of particular significance, since, appearing two years after the first edition of this book, it may, perhaps, be taken as directed specifically against the view here set forth, and as a clear affirmation of the position which I am attributing to Mrs. Robinson.[2]

Mr. Kaldor is even more illuminating. Like many others, he has evidently regarded imperfect and monopolistic competition as merely English and American equivalents for the same thing (his comparison is braces and suspenders). One might hope, therefore, that he would reply to the argument immediately above — that Mrs. Robinson's "imperfect" competition contains no monopoly — by presenting the evidence that it does, thereby bringing the two theories together. Instead, he brings them together by removing the monopoly also from monopolistic competition and asserting that the residue, being "a great step forward," should be placed to my credit whether I agree or not.[3] This is generous indeed, but I must still ask to have this particular step attributed elsewhere, because it is not what I have been trying to say.

[1] "Some Notes on Ideal Output," *Economic Journal*, Vol. xlv, p. 20.

[2] Mr. Sraffa in 1926 had laid great stress on monopoly, had issued a call to "abandon" competition, and had virtually abandoned it himself. (Cf. below, p. 311.) It is at least possible that the denial of monopoly by Mrs. Robinson and Mr. Kahn is a reaction from this other extreme. But why abandon either one?

[3] ". . . to have shown that the monopoloid situations of the real world are quite compatible . . . with the *complete absence of particular advantages vested in particular people* (my italics), I have always regarded as one of the great achievements of the Theory of Monopolistic Competition. . . . [It] has shown us . . . that monopolies of various degrees can exist *without any "unique advantage" at all* (my italics) . . . [this] was a great step forward in economics; and it should be placed to Professor Chamberlin's credit despite his present disclaimer." (*Loc. cit.* p. 523.)

Mr. Kaldor uses much the term "institutional monopoly" by which he appears to mean no more nor less than what has traditionally been meant in economic literature by monopoly,[1] and what is meant by it in this book. That such monopoly, in his understanding, is a thing quite apart from the theories of imperfect and monopolistic competition appears explicitly in his formulation of the "four basic assumptions" of these theories, one of which is "that no producer possesses an 'institutional monopoly' over any of the varieties produced."[2] Could anything be further from the central thesis of this book, as elaborated especially in Chapter IV above? Could anything provide a better illustration, not merely of the proposition that "imperfect" competition does not view the economic system as a blend of monopoly and competition, but also of the fact that monopolistic competition has been frequently and carelessly interpreted in the same way?[3]

What, now, are some of the consequences of this difference in viewpoint? I shall consider only three points. The first has

[1] "Market Imperfection and Excess Capacity," *Economica*, Feb. 1935. p. 44.

[2] *Ibid*, p. 35. "Institutional monopolies" may, of course, be added into the picture, as Mr. Kaldor does briefly on p. 45, where he says that, although "by no means essential [they] may even be directly responsible for a large part of market imperfection" *as shown* in my own Appendix E! Again it is evident that Mr. Kaldor found no such idea in *Monopolistic Competition* until he reached the last of the appendices.

[3] In his reply to this chapter in its earlier form, Mr. Kaldor, protesting my interpretation of monopolistic competition, points out that, if it were to be accepted, the widely used measurement of the degree of imperfection of competition in terms of the elasticity of individual firms' demand curves "certainly cannot be used to denote the relative strength of the 'monopoly' and 'competitive' elements in a given situation, in the sense which Professor Chamberlin has in mind" (*loc. cit.*, p. 256). This is good evidence that he is now aware of his initial misinterpretation — and the widespread use of Mr. Lerner's measure of the "degree of monopoly" is further evidence of how general the misinterpretation has been. I agree entirely with Mr. Kaldor that such an index cannot be used, and have never myself sanctioned or used it. It measures, under simplified assumptions, only one of the many facets of monopolistic competition (some of which are qualitative and not subject to measurement at all); and it is thus quite completely mischievous in its implications. The conclusion is evidently to abandon the index, not to misinterpret the theory in order to retain it. For a fuller discussion of the "degree of monopoly" see my article, "Measuring the Degree of Monopoly and Competition" in *Monopoly and Competition and Their Regulation*, E. H. Chamberlin, ed., London and New York, 1954; (Essay 4 in *Towards a More General Theory of Value*, with a Supplementary Note on Cross-elasticity).

to do with profits. Within the "completely arbitrary" boundary of a "commodity" or "industry," under imperfect competition, all profits are competitive to Mrs. Robinson.[1] It follows that, by defining "industries" rather broadly, the whole problem of monopoly profits can be made to disappear entirely. Contrast this with the view of profits which emerges from monopolistic competition: throughout the economic system are to be found profits arising from the control of the outputs of particular products (greatly affected, of course, by selling outlays and product variation), monopoly profits in the true sense that they would not be there if competition were pure. A theory of profits which adequately accounts for them has yet to be written.[2] When it is written, it seems that it can hardly fail to alter our views as to the relation between monopoly and the public interest. But the problem cannot even be posed, let alone answered, in terms of an "imperfect" competition in which no monopoly is to be found.

The second point has to do with "competitive" norms. "Free enterprise" has too long been loosely identified with "competition." In economic theory the identification has been with "perfect" or with "pure" competition. Yet it must be obvious that the typical outcome of free enterprise is not pure competition, but monopolistic competition. Commodities are differentiated partly by their very nature (without regard to demand), and partly in response to differences in buyers' tastes, preferences, locations, etc., which are as much a part of the order of things *within* any broad class of product as they are *between* one class of product and another. Heterogeneity from these causes is vastly increased by business men under "free enterprise," in their efforts further to distinguish their commodity from others and to manipulate the demand for it through advertising. In other words, an essential part of free enterprise is the

---

[1] *Imperfect Competition*, Chaps. 7 and 9.

[2] I do not myself pretend to have presented any such theory, having merely included in the cost curve of the individual firm whatever payments are necessary to obtain the resources it uses, including the services of the "entrepreneur." Actual profits in excess of this amount may, of course, be a substantial factor influencing the supply of entrepreneurial services generally.

attempt of every business man to build up his own monopoly, extending it wherever possible and defending it against the attempts of others to extend theirs.[1] There is no tendency for these monopolies to be competed out of the picture; on the contrary, they are as much a part of it as is the competition which restrains them.

The explicit recognition that product is differentiated brings into the open the problem of variety and makes it clear that *pure competition may no longer be regarded as in any sense an "ideal" for purposes of welfare economics.* In many cases it would be quite impossible to establish it, even supposing it to be desirable. Retail shops, for example, could not all be located on the same spot, and personal differences between actors, singers, professional men, and business men could not be eliminated. But even where possible, it would not be desirable to standardize products beyond a certain point. Differences in tastes, desires, incomes, and locations of buyers, and differences in the uses which they wish to make of commodities all indicate the need for variety and the necessity of substituting for the concept of a "competitive ideal" an ideal involving both monopoly and competition. How much and what kinds of monop-

---

[1] "Freedom," in the sense of freedom from social control, may evidently lead also to agreements and to various forms of associative action between the individual economic units, whether firms or individuals. Such agreements are obviously monopolistic, and must clearly be added to the picture here given of the economic system as a blend of monopoly and competition. However, they form no important part of the subject matter of this book. The danger to be avoided is to conceive of the system as "competitive" in the absence of such agreements.

In the same way, although "large units" frequently possess monopoly power, it is not to be supposed that to break up such units would establish a competition unalloyed with monopoly. On the contrary, "atomistic" competition would almost certainly involve an *increase* in product differentiation through abolishing such standardization as now takes place (in order to achieve economies of scale) within large units. Monopoly elements arise (in part) from heterogeneity of product, not from mere size, and an economic system composed of very small units would certainly be one of monopolistic, not of pure or perfect, competition. Indeed, it might well involve an *increase* in the aggregate of monopoly power exercised, consistent with its distribution among a larger number of individuals. (Problems of measurement, however, preclude giving precision to such quantitative comparison.) Certainly, even assuming standardization in some degree to be desirable, and therefore specifically imposed by social control, it could actually be achieved only within definite limits, and hence could reduce only partially the monopoly elements in "atomistic" competition.

oly, and with what measure of social control, become the questions.[1]

Furthermore, the "ideal" adjustment of products and of selling outlays, as well as the conventional price and output analysis, must be explicitly recognized as a part of the welfare optimum. These added elements are, in fact, probably more variable than prices; yet the familiar problem of allocating resources in order to maximize "welfare" assumes (1) products as given, and (2) selling costs as totally absent. With respect to the first, there are ignored, not only the product adjustments made by individual firm, but also the change in the product composition of the system every time the number of firms changes with a flow of resources, such change arising from the fact that each new firm produces a new product. With respect to the second, it seems clear that selling costs can be disposed of neither as wholly wasteful, nor as wholly on a par with production costs, either of which would be a simple solution; in fact, the difficult problem must be faced of finding both quantitative and qualitative criteria for judging them and integrating a part of them into the welfare ideal. Both of these factors arise from the monopoly elements inherent in a differentiated product, and for this reason there seems to be no ground for hope that an adequate treatment of them will emerge from a theory of "imperfect" competition, in which no monopoly is recognized to be present.[2]

A final point has to do with one specific competitive norm. Mrs. Robinson defines "exploitation," with Professor Pigou, as a wage less than the marginal physical product of labor valued at its selling price,[3] and devotes a great deal of space to com-

[1] Cf. D. H. Wallace, "Monopolistic Competition and Public Policy," *American Economic Review*, Vol. 26, supplement, p. 77; and my own "Product Heterogeneity and Public Policy," *ibid.*, Vol. 40, no. 2 (Proceedings). (The latter appears also as Essay 5 in *Towards a More General Theory of Value.*)

[2] "Imperfect" competition suggests, rather, the removal of the imperfections. Cf., for instance, *Imperfect Competition*, pp. 284 ff.

Mr. Lerner's *Economics of Control* is the most recent example of welfare analysis whose optimum is defined with exhaustive thoroughness in terms of the perfectly competitive criterion; and is therefore fully subject to the criticisms above. [3] Pp. 282–283.

paring the results under imperfect competition and under monopsony with this criterion. She shows that labor inevitably gets less than this under imperfect competition, since it is paid according to its marginal product multiplied by marginal revenue, which is smaller than its marginal product multiplied by price. The conclusion is, of course, that labor is "exploited" very generally, according to this definition.

Now it seems evident that not only labor, but *all* shares, receive under monopolistic competition less than the market equivalent of their marginal physical products, the reason being that the argument applied to labor could also be applied to *any* share, and that the total incomes for the factors composing any firm, computed according to the competitive criterion of marginal productivity, add up to more than the total revenue of the firm.[1] The fact that some one share receives less than its marginal product does not mean, then, that some other one receives more (as it would under pure competition); they *all* receive less, being paid, one and all, according to a different principle. Mrs. Robinson clearly holds this view for the individual firm, with the significant difference that she does not include entrepreneurial services as one of the factors.[2] To the entrepreneur is reserved the rôle of exploiter, a rôle very easy to put off upon him in her analysis through identifying him with the firm.

This implicit identity of entrepreneur and firm runs throughout the argument. It is held (page 408) that "the marginal product of the entrepreneur to the firm has no meaning," for the evident reason that he is one and indivisible.[3] To say that

---

[1] Cf. above, p. 182; and Mrs. Robinson in "Euler's Theorem and the Problem of Distribution," *Economic Journal*, Vol. xliv (1934), p. 411 and *passim*. "Exploitation" is discussed further by Mrs. Robinson in her *Essay on Marxian Economics*, Chapter 9 on "Imperfect Competition"; and in my *Towards a More General Theory of Value*, Essay 16, "Mrs. Robinson's Recent Visit to Monopolistic Competition."

[2] "Euler's Theorem," p. 411. In note 1 she says that "in the present context cost is reckoned excluding profit."

[3] In one brief recognition of the possibility that his services may be varied there is a curious attempt to preserve the indivisible unit. "When the entrepreneur's earnings vary with the amount of effort which he supplies to his firm the unit of entrepreneurship from the point of view of the industry is best regarded as a single entrepreneur doing that amount of work whose marginal cost

"the size of the firm is uneconomically small" under imperfect competition is taken as synonymous with saying that "the ratio of entrepreneurs to other factors is higher than that which would give minimum cost." [1] All that is meant really is that the ratio of *firms* to factors is higher than that which would give minimum cost. It seems to have been overlooked that the increase in the number of firms (under monopolistic as compared with pure competition) affects not only the number of entrepreneurs, but the number of laborers, of general managers, of plants, and of other factors as well. It is resources in general which are redundant (i.e., again by purely competitive criteria), and *a priori* there is nothing to indicate which particular one, if any, is increased relative to the others.

As for the entrepreneur, the argument runs that he has an income in excess of the value of his marginal product to an "industry" because, if the entrepreneurial services employed in one firm were removed, and the other factors composing this firm distributed among the other firms, so that the number of firms was reduced by one, the economies resulting from a larger output per firm would act as an offset to the loss of entrepreneurial services and diminish accordingly the loss of product. Indeed, they might even be so great that the product would increase, thus indicating that the value of the marginal product of entrepreneurship in the "industry" was negative, a possibility which Mrs. Robinson suggests and Mr. Kahn develops at some length. The reasoning, however, applies not merely to entrepreneurship, but with equal force to any of the other factors. Any factor could be shown to have an excess of income over the value of its marginal product to the industry if, at the same time that a small quantity of it were removed, the resulting loss of product were offset by reorganizing the remaining resources

---

to him is equal to its marginal product to the firm" (p. 409, note 2). Thus is the actually divisible entrepreneur rendered indivisible in order to fit the logic whereby he becomes the exploiter.

[1] P. 413. Mr. Kahn (*loc. cit.*, p. 23), cites Mrs. Robinson's demonstration with approval and takes it as a starting point for a further analysis of entrepreneurial income under "imperfect" competition.

in the industry (including entrepreneurial ability) on a "more efficient" basis through increasing the degree of standardization of the product and reducing the number of firms. In fact, however, *the number of firms in the "industry" will be governed by the strength of the monopoly elements involved, and cannot be manipulated in this way.* But the whole procedure is illegitimate anyway, because the change in the number of firms which *accompanies* the variation in the amount of a factor, and therefore affects the so-called marginal product, has no necessary connection with such variation at all. With respect to entrepreneurs, the argument no longer stands if we drop the assumption that varying entrepreneurs and varying firms are one and the same thing, and recognize that, in modern economic society, "entrepreneurship" seems to be as highly divisible and capable of being redistributed as any factor.[1]

It would seem that, if entrepreneurship is taken to be divisible, there is no one left to assume the onus of "exploitation." Indeed the search for an exploiter appears as a misdirected effort arising out of the extension of a competitive criterion of exploitation into a field where it is rendered inappropriate by the presence of monopoly. Whatever may explain the extension in this case, it seems likely that purely competitive concepts and theories will be more readily applied to "imperfect" than to "monopolistic" competition. Where monopoly elements are present, failure to call them by name risks forgetting that they are there and falling into modes of analysis appropriate only if the problem is a competitive one.

[1] The development which the theory then takes is indicated in Appendix B below, p. 230; especially pp. 250–252, and 259.

APPENDICES

APPENDIX A
MATHEMATICAL THEORIES OF DUOPOLY AND OLIGOPOLY

COURNOT stated the problem of duopoly as follows:[1] The quantity sold by each of the two competitors being, respectively, D_1 and D_2, the total amount produced will be $D_1 + D_2 = D$, and the price

$$p = f(D_1 + D_2) = f(D).$$

Assuming that there are no expenses of production, the profits of the two sellers are, respectively,

$$D_1 \cdot f(D_1 + D_2) \text{ and } D_2 \cdot f(D_1 + D_2).$$

Since each one can influence directly only his own supply, he will seek to maximize his profits by adjusting it at the point most advantageous in the light of the amount being offered by his rival. The profits of the first seller will be a maximum when

$$\frac{d \cdot D_1 f(D_1 + D_2)}{dD_1} = 0,$$

and those of the second will be a maximum when

$$\frac{d \cdot D_2 f(D_1 + D_2)}{dD_2} = 0.$$

Differentiating, the following equations are obtained:

$$f(D_1 + D_2) + D_1 f'(D_1 + D_2) = 0$$

$$f(D_1 + D_2) + D_2 f'(D_1 + D_2) = 0.$$

From these, the conclusion is at once drawn that

$$D_1 = D_2,$$

and also, by adding them, that

(1) $$2f(D) + (D)f'(D) = 0.$$

It is evident that the solution is perfectly determinate. This may be transformed into

$$D + 2p\frac{dD}{dp} = 0,$$

and a similar equation obtains for any number of producers, n, the general form being

$$D + np\frac{dD}{dp} = 0,$$

[1] *Loc. cit.*, above, p. 32.

from which it follows that the value of p becomes constantly smaller as the number of sellers increases.

This may be applied to the simple hypothesis where $f(D_1 + D_2)$ is a straight line, and the solution is seen to be that which we have reached in our earlier exposition. Taking the equation of the line to be

$$\frac{p}{p_0} + \frac{D}{D_0} = 1,$$

p_0 and D_0 being the intercepts on the axis of p and D, respectively, we have

$$p = p_0 \left(1 - \frac{D}{D_0}\right), \text{ or}$$

$$p = \frac{p_0}{D_0} (D_0 - D).$$

Substituting in (1),

$$2 \frac{p_0}{D_0} (D_0 - D) + D \quad - \frac{p_0}{D_0}) = 0$$

$$2(D_0 - D) - D = 0$$

$$2D_0 - 3D = 0$$

$$D = \tfrac{2}{3} D_0$$

$$D_1 = D_2 = \tfrac{1}{3} D_0.$$

To this solution, Pareto has made two objections.[1] In the first place, since of the three variables p, D_1, and D_2, the last two have been chosen as independent by writing

$$p = f(D_1 + D_2),$$

one must continue to treat them as such. That is to say, the derivatives of each of the expressions $D_1 f(D_1 + D_2)$ and $D_2 f(D_1 + D_2)$ with respect to *both* D_1 and D_2 must be equated to zero, and the result is the four equations,

(2) $$D_1 f'(D_1 + D_2) + f(D_1 + D_2) = 0$$

(3) $$D_1 f'(D_1 + D_2) = 0$$

(4) $$D_2 f'(D_1 + D_2) = 0$$

(5) $$D_2 f'(D_1 + D_2) + f(D_1 + D_2) = 0.$$

[1] "Économie Mathématique" in the *Encyclopédie des Sciences Mathématiques*, Tome I, Vol. IV (1911), p. 606, note. *Manuel d'Économie Politique*, pp. 595-602, The former contains his specific criticism of Cournot.

Cournot was able to obtain a solution only by discarding (3) and (4). It is then shown that the four equations solved simultaneously give absurd results.

In the second place, the price is not a function of the sum $(D_1 + D_2)$, but is simply a general function of the two variables $f(D_1, D_2)$. The problem is then to maximize

$$D_1 f(D_1, D_2) \text{ and } D_2 f(D_1, D_2).$$

The derivative of each with respect to both D_1 and D_2 must be equated to zero, and we have four equations which reduce to

$$f = 0, \frac{\partial f}{\partial D_1} = 0, \frac{\partial f}{\partial D_2} = 0.$$

Since there are now three equations to determine the two unknowns D_1 and D_2, the problem is insoluble because it is "too determinate." This conclusion is concurred in by Zawadski.[1]

I am unable to agree with either of these criticisms. It was not an error for Cournot to neglect equations (3) and (4) above; on the contrary, it is an absurdity to include them. Equation (3) is legitimate only if the first producer can set his rival's supply as he pleases; equation (4) is legitimate only if the second producer can set the supply of the first as he pleases. Indeed, Zawadski states the problem in exactly this way — each producer, being able to affect *both* supplies, will choose the value of D_1 and the value of D_2 most profitable to himself.[2] Applying this to our first illustration (Fig. 5), if each producer had this power he would at once make his rival's supply zero and set his own at OA. It is nonsense to differentiate the profit of one of the producers with respect to the supply of the other. This applies equally to the more general solution when one takes $p = f(D_1, D_2)$. The influence of either producer on the supply of the other is only *indirect* and through his control of his own supply. All this is contained in the two equations (2) and (5) which Cournot used.

As to the second criticism, there seems to be nothing gained and a good deal lost by substituting $f(D_1, D_2)$ for $f(D_1 + D_2)$. The former is simply a more general form of the latter, and since the latter is known it had better be used. By using $f(D_1, D_2)$ one discovers that the problem may have a solution; by using $f(D_1 + D_2)$ one arrives at the solution itself. Pareto regards the use of $f(D_1 + D_2)$ as a capital blunder, arising from "l'oubli de la dépendance des phénomènes économiques."

[1] *Les Mathématiques Appliquées à l'Économie Politique*, pp. 68-75.
    Ibid., p. 73.

If it is meant that D_1 and D_2 are dependent on each other, this is by no means inconsistent with taking p as a function of their sum.[1]

Duopoly is treated at length by Amoroso,[2] whose conclusions differ in no essential respect from those of Cournot. Edgeworth takes him to task in his review,[3] even suggesting that the section on duopoly be omitted if the book be translated into English.

An analysis of the problem has been made by G. C. Evans,[4] who, like Cournot, develops his theory of competition by first considering two producers and then enlarging their numbers. He takes in succession three different postulates, each of which gives a determinate solution. Since a quadratic supply curve,

$$q(u) = Au^2 + Bu + C,$$

is carried throughout the analysis, the conclusions involve this function. They are, however, easily compared with those of other writers and with my simpler illustration.

The first postulate is Cournot's, and the results correspond. The second is that "each producer tries to determine the amount of his production per unit of time so as to make the total profit a maximum." That is, it is the *joint* profit which is maximized. The solution is the monopoly one, of course; in fact, it is *defined* as "coöperation." The third postulate is that "each competitor regards the price as fixed and tries to make his profit a maximum." The profit of each is differentiated with respect to his supply the price being constant. Price falls in this case, and, the demand curve being a straight line, the supply proves to be exactly double what it would be under monopoly conditions. (Cf. the solution above, page 36, where each producer acts as though he had no influence on the price.) General equations are then presented for n producers under each hypothesis, and it is shown that

---

[1] Cf. the solution of Bowley, below, p. 225.

Erich Schneider ("Zur Theorie des mehrfachen Monopols, insbesondere der des Duopols," *Archiv. für Sozialwissenschaft und Sozialpolitik,* Vol. 63, Heft 3 [1930], pp. 539–555; also Vol. 64, Heft 2 [1930], p. 380) has also criticised the argument of Pareto. He concludes against it on the ground that it ignores the interdependence of D_1 and D_2, defending Cournot (and Wicksell). In another article ("Drei Probleme der Monopoltheorie," *Zeitschrift für Nationalökonomie,* Band II, Heft 3 [1931], p. 382) he develops a special case along the lines of Cournot.

[2] *Lezioni di Economia Matematica* (1921), pp. 258 ff. Cf. also a recent article, "La Curva Statica di offerta," *Giornale degli Economisti,* Vol. LXX (1930) especially pp. 11–20.

[3] *Economic Journal,* Vol. XXXII (1922), p. 400.

[4] "A Simple Theory of Competition," *American Mathematical Monthly,* Vol. XXIX (1922), p. 371. Cf. also his *Mathematical Introduction to Economics* (1930), Chap. III. C. F. Roos ("A Mathematical Theory of Competition," *American Journal of Mathematics,* Vol. XLVII [1925], p. 163) has presented a dynamic development of the theory.

when their numbers are very large the results given by the first and third postulates are approximately the same; whereas coöperation always gives a supply about half of what it would be in either case of competition.

Professor Bowley has given equations strikingly similar to those of Cournot, but differing in that D_1 is considered as a function of D_2.[1] He assumes a definite function for the demand curve, a straight line,

$$p = c - k(D_1 + D_2),$$

and adds supply lines, $p_1 = l_1 D_1$ and $p_2 = l_2 D_2$. The first seller varies D_1 to maximize

$$D_1(c - k(D_1 + D_2) - l_1 D_1).$$

The second varies D_2 to maximize

$$D_2(c - k(D_1 + D_2) - l_2 D_2).$$

The derivative of the first with respect to D_1 and that of the second with respect to D_2 give the two equations,

$$c - 2(k + l_1)D_1 - kD_2 - k \frac{dD_2}{dD_1} D_1 = 0$$

$$c - 2(k + l_2)D_2 - kD_1 - k \frac{dD_1}{dD_2} D_2 = 0.$$

The conclusion is that the equations cannot be solved unless D_1 is known as a function of D_2, "and this depends on what each producer thinks the other is likely to do." Let us first note that, neglecting the last term, the solution is determinate, and is, in fact, Cournot's. To compare with my own earlier illustration, if l_1 and l_2 are set equal to zero (to eliminate the cost of production), the two equations give the familiar result,

$$D_1 = D_2 = \tfrac{1}{3} \cdot \frac{c}{k}$$

$\frac{c}{k}$ being the intercept on the axis of D.

What, now, is the significance of the last term? My interpretation is given only with hesitation. The solution yielded when uncertainty as to "what each producer thinks the other is likely to do" is eliminated being Cournot's, it seems hardly possible to interpret it as compassing elements of uncertainty outside of the limits of Cournot's putting of

[1] *The Mathematical Groundwork of Economics* (1924), p. 38.

the problem. D_1 is clearly not a function of D_2 as Cournot conceived of the moves of the two sellers. Each knew the amount his rival was putting on the market and adjusted his own accordingly, the other remaining unchanged. (The fact that the amount supplied by one depends on the amount supplied by the other is expressed in the equation $p = f(D_1 + D_2)$ and does not, in itself, make D_1 and D_2 functions of each other.) But if neither one *knows* the amount his rival is offering, he will not *know* how much to offer himself. D_1 and D_2 are then functions of each other and the problem cannot be solved, which is only equivalent to saying that the two might stand opposite each other indefinitely, each waiting for the other to begin. As soon as one makes an offer, however, D_1 and D_2 are no longer functions of each other, the last term drops off, and price moves to its determinate position. If this interpretation is correct, the difference between Cournot and Bowley is slight.

FIGURE 34

Professor Hotelling has presented an ingenious mathematical solution for duopoly under the assumption that the product is not standardized.[1] He strongly endorses the idea that "a market is commonly subdivided into regions within each of which one seller is in a quasi-monopolistic position" and argues that this factor puts stability into the otherwise indeterminate solution of duopoly. "It is the gradualness in the shifting of customers from one merchant to another as their prices vary independently," he says, "which is ignored in the examples worked out by Cournot, Amoroso and Edgeworth. The assumption, implicit in their work, that all buyers deal with the cheapest seller leads to a type of instability *which disappears when the quantity sold by each is considered as a continuous function of the differences in price.*"[2]

He considers an illustration in which the buyers are supposed to be "uniformly distributed along a line of length l, which may be Main Street in a town or a transcontinental railroad. At distances a and b respectively from the two ends of this line are the places of business of A and B (Fig. 34). Each buyer transports his purchases home at a cost

---

[1] "Stability in Competition," *Economic Journal*, Vol. XXXXI (March, 1929) p. 41. Hotelling's article appeared several months prior to the first publication of my own chapter on Duopoly (including this appendix) as an article in the *Quarterly Journal of Economics* (November, 1929). It was not mentioned in my article because I had held to the assumption of a standardized product throughout, and it seemed to relate to a phase of the problem which had been reserved for another portion of this book. (Cf. above, pp. 100–104.) It is now included at this point because the argument is mathematical.

[2] *Ibid.*, p. 44 (italics mine).

c per unit distance. Without effect upon the generality of our conclusions we shall suppose that the cost of production to A and B is zero,
and that unit quantity of the commodity is consumed in each unit of
time in each unit of length of line. The demand is thus at the extreme
of inelasticity. No customer has any preference for either seller except
on the ground of price plus transportation cost. In general there will
be many causes leading particular classes of buyers to prefer one seller
to another, but the ensemble of such consideration is here symbolised
by transportation cost. Denote A's price by p_1, B's by p_2, and let q_1 and
q_2 be the respective quantities sold. . . .

"The point of division between the regions served by the two entrepreneurs is determined by the condition that at this place it is a matter
of indifference whether one buys from A or from B. Equating the
delivered prices we have

$$p_1 + cx = p_2 + cy.$$

Another equation between x and y is

$$a + x + y + b = l.$$

Solving we find

$$x = \tfrac{1}{2} \left(l - a - b + \frac{p_2 - p_1}{c} \right),$$

$$y = \tfrac{1}{2} \left(l - a - b + \frac{p_1 - p_2}{c} \right),$$

so that the profits are

$$\pi_1 = p_1 q_1 = p_1 (a + x) = \tfrac{1}{2} (l + a - b) p_1 - \frac{p_1^2}{2c} + \frac{p_1 p_2}{2c},$$

and $\pi_2 = p_2 q_2 = p_2 (b + y) = \tfrac{1}{2} (l - a + b) p_2 - \frac{p_2^2}{2c} + \frac{p_1 p_2}{2c}.$

" . . . Each competitor adjusts his price so that, with the existing
value of the other price, his own profit will be a maximum. This
gives the equations

$$\frac{\partial \pi_1}{\partial p_1} = \tfrac{1}{2} (l + a - b) - \frac{p_1}{c} + \frac{p_2}{2c} = 0,$$

$$\frac{\partial \pi_2}{\partial p_2} = \tfrac{1}{2} (l - a + b) + \frac{p_1}{2c} - \frac{p_2}{c} = 0,$$

from which we obtain

$$p_1 = c\left(l + \frac{a - b}{3}\right),$$

$$p_2 = c\left(l - \frac{a - b}{3}\right);$$

and
$$q_1 = a + x = \tfrac{1}{2}\left(l + \frac{a - b}{3}\right),$$

$$q_2 = b + y = \tfrac{1}{2}\left(l - \frac{a - b}{3}\right).$$

"The conditions $\partial^2\pi_1/\partial p_1{}^2 < 0$ and $\partial^2\pi_2/\partial p_2{}^2 < 0$, sufficient for a maximum of each of the functions π_1 and π_2, are obviously satisfied."

In the particular example chosen, $l = 35$, $a = 4$, $b = 1$, and $c = 1$. If these values are substituted in the equations we get

$$p_1 = 36, \qquad p_2 = 34, \qquad q_1 = 18, \qquad q_2 = 17.$$

The determinateness of the result, however, is not due, as is supposed, to "the gradualness in the shifting of customers from one merchant to another," symbolized in the illustration by c, the transportation cost. If c is put equal to zero, the price is still determinate — at zero this time because there are no costs. It would be carried to that point by competitive underbidding and would remain there because, if either seller were to raise his price again, he would surrender the entire market to his rival. (The equations which Hotelling employs cannot be used to show this, since they are valid only for the case where $c \neq 0$.) This is the answer *if the other assumptions of the problem are retained,* in particular these two: (1) that "each competitor adjusts his price so that, with the existing value of the other price, his own profit will be a maximum," and (2) that either seller is able to supply the entire market alone. It is evident from Chapter III that the first of these restricts the problem to only one of several possibilities. As to the second, although not mentioned explicitly by Hotelling it is necessary to his conclusions. It is, indeed, the key to the determinateness of his solution, as may now be shown.

Let us assume a maximum output for each seller of something less than 35, say 20, *retain the supposedly crucial element c,* and observe the result. Under "equilibrium" conditions, B is making a profit of 578. But by raising his price from 34 to, say, 50, he could sell 15 units and enjoy a profit of 750, for A could not under any circumstances sell more than 20. Since absolute inelasticity of demand is assumed in the illustration, the upper limit to such a move would be infinity. If the demand were taken to be elastic, however, the upper limit would be finite and oscillation would take place between this upper limit and a lower one in the familiar manner described by Edgeworth.[1] It should be noted that in Edgeworth's illustration the limited output of each seller is crucial to his argument. (Cf. above, pp. 37 ff., especially the statement, "He need not fear the competition of his rival, since that rival has already done his worst by putting his whole supply on the market." Cf. also my own argument on page 43, ". . . if either alone could supply *OB* or more, the other would at once eliminate himself completely were he to set any price higher than zero. The price would therefore be stable at the purely competitive level (zero in our illustration)." It appears, then, that it is the *unlimited supply* of each seller which creates stability in the example before us. Hotelling's thesis that it is due to the fact that the product is differentiated is invalid.

It is true that differentiation of the product makes for greater stability in the sense that it raises the lower limit of possible indeterminateness. It was observed by Edgeworth that "the extent of indeterminateness diminishes with the diminution of the degree of correlation between the articles." [2] This is also apparent from Hotelling's equations and from my own argument above, p. 101.

Finally, reference may be made to J. Tinbergen ("Bestimmung und Deutung von Angebotskurven: Ein Beispiel," *Zeitschrift für Nationalökonomie*, Vol. I, Heft 5, p. 676), who presents a statistical example in which he follows Cournot.

---

[1] Hotelling, in fact, qualifies his determinate solution, pointing out that "prices other than the coördinates of the equilibrium point may obtain for a considerable time." But he seems to have in mind only tacit understandings to maintain prices above the equilibrium point, and argues that such understandings are "notoriously fragile."

[2] Papers, Vol. I, p. 121.

APPENDIX B

THE COST CURVE OF THE INDIVIDUAL PRODUCER [1]

THE long-run average cost curve of the firm must be interpreted as the *joint* result of the proportions of factors employed and of their aggregate amount. It will be held below that the common practice of treating proportions and size as separate problems has caused the current theory of the subject to go seriously astray, mainly through its becoming almost entirely a theory of proportions.

As a part of this development the erroneous thesis has come to be widely held that under the "perfect divisibility" of theory, as applied to the factors of production, there would be no economies or diseconomies of scale. From this absence of economies and diseconomies there follows directly (under the assumption of pure competition) an economy without firms. The reason is that, efficiency being the same at all outputs, the size of the firm is indeterminate, hence the number of firms also; so that the very concept of a firm has ceased to have any meaning. As a further consequence the state of competition cannot be defined, since the number of sellers is not discoverable.

There has been concern in many quarters over this alleged propensity of the firm to disappear theoretically, and many strange and even wonderful lines of analysis owe their inspiration to it. It will be argued that these developments were not necessary — the firm exists, in theory as well as in fact. This simple proposition, if established, should lead beyond itself to a reconsideration of those lines of thought which have derived both (*a*) directly from the "imperfect divisibility" thesis of economies, and (*b*) from the unnecessary attempts to escape from its consequences. The analysis will be carried out initially in terms of unit cost curves, and reformulated later in terms of the indifference curve technique, where the two methods will be related to each other.

1. "PLANT" AND ENVELOPE CURVES

The variety of U-shaped cost curve for the individual firm which assumes a fixed "plant" has become a textbook commonplace. It is reproduced for reference in Figure 35, where cost per unit of product

[1] This appendix replaces a shorter treatment of the subject in editions prior to the sixth. It is a reprint, with only minor changes, of an article entitled "Proportionality, Divisibility and Economies of Scale," from the *Quarterly Journal of Economics* for February 1948. See the same journal, February 1949, for comments on this article by A. N. McLeod and F. H. Hahn and a reply by the author. (This Appendix together with the replies to the two comments appears as Essay 9 in *Towards a More General Theory of Value*.)

is measured on the vertical axis and output on the horizontal one. The prices of the factors are taken as given for the firm in question, that is, as not influenced by its own adjustments to different outputs.[1]

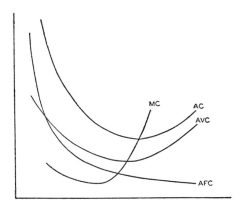

FIGURE 35

The curves of average fixed cost, average variable cost, average (total unit) cost and marginal cost are indicated by appropriate letters.[2]

Remembering that a similar set of curves may be drawn for each and every fixed aggregate of factors,[3] hereafter called a "plant," let us carry forward only the *AC* curve, henceforth labelled *PAC* for "plant average cost."

In order to describe completely the cost conditions under which any particular good may be produced, it seems evident that thousands of such *PAC* curves would be required. Let us begin by showing only five of them in Figure 36, assuming for the moment that these five

---

[1] Thus the influence upon the cost curves of monopsony in the purchase of factors is not within the scope of this analysis. It should also be clear that we are dealing with production costs only. The behavior of selling costs — those devoted to creating or increasing the demand for a product, as distinct from creating the product itself — is a different matter. But the selling cost curve may be added directly to the production cost curve. (Cf. above, Chaps. VI, VII.)

[2] For a full discussion of these curves and their derivation see, for example, Garver and Hansen, *Principles of Economics*, Chap. 5; Boulding, *Economic Analysis*, rev. ed., Chap. 24; Stigler, *Theory of Price*, Chap. 8.

[3] The possibilities include not only plants of different size (aggregate investment) but also of different qualitative or technological character (for each investment total). They also include different possible assumptions as to how the total resources used are apportioned as between the fixed and variable categories. *All* factors being variable in the long run, what is taken to be fixed and what variable in any particular case is in a sense arbitrary, depending upon the nature of the problem and of the decisions to be taken by the entrepreneur.

constitute all possibilities. The optimum manner of producing all
outputs is then given by the heavy line in three "scallops," made up
of portions of PAC_1, PAC_3, and PAC_5. It is simply the lowest point
on *any* curve for each output, discovered by measuring upwards from

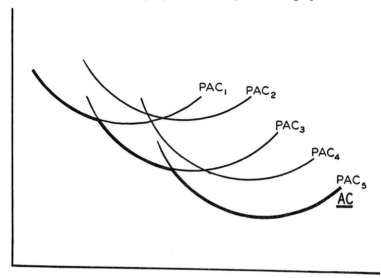

each point on the *x* axis until a plant curve is encountered. This scalloped curve of optimum average costs, being more general than any
of the plant curves, we shall now designate as the curve of average
costs, or AC.[1]

---

[1] The possibility of choosing the best plant for each output (evidently to be
associated only with the "long-run"), rules out portions of curves PAC_1, PAC_3,
and PAC_5, and all of curves PAC_2 and PAC_4. These latter curves, although not
forming a part of AC, are not without significance. In the first place, it would
not be possible from the outset to omit such curves on the plea that they lie entirely above AC, for we do not yet know where AC is. To draw them in, therefore, as has been done, clarifies the manner in which the AC curve was discovered.
In the second place, in so far as the plant cannot be varied in the "short-run,"
not only may the lighter portions of curves PAC_1, PAC_3, and PAC_5 be significant
for short-run problems, but also curves such as PAC_2 and PAC_4. This is true
because the long-run situation to which it is assumed adjustment cannot be
made in the short-run involves not merely variations in output along given plant
cost curves which contribute to the AC curve, but also changes in amounts of
factors and in techniques, which redefine all plant curves and hence the AC curve
itself. If AC in our diagram is taken to be the *present* long-run average cost
curve, then curves such as PAC_2 and PAC_4 may represent plants built under
earlier long-run optimum conditions. It would seem that any short-run period

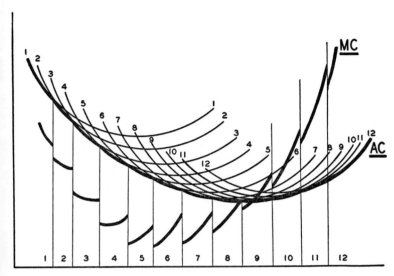

FIGURE 37.

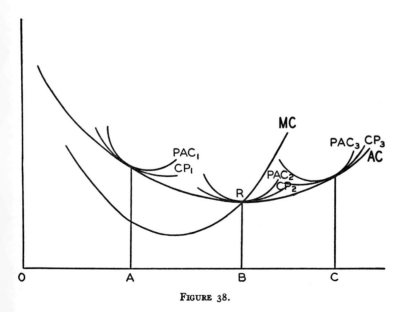

FIGURE 38.

   The next step must be to consider the more general case where the plant possibilities are more numerous; and the limiting case where they are so numerous and so "close together" as to make it legitimate to treat them as continuously variable. In Figure 37, we have a number of plant curves drawn close together, and an AC curve of tiny scallops composed of small segments of the plant curves. Segments of the plant marginal cost curves for each plant corresponding to the range of outputs within which it contributes to the AC curve are also drawn, constituting a discontinuous marginal cost curve, MC, to the general average cost curve.[1] The numbers along the base line indicate the range within which the indicated plant average and marginal cost curves contribute to the AC and MC curves.

   In Figure 38 the number of plant possibilities has been multiplied to the point where they may be considered as continuous, so that AC and also MC have become smooth curves. Three of the theoretically infinite number of plant curves are drawn in: PAC_1, PAC_2, and PAC_3, for the plants best adapted respectively to producing the outputs OA, OB, and OC. (Let the curves CP_1, CP_2 and CP_3 be ignored for the present.) Under the assumption of continuity, even a very small movement along the AC curve involves a change in the plant as well as in the variable factors used with it — in other words, *all* factors, as well as their proportions to each other, are continuously variable. This is the familiar "envelope" cost curve.[2]

   Whether the AC curve is continuous or not will be a question of fact in any particular economic situation; but always it will be true

---

would include such plants, and that short-run economic analysis should not confine itself, as it usually does (at least by implication), to those curves of fixed equipment which touch the "envelope" or long-run curve.

[1] In case the marginal revenue curve for the firm cuts more than one segment of this discontinuous marginal cost curve, equilibrium will be defined by the intersection which yields the *highest* of the several relative profit maxima; and there would be "multiple equilibrium" only if two or more of the maxima were identical. Mr. Higgins has analyzed this problem differently ("Indeterminacy in Non-Perfect Competition," *American Economic Review*, September 1939, pp. 471–473).

[2] We have here an advance indication of the nature of the fallacy that economies of scale disappear with perfect divisibility of the factors. (Assuming the "variable" factor to be finely divisible), "perfect divisibility" is achieved when the "plant" possibilities are continuous, and is therefore defined by the limiting position of the AC curve as the number of "plants" approaches infinity. Economies of scale would be eliminated by perfect divisibility only if the envelope curve were a horizontal line, i.e. if all the plant curves had the same minimum value. The issue then turns on the location of the plant curves. There seems to be general agreement that they are located as drawn, although, of course, this may not be taken for granted without begging the question. It will be discussed **further on.**

that this curve should be looked upon, not as a separate construction, drawn in a particular way with reference to the plant curves, but as made up of segments of the plant curves themselves. It is composed of plant curves: it *is* the plant curves. The problem therefore is *not*, having drawn all relevant plant curves, to draw in the envelope curve, either through their minimum points (wrong, of course) or tangent to them, or in some other way. It is merely to draw in all the plant curves. The envelope curve is there already, and the question of how to draw it does not arise.

The urge to give significance to the minimum points on the plant curves is perennial,[1] yet they are clearly of no (long-run) significance whatever. Unless the plant curves are spaced very far apart, their minimum points will not even lie on the *AC* curve; and even in the unusual case of a great gap between some particular plant and the next possible larger one, such that the minimum point on the first *PAC* curve lay within the segment it contributed to the *AC* curve, this minimum would be no more significant than any other point. It is evident that in this matter there has been, and continues to be, a serious confusion between two different optima which are quite unrelated: the optimum way of producing a given output and the optimum way of utilizing a given plant.

2. DIVISIBILITY AND ECONOMIES OF SCALE

With this preparation we may now turn to our central problem, which is the U-shape of the *AC* curve and its explanation. Let us consider the falling and rising phases of the curve in turn.

The plant curves which compose the average cost curve have, for a time, successively lower minima, and hence define a downward course for the latter until its minimum is reached, primarily for two reasons: (1) increased specialization made possible in general by the fact that the aggregate of resources is larger, and (2) qualitatively different and technologically more efficient units or factors,[2] particu-

---

[1] Beginning with the now classic argument between Professor Viner and his admirably obstinate Chinese draftsman (*Zeitschrift für Nationalökonomie*, Band III, Heft 1, page 36 note). Not only does the envelope curve there drawn pass through the minimum points of the plant curves, but it is suggested that it may be significant only at these points!

[2] Incidentally, the product itself ordinarily undergoes qualitative change, often quite drastic, as a function of the scale of production, thus calling into question the whole concept of "economies of scale," since what is produced more economically, say under mass production methods, is not at all the same thing as what is produced by the simpler methods of small scale industry. This is a phase of the general problem of "product variation," to which little enough attention has been paid in economics. Unfortunately, it cannot be developed here, where the usual assumption of a "given" product for each firm is made.

larly machinery, made possible by a wise selection from among the greater range of technical possibilities opened up by the greater resources.[1] These two explanations overlap substantially (machinery, for instance, being often the expression of further "specialization" in the capital factor); and numerous other reasons, probably of lesser importance, could certainly be added. On the positive side we shall be content here, however, with the above summary statement, since our main purpose is the negative one of refuting the "imperfect divisibility" explanation, which has so largely pushed into the background the one just given.

The explanation of economies of scale as a matter of imperfect divisibility of factors derives from an approach to the problem which, by contrast with that just summarized, stresses proportionality. There is a certain optimum proportion of factors; and, because factors may be had only in discrete units, some of them quite large or "lumpy," this optimum proportion is attainable with precision only when the aggregate of factors is large. Thus the relative inefficiency of small-scale production is explained merely as a matter of failure to achieve the optimum proportions. With perfect divisibility, it is argued, they could be realized by subdivision for *any* aggregate, no matter how small, and economies of scale would be nonexistent. *Ergo*, economies are explained by imperfect divisibility.

The fundamental fault with this argument is that it omits the effect of "divisibility" upon efficiency. But before going into this matter, the extent to which the explanation has been turned into a tautology, by including in the *definition* of divisibility the requirement that efficiency be unaffected, should be made clear. Professor Stigler reflects this recent trend when he states explicitly: "It is tautological that economies of scale rest on indivisibilities, for an indivisible productive service is *defined* as one which is not equally efficient in all sizes (measured in terms of output)." [2]

Much more common is a treatment in which the tautology, though

---

[1] The downward course of the curve follows, as stated, from successively lower plant curves; movement along the curve, however, involves *both* more efficient plants *and* their more efficient utilization, until at the minimum point we have (a) the most efficient plant (b) most efficiently utilized.

[2] *The Theory of Price* (1946), p. 202 note. (Italics supplied.) It should be added that with Stigler the tautology is incidental rather than fundamental. At an earlier point (p. 133) it is not mentioned; and he lists both (a) indivisibilities and (b) the "human factor," this latter being illustrated by specialization and by the problems of management. But the "human factor" is at once transmuted back into indivisibilities. The arguments are dubious (and only too familiar). For example, management, although described as more than doubled (sic) while labor is doubled, is nevertheless called "indivisible," apparently for the reason that it is "used more intensively." (If "more than doubled," it would be used

not explicitly acknowledged, is nevertheless equally present. Thus Mr. Kaldor states that "it appears *methodologically convenient* to treat all cases of large scale economies under the heading 'indivisibility';" and in order to bring a refractory case under the rule, immediately explains that it may be "not so much the 'original factors,' but the specialized functions of those factors, which are indivisible." [1] Divisibility is thus *defined* to include the availability for small scales of those "specialized functions" which depend in fact upon large-scale operations, "specialization" being of the essence of economies of scale. To affirm now that where everything is "perfectly divisible" economies of scale are completely absent is merely to repeat oneself.

Similarly, Mr. Lerner's exhaustive analysis of divisibilities in relation to the welfare problem leans heavily on the proposition that under perfect divisibility of "factors, products and methods of production," economies of scale are absent, and far-reaching conclusions are drawn from the alleged resulting conditions of constant cost. Here the explicit inclusion of "methods of production" automatically takes care of the efficiency problem, since the "divisibility" of this item "permits any particular method of production, involving certain proportions between factors and products, to be repeated in exactly the same way on a larger or on a smaller scale." [2] The phrase "in exactly the same way" clearly means with exactly the same efficiency (otherwise economies of scale would remain even with the perfect divisibility of "method"). What is being *assumed* is that the superior methods made possible by a larger aggregate of resources, such as assembly lines, are equally available with smaller aggregates — in other words, "divisibility of method" is simply a euphemism for "absence of economies."

Professor Knight has given the earliest statement of the divisibility argument of which I am aware, perhaps the one from which, in view of his great influence, the more explicitly tautological formulations of recent years have evolved. He argued that "*If* the amounts of *all* elements in a combination were freely variable without limit and the product also continuously divisible, it is evident that one size of combination would be precisely similar in its workings to any other

---

less intensively.) However, it is finally held that the envelope curve "usually" descends to a minimum and rises again, for reasons which include those given in this appendix.

[1] "The Equilibrium of the Firm," *Economic Journal*, Vol. 44, p. 65 note. (Italics supplied.)

[2] *Economics of Control*, p. 143. On the absence of economies of scale under "perfect divisibility," see pp. 165–167 and *passim*. On the principle that a change in scale will not change the marginal productivity of any of the factors, see pp. 144, 154 and *passim*.

similarly composed." [1] Such a proposition is "evident" only if the effect upon efficiency of dividing factors is ignored; in other words, if the issue of economies of scale is assumed away.

Let us pass from the question of tautologies to still another false approach to the problem: a common line of reasoning which holds that there is something in the "mathematics" of divisibility which washes out the economies. I have encountered this again and again in discussing the matter with students and with colleagues — indeed, it would seem to be not unreasonable to ascribe the ascendency of the divisibility thesis in recent years in some measure to the ascendency of mathematics, not merely as a tool, but often as a substitute for economics. In the present instance it is a bad substitute — and it is not even mathematics. To assume that factors are "perfectly divisible" carries with it no implication whatever as to how their efficiency will be affected in the process. In other words, mathematics as such contributes literally nothing to the question at issue.

The *actual* economic function is discontinuous in any event, and from the point of view of mathematics, to assume "perfect" divisibility is merely to substitute a smooth function for it. Unless the substituted function follows closely the one which expresses the economic realities, the results derived from its use will be worthless. A mathematician called in for consultation as to how to draw the continuous cost function for the firm under an assumption of perfect divisibility would be obliged to ask the economist what divisibility meant concretely in the problem at hand, and how it would affect efficiency. Only when the economist had told him could he proceed; the question is one of economics, not mathematics. [2]

[1] *Risk, Uncertainty and Profit*, p. 98. (Italics in original.)
[2] Mr. Kaldor must again be cited in this connection. "We see therefore," he says, "that the mathematical economists in taking 'perfect competition' as their starting point, weren't such fools after all. For they assumed perfect divisibility of everything; and where everything is perfectly divisible, and consequently economies of scale completely absent, 'perfect competition' [instead of monopolistic competition] must necessarily establish itself solely as a result of the 'free play of economic forces.'" ("Market Imperfection and Excess Capacity," *Economica*, February 1935, p. 42. The absence of economies of scale is crucial to his argument, which, however, involves other matters as well. Cf. above, pp. 198–199.) Here not only are economies of scale cast out, but monopoly as well; and "mathematics" appears as a sort of mad queen striding about the economic croquet grounds and shouting "Off with their heads!" Perhaps it should be recalled that when Alice's patience with such procedures had worn thin she retorted, "Stuff and nonsense! . . . Who cares for you?" (and promptly woke up).

Unfortunately, this identification of mathematical economics with "perfect competition" is not limited to Mr. Kaldor. Closely related is the idea that "economic theory" is the theory of perfect competition, monopolistic competition having to do, by contrast, with "reality."

What, if anything, does divisibility do to efficiency? — that is the question; and the answer depends in part on what we mean concretely by "dividing up" a factor.[1] A further question must be answered: what is to be done with the case where a factor *cannot* be divided, and hence where the question of its efficiency in fractional units does not arise?

Let us begin with the case where divisibility is in some sense possible, and suppose that under the most efficient conditions of production for the firm (the minimum point on its envelope cost curve) there were 100 laborers employed, assuming further, in order to simplify the problem, that no other factors of production are involved. There is no difficulty whatever in dividing the total labor force into any fraction which has a whole number for the numerator and 100 for the denominator, by merely taking the proper number of units. Until a single unit is reached, this is what "division" means concretely, and we know very well its effect upon efficiency: the fewer the laborers the less specialized they will be and hence the less efficient, for reasons explained in detail by Adam Smith — briefly, that they would achieve less "dexterity" and that they would lose more time "in passing from one species of work to another." Plotting the unit costs of the outputs in question, we obtain a discontinuous series of 100 dots, each one a point on the falling phase of the average cost curve. "Full divisibility" of the labor force of 100, whatever it may mean for the intermediate points, must *include* the fractions 1/100, 2/100 . . . 100/100, and there is no avoiding the conclusion that these points must lie on the curve. This being so, it would appear that what happens between them is really of minor importance, for as long as it is established that the curve of perfect divisibility must pass through these points, it is, for practical purposes, defined: it is perfectly clear, for instance, that it cannot be the horizontal line which negates economies of scale.

But let us look into the further divisibilities involved in *fractional* units of a factor. There are a number of ways in which units of different economic entities may be "divided." The commodity beefsteak is infinitely divisible by the use of a meat cleaver; a steam boiler may be "divided" in manufacture by making it smaller (or larger), and again the gradations are infinite. The reflection that neither of these processes is available for the labor factor is not made in order to be facetious, but to make clear that the interpretation to be given to divisibility is not derived from the mathematical blue, but from the economic realities of the problem at hand.

[1] The analysis of divisibility has gained in clarity through the helpful criticisms of my colleague, Dr. A. E. Monroe.

It would appear that one meaningful and realistic way to divide a unit of labor is on a time basis.

Let us suppose that an output is desired intermediate between that provided by 50 laborers and by 51 laborers. If laborers may be hired on a part-time basis, either directly, or indirectly by contracting out certain types of work, the matter becomes simply one of inquiring into the efficiency of production under such arrangements and filling in the gaps. The most favorable circumstances would seem to be where a worker could be hired part-time with an effect upon efficiency such that cost per unit of product at the intermediate point would conform to the trend, that is, lie on the smooth curve drawn through our original 100 points. This would involve the application, to ranges between any two of these points, of the same type of analysis as that just developed for the range from 0 to 100 laborers. Thus, if we assume a "fractional unit" of labor to be five minutes, there will be roughly 100 of them to the day, and 10 such five-minute units of labor will be generally less efficient than 100, for the same reason that 10 days labor will be less efficient than 100 days. This conclusion makes efficiency depend upon the *amount* of a factor, the size of the unit being completely arbitrary. It is certainly the simplest and would seem to be the most defensible *general* assumption as to the effect of divisibility upon efficiency in the problem at hand.

It should be noted that, as a consequence of this interpretation, the efficiency of a fractional unit depends upon the total amount of labor to which it is *added*. It is different at every point on the curve, and corresponds approximately to the efficiency which obtains at the point where the division takes place, not at that which obtains at some other distant point, such as the minimum one on the cost curve. For example, because 50 whole laborers might be thought of as arithmetically equal to 100 half-laborers, one may not conclude that their efficiency will be that of 100 whole laborers at the minimum point because the number of "units" is the same. Their number being *actually* 50, each will have to master more operations than if there were 100 and shift more frequently from one to the other, and so on. For these and similar reasons they will be less efficient.

Nor is there an escape from this conclusion by the alternative of actually hiring 100 laborers for half time. In this case there will be inefficiencies because of the hiring, training, and maintaining of twice as many workers as necessary, of the change-overs from one worker to another, and so forth, so that the results would in fact be worse, not better, than with 50 whole laborers. One need only contrast the extreme of one person working eight hours a day with 96 persons succeeding each other in five minute shifts, to see that subdivision, although it may reproduce for smaller outputs the same number of "units" as under the optimum output, will not reproduce the same conditions of efficiency.

From this example of units which are too small, we are led to a consideration of the very real complications which are introduced by the size of the unit. To produce any particular output most efficiently it is clearly not a matter of indifference whether there be a single laborer working 100 days, 100 laborers working one day, or 10,000 laborers working for 4.8 minutes. The envelope curve requires by definition that for each output the units of the factors be always chosen so as to achieve maximum efficiency. (They will evidently be of diverse sizes in such a broad category as "labor.") But if the size of the unit matters, we have still another problem of divisibility: a fractional unit may involve a loss in efficiency merely because it is fractional — because, for instance, the time lost in starting and stopping work is the same for a part-time as for a full-time worker. In this case, wherever a fractional unit appears in our hitherto smooth curve, there will be a slight break to a higher point and within the range of the divided unit a more rapid descent to the smooth curve at the point where a whole unit is again reached. Such considerations may be important where the divided units are large relative to the total, but the inefficiencies of such fractional units would always be averaged over *all* units, and would usually become inconsequential for anything but the smallest outputs. Herein lies the justification in most cases for ignoring them, and considering that the efficiency of part-time workers conforms to the trend, that is, that unit cost is a *continuous* function of output. (Wherever the inefficiencies were consequential, an alternative would be to fit a smooth curve to the actual data.)

In addition to the time basis just discussed, another meaningful and realistic way to achieve continuous divisibility of a factor is to change it qualitatively. Instead of part-time laborers, more (or less) efficient laborers, or perhaps just *different* ones, are now the answer. The fact that human beings are strikingly diverse in their capabilities and economic attributes is a commonplace, and there would surely be no dissent from the proposition that the general factor "labor" is continuously divisible in the sense here discussed; it only remains to call to mind the effect of such divisibility on economies. Here, too, I believe there would be general agreement that such qualitative considerations yield in themselves an important new source of economies of scale. The reason is that the employment of more highly specialized and superior abilities is often conditioned upon larger outputs, since the units in which such abilities are embodied are too large to be fully utilized for small ones. Hence the "division" of an aggregate of "labor" corresponding to minimum cost conditions (as in our earlier case of one hundred laborers) will diminish efficiency by narrowing the choice of the types of units used. Such units may, of course, be divisible on a time basis, in which case our earlier analysis will apply as an alternative to substituting less efficient units, and the better possibility chosen.

An analysis parallel to that for human beings may be made for machines (also for land), and need only be indicated briefly. Just as it does with the number of laborers, specialization increases with the number of machines, both in the manner of use of identical units and in the construction and design of different ones. "Fractional" units on a time basis are again possible in some degree through rental, sharing, or contractual arrangements, although these considerations are probably not of great importance in the ordinary operations of manufacturing. Where they are present the analysis already given for labor seems applicable without important modification.

It would appear that by far the most meaningful and important interpretation of divisibility in the case of machinery and capital equipment is in terms of qualitative change. While human beings are diverse by nature and training, capital instruments are so by manufacture. Variations in design are infinite, and all machines are also continuously divisible in a new dimension of physical size, with important consequences, of course, for efficiency. It would appear that continuous divisibility in the capital factor would be completely general, were it not for economies in the production of capital instruments themselves through concentration on a limited number of models, thus creating the possibility of "gaps" between the different types of units available to the firm. Wherever such gaps occur (unless a fractional unit is to be had on some other basis, such as time), particular units will be used with varying degrees of intensity over a certain range by changing the quantities of other factors employed with them, and the result will be a scalloped curve as in Figure 37. In large organizational complexes, however, such gaps are almost certain to come at different points for different types of equipment, thus shortening the scallops and perhaps reëstablishing complete divisibility of capital outlay at all points.

So much for the question of continuity; what now of the shape of the curve — the effect of divisibility upon economies in this case of qualitative change? Here again, as for labor, I believe there would be general agreement that larger outputs widen the choice of units, constantly opening up new and more efficient technological possibilities which would be too costly for smaller outputs, because too badly underutilized. Hence, to look at the matter the other way around, the division of an aggregate of capital, as of labor, corresponding to minimum cost conditions will diminish efficiency by narrowing the choice of units used.

Let us turn now to the case where a unit, or a factor, is not divisible at all. Thus it may be said that, although the general factor "capital" is divisible, the particular machines in which it is embodied are not, and that this is the source, or at least a source, of economies of scale. But there appears to be no truth in this proposition. Evidently, if a machine may not be divided, the "amount" of it must be held constant so long as it is used at all, and the amounts of other factors used with it will be varied, yielding a U-shaped plant curve with economies in its descending phase. However, in the case of continuous qualitative variation, movement along the envelope curve involves constant passage from one such curve to another, and the descending phase of the envelope curve is the result, not of the *shapes* of the plant curves composing it, but of their *position* relative to each other. This is clear at once when it is recalled that if the U-shaped plant curves all had the same minimum value, the envelope curve would be a horizontal line.

In the alternative case where substantial "gaps" exist between the units of a factor, or between "plants," the contribution of particular plant curves to the long-run average cost curve will be finite, and perhaps substantial. It may then be said, of course, that each "scallop" is governed by the laws of the fixed factor analysis, as symbolized in Figure 35. But, as in the case of continuity, the particular *portion* of any plant curve which contributes to the long-run average cost curve is governed by the position of the plant curves relative to each other, not by their shape. Thus again, if all plant curves had the same minimum value, the *AC* curve would be made up of segments around these minimum values; there would be as many rising as falling portions, and a smooth curve fitted to it would be horizontal. Even in the case of "gaps" we may conclude, therefore, that the trend of the curve is governed by the nature of the movement from plant to plant, rather than the movement within any particular plant curve. At the same time, there is no objection, of course, to saying that the behavior of the curve within any particular (perhaps substantial) segment is governed by the fixed factor analysis.

There *is* objection, however, in any case, to saying that the economies in the falling phase of a plant curve are explained by the *indivisibility* of the fixed plant, interpreting this to mean that if the plant were divisible there would be no economies. Such a proposition is part and parcel of the tautological conception of the problem, which derives in turn from the premise that if the same (allegedly "best") proportions are reproduced for all outputs, there will be no economies (or diseconomies) of scale. The prevalence of this conception of divisibility as including "without loss of efficiency," is evidently the measure of how sweeping has been the victory of proportions over size in the explanation of economies; whereas at best, divisibility here, if meaningful at all, would make possible the reproduction for smaller outputs of the conditions at the minimum point on the plant curve *only with respect to proportions*. All the forces discussed above which affect efficiency and which are a function of *size* would remain. The real objection, however, to explaining the shape of a plant curve in terms of "indivisibility" is that it has no meaning. If a factor is indivisible, that is the end of the matter: there is no way of finding out how dividing it would affect its efficiency.[1] If by divisibility is meant merely the substitution of a smooth curve for the actual scalloped one, the substituted curve must at least be a reasonable fit to the one it replaces, and not involve an arbitrary assumption which carries it off on a tangent.

It may be added that in many cases where a factor *is* not divided, the reason may be, not that it is indivisible, but that to "divide" it (by, let us say, sharing it part-time with some one else) would entail a greater loss in efficiency than to have it standing idle a part of the time. In this case, using it as an indivisible unit *increases* efficiency.

In summary, it appears that indivisibilities play no part whatever in explaining economies of scale. Where all factors are perfectly divisible, efficiency remains nevertheless a function of size; so that the envelope curve, whether smooth or scalloped, descends to a minimum in its first phase. Where particular factors, or units of factors, remain fixed for substantial portions of the long-run average cost curve, and where this introduces scallops, the "trend" will be the same, and for the same reason. And where the segments of the long-run average cost curve to which the fixed factor analysis applies are substantial, to attribute the economies (or diseconomies) within this range to "indivisibility" is either tautological or meaningless.

3. PROPORTIONALITY AND DISECONOMIES OF SCALE

Let us turn now to the behavior of the AC curve to the right of its minimum point. Here again the proportionality thesis has badly falsified the picture, both as to whether the curve rises, and, if it does, as to why.

---

[1] In the same way, if horses cannot fly, there is no way of finding out how **high** they could fly, if they could.

The matter is of crucial importance for purely competitive theory [1] since, unless the curve rises, the number of firms is indeterminate, instead of being the "large number" required for pure competition. Faced with this consequence of the sweeping proportionality thesis which divorces efficiency from size, Professor Knight, having just affirmed that "these things (proportionality and size) must imperatively be kept separate," finds, two sentences further on, that they cannot be, and so *postulates* the contrary [2] — an expedient which ought to indicate that something is wrong with the principle of separation.

Mr. Kaldor, up against the same difficulty, attempts to solve it within the proportionality formula. He asserts that, "as diminishing returns to *all* factors together are not conceivable," the optimum size of the firm cannot be determined unless at least one factor is fixed,[3] and therefore seeks a fixed factor such that "*only one unit* (of it) can do the job." Analyzing the functions of entrepreneurship into uncertainty-bearing, supervision and coördination, he agrees that the first two are variable, and settles upon the last as the fixed factor, holding that it is a unit because it involves a "single brain." Boards of Directors are almost a fatal rock and are finally admitted to be variable; but it is maintained that in spite of their plurality they conform to the requirement of a "single brain." The firm is then defined as a "productive combination possessing a *given* unit of coördinating ability.[4] Yet if it has to be "given," it is fixed only by

---

[1] In contrast, it is of much less importance for the theory of monopolistic competition, in the sense that elements of monopoly will usually (but not always, cf. above, p. 78, note and p. 161) define equilibrium for the firm to the left of the minimum point on the production cost curve. However, the shape of the curve beyond the immediate vicinity of equilibrium must always be important as a part of explaining and understanding the economic system in the broadest sense.

[2] "For the competitive system to work, it is necessary to postulate . . . that an establishment of relatively small size in proportion to the industry as a whole is more efficient than a larger one." *Risk, Uncertainty and Profit*, p. 98.

[3] "The Equilibrium of the Firm," p. 66.

Professor G. J. Cady, in his *Entrepreneurial Costs and Price*, seems to hold to this position so firmly that he mistakenly describes it (p. 7 note) as an "implied assumption" of my own Appendix B (earlier editions).

[4] "The Equilibrium of the Firm," p. 69. (Italics supplied.) Mr. Kaldor labors to show that there must be a *single unit* at the top; but even granting this dubious proposition (Who is it in the corporation?), it would seem that all that is established is hierarchy within a variable factor. As the firm expands, resources are added to the Chief Accountant as well as to the mythical "Chief Coördinator." It would perhaps be as relevant to point out that they are also added to the tallest man in the organization, or to the one with the broadest grin.

The entrepreneur as a fixed and indivisible unit seems firmly imbedded in the theory of the firm in England, and a theory of exploitation has been erected upon

assumption, as any factor other than coördination might equally well have been.

But coördination, as white-headed boy destined to contain the firm within limits, fails us in the end, even with Mr. Kaldor, for it is finally discovered to be an "essentially dynamic function," which, with the approach of the stationary state, suffers a euthanasia, leaving us again with the size of the firm "infinite (or indeterminate)." His final conclusion therefore is that "long-period static equilibrium and perfect competition are incompatible assumptions." How much simpler it would all have been if "diminishing returns to all factors," in the sense of rising costs when all are increased together, had not been barred as an absurdity!

Without accepting the proposition that a fixed factor is *necessary* in order to make the curve rise, it may be granted at once that if there *is* a factor which for some reason *is* fixed in any particular case, the curve will rise as in the plant curve analysis of Figure 35. "Entrepreneurship," however defined, appears to be variable; but if a particular entrepreneur does not wish to expand it in his own firm because he does not want to share with others certain functions which he performs, then the size of his firm will be limited by his ability to perform these functions, or by his available capital and borrowing ability, or by both, after the manner of the plant curve analysis.[1]

---

this concept, which I have criticized above, pp. 182–183, 215–218. It is interesting to compare Mr. Kaldor's reduction of the variable factor coördination to the required unitary basis with Mrs. Robinson's similar conversion of an admittedly divisible entrepreneur (cited above, p. 216, note 3).

[1] Mr. Kalecki's "principle of increasing risk" (*Essays in the Theory of Economic Fluctuations*, Chap. 4) seems to come under this heading. With a *given* amount of owned capital, an individual entrepreneur may extend his borrowings only at progressively higher rates of interest, as illustrated by the higher rate on second as compared with first mortgages, etc. But the extension of the argument to the corporation is not convincing. In seeking to show, as he must, that there is a limit to the *amount* of "ordinary shares," Mr. Kalecki only demonstrates that the promoters of a new company or the original shareholders of an existing (profitable!) one will not admit new shareholders on an equal basis with themselves, which is quite a different matter. The possibility of expanding common stock by offering to the *existing* body of stockholders rights to subscribe to the new shares is also ignored.

The "principle of increasing risk," combined with the fact that the private capital of various entrepreneurs is not the same, must certainly play a part, as Mr. Kalecki contends, in explaining the coexistence of large and small enterprises in the same industry. But in (correctly) dismissing imperfect competition as a factor contributing to the explanation of this diversity (p. 98), he has apparently committed the common error of identifying imperfect and monopolistic competition, and (incorrectly) dismissed the latter also. On this matter the reader is referred to pp. 209–210 above. Uniformity of conditions as between firms is of the essence of imperfect competition; diversity, of the essence of monopolistic

All factors being variable on the envelope curve, it is evident that the *general* explanation of why it rises cannot be in terms of a fixed factor. Yet there seem to be solid reasons why it should rise, and no reason to reject them merely because it is mathematically possible to subject the proportions at the minimum point to multiplication! The question is again: what does multiplication do to efficiency?

The plant curves which compose the average cost curve have, after a certain point, successively higher minima, and hence define an upward course for the average cost curve because of the greater complexity of the producing unit as it grows in size, leading to increased difficulties of coördination and management. More elaborate systems of control are made necessary by impersonal relations. They are costly in themselves, and lead, furthermore, to a rigidity of procedure and the stifling of individual initiative. Mr. E. A. G. Robinson has used as an apt analogy from the army: "A mistake made by a platoon commander demands only an instantaneous 'As you were!' A mistake made by an army commander may require days of labor to set right." [1] Again, this line of analysis is familiar [2] and need not be defended at length, especially since the proportionality thesis, in which our primary interest lies, has proceeded not so much by denying or criticising it as merely by ignoring it.

It is important to avoid identifying the emergence of the problems of coördination arising from increasing complexity with the minimum point on the cost curve. Where they first become important will depend upon the product in question and the techniques and circumstances under which its production is undertaken at different times and places, but in general they will begin to appear for quite small outputs, as one element in the total picture of efficiency described by the *AC* curve. In the early stages they are submerged by the overwhelming gains from further specialization and more efficient tech-

competition (above, pp. 110–113). Under monopolistic competition, where different producers produce *different* products under *different* circumstances of cost and demand, the *expected* result would be firms of all sizes; and it seems most likely that the diversity associated with the different capital resources of different entrepreneurs would adapt itself to the more fundamental diversity arising from such "product" heterogeneity. Thus an entrepreneur of small resources would establish himself in a situation where the market was limited, etc.

Incidentally, Mr. Kalecki, in his matter-of-fact statement that imperfect competition cannot account for diversity, has provided important corroborative evidence for my own interpretation (above, pp. 208–211) of the nature of "imperfect" competition, and therefore of the vital differences between Mrs. Robinson's theories and my own.

[1] *The Structure of Competitive Industry*, p. 44.

[2] The reader may be referred to Robinson, *loc. cit.*, and to J. M. Clark, *The Economics of Overhead Costs*, pp. 131ff.

niques already discussed. But since these latter tend to exhaust themselves with larger aggregates, whereas complexity steadily increases, it appears certain that the diseconomies must *sooner or later* outweigh the economies, and beyond that point predominate. The forces making for economies and for diseconomies are in balance at the minimum point on the *AC* curve; the latter predominate to the right of it.

From this approach the central principle again emerges that there is no "most efficient proportion of factors" independent of output. If the descending curve had been explained by a failure to achieve the "best proportions" because of indivisibilities, it might follow that when output was large enough the difficulties would be overcome, and that beyond that point there would *a fortiori* be no further problem. But our position, developed above, has been that the proportion of factors corresponding to the minimum point on the *AC* curve is *not* the "best proportion," but only the best for that output. This is a very different thing, and gives no warrant for multiplying it. Already at this output the influence of complexity is playing a part; and because it is a force in itself making for higher costs at the minimum point, the other influences which make for economies must also be present in an offsetting role. From this point of view, since *both* forces are present in *both* directions from the minimum, there is no more reason to think that the conditions of efficiency which characterize the minimum could be extended to larger than to smaller outputs.[1]

---

[1] It is sometimes argued that a policy of decentralization may be adopted beyond the minimum point, reproducing the conditions there found in substantially independent units, and thus eliminating, almost by definition, the problems of complexity. The question is whether the firm, as the "control unit," can divest itself *completely* of control over its component parts; for unless it can, conditions are not duplicated. Decentralization and delegation of authority are well known expedients of large (also of small) organizations; yet there must always be a residue of authority in central hands, including the vital one of choosing those to whom authority is to be delegated. In so far as decentralization is an effective means of combating the diseconomies of size, far from being denied, it is, of course, included by definition in the envelope curve at all points. Its importance will vary with techniques and circumstances, and its effect may often be to postpone net diseconomies far beyond the scales of production to be found in reality. It is contended only that the curve does turn up somewhere.

It should be noted that, in so far as the diseconomies are postponed, the conclusions of this line of argument are disastrous for purely competitive theory, since pure competition will result only if the curves *actually* turn up for scales of production which are small relative to total output. (Of course the product must also be homogeneous.) This is the difficulty which Professor Knight surmounts by merely assuming it away. (Above, p. 237).

4. CONSTANT PROPORTIONS AND HOMOGENEITY

We have now to inquire into the effect of holding the proportions of factors constant while varying their aggregate amount. It must be recalled that the envelope curve is characterized by complete variability throughout as to what factors are chosen, in what amounts, and hence in what proportions to each other. It gives merely the optimum for each output. If, to the right of its minimum point, it rises when resources are applied *most effectively* to the overcoming of increased complexity, then a curve of unit costs restricted by the arbitrary requirement that the proportions of factors which is optimum for the minimum point be maintained for the larger outputs, will rise still more rapidly. If, for instance, a "managerial" or "supervisory" or "coördinating" factor is distinguished, and its proportion to the others increased with increasing size, the envelope curve will reflect this adjustment. Since cost per unit rises beyond the minimum with the managerial factor increasing more rapidly than the others (the envelope curve), it will rise even more steeply if the managerial factor is increased by the lesser amount necessary to maintain the proportions constant.

This curve of constant proportions, labelled CP, is shown in three different locations in Figure 38 (page 233). Let us first consider CP_2 at the minimum point of the AC curve in its relation to the relevant plant curve PAC_2 and to the AC curve. As output is varied from OB, we know that PAC_2 in general rises as it does above AC in either direction because the restriction has been imposed that one complex of factors, the "plant," is held fixed at the amount appropriate to the OB output, whereas no restrictions whatever are imposed along the AC curve. A similar proposition may now be made for the CP_2 curve. As output is varied from OB, CP_2 will in general rise above AC in either direction because a restriction of another sort has been imposed: that the *proportions* of factors remain as defined for OB, whereas no such restriction is imposed along the AC curve. All three curves are tangent to each other at R. If along the envelope curve the proportions of the factors change very slowly with variations in output, CP_2 will diverge from AC on either side of R more slowly than will PAC_2, and will thus lie between PAC_2 and AC, as shown in Figure 38. If, on the other hand, the proportions of the factors change rapidly along the envelope curve, CP_2 will diverge from AC on either side of R more rapidly than will PAC_2, and will thus lie above PAC_2 as well as above AC.[1] There appears to be no *a priori*

[1] I am indebted to Mr. Joseph Lerner for the suggestion of this second possibility. See his article, "Constant Proportions, Fixed Plant and the Optimum Conditions of Production," *Quarterly Journal of Economics*, Vol. LXIII (1949), p. 361.

rule to indicate which of these two results is the more likely; only the first is illustrated in Figure 38.

These same curves may be drawn from any point on the envelope curve, and are drawn in Figure 38 for illustration also at outputs OA and OC. The relation of the plant to the envelope curve at each of these points has already been discussed. The CP curve will in each case lie above the AC curve on either side of their point of tangency, because the proportions which define it are those which are optimum respectively to OA and OC, but which are at all other points inferior to those given by the envelope curve. As before, it is drawn in each case below the plant curve, although the positions of the two might equally well be reversed, as just explained.

From the CP_2 curve drawn at the minimum point, it would now appear that when the proportion at that point is reproduced in smaller or larger aggregates, assuming this to be continuously possible, far from collapsing the envelope curve to a horizontal line, it would have an *opposite* effect, giving results which at all points other than the minimum would be inferior to the envelope curve (and perhaps inferior even to the plant curve from the same point).

There seems to be no reason why entrepreneurs should ever have any interest in maintaining the proportions of factors constant. With maximum flexibility, they will seek the conditions of the envelope curve. In so far as they are obliged to hold various complexes of factors constant in "short periods," they will move on curves symbolized by the various PAC curves. In so far as factors may be varied slowly over intermediate periods, they will move along curves intermediate between the PAC and AC curves, expressing partially the full possibilities contained in the envelope curve. But unless they harbor an interest in the mathematics of homogeneity which submerges their ordinary entrepreneurial objectives, they will have no reason to pursue the possibilities illustrated by the CP curves.

The economist, however, is interested in the homogeneity of the production function as a part of the problem of distribution, and in this connection it is the CP curves, not the plant or envelope curves, which are relevant. The firm will be in equilibrium under pure competition at the minimum point of the *envelope* curve; Euler's theorem will apply approximately at the minimum point of the *constant proportions* curve; and it is because these two points coincide that Euler's theorem applies to equilibrium conditions. In spite of the fact that entrepreneurs will not actually make adjustments along the CP curve, it remains true, nevertheless, that if each factor included in the cost curve is paid according to its marginal product at equilibrium, the total product of the firm will be exactly distributed among them without excess or defect.

A similar proposition will be true under monopolistic competition with marginal *revenue* product substituted for marginal product. However, for those whose knowledge of Euler's theorem is rudimentary or zero — in short, for those who take it on faith and associate it with constant cost, the fact that equilibrium for the firm involves conditions of decreasing cost is troublesome. Let us consider the case where demand and cost curves are tangent, as in Figure 39, equilibrium output being *OA* and equilibrium price *AP*. Plant, constant proportions, and envelope curves are drawn in, all tangent, as already

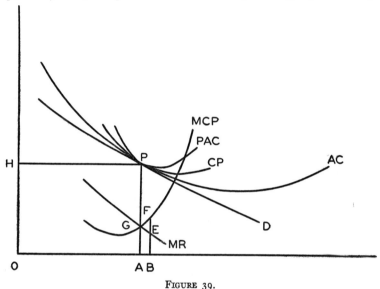

FIGURE 39.

explained, to each other and to the demand curve at *P*. The marginal cost curve to the *CP* curve, labelled *MCP*, has been drawn in, since this is the one which is significant for our purposes. It intersects the marginal revenue curve *MR* at *G* (as would the other two marginal cost curves also, were they drawn in). At equilibrium, total outlay for factors and total revenue product are both equal to the rectangle *OAPH*. If now a very small change in the outlay for factors were made, their proportions being held constant, the increase in physical product would be, say *AB* (magnified in the diagram in order to make it visible); the increase in outlay would be *ABFG*, and the increase in revenue product *ABEG*. If these increases are made smaller by letting *B* approach very close to *A*, the discrepancy *EFG* is sharply diminished, until for very small variations around *G* it may be neglected: the increase in revenue product is approximately proportional to the increase in the outlay for factors. Again, Euler's theorem is applicable under equilibrium conditions, although these conditions are defined without reference to the *CP* curve. It follows that if each factor included in the cost curve is paid according to its marginal *revenue product* at equilibrium, the total *revenue product* of the firm (*OAPH*) will be exactly distributed among them without excess or defect.

As an alternative, the curves might be redrawn, measuring along the *x* axis not physical product but revenue product: "dollar's worth of product." At equilibrium (output *OA* in Figure 39), the cost of producing a "dollar's worth of product" is exactly one dollar (since price equals cost), whereas on either side of equilibrium it is more (since cost is greater than price). The three cost curves would now all be tangent at their *minimum* points (equal to one dollar), and the demand curve would be horizontal and tangent to them at this point, since a "dollar's worth of product" will obviously always sell for a dollar. The case thus appears explicitly as one of approximately constant cost at equilibrium — constant cost of producing *revenue product*.

But suppose the curves are not tangent? — for I have myself insisted that the "tangency solution" is of only limited applicability, the general situation being one of "diversity," including non-tangency.[1] By adding *all* actual profits (including the excess over the "minimum") into the cost curve, equilibrium can always be identified with a condition of tangency; and although this would *certainly not be legitimate as a general procedure*, it appears to be unobjectionable for present purposes. Here the question is not one of the *determination* of equilibrium, since in the non-tangency solution equilibrium must already have been defined before the new curve including total profits could be drawn. Thus *actual* profits are not being "treated as a cost," and the host of issues raised by that problem is avoided. We are interested only in knowing the relationship between what factors actually receive and their marginal revenue products. There is no doubt as to the income which entrepreneurship actually receives, and it may be treated for our purposes as the price paid for the factor in question. The conclusion is, as already developed, that under equilibrium conditions *all* factors, including entrepreneurship, receive their marginal revenue products to the firm, and that, by this rule, the total product of the firm is exactly used up.[2]

[1] Above, pp. 110–113.

[2] The significance of this proposition for distributive theory and welfare economics has as yet hardly been touched, although a substantial literature has

5. SUMMARY: PROPORTIONS AND SIZE

Let us now consider more specifically the central proposition that proportions and size are functionally related, and the nature of the errors which flow from treating them as if they were not.

The problems of proportions and size may be legitimately "separated" only in the sense that a relative optimum may be formally defined for each, the other being held constant at an assumed value. Thus we have the optimum proportion for any given size (total outlay) and the optimum size for any given proportion, the former being discovered most effectively by the indifference curve technique but appearing as a point on the envelope curve; the latter being given by the minimum point of some particular *CP* curve, not in general on the envelope curve at all. Such partial solutions are "legitimate" only in the sense of being consistent with a recognition of the ultimate functional relationship between the variables in question. In the problem at hand each of them has only very limited meaning or value in itself. Certainly assent cannot be given to keeping proportions and size separate in the sense of stopping short with such partial analyses. Since in the general problem they are both variable, the optimum (minimum) cost conditions for the firm can be found only by bringing them together again.

Before proceeding with this *general* problem, it should be recognized that both proportions and size are variables in certain *partial* analyses as well. When one factor (or complex of factors) is held constant at an assumed amount while others are varied relative to it, movement along the "plant" curve involves constant change in proportions and *also* in size (total outlay). This fixed factor analysis is highly important [1] (and certainly unobjectionable!), yet it would be ruled out by a strict interpretation of the dictum that proportions and size must be kept separate.

Our main concern, however, is with the general analysis, in which all factors are variable on the envelope curve. To rule, as is commonly done, that the "best proportions" are a separate problem the solution of which opens the way to a second distinct problem of scale, defined as the reproduction of these "best proportions" for all aggregate outlays, is not to break up a complex problem into its parts, but to misconceive it completely. The reason is that the procedure

---

developed around the erroneous theme that the "hired factors" are exploited by entrepreneurs. (Cf. above, pp. 215–218.)

[1] It is one of the deficiencies of the indifference curve technique, which by some seems to be regarded as having superseded cost curves, that in it this problem is lost from view.

which finds the best proportions yields also the best total outlay and *vice versa*, for it is the single procedure in both cases of finding the minimum point on the envelope curve. To define the question of scale, as is commonly done, in terms of reproducing these optimum proportions at other outputs (the *CP* curve) is to create a wholly artificial problem. To go further and rule, as is commonly done, not only that the "best proportions" are independent of size (coincidence of the *CP* and envelope curves), but also that (under the "perfect divisibility" of theory) they are no better at one size than at another (collapse of the *CP* curve to the horizontal), is to "separate" the two elements involved by the extreme but effective expedient of liquidating one of them completely — thereby also wiping out the firm, and creating this time a whole host of artificial problems.

Historically it would appear that this state of affairs has evolved out of the very old practice of interpreting the "fixed factor" approach to diminishing returns as one involving proportions alone, size being regarded as not changing, probably through unconsciously associating it with the *fixed* factor. For small changes in a variable factor the total outlay for which is in turn small relative to that for the fixed ones, the error involved in this interpretation may not be great, but by extension it soon becomes prodigious. Thus, if "management" is five per cent, and all other factors ninety-five per cent, of the total outlay, a doubling of all others not only changes their proportion to management, but virtually doubles the total outlay. *Yet in all such cases, and indeed whenever a fixed element no matter how unimportant can be identified, the common practice has been to attribute the whole result to proportions.*[1] From this it has been an easy step to attribute the whole result to proportions, even when there is no fixed factor, as on the envelope curve, so long as the proportions change at all with the changing total outlay.[2] Proportions

---

[1] Examples abound; cf., for instance, Boulding, *Economic Analysis*, p. 491; rev. ed., p. 677. Boulding's whole treatment is typical in its rigid insistence on the separation of proportions and size, with the usual result that proportions take over. "Variability of returns to scale" are not absolutely denied, but are described as "difficult to prove," and when mentioned at all are always on the defensive. It is strange indeed that Boulding himself seems only faintly impressed by his own breath-taking example from nature (which ought to convince anyone) of a flea which, increased to the size of a man (proportions constant), not only could not "jump over the Capitol," but would collapse on the spot; his own cautious conclusion being only that "the *possibility* of genuine departures from homogeneity in the production schedule must therefore be taken into consideration." (P. 493, rev. ed., p. 678; italics supplied.)

[2] In the flea example of Boulding this would mean that if the flea were increased in length and breadth by 100, but in height by only 99, its collapse would be attributed *entirely* to the change in proportions and not at all to size!

have now won the day completely: since they explain all economies, it is evident that nothing remains to be explained by scale, and so we have the dictum that economies (and diseconomies) of scale do not exist. The fact that they do has then been squared with the theory that they do not by the thesis that it is "imperfect divisibility" which accounts for them by interfering with the right proportions at all outputs; and finally the whole preposterous structure saved only by the happy expedient of turning it into a tautology.

How much better to have recognized from the first that when both proportions *and* size change, the effect upon costs is the effect of neither alone, but of both together! There is no element of the problem which does not fall readily into place once this has been done.

6. THE INDIFFERENCE CURVE ANALYSIS

The purpose of this section is not to add anything to the foregoing argument, but merely to interpret it in terms of the alternative indifference curve technique. A production function for two factors gives a surface in three dimensions, like a hill rising out of a level plain. It will be helpful to think of Figure 40 as a map, and of the various lines as roads or paths on this hill which rises to the northeast of O, the axes OA and OB being level roads in the plain. Quantities of the two factors are measured east and north along these two lines as indicated, and any point on the map northeast of O represents a certain combination of the factors. We may, for convenience, think of the plain as being located at sea level. The third variable is altitude; and the height above sea level of any point on the hill will represent the amount of product produced (under optimum conditions) by the combination in question. With larger aggregates of factors used as one moves to the northeast, the hill evidently gains in height. Contour lines, showing equal heights above sea level, are familiar to map readers, and the indifference curves labelled $I_1, I_2, I_3,$ and I_4 are such lines, or paths, around the hill. From each of them may be read the different combinations of factors which will produce the same output, equal to the height at which the contour was drawn.

The prices of the factors are taken as given throughout, and we may now assume a given total sum of money and mark off the quantity of factors it will buy. Supposing the sum to be one thousand dollars, if it were spent entirely on factor A it would purchase (say) the quantity OA_1; and if it were spent entirely on factor B, it would purchase (say) the quantity OB_1. If we now draw the straight line A_1B_1 on the map, any point on it will indicate a combination of the two factors which could be purchased for the sum of one thousand dollars. This straight line will cut across many contour lines and will be tangent to the highest one it touches, the point of tangency giving the highest altitude reached on the path A_1B_1, that is, the largest amount of product which can be obtained for one thousand dollars. A_2B_2, A_3B_3 and A_4B_4, further out from the origin, are constructed similarly for larger total outlays, and similarly each will be

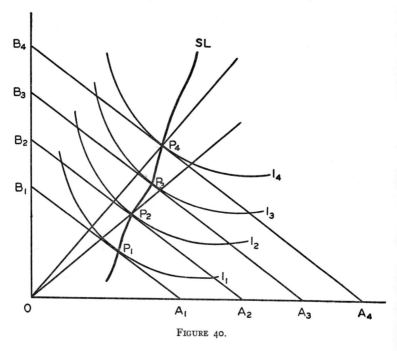

FIGURE 40.

tangent to a contour line at its highest point, indicating the maximum output obtainable for the total sum represented.

Since at each of these points of tangency the total product is a maximum for the outlay, and the total cost a minimum for the output, in question, the cost per unit will evidently be a minimum, both for outlay and output. Any other point on the constant outlay line involved would give a smaller product for the same outlay; any other point on the indifference curve involved would give the same product for a larger outlay. Each point of tangency corresponds, therefore, to a point on the envelope curve, and the wavy line, labelled *SL* for scale line, which passes through all the points of tangency corresponds to the envelope curve. From it we can read off a series of optimum combinations of the factors for different outputs; and, the heights of the indifference curves on the production surface being known, we can associate each combination with the output it produces.

Since the application of a certain minimum amount of factors is necessary in order to obtain any product at all, one would not, in departing from O, begin climbing the hill at once. The scale line does not therefore pass through O (although one frequently encounters the conviction that it is "mathematically" necessary for it to do so), but begins at a point discontinuous from it, as drawn in Figure 40. Nor is there any reason for it to begin in such a way that its extension backwards would pass through O. The point is of major importance, since the belief that the line must pass through O, and the fact that it is usually drawn that way, must contribute substantially to the propensity to regard it as a line of approximately constant proportions, and from this to take the further step of treating the production function as approximately homogeneous.

Let us now consider straight lines from the origin through various points on the scale line. For illustration only two are drawn in Figure 40, through points P_2 and P_4. Each of these paths up the mountain involves a constant ratio between the factors (equal, of course, to that obtaining at its intersection with the scale line). They are the equivalent of our CP curves in Figure 38: just as any output except the one at a point of tangency of the two curves in Figure 38 may be produced more cheaply by moving from the CP curve to the envelope curve, so here any output on a constant proportions line, except at its point of intersection with the scale line, may be produced more cheaply by moving along an indifference curve to the scale line. Or, alternatively, the same outlay can be made to produce more product by moving along a constant outlay line of the AB type to a higher altitude at its intersection with the scale line. This will be true no matter on which side of the scale line the constant proportions line lies; that is, whether, in walking up the hill from O along the path OP_2, the scale line lies to the right (before P_2 is reached) or to the left (after P_2 is passed). The scale line is always the optimum.[1]

---

[1] "Plant" cost curves are derived, of course, from cross sections of the surface taken so that one factor is held fixed. Thus if factor B is the plant and factor A is variable, the plant curve tangent to the envelope curve at P_2 would be derived (as in Figure 35) from the factor prices combined with physical data given by the path on the surface traced by a line through P_2 parallel to OA (not drawn in the figure). If A were fixed and B variable, the line would be parallel to OB. The "profile" of such lines, as seen from OA or OB, and usually divided through by the quantity of the variable factor for each output, is the curve common in presentations of the fixed and variable factor approach to diminishing returns. From any point on such paths (except their intersection with SL) it would evi-

Since homogeneity involves the relationship of all three variables to each other, it is impossible to tell from Figure 40 whether its conditions are fully met, without knowledge of the altitudes involved. For homogeneity in the first degree, it would be necessary for the scale line, under every possible assumption as to the prices of the factors (hence the slope of the AB curves), to be a straight line passing through O (as OP_2 and OP_4, *not* as SL), not only in the two dimensions pictured, but also in the third one of altitude. This would mean that, as one walked up the hill from O in any direction whatever, keeping a straight line on the map, the gradient of his path would never change. (It would, of course, in general, be different in different directions.) If this were true, it would follow that at any point (combination of factors) whatever on the surface, the total product would be exactly used up if each factor were paid according to its marginal productivity (Euler's theorem).

The condition is equivalent to constant unit cost, and we know from our earlier analysis that the production function of the firm is not of this type. On the contrary, not only do the proportions of factors change in the scale line path, as in SL as drawn, but the gradients of the constant proportions paths (as with most hills in reality) rise slowly at first, reach a maximum and then decline. On the actual surface, as one travels on any path, say OP_4, away from O, he will, after passing the steepest gradient but before reaching the top of the hill, come to a point beyond which he will be unable any longer, because of the curvature of the hill, to see the point O. (The height of his eyes from the ground must be neglected.) At this point the gradient of his path will momentarily be that of a straight line *through space* from O, and the production function will be approximately homogeneous for very small movements along the constant proportions path. There will be such a point on each of the lines radiating from O, and their locus (not shown in the figure) may be thought of as the path which one would follow if he were to move along the hill in such a way as just barely to keep O from passing out of sight; or alternatively, as the horizon if one stood at O and surveyed the hill. This is the path of approximate homogeneity (constant cost), and its intersection with the scale line gives the horizon point on that line as well, in other words, the minimum point on the U-shaped envelope cost curve of the firm. Let us assume this to be at P_4. The constant proportions line OP_4 will now correspond to the CP cost curve which is tangent to the envelope curve at the minimum point for both.

---

dently be advantageous to move along either an indifference contour or a constant outlay line in Figure 40 until SL was reached.

So far we have considered altitude as physical product, or as physical product multiplied by a *constant* price, thus conforming to the situation of the firm under pure competition. Under monopolistic competition the price varies with output, being lower as the output sold by the firm increases. If each output is multiplied by the price at which it is sold, the resulting *revenue product* may be substituted for physical product in our analysis so far, and a different surface will result. The contour lines (indifference curves) of this surface will be the same as before, since the output (altitude) for each is simply multiplied by its marginal revenue; and therefore the scale line will not change. (The envelope cost curve is evidently not altered by a change in the demand curve.) But the *height* of each contour line is differently defined; and since the price of the product steadily decreases with greater distance from O, the altitude of this surface (now defined by revenue product) will fall off earlier and more rapidly, with the result that the horizon viewed from O (that is, the line of approximate homogeneity) moves nearer. Let us suppose it to intersect the scale line at P_2, and we have here a point of momentarily constant (minimum) cost of producing, not a unit of product, but a unit of *revenue* product. In terms of our earlier Figure 39 where the base line measures physical product, this is the point of tangency of the demand and cost curves.[1] The constant proportions line OP_2 corresponds to the CP cost curve drawn tangent to the envelope cost curve for the output in question. At this point, the *revenue production* function being approximately homogeneous for small variations along OP_2, the total revenue of the firm will be exactly used up if each factor is paid according to its marginal *revenue* product.

[1] Defining the cost curve for this purpose, as explained earlier, to include the remuneration of *all* factors, entrepreneurial as well as hired.

APPENDIX C

PURE SPATIAL COMPETITION

THE problem of pure spatial competition is defined very simply. Just as a seller's market is large or small depending upon the price he sets, so it varies with the location he chooses. People not only buy where prices are cheapest; they also trade at the shop which is most conveniently located. The analysis of prices ordinarily assumes that the other bases of competition than that of price "remain equal"; it is now proposed to assume that prices and everything else but location "remain equal" while sellers attempt to secure a market for their goods solely by adjusting their places of business.

In its most general form, the problem is one of the locational adaptation of *both* buyers and sellers to each other. In any urban area, for instance, there is mutual adaptation between the distribution of shops and the distribution of population. On the one hand, buyers tend to locate, *other things being equal*, near the places where things are sold; on the other hand, sellers are seeking out the buyers, each trying to locate his shop so as to reduce to a minimum the inconveniences of trading with him. We may begin, however, with the assumption that the distribution of population is given, and it will appear that but little modification of it is needed. The distribution of shops is sufficiently well adapted to the needs of customers to enable them to choose their places of residence with other things primarily in view.

The fundamental question is whether sellers (of the same commodity) will tend to concentrate at one point or to disperse over the area so as to give a maximum of convenience to the buyers. Let us begin by assuming the buyers to be uniformly distributed; and the problem will be simplified (without affecting the nature of the conclusions) by considering them as distributed along a line instead of over an area. It has been shown by Professor Hotelling [1] that, where buyers are distributed along such a line, and where there are but two sellers, these latter will, contrary to expectations, locate as close to each other as possible, instead of at the quartile points of the line where convenience to the buyers would be a maximum. In Fig. 34 (p. 226), for instance, it is seen at once that, since the market of each of the two sellers, A and B, extends half way towards the other, either one could enlarge his market by a move in that direction. (The final equilibrium point may, in fact, be defined with precision. It would be located at the center of the line, since, if it were elsewhere, the seller whose market were smaller would move to the other side of his rival, and such moves would continue until both were established at the midpoint.) This is a conclusion of great importance, but Professor Hotelling is in error

---

[1] "Stability in Competition," *Economic Journal*, Vol. XXXXI (1929), pp. 52-53.

when he generalizes it for large numbers. He argues that "if a third seller C appears, his desire for as large a market as possible will prompt him likewise to take up a position close to A or B, but not between them," and reaches the conclusion that "as more and more sellers of the same commodity arise, the tendency is not to become distributed in the socially optimum manner but to cluster unduly." As soon as there are three, however, the one who is caught between the other two will move to the outer edge of the group, and a series of such moves, always by the one left in the center, will disperse the group. For three sellers, the outcome seems to be that two of them, say A and B, would be located at the quartile points and the third, C, at any point between them. Dispersion would go at least this far, for if we suppose either A or B to move towards the center in order to enlarge his market, his place would promptly be taken by C. We may conclude that, although there might be continual shifting amongst the sellers in their attempts to occupy the best places, no buyer would ever have to travel more than 1/4 of the length of the line in order to make a purchase. Ideally he should have to travel no more than 1/6, for convenience is maximized if the three sellers are located at points which are 1/6, 1/2, and 5/6 of the distance from one end of the line to the other.

As the number of sellers increases, they may group in twos (we have just seen that C may locate next to A or B), but any group of three or more would be broken up in the manner already described. Taking the length of the line as unity, the general conclusion for n sellers is that the space between the last sellers at either end and the ends of the line can never exceed $1/n$ (if the number of sellers is odd, it cannot exceed $\frac{1}{n+1}$), and that the space between any two sellers can never exceed $2/n$, this limit being reached only in the extreme case where sellers are grouped by twos. The distance traveled by any one buyer can therefore never exceed $1/n$, or twice what it would be under the ideal distribution of sellers, where it could never exceed $\frac{1}{2n}$. However, there is no more reason for the sellers grouping by twos than for their dispersing.[1] It has been shown that where a seller finds himself between two others (as C in the example above) it is a matter of indifference at what point he locates, and if we suppose him to choose the midpoint so that the sellers are distributed at equal intervals along the line, the result is but little different from the ideal. If there are nine sellers, they will be distributed at intervals of 1/10, 2/10...9/10 along the line, compared with an ideal distribution at intervals of 1/18, 3/18

[1] With the exception that there must be two sellers at each end. Although the remainder of this paragraph gives values for the intervals which are inaccurate for this reason, it is left as in the first edition. For further discussion of this matter and of the spatial problem in general see "The Product as an Economic Variable," *op. cit.*, esp. pp. 17 ff.

...17/18. The markets of the two end sellers will be 3/20 each, of the other seven 1/10 each, compared with an ideal for all of 1/9. The distance traveled by a few buyers at the ends of the line will be 1/10 $\left(= \frac{1}{n+1} \right)$; but aside from these the maximum is 1/20 $\left(= \frac{1}{2\,(n+1)} \right)$, compared with an ideal of 1/18 $\left(= \frac{1}{2\,n} \right)$. In summary, two sellers will concentrate at a point, but dispersion begins when there are three, and, for fairly large numbers, the distribution approximates closely the ideal which maximizes the convenience of the buyers.[1]

Wherever, for any reason, population is unevenly distributed, it is evident that the distribution of stores will conform to it. This is a proposition which is of great importance in the light of the interpretation which must now be given to the phrase "distribution of population." As used throughout the argument, it must be understood to include not only the location of residences, but also the changing location of buyers in going to and from work, amusements, and other pursuits. Obviously many purchases are made at points more convenient to travels than to places of residence. Wherever, then, the "population" is more dense, a piling up of shops is to be expected. Such concentration is cumulative, within limits, for shops draw both purchasers and the people who are employed in them, and these, in turn, afford a market for more shops. We must, however, avoid falling into the error of explaining the "shopping district" and similar concentrations of sellers as due wholly to the concentration of buyers in these districts. The question to be explained is how such a concentration of buyers got started in the first place.

The general argument for dispersion applies to the sellers of any one good — strictly speaking, only to sellers of a perfectly standardized product. It is obviously for the convenience of buyers that *different* products be sold in proximity to each other, and herein lies the explanation of most of the concentration actually found in retail trading. The simplest form of such concentration is the individual shop itself, which, by offering a variety of merchandise, enables the buyer (*a*) to economize time by making many purchases under one roof, and (*b*) to "shop," i.e., to make comparisons of price and quality before purchasing.[2]

---

[1] In generalizing his thesis of excessive sameness, Professor Hotelling points out its applicability in other fields. For instance, just as two sellers move together on the line, so the Democratic and Republican parties make their platforms as nearly alike as possible in their competition for votes. It may now be added that where there are more than two parties a dispersion takes place analogous to that of the sellers on the line. In France, for instance, the parties are not all grouped at the Center, but range, with fair diversity, from extreme Left to extreme Right.

[2] Such concentration is also accounted for, of course, by the limitations to the market for any one variety of product, compared to the most efficient scale of retail selling.

There is naturally a strong tendency in connection with (*a*) to group products which are jointly demanded, such as different kinds of groceries, of drugs, of clothing, etc.; and in connection with (*b*) to group products which form a composite supply, i.e., which are substitutes for each other, such as different brands or varieties of the same general class of goods. Concentration is carried further by the grouping of stores, and this takes place according to the same principles. Stores of quite different types cluster together so that buyers may make many purchases in one district, and these clusters tend to be dispersed according to the rule already laid down for single products. Furthermore, stores selling similar products tend to group in order that people may "shop." Instances are the theater district and the automobile district. The "shopping district" combines on a grand scale the two principles of grouping (*a*) widely different products, and (*b*) many varieties of each. As has already been pointed out, such a concentration may be highly cumulative.

We pass now to some other considerations. Our analysis has assumed that prices, among other things, remain equal while spatial competition takes place. The number of sellers engaged in the competition and the scale of production of each will depend upon the relation between cost and the prices assumed. Whatever these prices, both the number of sellers and the scale of production will adjust themselves as described earlier (p. 108), so that prices and costs are brought to an equation, except that where population is concentrated the relative scarcity of land may act as a barrier to the adjustment and lead to a generally larger scale of production and higher rents. (Cf. above, p. 112 and Appendix D.) The relation between the uneven distribution of buyers and sellers on the one hand and urban rents on the other, under our present assumptions of pure spatial competition, may now be traced more in detail.

A moderate concentration of population may require no modification in our general conclusions. If there is room enough, the result may be simply a multiplication of shops of the same general size and rate of profits, and paying no higher rent than the land would yield for residential or other purposes. If any seller enjoyed temporarily a larger volume of business and larger profits, he would be obliged to share his market with competitors who would locate near by. Such competition would force the same volume of business here as could be secured in less densely populated districts, and rents could be no higher, since one location would yield no larger market than any other.

But the concentration may be so great in an area so small that there is not room for all the sellers who would naturally be attracted. The levelling effect of competition on profits and the resulting tendency towards a uniform scale of production is then restricted by the impossibility of piling stores on top of each other. Competitors are unable to make incursions upon the larger markets afforded to those who first secured locations in the district. But they can prevent them from enjoying the increased profits arising out of a larger scale of production and diminished unit costs — profits which would ordinarily be eliminated by an increase in the number of stores. Their bidding for the sites forces these gains into the hands of the landowners in the form of rent.

Variations in the scale of production, in rents, and in profits also take place from unevenness in the distribution of population, not in the sense of the existence of certain areas where it is on the whole more dense, but in the sense that the markets of different sellers fit into each other in highly irregular fashion. It has been tacitly assumed that buyers move towards sellers in a straight line, and therefore that sellers could distribute themselves so that their markets would be of approximately the same size. The vagaries of streets, however, introduce inevitable irregularities. If a certain corner is passed by 8000 people daily, it affords a better market than the nearest possible location (next door, but not on the corner), where 5000 people pass daily. *Other things being equal,* its sales will be greater in the proportion of 8 to 5 and profits will be larger. Since competitors will not have the alternative of sharing in this market by setting up for themselves next door or near by, they will bid for the occupancy of the better site and thus put into the hands of the landowner all of the extra gains which it affords. Competition levels profits by converting a portion of them into rent. And the tendency towards a uniform size is modified by the fact that markets are to a degree concentrated at *one spot* and not spread over an area which can be divided.

Again, it might seem that if a seller's nearest competitor were at a considerable distance, it would be almost a matter of indifference which one of a dozen adjacent sites was chosen. And so it might be, if his trade came entirely from those whose *residences* were in the vicinity of his store. But many of those living nearest to him pass other stores in their daily travels. Also a particular location within the district at a street intersection may bring him a large volume of business from people passing through which he would otherwise miss entirely. Such factors as these give varying importance to different sites, even though they be adjacent, and corresponding variations in their rents. It is obvious that any location giving an unusually large market will have that market cut into by a competitor if there exists an available site which will allow sufficient incursions to pay the ordinary rate of profits; so that, except in very congested districts, there is a definite limit to the volume of business secured by any single seller. The more "smooth" the distribution of population — that is, the more alike are the opportunities afforded by a number of contiguous sites — the smaller will be the deviations from the "normal" size.

These irregularities in markets may cause variations in profits instead of in rents. If a market is so large as to yield exceptional profits to one merchant, and yet not large enough to give the ordinary rate to two, the seller who happens to get there first may succeed in keeping the extra profit, providing there are several sites which are about equally attractive. There could be no rent in this case beyond that given to the land for other uses, say residential purposes, for the competition of landowners would reduce it to that level. The higher rate of profits could not be diminished by a new competitor, for he, as well as the first seller, would lose by his entrance. The forces tending to give surpluses resulting from irregularities of this sort to the landlord or to the tenant are probably mixed in most cases, so that there may be variations in both rent and profits throughout the area on this account. Since those competing for a site are usually few, there is room for bargaining, and this may divide the gain or throw it one way or the other.

APPENDIX D

URBAN RENT AS A MONOPOLY INCOME[1]

THE theory of monopolistic competition applied to the field of retail selling yields an explanation of urban site rent which is at odds with the usual one. Urban rent for retailing purposes[2] is a different sort of income from agricultural rent — in fact, although the two types are ordinarily thought of as analogous, the only resemblance between them appears to be that they are both paid for the use of land. Agricultural rent is a purely competitive return; urban rent a purely monopolistic one. The former can and does exist under pure competition; the latter is due entirely to the monopoly elements in monopolistic competition.

Barring conceivable cases where the soil or rock is particularly able to support the weight of a large building, a business site confers no advantages analogous to superior fertility in agricultural rent. One site is capable of *producing* as large a quantity of retailing services as another — there are no differences in fertility and no scarcity whatever of the best land in this respect. Marginal and sub-marginal land anywhere — free land — is as "fertile" for selling purposes as the best site in the heart of the shopping district of New York. It could equally well provide the same retailing facilities, and would if the services there produced could be sold.

The rent of urban land is explained wholly, that of agricultural land partly, by the factor of location. Yet the locational advantage adhering to a business site is not the same as that which forms a part of the explanation of agricultural rent. Agricultural land bears a higher or lower rent according as it is near to or far from the market where its product is sold. It is always *at a distance* from the market. Urban land carries its market with it, — those buyers who find it most convenient to trade at the location in question, — and its rent is high or low depending upon the size and nature of this market. Agricultural rent arises because the product of some lands can be produced and transported to the market at a total cost which is less than the market price, the product of all lands being sold indifferently to the same group of buyers in the competitive market. Urban rent arises because a piece of land can *sell* more — is better located within a certain trading area with reference to a *part* of the buyers. The market for

---

[1] Cf. above, p. 112.

[2] The problem of rent for residential or manufacturing sites is not considered.

the product of agricultural land is a purely competitive one — there are a large number of buyers and sellers, and the product of one piece of land is not differentiated from that of others. The retail market, on the other hand, contains monopoly elements, for the factor of convenience differentiates the product spatially. The movements of buyers being impeded, the "product" of each site contains an element of convenience to a certain group, and the seller locating on the site has a monopoly of its product, the full value of which he is obliged by the competition of others for its use to pay into the hands of the landlord. If buyers moved freely over the entire area, as they would if the market were a purely competitive one, the differences in urban rent and in land values would entirely disappear.

A simple illustration will bring out the difference. Consider the rent of a piece of agricultural land located at such distance from the central market that the transportation cost of its product is 10 cents per bushel. If the transportation cost on marginal land is 30 cents per bushel, the rent of this piece of land (neglecting differences in fertility) would be 20 cents per bushel. Since the central market is composed of a large number of buyers and sellers, it is purely competitive, and every seller is assured of disposing of whatever quantity he produces at the market price. The demand curve for his own product is always a horizontal line. He can sell an amount indefinitely large (compared to the amount it will be profitable for him to produce) at the market price, say $1.00 per bushel. Or, subtracting transportation charges, we may say that the demand *at his farm* is indefinitely large at a price of 80 cents.

Contrast this with urban site rent. The ordinary rent reasoning does not fit at all. Rent is not paid in order to save transportation charges. It is paid in order to secure a larger volume of sales. Buyers and sellers alike are scattered over a wide area. Movement among them is so impeded that one place within the area gives advantages in securing the custom of a portion of the buyers. It affords a market which is, to a degree, distinct from the whole. The amount of product each seller can dispose of is not indefinitely large at the prevailing price. It is very definitely limited by location; if it were not, department stores would locate in the outlying districts, secure the same volume of business, and increase their profits by the saving of rent. If we regard the whole area as one market, it is clear that rent is paid because it contains elements of monopoly. Spatial differentiation results in demand curves for the goods of individual sellers which have a negative slope instead of being perfectly horizontal. Since urban site rent would disappear if they were horizontal, we must conclude that it is due to the monopoly elements and is a pure monopoly return.

There is no extensive margin in urban site rent. This concept has to do with a situation where the product of lands of *different* grades is sold in the *same* market, whereas urban rent arises from the products of lands of the *same* grade being sold in *different* markets. Low rent sites are not poorer sites in the same sense that marginal land is poorer than the best agricultural land. The costs of producing on them are not higher; rather, the market they afford is smaller. Two sites have different rents to the degree that they are in different markets, and to exactly this same degree the concept of an extensive margin is meaningless as applied to them.

The rent on any urban site is an expression of the value of the monopoly privilege of providing retail services *at that particular place.* Competition among entrepreneurs to secure these monopoly gains is the force which puts them into the hands of the landlords. In the cost curves dealt with above, the rent has always been included as one of the costs from the individual seller's point of view, and profits have been treated as the residuum. From the landlord's point of view, the business man's profits may be included as a cost, and the residuum will be rent. Diagrammatically it would appear as the profit surpluses in earlier graphic presentations.

If buyers were distributed uniformly over an entire city area, there would be no differences in rent. Sites would everywhere have about the same advantages, and demand curves would be similarly placed relative to cost curves. (If the rent given to the land for other, say residential, purposes were included in the cost curve, the demand and cost curves would be tangent to each other.) It is the concentration of buyers in particular districts and on certain streets or corners, and the relative scarcity of sites in these places, which establishes the demand curves for the services there provided in a position further to the right than elsewhere, and gives to each particular site the surplus for which it is responsible.

We must guard against an inaccuracy in conceiving of the differences in rent as measuring simply differences in the volume of business afforded by each site. This would be true only if the product were differentiated in no other way than spatially and if prices throughout the area were uniform. Rent would then constitute an exact measure of the economies of large-scale production, for the sites affording the largest markets would be more valuable only if, and to the degree that, this larger volume could be produced at a lower cost per unit. It would be this amount which the landlord could exact and which the competition of business men would put into his hands. In fact, no such conclusion as to the economies of large-scale production can be drawn. Rent is an expression of the relative *advantages* afforded by different sites, and these advantages are dependent only in part on relative volumes of business. Other factors are the prices which can be charged, and the type of business which can best be conducted on the location.

As has been argued in Chapter V, there is no *a priori* reason for believing that prices will be the same throughout a retail areaunless the distribution of buyers is a random one. Wide differences in sales volume are evidence enough that it is not a random one quantitatively. Neither is it qualitatively: the customers of any one store are not in general a random sample of the whole body of purchasers. Near Harvard Square students predominate; near Central Square, workers; in the shopping district, women. Such factors may or may not lead to price variations. Each merchant must decide for himself whether his profits will be greater by setting a high, a moderate, or a low level of prices for his goods. To the degree that the site dictates the policy to be followed, the larger or smaller profit it thus makes possible will be reflected in the rent.

In addition to this price factor, all the other types of differentiation are present at the same time and have their effect upon rent. The quality of goods sold in different districts varies over a wide range with the class of trade, and various types of merchandising methods bear no resemblance to each other. Furthermore, the product may change qualitatively as the scale of production changes. A large department store offers, among other things, a wider variety of choice within any class of goods than the smaller shop. It also sells convenience in a different sense from that already considered, through providing for many kinds of purchases under one roof. These are not economies of large- as compared with small-scale production *of the same thing*, but changes in the product itself. No conclusions with regard to the economies of large-scale production can be drawn in the retail field without reckoning with these factors of variations in price and quality.

Qualitative variations in the type of retail service provided — the "product" — mean variations in cost curves, and such variations are determined in part by the location of the site in question. In so far as they are so determined, they are a factor entering into the determination of its rent. To sum up the theory simply: each site tends to be put to the use whereby it will yield the maximum total return over the costs involved in utilizing it. These costs include, among other things, such returns in the form of profits as are necessary to attract business ability. The differential remaining, which is due to the superiority of the profit-making opportunities afforded by one site as compared to another, is rent, and is put into the hands of the landlords by the competition of entrepreneurs for the best opportunities.

APPENDIX E

SOME ARGUMENTS IN FAVOR OF TRADE–MARK INFRINGE-MENT AND "UNFAIR TRADING"

THE analysis of patents and trade-marks in Chapter IV leads to the conclusion that the protection of trade-marks from infringement and of business men generally from the imitation of their products known as "unfair trading" is the protection of monopoly. To permit such infringements and imitations would be a step towards purifying competition by the elimination of monopoly elements. Reasoning, then, from the premise that competition is good and monopoly bad, the conclusion would be that "unfair" competition (in this sense of the imitation of competitors' goods) ought to be permitted and even encouraged. Let us examine the argument further.

Although trade-mark infringement and unfair trading have a different legal origin, and still may be distinguished technically, the former may, for our purposes, be considered as a type of the latter and the whole discussion brought under a single head. The fundamental rule of law is that no one has the right to pass off his goods as the goods of a rival trader.

The methods whereby this may be attempted are various. The successful name or trade-mark itself inevitably has a host of imitations to contend with. For example, "Gold Dust" was held infringed by "Gold Drop," "Lacto-Peptine" by "Lactopepsine," "Uneeda" by "Iwanta," etc.[1] The Waltham Watch Company was protected against the use of the geographic name "Waltham" by another manufacturer locating in the same city, in such a way as to confuse the two products.[2] Even purely descriptive words or phrases may not be used by one producer where they already have associations with the goods of a competitor "unless accompanied with sufficient explanations or precautions to prevent confusion with the goods of the original manufacturer or vendor."[3] In addition to the imitation of names, labels and packages are imitated in general make-up and appearance, color, size, and shape. The degree of ingenuity which has been displayed in many cases is remarkable, and

[1] For many interesting cases of infringements, with illustrations, see Rogers, *op. cit.*, pp. 123 ff.; Dushkind, *Handbook on Trade-Marks*; and Thomson, *Trade-Marks*. Almost any copy of *Printer's Ink* will contain accounts of one or two cases of unfair trading currently before the courts.

[2] American Waltham Watch Co. *vs.* United States Watch Co., 173 Mass. 85; 53 N. E. 141; 43 L. R. A. 826.

[3] C. A. Briggs Co. *vs.* National Wafer Co., 102 N. E. 87; 215 Mass. 100.

it is a matter of nice discrimination just how far one may go and still keep within the law. There are cases in which it has been held that the shape of the product itself cannot be copied, as with a medicine in tablet form (Cascarets)[1] and padlocks.[2] In Coca-Cola Co. *vs.* Gay-Ola Co.,[3] the defendant was enjoined from copying the artificial color of the plaintiff's beverage when it was demonstrated that the imitation was unnecessary since other colors could equally well have been used.

In all these cases, there can be no question as to what the law is doing. It is preserving, not competition, but monopoly. When one producer copies the name, symbol, package, or product of another, the result is goods more nearly standardized, and, if the imitator is successful, a reduction in the profits of his rival. These profits (in so far as they exceed the necessary minimum) are, as has been shown in Chapter IV, due solely to monopoly elements. For if the goods were *perfectly* standardized, buyers would have no basis for discrimination; one producer could secure no larger volume of sales than another and hence no larger profits (exclusive of rents of land and of superior business ability). They are due to the dissimilarity, not the similarity, of the goods, hence to the monopolistic, not the competitive, elements. They must not be confused with the temporary profits which a producer might earn under pure competition during the interim before competitors appeared, or even for a time afterwards, because of his advantage in being first in the field. These tend to be eliminated; not so with the permanent profits made possible by trade-mark protection. The latter are due, not to the "imperfection" of competition, in that the system does not adjust itself promptly to new conditions; they are due to the permanent "imperfection" (if such it must be called) that it never adjusts itself at all — the law prevents it.

It is interesting to note that competition has no *prima facie* case in court. The right to goodwill is the fundamental legal right, and competition is "tolerated" only as a matter of policy on account of its supposed social benefits.[4] Economically, however, the *prima facie* case is in favor of competition, and (unregulated) monopoly is generally recognized as against the social interest. Exceptions there are, but they are by no means to be taken for granted. Monopolies protected by the patent law, for instance, are often justified on the ground that they stimulate invention. It must now be asked on what grounds, if any, monopolies protected by the law of unfair competition and of trade-marks may be justified.

[1] Sterling Remedy Co. *vs.* Gorey, 110 Fed. 372 (C. C. N. D. Ohio).
[2] Yale & Towne Manufacturing Co. *vs.* Alder, 154 Fed. 37 (C. C. A. 2nd Cir., reversing 149 Fed. 783).
[3] 200 Fed. 720 (C. C. A. 6th Cir.).
[4] Cf. Wyman, *Control of the Market*, Chap. II.

The protection of the law may be regarded as given (*a*) to the producer, or (*b*) to the consumer. Let us consider first the producer. There seem to be no grounds upon which he may justly claim such protection. Given that the consumer is equally satisfied with the goods of two sellers, the entrance of the second into the field must be regarded as the natural flow of capital under competition to check the profits of the first and to adjust the supply of the commodity to the demand for it at cost. Lord Hardwick, in 1742, put it plainly when he declined to enjoin a trader from using another's mark, saying:

> Every particular trader has some particular mark or stamp; but I do not know of any instance of granting an injunction here, to restrain one trader from using the same mark with another and I think it would be of mischievous consequence to do it.
>
> An objection has been made, that the defendant, in using this mark, prejudices the plaintiff by taking away his customers.
>
> But there is no more weight in this, than there would be in an objection to one innkeeper, setting up the same sign with another.[1]

A producer has no right to exclude others from manufacturing and selling the same product, even the *identical* product. He can claim protection only against anyone forging his name, and it seems to be the *theory* of the law that he be protected only in this respect. The Court in Ball *vs.* Broadway Bazaar [2] defined a trade-mark as "any sign, mark, symbol, word or words which indicate the *origin* or ownership of an article *as distinguished from its quality*, and which others have not the equal right to employ for the same purposes." Legal cases and text books agree that the function of the trade-mark is to show origin, to identify. The question is, where does identification leave off and differentiation begin? There would be *mere* identification, without further differentiation of product, in the case of two competing goods, identical in every respect, — as to color, shape and design, labels, marks and names, everything excepting only an inconspicuous identification mark or the name and address of the producer. Obviously "protection" which went no further than this would have no economic value to the producer, for it would mean no more to the buyer than does the slip found in a container (and which identifies perfectly), "Packed by No. 23." Except where the buyer deals directly with the seller, as in retail trade, and where personal relations therefore enter in, origin is of absolutely no significance to him *except* as it indicates quality. The purchaser of "Lux" probably does not even know that it is made by Lever Brothers Company, to say nothing of caring

---

[1] Cited in Rogers, *op. cit.*, p. 272. Rogers regards this as an indication of the lax development of the "judicial conscience" at the time.

[2] 194 N. Y. 429; 87 N.E. 674. (Italics mine.) See also G. W. Cole Co. *vs.* American Cement & Oil Co., 130 Fed. 703 (C. C. A. 7th Cir.)

whether it is or not. If the identical product were made by another company, put up in the same box and given the same name so as to guard against his being foolishly deluded, he would be equally ready to take it. The name stands for a certain quality, a certain product, not a certain producer, and to permit only one producer to use the name is to grant him a monopoly of this product. The law does vastly more than to identify.

Let us turn to the consumer. It will be said at once that trade-marks are necessary in order to protect him against deception and fraud. If producers were free to imitate the trade-marks, labels, packages, and products of others, no one would have any incentive to maintain the quality of his goods, for they would inevitably be imitated by inferior products at lower prices, put up to look identical. It is evident at once that, in fields where differentiation is possible, the consumer needs legal protection against inferior quality. The law of trade-marks and unfair trading safeguards him by putting a premium on differentiation and protecting the monopolies thereby established. Equally effective, however, would be a policy of permitting imitation provided only it were perfect, or of defining standards of quality by law. The former is, perhaps, condemned by its impracticability. The latter, however, has large possibilities, especially in the case of staples, where trade-marks and brands are patently useless so long as quality is assured. The consumer is defrauded only if goods actually different are deceptively similar. So long as he is able to recognize a variety of product, a package, or a mark, and to know that it is of the same quality as others like it, he is fully protected.

A final argument in favor of trade-mark protection might be that it stimulates variety and hence gives the consumer a wider choice. This is desirable, to be sure, but within limits. The question is one of weighing variety at a higher price against a more uniform product at a lower one, and theory affords an answer neither as to how far differentiation will "naturally" be carried, nor as to how far it should be carried. (The fact that it *is* carried to a certain point is no indication that this is in accord with the wishes of consumers, for producers are prevented by the law from directing resources freely into the channels where a strong demand is creating large profits.) However, in so far as individual initiative would be checked in the creation of variety by allowing perfect duplication, there is reason to believe that such a check would not be without advantages. Since less monopoly could be created, there would be less attention given to trying to create it and correspondingly more to production. There might be fewer "business" men and more laborers. Useless differentiation would be discouraged. Complete standardization would not follow, for the consumers' desire for variety would still have its natural effect in guiding production. As to innovations, there would still remain the possibility of a patent for a limited period if a new idea were significant enough, and, in any case, the "enterprise" profit accruing temporarily to the first producers in any field before competitors have had time to appear. If this were insufficient, the exclusive use of a trade-mark might be granted for a limited period, under the same principle as that of the patent law, say for five years, after which anyone could make the identical product, and call it by the same name. The wastes of advertising, about which economists have so often complained, would be reduced, for no one could afford to build up goodwill by this means, only to see it vanish through the unimpeded entrance of competitors. There would be more nearly equal returns to all producers and the elimination of sustained monopoly profits. All in all, there would be a closer approach to those beneficent results ordinarily pictured as working themselves out under "free competition."

APPENDIX F

THE DEFINITION OF SELLING COSTS

THE analysis of Chapter VI, which aims to distinguish selling costs from costs of production and to refine the distinction, is, I believe, correct in the main; but it is inadequate, and thus misleading, by its failure to recognize clearly and to discuss one of the main issues, *viz.*, that of distinguishing between selling costs and costs of *changing* the product.

Several definitions of selling costs are given,[1] and they all involve the creation or shifting of demands for products. One might say that a *given* product always seems to be tacitly assumed (there are constant references to "a product," "the product," etc.); and if the product were actually a *datum*, there could indeed be no problem of changing it, and hence no problem either of the costs of change.

However, when the variability of the product is recognized, (as it must be), possible confusion arises from the fact that *changing* it in general changes the demand for it (since it is then a *different* product). To point out that an expenditure "changes the demand," therefore, does not necessarily establish that it is a selling cost. On the contrary, if an expenditure shifts the demand curve to the right, it remains an open question (so far) whether the expenditure has resulted in a new product for which there is a stronger demand (and is therefore a production cost for the new product) or whether it has merely increased the demand for the old one (and is therefore a selling cost of the latter). Indeed the possibility appears that it may quite arbitrarily be regarded as either the one or the other. This is the primary matter which needs looking into.

The product as an economic variable has been discussed in limited degree in the present volume, and much more at length elsewhere.[2] Here there need only be recalled the broad sense in which the word "product" is used.[3]

The issue with which we are concerned may be illustrated by the well-worn example of the "fins" on American automobiles. Are they a part of the cost of *producing* an automobile with fins, or are they a cost of *selling* an automobile which is conceived as being without fins?

---

[1] Pp. 117, 123, and 125.

[2] See esp. "The Product as an Economic Variable," Essay 6 in *Towards A More General Theory of Value*, or *Quarterly Journal of Economics*, February 1953.

[3] See above, pp. 71–72, 78, and *passim*.

It is a common practice, especially among English writers on this subject, to speak critically of the supposedly more superficial aspects of product differentiation, and to relegate all expenditures of this sort to the category of selling costs. Thus Kaldor includes among selling costs "excess expenditures" (whatever that is) "on quality and on more variety, 'style' costs, costs of expensive package, and so forth." [4] This position seems utterly indefensible. What is "excess" quality anyway? — Simply more than Mr. Kaldor or someone else thinks necessary? And as for fancy packing are we to call it a selling cost merely because it is "fancy"? Why is the cost of gift-wrapping an article bought as a gift, a selling cost, whereas wrapping another article in brown paper is not? As for style, are we to say that any expenditures upon clothing beyond those necessary to produce a minimum "utility" suit or woman's dress is a selling cost? What seems to be involved is simply a general antipathy to any expenditure which goes beyond what might be called "basic engineering." [5] Furthermore everyone's judgment on such matters will be different. Many people may even like and be willing to pay for what Mr. Kaldor calls "excess" quality. The camel on the package of cigarettes no doubt plays its part in "selling" the product, but if we call it a selling cost there is no stopping place. The cellophane around the package too may be called advertising — in fact it has been by many. Even the package itself may be advertising. It is indeed a possible example of "fancy packaging," since many cigarettes are on occasion sold individually without package at all.

In a restaurant the cost of preparing and serving a meal seems clearly to be a cost of production. But is the bill of fare, considered as information, production or selling? And what if it is printed as an advertisement in a newspaper? Where do costs of production end and costs of selling begin?

It seems quite possible by such examples to be led to the conclusion that the boundary line is entirely arbitrary. Indeed Mr. Kaldor is one who holds that it is. "No sensible distinction can be drawn,"

[4] "The Economic Aspects of Advertising," *Review of Economic Studies,* Vol. XVIII (1959–50), p. 24. Mr. Kaldor's article deals with many aspects of advertising beyond those which are considered here, and is "must" reading for anyone interested in the general subject.

[5] In the same way there is certainly an adverse "value judgment" in the usual discussion of information as afforded by advertising. Although generally defended within limits and with qualifications, what is in mind seems to be mainly "technical" information. Yet the fact that a certain prominent athlete or movie star smokes a certain brand of cigarettes is just as much *information* as statements about the quality of the tobacco or the filter — and it may be much more important to the buyer.

he says.[6] At one extreme, all costs could be looked upon as selling costs, since they all have the effect of raising the demand curve. The example he gives is that "every lump of coal on its way from the bottom of a mine in Durham to a drawing-room in London is continuously 'shifting its own demand curve' upwards or to the right as it travels along." But this is ridiculous, and I think the example is even well designed to reveal where the error lies. If the coal car *really* pushed its demand in front of it, it would do so no matter in what direction it was going — away from London as well as towards London. In other words the reason why the coal car is headed for London is that the demand for coal is already there. It does not create the demand — it goes to meet the demand. The cost of shipping the coal is a cost of production, not of selling. More generally, the cost of producing a product does not automatically create the demand for it. If it did, no one would ever go bankrupt for lack of a market. The conclusion must be that all production costs can *not* be regarded alternatively as selling costs. It is a conclusion of the utmost importance, for it bars disposing of the category of selling costs by simple demonstration that it is meaningless: that *all* costs are in some sense costs of selling.

It is, nevertheless, true and consistent with this that there is a sense in which all selling costs may be regarded as costs of production. The costs of televising a baseball game paid by a brewing company which offers the spectacle free to all (in the United States) would seem to be advertising, and so a selling cost without question. On the other hand, it might be regarded simply as the cost of production of a television program — e.g. in England, where (I understand) television entertainment has for years been paid for as such by a system of taxes on the owners of television sets; and other methods of marketing such entertainment are clearly conceivable.

In the same way, an advertisement for Camel cigarettes on a billboard might be regarded as a product, provided free of charge of course, and conferring upon everyone the privilege of looking at it as he drives past. To be sure, it is a product that nobody wants, but a product none the less. In a similar way, all advertising and selling activity may be regarded as producing "products" or services of some kind (which, if offered separately for sale as such might bring prices ranging from substantially above cost to zero or even negative amounts).

How, then, are we to distinguish between costs of production *tout court*, and costs of selling (recognizing at the same time, as we must, that the latter too may be regarded as the cost of producing *some-*

[6] "Economic Aspects," p. 22.

thing)? The criterion which I propose is one to be got from the market itself. The question is simply: what does the buyer buy, and what does the seller sell? Exactly what is it that is the subject of the "contract"? Viewed in this way a line of distinction is clearly indicated: everything that goes along with the product when it is sold (including services), and makes up what we might call the "package" which passes from seller to buyer, is included in the product, and its cost is a cost of production. Outlays on items separate from this "package," and separately distributed, are selling costs.

By this criterion, the television program in the United States is clearly a selling cost. It is distributed independently, so that many people who receive it do not buy the beer, and many people who buy the beer do not receive the television program. The menu on the table in the restaurant is a cost of production, but posted on the window for the benefit of those outside, it becomes a selling cost. The camel on the package of cigarettes is a cost of production because everybody gets one, but on the billboard it is not. The cellophane, the package, and in general, "excess" quality, fancy packing, and style are all clearly a part of the product by this definition.

Such a criterion is certainly not arbitrary; and it has the merit of being realistic and in accord with common sense, avoiding for instance the absurdity of saying, in the beer example, that the "product" consists in a bottle of beer plus a fraction of a television program. Since there is a border line, there will naturally be borderline cases; but to recognize difficulties in applying the principle to particular examples is a vastly different thing from saying that all is arbitrary and that there is no principle, so that the distinction between production and selling costs vanishes.

Borderline cases reduce for the most part to questions of exactly what it is that the buyer buys — what is he offered *as a buyer* which he would not be offered otherwise?

Advertising seems clearly to be ruled out here, since it is offered generally, and not merely to those who buy. It is consistent with this that those who do buy pay in the price of the product enough to cover selling costs on the average; the point is that they do not have to pay in order to get the advertising, and that others who do not pay may get it (in both cases, whether they want it or not): it is therefore not a part of the "contract." It should be noted that advertising is ruled out whether or not the services in question, e.g., the television program, might be marketed separately at a profit.[7]

---

[7] Thus it departs from Mr. Kaldor's suggested definition of selling costs (one of several, not wholly consistent with each other) as the costs of those "products" or services which would not pay their way if sold separately (Kaldor,

Turning attention then to the "contract" itself, questions of exactly what it is that the buyer buys arise only for the reason that products (and services) are actually composites which may be broken down (at least analytically) into parts almost indefinitely, so that the individual buyer almost inevitably buys or at least pays for elements in the composite which he would rather not have. He may or may not succeed in avoiding them. He will succeed where he has the option of refusing the elements in question at the moment of purchase. A simple example would be credit and delivery in retail trade wherever these services are provided to all if they wish them, but may be refused by those who prefer to pay cash, and carry their purchases with them. But he will not succeed where the elements in question are incorporated into the product and cannot be separated from it. So it is with the tail fins. The ones on my own car seemed to me particularly ugly when I bought it (and they still do); yet I liked the car for other reasons, and bought the fins along with it because there was no alternative.

Both these cases have in common with that of advertising, that buyers as a group are being "assessed" for a share of the global cost of something which they may not want, and are precluded from obtaining exactly what they do want at an appropriately adjusted figure. However, the elements in question are being offered *only to buyers*, and therein lies the important distinction from advertising.

It should not be overlooked that the case may also be put in reverse: many buyers might like to have (and be willing to pay for) elements in the composite product which are *not* offered to them. They might, for instance, prefer to have credit and delivery service at a shop where they must pay cash and carry the purchase themselves; but where they trade for other reasons, such as convenience, superior quality, and so on. Of course, in so far as it is practicable, parts of the product may be sold separately with a corresponding adjustment in price (an extra charge for delivery, for instance); and in so far as this is done, the general problem is diminished in importance.[8] The adaptation of "products" by different sellers to the gen-

---

"Economic Aspects," page 23, last sentence). Such an approach begs the whole question of waste: selling costs are made wasteful *by definition*.

[8] Mr. Kaldor identifies the divisibility of all products and the separate pricing and sale of each element in this way with "perfect" competition ("Economic Aspects," p. 3), holding that "if they happen to be sold together, the price of the whole could never be different from the sum of the prices of its parts," a proposition which evidently rests heavily upon the absence of economies of scale. One can only marvel at the magical quality which can be infused into economics by merely "assuming perfect competition," especially when, as with Mr. Kaldor, economies of scale are made to disappear also by waving the wand of perfect divisibility-without-loss-of-efficiency.

eral demand for "variety" should also not be overlooked. (Thus some shops will sell for cash and others offer credit, etc.) But the fact remains that the experience of finding on the market a product or service which is *exactly* what the individual buyer wants in every detail must be a rare one indeed. What we typically find, to meet the actual diversity of wants, is a standardized product, cheaper because of economies of scale, but corresponding only imperfectly to what is wanted by any particular buyer. This principle of compromise between economies of scale on the one hand and the demand for variety on the other is a familiar one in the theory of the product as a variable.[9]

The broad meaning of the word "product" in the general analysis must be constantly borne in mind; in the above discussion credit and delivery must be considered as simple illustrations to cover the whole spectrum of product variations.

The fact that buyers may get different products at the same price, so that some get more than others (as with delivery), has often been mentioned as a mild form of discrimination — a rough equivalent of getting the *same* thing at *different* prices. No doubt there is a failure of prices to correspond with precision to costs, but it should be recognized that this failure is very general. For example, in retail trade, buyers purchase a different amount of convenience with every variation in their distance from the product, and again the argument is very general, applying as it does to "economic" as well as to geographical distance. The problem is evidently a highly complex one, but new light is certainly thrown upon it by the recognition that few people either (1) get exactly what they want, or (2) pay exactly the cost of producing it for them. In this area there is clearly room for discussion as to (1) just what it is that the buyer gets and (2) just what it is that he pays for it — hence for borderline cases.

A question might be raised as to certain types of advertising which add prestige to a product, or which in one way or another lead to greater appreciation on the part of those who buy it and own it. Although it is the result of advertising, such added "utility" might be considered a part of the product and therefore a cost of production in the sense that every buyer gets it, even if some care nothing about it. We seem to have here merely another example of one element of the composite product which the buyer gets even though he would rather not pay for it.

Finally, we may mention a borderline problem possibly arising out

---

[9] For further discussion and further consequences of the principle, see "The Product as an Economic Variable," *Towards a More General Theory of Value*, *pasism*, esp. pp. 117–120 and 129–131.

of the fact that a given change in a product may not be worthwhile unless it is advertised (certainly it cannot be advertised unless it is actually made), and that all costs of making the change and telling the public about it may not be clearly allocable. The cost of the tools and dies and labor to put fins on a car is clearly a production cost; and persuading the public that this is what it wants seems clearly a selling cost. But the cost for instance of the time of executives discussing the whole project may be allocated only arbitrarily.

Although borderline problems such as those mentioned may cause concern for certain purposes, it should be noted that the purely technical problems which they raise are easily resolved. Hans Brems has shown [10] that certain problems of product variation may be treated diagrammatically in exactly the same way as selling costs in Figure 22 (page 142) above. For example, assuming a certain "minimum" product, successive expenditures on improving it and so increasing sales may be shown exactly as are selling costs in Figure 22 for the price OF; thereby discovering the "optimum" product for any given price. Similarly, product improvement and selling costs can be *combined* in the same analysis: beginning with a minimum product and no advertising, expenditures may be made on both together, always assuming the best distribution between them and the optimum use of resources generally. When this is done for each possible price, we get a *locus* curve [11] of optimum expenditure on quality improvement *and* selling cost for each price, from which we obtain the best price, and so the optimum for the firm of the *four* variables of selling cost, product, price, and output. Evidently the final result should be the same no matter which way the borderline cases between product variation and selling costs are thrown.

This purely technical result is not surprising, and is evidently quite independent of the discussion above as to the importance of maintaining the distinction between selling costs and costs of production.

[10] See bibliography below, No. 485.

[11] The use of such locus curves and the method of obtaining through them the final solution for several variables is explained in detail at several points above. For the present problem see especially pp. 146–148, where the "solution" of the whole problem is given in words, but not in diagrams. Thus Figure 24 (p. 148) displays merely the "characteristics of the optimum," and not the locus curves which would be used to obtain it. As early as 1934, Mr. Henry Smith developed locus curves under the assumption that advertising costs were subtracted from price, instead of being added to cost. The problem turned out to have unsuspected complications, however. (See Bibliography below, Nos. 373, 491, 1384, 852. My own part in the discussion of these is reproduced in *Towards A More General Theory of Value*, Essay 8, and the complications are discussed esp. pp. 158–159. See also T. H. Silcock, Nos. 1355, 1356.) Attention should also be called to Buchanan's use of the locus curve technique, (No. 487) where the selling costs are, as in my own case, added to production costs.

APPENDIX G

NUMBERS AND ELASTICITIES *

Most economists would I think give ready assent to the general proposition that the larger the number of sellers in a market, the greater the elasticity of demand for each seller. It is the purpose of this appendix to show by a few simple examples that the proposition is true only under certain special assumptions. It is important to realize what these assumptions are, for those who accept it are presumably making them, even though perhaps unconsciously. As a statement of general principle, it is simply not true at all, and only harm can result from its indiscriminate acceptance.

It is well known that the elasticity of a curve at any point is given by the ratio of two segments of a tangent to it at that point: the segment extending to the x axis, divided by the segment extending to the y axis.[1] Thus in Figure 41, the elasticity of DD at P is PA/PB.

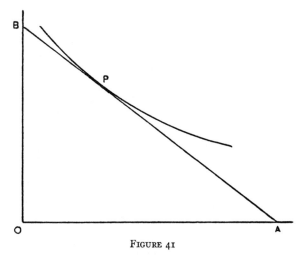

FIGURE 41

This method of measuring elasticity will be used in the early part of this appendix. In fact the simplest procedure is merely to deal directly with a straight line demand curve, whose elasticity by this rule evidently moves from ∞ at the y intercept to unity at its midpoint and on to zero at the x intercept.

* Reprinted with permission from *Festskrift til Frederik Zeuthen*, Copenhagen, 1958.
[1] A proof is given in Marshall's *Principles*, Mathematical Appendix, p. 839.

The most mischievous effect of the principle which is here being challenged is surely to be found in the area of product differentiation,[2] and this phase of the matter will be discussed briefly later on. Our first concern will be to look into the simpler case of a homogeneous product, where it might be thought that the direct correlation between numbers and elasticity was almost axiomatic.

Those who hold for this direct correlation are, perhaps without knowing it, Cournotists in the sense that they are concerned with the elasticity of one seller's demand curve under the assumption that the quantities offered by the other sellers do not change. And even within this Cournot framework they are making the further assumption that the price, and hence the total quantity sold, remains the same as the number of sellers is increased, so that each seller provides a smaller fraction of the fixed total sales. Under these conditions it is true. Thus in Figure 42, where *P* is the mid-point of the

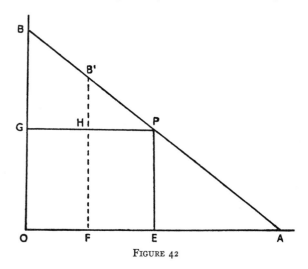

FIGURE 42

straight line demand curve *BA*, and costs of production are assumed absent, if output *OE* is in the hands of one seller, the price will be *EP* and elasticity is *PA/PB*, or unity. If *OE* is divided equally between two sellers, each providing *OF* (= *FE*), and if each takes his rival's supply as a datum, it is as if he ignored that part of the diagram to the left of the dotted line *FB'*, taking *FB'* as the *y* axis for his own calculations. The elasticity of his demand curve at *P* is therefore *PA/PB'*, or 2. Continuing this procedure, it is evident that the

[2] See, for instance, above, pp. 196–199.

elasticity at *P* for any one seller, as *OE* is divided among a larger and larger number, is in this simple example numerically equal to the number of sellers, and so approaches ∞ as their numbers become very large.

Another way to state the same result is in terms of the formula for elasticity, $\varepsilon = pdq/qdp$. In the present example, both p and dq/dp are constants, while q (for the individual firm) approaches zero as the number of firms approaches ∞ · ε therefore approaches ∞.

The result so far, however, has been obtained by holding price, and hence total sales, constant. *EP* is in fact the equilibrium price *only* for one seller, and if we now ask what happens to elasticity of demand for the individual seller *at equilibrium*, the answer is different. The equilibrium for two sellers is shown in Figure 43, where

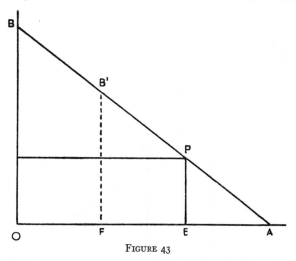

FIGURE 43

$OF = FE = EA$. Each seller supplies OF ($= FE$) and the equilibrium price is *EP*. Elasticity of demand for the individual seller is $PA/PB' = 1$, just as it was for a single seller, and it remains at unity *under equilibrium* as the number of sellers increases, so that its limiting value as the number of sellers approaches ∞ is still unity. Larger numbers do not mean higher elasticities *at equilibrium*, and it would seem that the question of how elasticity behaves at equilibrium would be more important than how it behaves at some particular, and arbitrarily chosen, price.

If we leave Cournot and now shift to the more familiar — and more realistic — assumption of price competition, the answer is still different. In Figure 42, the equilibrium price for a single seller is, as before, *EP*, and $\varepsilon = 1$. But with two sellers, each disposing of *GH* (= *HP*), either one may by a slight reduction in price increase his sales discontinuously from *HP* to *GP*, taking away all of his rival's customers. Since he will sell nothing at a price higher than *EP*, and will sell *GP* at a price infinitessimally lower, we may say that his demand curve is approximately the discontinuous line *GPA*. At the price *EP*, however, since his sales are only *GH*, he is located at *H* rather than at *P*, the segment *HP* representing the finite increment of sales which he gains by an infinitesimal price reduction. Although his actual demand curve has a corner at *P* and intersects the *x* axis at *A*, a "tangent" to it at *H* intersects the *x* axis at ∞. Elasticity at *H* is therefore $\infty/GH = \infty$.

Alternatively, we may refer to the coefficient pdq/qdp, and note that in this case p and q are constants while dq/dp becomes ∞, since $\triangle q$ is constant and finite as $\triangle p$ becomes infinitesimally small. Therefore ε becomes ∞ with only two sellers. For two or any larger number of sellers it is always ∞, and so within this range is independent of numbers.

This second assumption of "price competition" is of course the one often associated with Bertrand and Edgeworth in the history of oligopoly theory, and the moral to be drawn from the different results obtained, as between this assumption and that of Cournot, is not that one is right and the other wrong, but simply that each is correct under its own assumptions.[3] In our present context we may say that these assumptions are reflected in different *definitions* of the demand curve; and since the curve is different in the two cases, its elasticity will naturally be different.

A number of other assumptions are possible,[4] and for illustration, one more may be noted quickly in passing. If each seller assumes that any price adjustment he makes will be followed by his rivals (a variety of "mutual dependence recognized"),[5] his demand curve will at all prices be a constant fraction of the total. Thus in Figure 42, with a straight line curve *BA* for the whole market, if there were

[3] See above, Chapter III, esp. p. 37.

[4] I have always been struck by Professor Zeuthen's highly original and ingenious development of multiple possibilities in Chapter II of his *Problems of Monopoly and Economic Warfare*, and have regularly given attention to it in my own teaching. Especially interesting is his discussion of varying "co-efficients of extension" into the markets of rivals on the one hand and into the "unsatisfied demands" on the other. Most of this analysis, of course, relates not to homogeneous, but to differentiated, products. This line of thought, pioneered by Professor Zeuthen, does not seem to me to have been given the attention it deserves in oligopoly theory.

[5] Above, pp. 46 ff.

two sellers sharing it equally between them, the demand curve for either one alone would be a straight line from B to E and passing through H (not drawn in the figure). No matter how large the number of sellers, as long as this recognition of mutual dependence holds, the elasticity of demand for any one will evidently be unity (under the assumption of straight line curves and no costs, as in Figure 42). The number must be "small," however, for as it increases, the impact upon any one seller of a move by another is lessened until it finally becomes negligible, and the assumption of mutual dependence recognized is no longer valid.[6]

This case makes an interesting contrast with the one immediately preceding. In both cases elasticity is independent of numbers over a certain range. In the present case it has a constant finite value over a range of "small" numbers including one; in the preceding case it has a constant value of ∞ over a range excluding one but including all larger numbers.

In sum, even in the simple case of a homogeneous product there appears to be no valid generalization as to the relation between numbers and elasticity. It is quite illegitimate merely to refer to the limiting cases of one seller (monopoly) and of a "large" number of sellers (pure competition), and to represent all that lies in between as some sort of smooth progression from one extreme to the other. What happens in the intermediate range of oligopoly is of the essence of the problem, and here we cannot escape the fact that a variety of different assumptions is both possible and legitimate. The behavior of elasticity depends on the behavior of the oligopolists. And this "intermediate range" embraces most of the economy.

Turning now to differentiated (or heterogeneous) products, let us first note that the whole character of the problem is transformed analytically. Here, since the product of each seller is different from those of others, there is in the nature of the case only one seller *for each product*. A larger number of sellers simply means a correspondingly larger number of products; and the nature of their interdependence, in so far as it is expressed in the elasticities of their demand curves, is not defined by numbers alone. It follows at once from the recognition of this simple truth that no generalization is possible as to the relationship between the number of sellers in a "group" and the elasticities of their demand curves.

An elementary confusion in this matter is between the *number* of substitutes and their *goodness*. *More* substitutes does not necessarily mean *better* substitutes in a sense which would increase elasticities. It may, of course, but it may just as well not. If every professor of

---

[6] The matter is discussed more fully, pp. 48–50.

economics in the world wrote a textbook, there is no reason to think that the demand curve for any one book would be any more elastic than it is at present (when, let us say, only about half of them do so). Indeed, since each professor might well have, and transmit to his students, some preference for his own text, demands might be less elastic than ever.

As another factor, who is there who has not found it more difficult to choose between twenty items on a menu card than between two? The labor involved in considering separately (or finding out about) each of a large number of competing items is a factor of prime importance very generally. Each buyer is probably able to consider effectively only a very few of them, so that more, although it would redistribute purchases, would not on the whole increase elasticities. Indeed it might well diminish them — the allegiance of the average buyer to some particular seller (product), might be strengthened by the larger number of alternatives he would have to try out in order to make a *rational* change. This must be a familiar phenomenon. Substitutes may be remote not only in the sense of being less good, but also in the sense of being across a threshold of awareness or availability, as in this example. Speaking generally, there could be no automatic effect of "more" substitutes upon elasticities when the fundamental principle is held in mind that substitution is entirely a matter of degree.

The concept of an "atomistic" economy is well known, and so also is its common identification with pure competition, which is surely an egregious error. Of course if the economy were composed of a limited number of homogeneous products, and if the sellers' side of the market for each were "atomized" so that each seller was small and there were many of them, the result would be pure competition. But the real world is a world of heterogeneous products, corresponding to the basic heterogeneity of human preferences. "Atomizing" large producers would in general mean replacing them by a larger number of smaller ones, *each producing his own variety* of product, and thus carrying product heterogeneity further than ever. With diverse human wants, an atomistic economy would necessarily be one of monopolistic, not of pure, competition, as each seller tried to fit himself into the most advantageous "niche" on a scale of "potential" products, corresponding to what is essentially a continuum of demand, analogous to the line along which buyers (and hence sellers) are located in the problem now to be discussed.[7]

It will be instructive to consider the general question of numbers and elasticities in terms of the familiar spatial analogy; and for

[7] See above, Appendix C.

simplicity we may limit ourselves to one-dimensional space — the familiar example of the distribution of sellers on a line (street) along which buyers are assumed to be uniformly dispersed. From conversations (and arguments) with others, including some in high places, I conclude that the view is widely held that, as the numbers of sellers (always equally spaced along the line) increases, so that the intervals between them are smaller, pure competition is approached as the limiting case. But this is easily shown to be untrue.

In the spatial problem all aspects of differentiation are resolved into one — that of convenience — by the assumption that the products of all sellers are identical except for being offered at different locations. A seller at any point on the line is more convenient to those buyers who are near him and less to those farther away. If we assume a general evaluation of convenience at some uniform rate, say a dollar a mile (which might express either cost of transportation (of buyer to product or vice versa) or an evaluation of the disutility of walking), the demand curve for any one seller at some particular point is a straight line whose slope depends on the uniform rate at which distance is valued. *BA* in Figure 44 is such a demand curve for

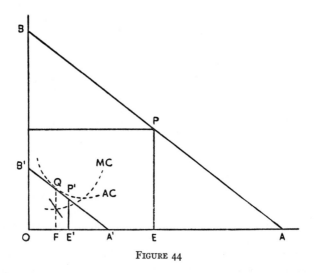

FIGURE 44

one seller, assuming some (arbitrary) total number of sellers, distributed at equal intervals along the line, and if we again assume an absence of cost curves, *EP* is his equilibrium price and *OE* the output. If the number of sellers now increases so that they are closer together, this demand curve for a single seller will move to the left, indicating his smaller market. It may move, for instance, to $B'A'$, so that the equilibrium price for each seller is $E'P'$ (ignoring for the moment the dotted cost curves). But its slope does not change, and elasticity is still unity at the equilibrium point. The number of firms may increase indefinitely, but even as it approaches the limiting value of ∞, elasticity at equilibrium is unchanged at unity. The example evidently involves special assumptions, and does not therefore prove that in the *general* case elasticity is *independent* of numbers. But since elasticity remains constant in this case, it does prove that larger numbers, with sellers "closer together," does not necessarily increase elasticities.

An objection may be raised that as sellers move "closer together," buyers will come to ignore the differences between them, so that the assumed valuation of distance at the fixed rate of a dollar a mile would no longer hold true. Now for those who wish to salvage pure competition at all costs, it is tempting to seize upon any argument, like this one, which appears to help. There are, however, several answers to it.

The argument may, perhaps unconsciously, confuse a decline in the *amount* of the "payment" as distance is less, with a decline in the *rate*. As for this latter, if it were true that for some reason people came to value distance at a lower *rate,* say one cent a mile instead of a dollar a mile, this would indeed represent a movement towards pure competition. But not so if, with sellers closer together, they valued it at one cent per 1/100 of a mile, which is no change in *rate* at all.

Again, the *uniform* rate is admittedly arbitrary. Actually, transportation rates may taper with distance because of terminal and other overhead costs. Or, the rate of disutility (of walking) may increase with distance because of accumulated fatigue; it may also decrease with distance within short ranges because of an initial inertia to be overcome in getting started at all, etc., etc. But such considerations do not lead to a discontinuous break to a *zero* rate for short distances.

Furthermore we are not concerned solely with rational calculations and measurements, but with market behavior, including the irrational as well. If people impulsively drop into the nearest shop (or buy the first product offered them without looking further), they are for our purposes putting a value on "distance." There is plenty of evidence that small distances are not in fact ignored. A simple example is that of the higher value of a location on the corner of two streets as compared to one next to it and hence on only one street. Shops could hardly be closer together than next to each other, and if people paid no attention to short distances, the corner location would not be more valuable.

One may observe finally, that in real life products are differentiated in many dimensions and not merely in the single one of (literal) space. Two shops next to each other in literal space sell products which are differentiated in other ways, either in attributes of the product itself in the narrower sense, or in the circumstances surrounding its sale (which is always a *part* of the product in our use of the word). Thus the identical product in the narrow sense (say the same brand of cigarettes) is not the same at all when sold in different shops. So it is that pure spatial examples exaggerate the possibility of products being *near* to each other. It should also be remarked that if in the case of a certain standard brand (of cigarettes), buyers are *actually* indifferent to other-than-spatial aspects of differentiation in their sale, they typically *do* buy them most conveniently, even though an alternative location is quite near by. They do not *in fact* ignore (spatial) differentiation, when it is slight.

To pass on to other matters, the introduction of a U-shaped average cost curve into the analysis, expressing economies of scale for the individual firm, would by familiar principles bring the movement of the demand curve to the left with larger numbers to a halt at a point where it became tangent to the cost curve. Such a cost curve is indicated by the dotted line AC in Figure 44, with the dotted marginal cost curve MC also drawn in. The intersection of marginal cost and marginal revenue is indicated below the point of tangency Q. It may now be noted that for all portions of the marginal cost curve MC where a tangent to it will cut the base line to the right of O, the elasticity of demand *at equilibrium* will actually *decrease* with larger numbers as the demand curve moves to the left to reach its equilibrium position of $B'A'$. This is a matter of simple geometry which the reader may test for himself by drawing a straight line marginal cost curve which intersects the x axis to the right of O, and observing the elasticities of demand at the outputs given by its intersection with successive marginal revenue curves as the demand curve moves to the left, say from BA to $B'A'$.

A final point in relation to cost curves is that their introduction decisively rules out the conception of increasing the number of sellers "indefinitely." This has been proposed by some under the belief (here held to be erroneous in any event) that if only the process were carried *far enough*, perfect elasticity (i.e., pure competition) would be achieved. Whether the product is homogeneous, as in the first part of this appendix, or heterogeneous, as in the latter part, the equilibrium *number* of sellers in any area of the economy will, assuming easy entry, be dictated in fact by economies of scale (together with the conditions of demand, of course). It is a part of the problem of equilibrium, and in the last analysis not subject to manipulation. One may, of course, under different assumed conditions, vary the numbers of sellers and inquire into the effect on elasticities, as has been done here. But in any given situation numbers are not subject to manipulation except hypothetically.

It is important to realize this, because of the common practice of conceiving the economy as essentially one of pure competition, via the assumption of perfect divisibility. This bit of magic allegedly performs the double service of wiping out economies of scale and providing as many sellers as might be desired by simply making the pieces smaller. It argues in effect that if a monopolist could (without loss of efficiency) be sliced into a thousand parts, each of which would compete with the others (if, like parts of an earthworm, they survived), he would no longer be a monopolist. This is not very illuminating, since if he cannot be so sliced (and without loss of efficiency), he will in fact continue to be a monopolist. Pure competition cannot be achieved by this route.

It has been the purpose of this appendix to show that as a general proposition numbers and elasticities are not positively correlated. Even with a homogeneous product, different assumptions give different results; and with product heterogeneity the relationships involved are still less subject to generalization. Finally, the introduction of cost curves makes the number of sellers a phase of the definition of equilibrium, and hence not subject to manipulation.

APPENDIX H

THE ORIGIN AND EARLY DEVELOPMENT OF
MONOPOLISTIC COMPETITION THEORY *

I. INTRODUCTION

THE purpose of this appendix is to say something about the more ultimate origins and influences contributing to the development of this book, first as a thesis [1] in 1927, and then in published form in 1933. Its relationship to the literature of the intervening period, in particular that of the controversies over increasing returns and the representative firm, will also be commented upon.

Information of this kind about a book ordinarily appears in greater or less detail in the preface, and if I had had any idea of subsequent developments, it would surely have been given in my own preface in 1933. This latter was in fact limited to a few general statements and a mere mention of the intermediate thesis stage, with acknowledgments of the help of several colleagues and especially that of Professor Allyn Young, under whose direction the thesis was written. The objective now (thirty-four years later!) is to spell out more fully the "intellectual history" of the book — to fill in a gap, the importance of which is, willy-nilly, attested by the fact that its very existence has led so many to fill it in (all wrong) by inference.

I have frequently been asked about the remoter origins of the theory, and have had in mind for some time saying something in print about them, but, although the spirit has been willing, the flesh was weak. The catalyst which finally brought action was an article on "The Erosion of Marshall's Theory of Value," by Mr. Peter Newman in the *Quarterly Journal*, November 1960 (although the particular issues there discussed are a small part of the whole subject taken up here). Mr. Newman describes how "Marshall's theory of value . . . was attacked vigorously and effectively soon after his death," and how "a new doctrine — the theory of imperfect competition — [rose] from the ashes." [2] The truth of the matter is that *Monopolistic Com-*

* Reprinted from the *Quarterly Journal of Economics*, November 1961.

[1] An account of the thesis as distinct from the book is of some interest because the former was not merely a manuscript put away in a drawer, but a bound volume in the Harvard University Library, freely available to all, including visiting scholars, etc. Library records show that it was in fact extensively consulted during the period 1927–1933, as well as later and down to the present time.

[2] *Op. cit.* p. 587. From later references to oligopoly and product differentia-

petition appeared at the particular time it did for reasons quite un-related to the "attack" in question and to the controversies on the laws of returns and the representative firm, mostly in the *Economic Journal*, which preceded chronologically the publication of the book in February 1933.

(It was unrelated also, in spite of frequent statements and a widespread impression to the contrary, to conditions of depression, either in postwar England or post-1929 United States. Mrs. Robinson writes: "The experience of slump conditions in the interwar period, which gave rise to Mr. Keynes's theory of employment, also led to drastic modifications in the orthodox theory of prices," i.e., to the "new type of analysis" which is "imperfect competition." [3] The fact is that *The Theory of Monopolistic Competition* was written at the height of "Coolidge prosperity," and is without reference to any particular period of business, either good or bad.)

Mrs. Robinson's *Economics of Imperfect Competition* appeared some months later in the year, as indicated by the reference to *Monopolistic Competition* in her Foreword; [4] and from the "intellectual history" of that book, which she spells out in some detail, it is clear that it was hers which, in Newman's phrase, "rose from the ashes" of the attack on Marshall. *Monopolistic Competition* was in fact quite outside the movement described by Newman, and regarded by him as so much responsible for the "success" of the new theories, as well as for their now "increasingly baroque appearance" (*sic*). Indeed, if monopolistic competition theory rose from the ashes of anything, it was twelve years earlier (1921), and the ashes were those of the Taussig-Pigou controversy as to whether "charging what the traffic will bear" in railway rates was to be explained in terms of monopolistic discrimination or in terms of joint costs.

II. Early Origins in Railway Rate Theory: Oligopoly

In 1921, as a graduate student at the University of Michigan, I took a course in Railway Transportation under Professor I. L. Sharfman, and wrote a course paper on the Taussig-Pigou controversy over railway rates. The conclusions reached were exciting to me, and they must have been to Professor Sharfman also, for I well remember that on his own initiative, he sent the paper to the *Quar-*

---

tion, as well as from the general context, it is clear that he is following a familiar practice of using imperfect competition in a broad sense to include monopolistic competition as well.

[3] *An Essay on Marxian Economics* (London: Macmillan, 1947), p. 73.

[4] London: Macmillan, 1933.

terly Journal of Economics from whence it was returned, no doubt with highly relevant comment to the effect that it needed more cultivation both intensive and extensive. Meanwhile, the paper has been lost (or mislaid), but perhaps even more important than the paper is a long footnote in the thesis (1927), evidently drawn from it and indicating clearly how the conclusions there reached served as a lead to further examination of the theoretical relationship between monopoly and competition.

The footnote is quoted below in full:

The distinction between pure competition and monopolistic competition has been of service to the writer in trying to reach a judgment of the Taussig-Pigou controversy over joint cost in the railway industry, and he suggests herewith a "compromise" solution. The gist of the argument is found in the *Quarterly Journal of Economics*, Feb., 1913, p. 378; May, 1913, p. 535; August, 1913, p. 687. A fuller statement of Prof. Taussig's case is in the same publication, July, 1891, p. 438, entitled "A Contribution to the Theory of Railway Rates"; of Prof. Pigou's in *Wealth and Welfare*, Chapter XII, and *The Economics of Welfare*, Chapter XV.

The issue is, simply, whether coal and copper are charged different rates in railroading because of monopoly or of joint cost, Prof. Pigou holding the former, Prof. Taussig the latter. Prof. Pigou states his argument thus: "If there are a number of competing sellers supplying transportation or anything else to several markets with separate demand schedules, and if the price in one of these markets is higher than in the other, it is necessarily to the interest of each individual seller to transfer his offer of service from the lower-priced market to the higher-priced market; and this process must tend ultimately to bring the prices in the different markets to a uniform level." (*Economics of Welfare*, p. 265) The reasoning is convincing where the market for each type of service is a *purely* competitive one so that competition takes the form of changing the *amounts* offered in each case. We believe, with Prof. Pigou, that unequal charges for coal and copper are due to monopoly.

But a very slight element of monopoly, through changing the processes of competition, will support Prof. Taussig's conclusion. Where producers *set prices* instead of *changing amounts*, it is not clear that they would *lower them* in the higher-priced market, and that the joint, or common, costs will be shared equally by the two commodities. In fact, it is impossible, logically, to show that they would. This argument is developed in detail later, especially pages 221 ff., and cannot easily be rendered into a condensed and at the same time convincing, statement here. [The reference is to a discussion of the "mutual dependence recognized" solution of oligopoly, ending with the following: "Under monopolistic competition it is impossible to eliminate from the calculations of any seller consideration of what his competitors are likely to do in response to his move, for the very simple reason that *what they do is a direct result of what he does*. The contrast with pure competition on this point is fundamental."]

Competition will force a single price in each market (a single rate for each commodity), so that inevitably each seller participates in all of them. He cannot secure an increased share in the more profitable market by offering a lower price, for his competitors will follow at once, and relative shares will be the same as before. He, therefore, sets such prices in each market as will make his total return a maximum, and, in doing so, he will take account of the strength of the demand in each case, charging "what the traffic will bear." If the total returns to each seller are large, there will be more sellers, rather than a readjustment of their price policies.

The writer is by no means convinced that all monopoly elements should be removed from the price system, — that rates should be uniform per ton mile *because* this would result under pure competition. If elements of monopoly are "natural" and inevitable, as in railroading, a case can be made for a price system which takes cognizance of them.[5]

A clarifying comment on the quotation is necessary because of the stricter definition of pure competition in the thesis (1927) than in the book (1933). In the former it was held that *any* price differences, even momentary, between units of a homogeneous product in the same market were incompatible with *pure* competition, so that *quantity* adjustments were the only ones possible.[6] "Setting prices" was possible only if the products are different or sold in (perhaps only momentarily) different markets.[7]

The "very slight element of monopoly" which would "support Taussig" was therefore the slight differentiation which would permit price adjustments, and which, combined with small numbers, would call for "mutual dependence recognized," thus checking any action of sellers towards destroying a discrimination which was mutually profitable. (Incidentally, this seems to me even now (1961) to be a valid theoretical explanation of charging what the traffic will bear in cases, of which railroading is a good example, where the number of sellers, if not one, is at least small.)

---

[5] Thesis, pp. 193–195.

[6] This strict interpretation of pure competition in terms of quantity adjustments only, later relaxed in my own case (cf. above, pp. 35–36 and accompanying footnote; see also pp. 42, 50), was in fact strictly maintained by Stackelberg (*Marktform und Gleichgewicht*; Berlin, J. Springer, 1934; see also Fellner, *Competition Among the Few*; New York: Knopf, 1949; p. 101). Hence it was that in the thesis, Edgeworth was considered a case of product differentiation (or "differentiated oligopoly"); but not in the book.

[7] In strict accuracy, it should be said that *price* adjustments, with mutual dependence *ignored*, were also held to be consistent with pure competition, *in the special case* that either seller could supply the entire market alone. In this case he would evidently gain (temporarily) by taking over the entire market at a (slightly) lower price, *and without creating a price difference*, since the other would make no sales at all. See thesis, pp. 74, 76.

It should be said further that the argument given as "supporting Taussig" is in fact not Taussig's at all. His position certainly confused joint costs (in the sense of fixed proportions) with mere overhead, or common costs. In the latter, as Pigou rightly pointed out, the proportions are not fixed, so that the true explanation of "charging what the traffic will bear" must be not "joint costs," but monopolistic (or oligopolistic, as held above) discrimination. The argument given as "supporting Taussig" would more correctly be described as "refuting Pigou," except, of course, for the case of pure competition.

(Finally, and parenthetically, the last paragraph of the quotation foreshadows a position definitely taken later on, viz., that monopoly elements are not something to be purged from the economy in favor of perfect competition as the welfare ideal, but that they necessarily play a part in the definition of the ideal itself.) [8]

The entire footnote, which in the thesis refers back, as explained, to the remoter origins of the book, was dropped from the book itself on the ground (as I remember it) that it seemed inadequate as it stood; and the urge to develop further either the special subject of railway rates or that of discrimination was lacking.

Before leaving Ann Arbor in 1922, I remember sounding out my beloved *maître*, Professor Fred M. Taylor, as to what he would think of trying to work out a synthesis between monopoly and competition as a doctor's thesis. He listened with benign attention, and went home to think it over. But the next day I had "Freddie's" honest, and I am sure carefully considered, advice that I had better look for something else.

III. Process, Structure, and Logic

Really serious work on the thesis at Harvard did not begin until "generals" were out of the way in the spring of 1924. The first and most obvious basis for a hybrid theory of monopoly and competition seemed to be that of numbers, with duopoly as an already recognized middle ground between the two extremes; and it is a fact that the "discovery" of what later became the second of the two phases of the

[8] In contrast with Mrs. Robinson, the welfare problem was no part of my original objective at all, and concern with it was at the vanishing point in both thesis and book. See, however, the 5th (1946) and later editions, pp. 214–215, and my *Towards a More General Theory of Value* (New York: Oxford University Press, 1957), Essays 5 and 16. A reference to "waste" (above, p. 109) clearly refers from its context *not* to production at any point to the left of the minimum point on the cost curve, as most often interpreted, but to production short of the "sort of ideal" (pp. 104 and 94).

problem, "product differentiation," arose in part out of trying to reconcile conflicting theories of duopoly, in particular those of Cournot and of Edgeworth. (A vestigial indication of this origin remains above in the paragraph beginning at the bottom of page 3 and carrying over to page 4.) The rather lengthy critical analysis of Edgeworth [9] was a natural by-product of this intensive study. The fact that two solutions with identical demand curves could be so different, merely because of quantity adjustments in the one case and price adjustments in the other, suggested what became a comprehensive inquiry into the descriptions by different writers of the processes by which the equilibrium price came to prevail. Evidently the curves alone do not give the answer. "The curves of demand and supply for a product, by their intersection, define the price at which demand and supply will be equated. But they are void of any explanation as to why the price should settle at that point. . . . Let the question be fairly asked — what will the price be and why?" [10]

The search for the "reason why" was given added impetus by the discovery that with some writers no reason was given at all. A perfect example of this question-begging type of answer is in Henderson, *Supply and Demand*, where, in the statement of the "law" one finds that "When at the price ruling, demand exceeds supply, the price tends to rise. Conversely when supply exceeds demand the price tends to fall." [11] Later what seems to be meant as a proof merely says the same thing over again.[12] It should be added that in this early period, I do not remember running across any of the more recent tautological solutions (although they may well have existed). In Henderson, for example, supply and demand are defined in such a way that either one *may* be in excess of the other, and this is clearly the case at any but the equilibrium price. The tautologies are, I believe, a reaction (perhaps unconscious) to the increasing awareness that the "law" in any meaningful sense is actually of only limited applicability. And so its "universality" is again solemnly affirmed in the proposition that supply and demand *must* always be equal because whatever is bought is also sold!

But *revenons à nos moutons*: why? The literature of economic theory was combed for examples of "competitive" markets, and of the logic in each case by which it was argued that, from some price divergent from the equating one, there would be a *movement* towards it. Among the markets analyzed and compared were those of Mar-

[9] Above, pp. 37–43.
[10] *Ibid.*, p. 12.
[11] (London: Nisbet, 1947), p. 18.
[12] *Ibid.*, p. 23.

shall (corn), Boehm-Bawerk (horses), Cournot (mineral water), Davenport (hats), Chapman (tea), Wicksteed (damson plums); and the general reasonings of dozens of others from Mill and Cairnes to J. M. Clark and Veblen.

In this excursion into market processes, among the most stimulating and provocative was that of J. M. Clark, and his paradoxical conclusion that "the retarded action of the market which permits different prices to prevail at the same time is not really an 'imperfection,' as theoretical economics has been inclined to regard it. On the contrary, it is an essential requirement, without which it could not produce its characteristic effects." [13] Must it really be said then that *imperfection* is necessary to make *any* market, even a *perfect* one, work? And if so, where does that leave us? The answers to these questions are surely to be found only in pure logic, and not in any appeal to real markets, since *all* of these latter we know to be imperfect in some degree. My own conclusion came to be that the argument was valid only in that happy hunting ground of paradoxes, the theory of oligopoly, and that *logically* large numbers were sufficient to produce both price *movements* and competitive results, without any retarded action or similar phenomena.[14] This would not deny, of course, that time lags, space lags, etc. do play an important part in the functioning of many actual markets; but it would deny that this was *necessary* or even *possible* if the market were perfectly competitive.

In the thesis substantial space was given, as indicated above, to a critical and comparative analysis of the markets and market processes of others, but only a small part of this detail remained in the book. Out of this whole phase, however, together with study of the fragmentary literature of duopoly at the time and intensive reading in the literature of business economics on how prices are made (to be noted below) came a number of the critical distinctions, as between: pure and perfect competition, numbers and differentiation as two distinct *kinds* of monopoly elements, quantity vs. price adjustments, direct and indirect influence, various *types* of certainty and uncertainty, short- and long-run interest in the market, time lags with and without recontract, and so on.

With regard to time lags, it may be noted that they were treated in the thesis as a species of differentiation: just as there might be a separation of sellers or (buyers) in space, the same was true in time. And so the concept of "temporal differentiation" appears repeatedly

[13] *The Economics of Overhead Costs* (University of Chicago Press: 1923), p. 417.
[14] Above, p. 49n.

in the thesis. It was not carried over to the book, and I have difficulty now in recalling the reason why it was not. My best guess is that it was dropped, as were many other things, in the interest of simplification, in order that the period of production of the book might have some finite end. It seems to me now to belong in the structure, and so to have been an unfortunate omission. Temporal differentiation, unlike spatial differentiation, would be a "one way street"; and, since it would be nullified by "recontract," the latter would have to be ruled out. There would have to be a succession of "final contracts," *exactly as in real life.* Without using the term, the "Note on Deviations from Equilibrium"[15] is an example of what could be called "temporal differentiation."[16] It is clear from what is here said that I should not now hold as I did then that the problem is unrelated to elements of monopoly.

Spatial differentiation as a distinct problem also received more extended development in the thesis than in the book. In particular, a section of Chapter V on "Pure Spatial Competition" contained an analysis in two dimensional space, showing among other things that sellers would first of all move towards concentration at a central point, and then disperse again (setting up, in the particular example given, a perpetual oscillation). In this case an adjustment in the text was made in the post-thesis period.[17] It was recognized that Professor Hotelling had "got there first" with his well-known article in 1929,[18] demonstrating the tendency (in one dimension) for firms, assumed to be initially dispersed along a line, to pile up at the central point, thus putting stability into the otherwise indeterminate problem of duopoly. Accordingly, my own treatment in two-dimensional space was scrapped, and converted (Appendix C) into a refutation of Hotelling's thesis of concentration, by bringing into the picture the evident counter forces working towards dispersion. The general conclusion was that the forces for dispersion begin to operate as soon as there are more than two sellers, and that "for fairly large numbers, the distribution approximates closely the ideal which maximizes the convenience of the buyers."

A further discussion of Hotelling's general thesis that the factor of differentiation generally puts stability into the otherwise indeter-

---

[15] Above, pp. 25–29.

[16] This analysis was carried much further in an article, "An Experimental Imperfect Market," Essay 11 in *Towards a More General Theory of Value.*

[17] Aside from this unique instance, the text of the book remained unaltered *by any post-thesis publications or materials.* (The latest item mentioned in the bibliography was in 1925; see below, p. 306.

[18] "Stability in Competition," *Economic Journal*, XXXIX (March 1929).

minate solution of duopoly was added to Appendix A,[19] where it was held that the thesis was invalid and that the stability in Hotelling's example was otherwise accounted for.

Perhaps the most important (and unexpected) subject to be omitted from the book after having been discussed at some length in the thesis was a section of Chapter V (24 pages) on "The Productivity Theory of Distribution." [20] It was omitted in 1933, again as a part of the process of simplification, in order to confine the book to the problem of value (in the narrower sense), without adding what appeared at the time to be an unfinished section on the more general problem of distribution. (See last paragraph of Chapter VII.) I believe that anyone reading Chapter VIII now, and noting the date at which it was added, would naturally assume that it was written after 1933 with the main purpose of rebutting Mrs. Robinson on some matters of definition of the marginal product, and in particular on the doctrine of exploitation. Of course, some of the material, and obviously most of the references, were added later. Yet, without using the word exploitation (and naturally without my knowing that any issue would ever arise over it), it contained in 1926 the principle of marginal revenue product (called marginal value product) and the principle, developed in detail, with diagrams, that the hired factors can get only their marginal value products under monopolistic competition, and that this is consistent with minimum profits for the entrepreneur. It contained also a fully developed envelope curve analysis, with diagrams, of the *long-run* cost curve with all factors variable (described as the one usually in mind in the thesis — see above, page 21, note 1), and a family of curves within it, tangent at any point, and obtained by allowing only one factor (as labor) to vary from that point while the others were held constant. (Such curves, with only one factor variable, are evidently necessary in order to define the value of marginal product and the marginal value product of the changing factor.) Having used the concept of marginal value product in 1926, I might perhaps lay claim to a place among the goodly company in Mrs. Robinson's Foreword of those who arrived at the concept at about the same time. But alas! I must confess that I found it in Marshall's Mathematical Appendix, Note XIV. Marshall does not draw a diagram, but he gives and discusses

---

[19] Above, pp. 226 ff.

[20] Its inclusion as Chapter VIII dates from the third edition (1938), after an earlier appearance in *Explorations in Economics* (New York and London: McGraw-Hill, 1936). It had also been given as a paper at the meetings of the American Economic Association in December 1933, and summarized in the *American Economic Review*, XXIV (Supplement March 1934).

at some length the algebraic formula.[21] Nor does he give it a name, but his reference to it as "the net product we are seeking" (in the case of monopoly) seems rather touching in retrospect.

IV. "COMPETING MONOPOLISTS" AND THE LITERATURE OF BUSINESS

Out of the comprehensive study of markets described above, there developed also a massive verification and elaboration of the idea, mentioned earlier as stemming from oligopoly theory, of a market for a commodity in the usual broad sense of the word being broken up in some degree into subdivisions so that individual sellers in the same market enjoyed some measure of isolation from each other. Typically the emphasis was still on the larger market, however. "Aside from scattered sentences here and there stating that trademarks, goodwill, convenience, habit, etc., must be taken into account as imperfections, economic literature contains no analysis of the kind here contemplated (i.e., of a market and a product for *each seller*). The usual point of view is that these things merely introduce friction into an otherwise perfect working of competition." [22] There follows the substance of note 2, page 69 of the first edition of the book, in which are mentioned Fisher, Marshall, Dobb, J. M. Clark, and A. B. Wolfe, all of whom (except A. B. Wolfe) refer explicitly to a separate *market* for each seller. There may well have been others, but I did not find them at the time, and find no reference to them in the thesis now. (Among these others might be mentioned Wicksell, who, in his *Lectures on Political Economy*,[23] has a very good brief passage (restricted to retailing), which was, according to Professor Robbins' Introduction, available in 1901 in Swedish. Of course, there were a number of others soon after, beginning with Sraffa in December 1926, some of whom appear in footnotes in the first (1933) and later editions of the book.

The transition from the idea of a competitive "market" in the conventional, broad sense being "broken up," so that each seller might be said to have some "limited," "partial," or otherwise qualified monopoly power, to the idea of a separate market for *each seller* as a monopoly *tout court*, so that the broader problem becomes one of a "group" of competing monopolists, is not an easy one, as has been made all too clear by the history of controversy in this field. It was achieved in my own case by an intensive foray in the thesis into

---

[21] *Principles*, p. 849.
[22] Thesis, p. 100.
[23] English translation (New York: Macmillan, 1934), I, 86–88.

the literature of patents and trade-marks.[24] The starting point was the position taken by Allyn Young in the chapter of which he was the author in Ely, *Outlines of Economics.* " 'Trade-marks, like patents, are monopolies in the strictly legal sense that no one else may use them. But, unlike patents, they do not lead to monopoly in the economic sense of giving control of one sort of business.' By means of a trade-mark a successful business man 'may be able to lift himself above the dead level of competition . . . he is able to obtain what might be called a quasi-monopoly. But because his power to control the price of his product is in general much more limited than that of the true monopolist, and because competition limits and conditions his activities in other ways, his business is more properly called competitive than monopolistic.' " [25] In rebuttal to this forthright statement by Young of the case for dichotomy, the general position was argued at length that there was no difference whatever between trade-marks and patents — perhaps not even in degree: "Each makes a product unique in certain respects; this is its monopolistic aspect. Each leaves room for other commodities almost but not quite like it; this is its competitive aspect." [26] There remains only to apply this general conclusion to the spatial problem and to all other aspects of differentiation, both of the product itself and of the conditions surrounding its sale, and the phrase "monopolistic competition," instead of appearing as a self-contradictory juggling of words, becomes the most elementary common sense. (There were lengthy arguments between Young and myself on the matter, and I am glad to be able to say that, before leaving for London, he told me that he accepted the criticism.)

The recognition of each seller as a monopolist *in the full sense of the word* — as having complete control over the supply of a *distinguishable* product (yet facing substitutes, of course, like any monopolist) — became the key to the whole analysis. There followed the substitution, for the more or less traditionally definite concept of an industry, of the more flexible idea of a "group" of competing monopolists; and the conception of an economic system consisting in a vastly greater number of products — one for each seller (except for the homogeneous output of a purely competitive market). Thus the entry or exit of sellers, in the problem of group equilibrium for instance, carries with it an expansion or contraction in the number of *products* in the whole system instead of merely a change in the number of producers for some given product.[27]

---

[24] Above, pp. 57–64.   [25] Cited above, p. 60.   [26] *Ibid.*, p. 62.

[27] The contrast with Mrs. Robinson's *Imperfect Competition* on this fundamental matter is total, and makes its contribution to almost every one of the

The conception of a market for each seller also reveals a problem of "diversity" far beyond anything that would be possible under pure competition, and beyond anything that would ordinarily be implied by the term imperfect. Under pure competition there could evidently be no diversity whatever on the demand side; and as to cost, diversity only in unit cost itself, size of firm (granted heterogeneity of factors) and possibly age of firm (if not ruled out by other assumptions). Imperfection, although it may be made to include more by definition, has the strong connotation of *general* "frictions," such as imperfect knowledge, irrationality, or immobility, exerting an influence rather evenly over the entire market. But with the recognition of a different product and market for each seller presumptions as to uniformity in *any* sense disappear, and we have diversity: as to prices, demands, new forces with respect to costs and size, products (in all aspects of this broad term, location, personality — including skill and "ability"), nature and degree of inter-firm relationships, market processes, etc., as the most natural and expected result.

In the thesis a great deal more attention was paid to this problem of "diversity" than in the book. Indeed, diversity between firms is recognized as so all-pervasive as to make the conception of demand and cost curves for an "industry," or for any category larger than a firm, fantastic and impossible. This position is maintained in fewer pages, but with equal force in the book.[28]

It is maintained in part because of diversity and because of selling costs, but also even in the simplified case of the "uniformity" assumption, and before selling costs have been introduced. It should be clear that the concept of a *group* equilibrium, even without selling costs, does not necessarily involve the concepts of demand and cost *curves* for the group as an aggregate.[29] It is true that one such

clashes between the two theories. See above, pp. 208 ff. Also, p. 198, n. 2. Mrs. Robinson not only *defined* her "commodity" as homogeneous, but obtained results to which she still adheres by *treating it analytically as if it really were.* (See Essay 16 in *Towards a More General Theory of Value*).

[28] See, for instance, above, pp. 9–10, 82–83, 102–104, 110–116, 149, 172–176. The strongest statement is at the end: "Wherever selling costs are incurred, — and they are incurred in some measure for almost all commodities, — to cast the price problem in terms of "competitive" demand and cost curves is not merely inaccurate; it is impossible. To assume such curves and to explain prices in terms of them is to go through an exercise which has nothing to do with the problem." (p. 174)

[29] With regard to demand, the following passages from the thesis indicate some of the difficulties:

"To add the demand curve for Fords and the demand curve for Packards gives a total which is a demand curve for neither Fords, Packards, nor 'automobiles in general.' It gives no clew whatever to the price of anything." (Thesis, p. 361). (*Footnote continued on next page.*)

set of aggregate curves for a differentiated product is drawn, on page 114, where it is attempted through their use to drive home the comparison between pure and monopolistic competition.[30] But here the cost and demand curves are first drawn for a purely competitive market, and then merely *assumed* (in order to bring out other aspects of the comparison) not to change when the product is differentiated.[31]

An aggregate demand curve for the more general market may seem to be implied in the group analysis (and uniformity assumption), where the DD' type of curve for the firm is defined as "a fractional part of the demand curve for the general class of product." [32] But the general curve cannot be obtained from DD' by multiplying this latter throughout by the number of sellers, for the number of sellers in the more general market is a variable. (It may be *assumed* constant for certain limited purposes, of course, as in the text at this point.) In sum, neither (1) entry and exit, nor (2) price, product, or selling cost adjustments (or all together), as a means of reaching a group tangency solution *requires* demand and cost curves *for the group* which would correspond to the familiar demand and cost curves for an "industry."

It may be of some interest, in view of the growing recognition of the problem of the "multi-product firm," that diversity was intra- as well as inter-firm in the thesis. After some extended discussion of the problems of diversity of product within the firm itself, both as to

---

"The amounts of different varieties of goods which would be demanded at various prices cannot, strictly speaking, be added to make up a total demand schedule, even assuming the prices of all varieties to be raised and lowered together in the construction of such a (total) schedule. The reason is that the total demand for any broad class of product depends in part on the varieties of which it is composed. It is not, in general, true that, although people prefer one variety to another, they will purchase the same amount of some close substitute if their exact desires cannot be met. A housewife's preference for halibut may be of such a nature that if it is not to be had, she will substitute meat or even vegetables instead of another kind of fish. Again, although many people may decide to go to the theatre before they investigate the entertainments offered, with many others the process is the reverse. They go because they wish to see a particular actor or play. A demand schedule for 'theatricals in general' is to this extent devoid of meaning. . ." (Thesis, p. 311, n.1)

[30] The fundamental difficulties of such comparisons are more fully discussed in *Towards a More General Theory of Value*, pp. 72–76.

[31] With respect to the demand curve, it was stated in the first edition (p. 115, n. 1) that "there seems to be no particular reason why it would change." But there is clearly a reason. The footnote was removed in the second edition, and in the second printing of the third edition was replaced by: "It would, in general, lie further to the right if wants were more exactly satisfied with a differentiated product."

[32] Above, p. 90. See also the accompanying discussion in a footnote.

demands and as to costs (from which latter the long quotation on railway rates above is taken), the following simplifying assumptions are made: "that the share of overhead which can most advantageously be apportioned to each product or class of product (within the firm) is about the same for different merchants in the same line of business, and that in setting their price policies, they apportion their overhead in this way. The cost curve for any commodity includes, therefore, such a proportion of the common costs of the business. Throughout the analysis, the cost curve may be interpreted as applying indifferently to (a) an individual commodity, or (b) a 'unit of business' in an establishment handling many commodities. In this latter case, the demand curve must be interpreted as a general average, or index number, of prices within the establishment." These are perhaps fairly reasonable assumptions, but it was certainly an awareness of their inadequacy, and inability to deal with the problem more adequately at the time which led to their omission from the book.

The last source to be mentioned among the ultimate origins of the book is that of substantial reading in the literature of Business Economics, in general, but also with some special reference to "distribution," to retail markets, and to the phenomenon of advertising.

With respect to the latter especially, the neglect by theoretical economics of a force of such overwhelming importance in the real world had long seemed to me an anomaly; and, as I remember it, the conviction that advertising was a *necessary* part of the hybrid theory I was trying to write was brought home with great force by the well-known footnote in Pigou, *Economics of Welfare*: "Under simple competition there is no purpose in this advertisement, because, *ex hypothesi*, the market will take, at the market price, as much as any one small seller wants to sell." [33]

A prime feature of *pure* competition then must be the total absence of advertising, an activity therefore logically attributed to tht *monopoly* elements in the situation — the existence for each seller of a market distinct from those of others, and which he tries to expand through selling efforts. It seemed clear at last why selling cost had been left out of economic theory. There was simply no place for it in the theory of competition, i.e., in the theory of "perfect" competition (which was widely regarded as *the* theory of the subject in its most abstract and general form). And on the other hand, under the prevailing dichotomy there was evidently no place either for such a highly competitive activity in the theory of monop-

[33] (London: Macmillan, 1929) 3d ed., p. 198.

oly. Yet how naturally selling cost falls into place in a theory whose very purpose is to analyze monopoly and competition in a framework of interrelationship, rather than of mutual exclusiveness!

Surely the major difference between thesis and book was that the treatment of selling cost was truncated in the former, stopping short at the end of Chapter VI, and containing only a promise of Chapter VII to come. This procedure was urged — I might better say insisted upon — by Young, since it was quite evident that the technical analysis of Chapter VII could not possibly be satisfactorily done (or even done at all) by the April 1 deadline. Chapter VI was much more detailed and longer than it later turned out to be, and even contained a part of what subsequently became Chapter VII. In the post-1927 revision, the formal organization of Chapter VII was brought into line with a completely reorganized Chapter V, the objective being that, section for section, Chapter VII should add to or correct the corresponding analysis of Chapter V, by making good the ("planned") deficiency of the latter as a piece of partial analysis from which selling costs had been explicitly assumed [34] to be absent.

A summary description of that standard appendage of a doctor's thesis, the bibliography,[35] will serve to point up the nature of the materials underlying the early development of the theory, as set forth in more detail above. It was divided into four sections: I. General Works and Journal Articles on Principles and Theory, including mainly English, French, Austrian, and American writers. The earliest item in this section was Cournot (1838); and the latest, a journal article of November 1925. II. The Theory of Duopoly: "The list here presented is complete to the writer's knowledge": twenty items, many of them mere fragments of no more than a few sentences or a page or two. The earliest item here was again Cournot, and the latest was Young's Review of Bowley in 1925. Others from this earlier period have been discovered since, but I should doubt if the number now known before 1926 would be more than twenty-five or thirty.[36] III. Books and Articles on Business Economics, includ-

[34] Above, p. 72.

[35] I.e., the bibliography of the most important works consulted for the thesis, not to be confused with the "Bibliography on Monopolistic Competition" in the book, beginning with the second edition (1936). For a description of the nature and limitations of this latter, the paragraph introductory to it should be consulted.

[36] It should be added that Chapter III on Duopoly and Oligopoly was never meant to be, as it has sometimes been described, a summary of the history of the theory; but, on the other hand, an analytical structure of the whole problem in its many phases and subdivisions, as it might have been written, for instance, even without reference to other writers at all. Since the "theory" of almost every writer up to that time had made the mistake, as I saw it, of iden-

ing many articles from *Printer's Ink, System,* and other leading business journals of the time. Included here are also bulletins from various Bureaus of Business Research and of the U. S. Government Department of Agriculture. IV. The Economic and Legal Literature of Patents and Trade Marks.

It should be noted that, in addition to the attempt to apply a rigorous logic to the existing economic analysis of markets, in general, even more important was the attempt to use the materials of business structure and behavior to suggest new hypotheses, and to provide illustrative materials for the new conclusions — in short, to incorporate into the general theory of value a type of economic activity hitherto beyond the pale of the general economic theorist. Increasing returns and the representative firm are, if anything, conspicuous by their absence.

A word more about the post-thesis period is called for to complete the picture.

In the Preface to the first edition it was indicated that the work of this period was mainly one of rewriting and of reorganization. Some of the descriptions given above of materials which disappeared in the process or were relegated to appendices will make clearer than before the nature of the upheaval which took place. Details of what was *mere* reorganization would not be of general interest, but the chapter subheadings in the present table of contents, as compared with those in the thesis, which were either absent or entirely different, will indicate the nature of the transformation. In particular, it might be noted that the analysis of oligopoly forces was much more widely dispersed and integrated with other phases of the whole subject in the thesis than in the book. In this respect it conformed to "reality" better than does the book, where the concentration of the analysis in Chapter III has had the unfortunate result of making it appear to many as a subject apart.

I have seen much comment and even criticism of the abstract character of the assumptions made in the theory, and of their remoteness from real life. It is true that every piece of analysis in the book is a partial one, carried out under definite assumptions as to other factors in the whole problem which are held constant; and for this very reason every one will ordinarily seem abstract and unreal when taken simply by itself. The explanation lies in a conscious attempt, for better or worse, to apply quite strictly the Marshallian instruc-

tifying his own particular set of assumptions with the whole problem, individual writers and the assumptions appropriate to their conclusions were related wherever possible to their position in the logical structure as a whole. (See above, p. 31)

tions to "go step by step, breaking up a complex question, studying one bit at a time, and at last combining his partial solutions into a more or less complete solution of the whole riddle. . . . The more the issue is thus narrowed, the more exactly can it be handled: but also the less closely does it correspond to real life. . . . With each step more things can be let out of the pound [of *Caeteris Paribus*] . . . , etc." [37] The case of oligopoly is a good illustration. The subject is first treated without product differentiation in Chapter III; it is combined with product differentiation, pp. 100–109; and finally selling costs, assumed absent up to that point, are added in, pp. 170–172.[38] In fact, I cannot think offhand of a more literal application of this phase of Marshallian method *"step by step"* to a more "complex problem" than the one at hand. Any "step" taken alone is bound to be unreal.

V. The Attack on Marshall

There is no intention here of entering more than ankle deep into the "increasing returns controversy," generally taken to date from Sraffa's *Economic Journal* article in December 1926,[39] nor into the debates on the representative firm dating from articles by Pigou and Robbins [40] (and continuing in this case right down to the present time). It would be easy merely to point out the obvious — that by simple chronology alone, as well as by the account of the book given above (and by inspection) neither one played any part whatsoever in the development of *The Theory of Monopolistic Competition*. The book may not, therefore, be interpreted as rising from the ashes of the "attack on Marshall" which preceded it. Nor did the book itself attack Marshall (as it might have by sheer coincidence) on any of the issues there involved.

There is no doubt, however, that there was an attack; *and that the literature of imperfect and monopolistic competition has been generally regarded as growing out of it.* One of the earliest (1934) of the many joint reviews of Mrs. Robinson's book and my own which did so much to identify them says in part: "We may take the book [*Monopolistic Competition*], therefore, as a useful summary of the advance achieved [*sic*]. Mrs. Robinson's book may be accepted in

[37] *Principles*, V,v,2. (8th ed., p. 366).

[38] For an analytical statement covering the entire book from this point of view, see *Towards a More General Theory of Value*, p. 68. (Or *Economica*, N. S., XVIII (Nov. 1951), 343.)

[39] "The Laws of Returns Under Competitive Conditions," XXXVI.

[40] Pigou, "An Analysis of Supply," and Robbins, "The Representative Firm," *Economic Journal*, XXXVIII (June and Sept. 1928).

the same light. Composed in the environment of Cambridge, it can be regarded as *even more authoritative* than the work from Harvard." [41] But this is too generous. The truth is (*caveat lector*) that in this matter *Monopolistic Competition* is simply without any "authority" whatsoever.

A few comments on the nature of the "attack" which actually took place should yield a better understanding of what did and what did not grow out of it.

First, it may be said categorically that what is now known as oligopoly was not a part of the attack at all. In the several cases where the question is raised, it is always for the same express purpose: to get rid of it. Sraffa wishes to "dispel the doubt" that in the case considered, "the equilibrium may be indeterminate," and after some argument concludes that it "is in general determinate," [42] clearly implying that there is therefore no cause for concern. Pigou makes clear at the outset of his article, "An Analysis of Supply," that "the difficult intermediate case of an industry in which x_r (output per firm) is neither small relative to y (total industry output) nor yet equal to y — a case involving some measure of indeterminateness — will be left out of account." [43] Harrod, in his "Notes on Supply," disposes of the matter in one short paragraph: "If the number of sources is greater than one but not great, it is difficult to determine the kind of demand with which each source is confronted . . . the demand curve and the increment of aggregate demand curve for the products of that source diverge; all sources may in this case yield an increase of output at decreasing supply prices in the short and long periods." [44] The above are three examples I have been able to find where the subject has been mentioned at all. In the usual case, there is nothing. Mrs. Robinson's well-known mention of the subject only to eliminate it,[45] is therefore strictly in the tradition. It is of interest

[41] "Economic Method and the Concept of Competition," W. H. Hutt, *South African Journal of Economics*, Vol. 2 (1934), p. 4. (My italics.) Mr. Hutt speaks of my book being "revised in the light of subsequent contributions and after correspondence with Dr. Kahn. . ." On "subsequent contributions" in the revision, see above, p. 299, n. 17. The "correspondence with Dr. Kahn" was limited to an exchange of letters on duopoly after the publication of my article, "Duopoly: Value Where Sellers Are Few," in the *Quarterly Journal of Economics*, XLIV (Nov. 1929).

[42] *Op. cit.*, pp. 547–549. (American Economic Association, *Readings in Price Theory*, pp. 194–195).

[43] *Op. cit.*, p. 240.

[44] *Economic Journal*, XL (June 1930), 239–240. (Also in Harrod's *Economic Essays*; New York: Harcourt Brace, 1953; p. 86). In strict fairness, this should probably not be described as "getting rid of" the subject, but only as an approach to the limiting case.

[45] *Imperfect Competition*, p. 21.

to note that Mr. Harrod, in his essay in the *Quarterly Journal* designed to set forth "the principal points of significance for economic theory in the doctrines relating to Imperfect Competition that have been recently evolved" [46] does not find oligopoly among them. On the contrary, his only comment is that "In the case of duopoly traditional theory has failed to provide a satisfactory solution." [47]

Second, as to the increasing returns controversy. Sraffa's basic "innovation" in this matter was with regard to industries, not firms. The attack was on the threefold classification in terms of increasing, decreasing and constant returns; and by skillfully undermining the first two as applicable to single commodities, it yielded the conclusion that (with few exceptions) "in normal cases the cost of production of commodities produced competitively . . . must be regarded as constant in respect to small variations in the quantities produced." [48] Indeed it seemed that it was this "best available" theory of "cost of production alone" which revealed the necessity "to abandon the path of free competition and turn . . . towards monopoly" in order "to study in greater detail the conditions under which exchange takes place in particular cases . . ." It is here that "we find (for the firm) a well-defined theory in which variations of cost connected with changes in the dimensions of the individual undertaking play an important part." And given constant costs for the industry, no problems seem to arise as to the effect of changes in industry output on the cost curve of the firm. The theory of the individual firm as a monopoly remained to be created by combining with this irreproachable constant cost curve a new analysis of demand.[49]

---

[46] "Doctrines of Imperfect Competition," *Quarterly Journal*, XLVIII (May 1934). (*Economic Essays*, p. 111)

[47] *Op. cit.*, p. 445. (*Economic Essays*, p. 114.)

There is good evidence that what was really bothering the British economists of this period was not the oligopoly problem as we know it today, but the prevailing identification (in England) of "duopoly" with the particular indeterminate solution of it by Edgeworth. (See Pigou, *Economics of Welfare*, p. 267.) A brief discussion and comments on his position will be found above, pp. 44–46.

[48] Sraffa, *op. cit.*, pp. 540–541. (*Readings in Price Theory*, pp. 186–187.)

[49] In my own case, the theory of group equilibrium, although similarly *presented* in terms of "constant cost" for the group, explicitly embraces increasing and decreasing costs as well, with a brief summary of the special factors involved in each one. The restriction to constant cost is largely for simplicity in exposition, on the ground that the additional elaborations to cover the cases of increasing and decreasing costs "need not be repeated at every stage of the argument." (Above, pp. 85–87.) With increasing and decreasing costs the cost curves of the firms (always including rents in the case of increasing costs) are raised or lowered respectively; and in general with expansion or contraction of the group (even under constant costs) their shape may not remain unaffected. But they will always be U-shaped.   (*footnote continued*)

Out of this extreme position the controversies developed: with respect to the laws governing industries, the relations of industries and firms (as to scarce factors, "external-internal" economies, and the like), whether industry equilibrium requires that all firms be in equilibrium or merely that their various disequilibria "cancel out," expansion of industries by increase in the number of firms as against increased output per firm, "equilibrium firm" vs. representative firm for the industry and the conditions of cost for such a firm at equilibrium, whether although the curve of unit cost of production was still descending at equilibrium it could be made to behave properly and turn up again at this point by adding in marketing expenses, etc., etc. I shall comment on only three matters: (1) "tangency," (2) the central role of the industry, and (3) the role of the demand curve of the firm in explaining the supply curve for the industry.

(1) The tangency solution which grew out of the increasing returns controversy emerged *six years* after Sraffa's 1926 article, in Mrs. Robinson's "Imperfect Competition and Falling Supply Price." [50] Sraffa had neglected the problem of entry (and by inference exit?), not through any oversight, but *deliberately,* and for what he regarded as good and sufficient reasons: heavy expenses where the good will of already established firms is a factor, and because it "can acquire importance only when the monopoly profits in a trade are considerably above the normal level," which in his analysis is already quite high.[51] In fact he argues at length and in some detail that producers (not in some, or even in a great many, industries, but *generally*) are more likely to raise prices than to lower them. Thus he not only excludes entry, but virtually eliminates price competition as well.[52]

Mrs. Robinson's analysis of the entry problem and her tangency solution of it emerges as a phase of her analysis of "falling supply price" in an industry, with the aim of contributing further to the discussions on this latter in the "Symposium" and in two articles by Harrod.[53] It is well known, and hardly needs to be summarized. If

---

In all this process, no conception is involved of a *cost curve* for the group as an aggregate. (See above, pp. 303–304, for discussion of this latter problem.)

[50] *Economic Journal*, XLII (Dec. 1932).

[51] *Op. cit.*, p. 549. (*Readings in Price Theory*, p. 196.)

[52] *Ibid.*, pp. 546–550. (*Readings in Price Theory*, pp. 193–196.) Demand elasticity remains, of course, as a measure of the strength of consumers' preferences, but its importance seems to express itself mainly with reference to price increases rather than decreases. In his "turn towards monopoly" Mr. Sraffa seems to have gone far indeed "in the opposite direction" in his elimination of competitive forces from the system!

[53] D. H. Robertson, G. F. Shove, and P. Sraffa, "Increasing Returns and

entry into an industry is possible, firms will enter or leave it according as actual industry profits exceed or fall short of "normal." Difficult entry simply means that the level of profits will have to be higher in order to overcome it. "The proposition that the industry is in equilibrium only when profits within it are normal is then reduced to a tautology." [54] It is acknowledged to fail only when entry is impossible in the sense that no level of profit, however high, will bring it about, in which case "we may say that the industry is always in equilibrium or never in equilibrium, whichever we please." The only point I wish to make here with respect to this much discussed "solution" is that it is only in this latter case of (1) no entry

---

the Representative Firm: A Symposium," *Economic Journal*, XL (March 1930). Harrod, "Notes on Supply," *op. cit.*; "The Law of Decreasing Costs," *Economic Journal*, XLI (Dec. 1931). The articles by Harrod appear also in his *Economic Essays*.

[54] "Imperfect Competition and Falling Supply Price," *op. cit.*, p. 547. She expresses indebtedness to Mr. Kahn for this proposition. It appears that Harrod had earlier given an example of equilibrium for the firm (in order to illustrate "the possibility of decreasing costs co-existing with competitive equilibrium,") but without reference to entry, and in which tangency was merely an accidental result. *Ibid.*, p. 548. Also Harrod, "The Law of Decreasing Costs," *op. cit.*, p. 572 and *idem*, "Decreasing Costs: An Addendum," *Economic Journal*, XLII (Sept. 1932), 492. (Also in Harrod, *Economic Essays*, pp. 94–96.)

Especially in view of the fact that so many regard the tangency solution as a kind of hallmark of monopolistic and imperfect competition, it is interesting to speculate as to why it was that, within the increasing returns genealogy, six years intervened between Sraffa's pioneering article and the "tangency" solution of Mrs. Robinson, limited as it was to a mere tautology. This is a guessing game, and my own guess would be that the explanation lies partly in (1) the exclusion of entry from the Sraffa "model," so that it was easily and naturally passed over in the subsequent discussion, and (2) the prolonged and agonizing struggle over reconciling "increasing returns" to the firm with "competitive" equilibrium for the industry. It is perhaps significant (and this would help to explain the meagre fruit) that when a "tangency" solution did emerge from this background, it was not in answer to a *direct* question as to the effects of entry and exit on the equilibrium of the *firm*, but (as indicated above) as a *by-product* of a question having to do with the shape of the supply curve of an *industry* — a question with which the increasing returns controversy was so heavily preoccupied.

Without all the "industry" impedimenta, "tangency" is really simplicity itself, and hardly merits being taken seriously as a discovery. Indeed it requires only economies of scale and a sloping demand curve for the firm; plus, in my own case, a sufficient possibility of substitutes to obtain it (hence by no means generally obtained), and in Mrs. Robinson's, any possibility at all, however limited, of entering the "industry." (One might, and should, add: emancipation from the preconceived notion that production *must* for some reason take place at the minimum point on the cost curve, without regard for demand conditions.)

at all (2) into an *industry*, that profits are not *by definition* competitive. The profits, however high, which arise from difficult or impossible entry into any *portion* of an industry are competitive so long as entry is at all possible into some other part of it. This astounding result follows from the fact that "normal" profits are an *industry* concept.

(2) There is no need to document in detail the omnipresence of the industry in the increasing returns controversy — its key position in *Imperfect Competition* is a convenient and sufficient index. Putting aside Book I on "Technique," only Books II and V deal with the firm as such. The other seven Books are centered on industries; and finally in Book X on "A World of Monopolies," we have a three-way comparison between a world of monopolized industries, of imperfectly competitive industries and of perfectly competitive industries. This is a different world from one in which each seller has a monopoly of *his own distinguishable product* and where various types of group relationships between them are envisaged. The difference between the two worlds is explained by the fact that one of them arose out of the increasing returns controversy and the other did not.[55]

(3) The role of "imperfections," expressed in the *demand* curve for the *firm*, in helping to explain the *supply* curve of the *industry*, seems to me another product of the increasing returns controversy which should not pass unnoticed. The idea is most clearly and simply stated in Mrs. Robinson's "Imperfect Competition and Falling Supply Price," already cited (or see *Imperfect Competition*, pp. 97–100), and it received the enthusiastic approval of Pigou three months later, with some further development and elaboration.[56] Let me try to summarize the essentials. Constant costs are assumed for the industry; cost curves for the firms are U-shaped, tangent to the horizontal cost curve for the industry, and do not change when the industry expands. Both cost and demand curves are uniform for all producers. At equilibrium, demand and cost curves for all firms are tangent, and at the same height above the cost curve for the industry. Now with increased demand there will be more firms, and all demand curves, again tangent to cost curves at the new equilibrium, may be, accord-

[55] Cf. above, p. 302, note 27.

[56] "A Note on Imperfect Competition," *Economic Journal*, XLIII (March 1933). Pigou discusses mainly demand relationships, and it should be noted that he concludes with an "observation" to the effect that Mrs. Robinson's aggregate demand function is "not identical" with the one of "ordinary elementary analysis," which evidently means in this context the one where product is homogeneous. It is in fact the *sum* of the amounts demanded for all the *different* products, each at the uniform price *p* which rules for all. But this important "observation" is not developed further.

ing to circumstances, either more elastic, less elastic, or of the same elasticity as before. The locus curve of these points of tangency, with expanding output and changing elasticities, will in the three cases be respectively downward sloping, upward sloping, and horizontal. All three are called supply curves, or curves of falling, rising, or constant supply price. Yet none can play any part whatever in the determination of price, since they cannot be drawn until after the price is known! Something is wrong here. Yet, without further discussion, let me simply say that the same problem in simpler form (without the changes in demand elasticity) had received earlier attention independently of the increasing returns controversy and with a very different conclusion. The reference is to pages 115–116 (especially 116) above (or thesis, page 308), where it is held that the locus of the points of tangency of demand and cost curves for the firms does not constitute a cost curve at all. Aside from the cost curves of the individual firms, the only true cost curve is the purely competitive one, and the points in question simply do not lie on this curve. From here on, the reader may be left to draw his own conclusions.

Third, the representative firm. There is lengthy criticism in the thesis of certain types of statistical studies of costs, in which the costs of different firms in an industry or trade are arranged in ascending order from left to right, with conclusions drawn from the resulting ogive curve as if it were a supply curve, which it plainly is not. The main points of criticism are the familiar ones of diversity of product, the fact that the costs in question include selling costs, that the firms are in different markets, etc. Here the phrase representative firm was used several times to indicate the modal firm, but for reasons just suggested no questions of the role of such a firm in price determination were raised. All of this material was dropped from the book and the concept of a representative firm does not appear. The word "illustrative" [57] has a totally different meaning — a meaning which is moreover made clearer by references in the context to diagram*s* (plural, hence those with and without profits above the minimum, with and without oligopoly forces, etc.), and to "levels appropriate for each."

A true "group equilibrium" under monopolistic competition would have to include these "illustrative" firms as well. The "tangency solution" of Chapter V is in fact based on several "heroic" assumptions, and designed simply to illuminate certain important aspects of the complex whole. Specifically, it is a prelude to the discussion of diversity, which "must now be explicitly recognized and related

[57] Above, pp. 111, 172.

to the conclusions established under the simpler hypothesis of uniformity." [58] In any group the final solution must be consistent with a wide variety of products, prices, costs, outputs, *and profits* [59]; and the further analysis of selling costs remains to be added: ("The theory must now be completed. . .") [60]

In all these matters there is no use looking for a "representative firm" *which will in some sense govern the group,* since it is the essence of the problem that each firm will be governed by *its own* economic environment. It should be clear by now that recognition of this element of uniqueness in the economic environment of each firm should not be misunderstood as a denial or denigration of any of the elements of interdependence between firms which exist, both in the cost structure by which the economic system is held together, and in the "maze of intricate problems" [61] on the demand side, especially when selling costs are brought into the picture.

I can see no escape (and no reason to try to escape) from the conclusion that the ubiquitous forces of oligopoly and of nonprice competition (to name only these) must be responsible for many loose ends, multiple optima and indeterminateness in one sense or another in "groups" and in the system, which must be expected either to assert themselves or to achieve a *de facto* stability thanks to inertia or other similar forces. The normal requirement for a group equilibrium that no resources could with advantage be transferred from one use to another would by no means dispose of all these problems.

The problem of time is not explicitly dealt with in the book, but it should be made clear also that neither is it lost sight of by rarefied assumptions of static conditions from which it is excluded. Typical of the underlying view is the statement with respect to cost curves: ". . . it is usually the long-run curve which is in mind; but the analysis is easily adapted to short-run problems by an appropriate interpretation of the content of the U-shaped curve." [62] Again, with reference to selling costs: "The curve of selling costs has [deliberately] been defined without reference to the period of time . . . like the curve of production costs, [it] must include such outlays and results as are relevant to the period of time taken into account by the business man when he decides upon his policies, and must be interpreted with reference to such a period." [63]

[58] P. 110.
[59] Pp. 111–113.
[60] P. 117.
[61] P. 139.
[62] P. 21n.
[63] P. 139.

Specifically, with respect to growth, and to that leading static-dynamic problem of Marshall — "movement" within a fixed aggregate — there is one rather enticing concept which was left open to further interpretation, viz., the amount of profit in the cost curve of the individual firm. It is defined as "the *minimum* profit necessary to secure the entrepreneur's services." [64] But this minimum might actually be negative during an early period of growth, or during any short period after which conditions were expected to improve. It is possible, too, that over-optimistic expectations which are beyond anything realistically attainable may keep some firms in business for a long time, only to be replaced as they disappear by others like them, and so provide a permanent "fringe" of unprofitable firms in the aggregate. Again, in a declining enterprise, minimum profits may be anything in excess of out-of-pocket costs. And so on. And to what extent is this minimum for one entrepreneur affected by the actual profits of others, or by expectations, even when actual profits, perhaps of all concerned, are nonexistent? The "minimum" certainly invites interpretation in terms of these and other dynamic problems.

VI. Marshall on Monopolistic Competition

Monopolistic Competition was an attack, not on Marshall, but on the theory of perfect competition. It was directed (1) against those "pure theorists" to whom the theory of our subject *is* perfect competition; but even more (because more numerous), (2) against those who simply regard "competitive" and "monopolistic" as separate categories, with different principles in each case and a clear line of distinction between them.

There has been much discussion in recent years as to how Marshall stood on these latter issues, and how he is to be interpreted in terms of them. Mr. Newman, for instance, complains that "much analysis, even of purely competitive conditions, that is today presented as Marshallian is quite foreign to his thought," [65] and I must say that I agree with him. But the question must also be raised of whether much of Marshall's analysis which *seems* to be in terms of monopolistic competition and which is being resurrected today as such, is not also "foreign to his thought" in the sense that it is *inadequate* as an expression of it.

But how are we to get an "adequate" expression of Marshall's thought? ". . . in the world in which we live," says Marshall, ". . .

---

[64] P. 77, also p. 76; and see p. 173 for the effect of selling costs on this minimum.

[65] *Loc. cit.*, p. 588.

every plain and simple doctrine as to the relations between cost of production, demand and value is necessarily false: and the greater the appearance of lucidity which is given to it by skilful exposition, the more mischievous it is." [66] The paraphrase is irresistible: Every plain and simple doctrine about Marshall is necessarily false, and the more lucid it is, the more mischievous — simply by attributing to Marshall theories more precise than they really were, or than he ever intended them to be. His well-known position on the limitations of the mathematical method in economics is quite to the point.

Marshall often "theorized" about situations by merely telling what business men did in real life; and this being so, it is easy to find particular markets, product differentiation (without the jargon), etc., emerging here and there (or *sub*merged in a footnote), because that's the way real life is. And, although, as observed by Mr. D. C. Hague in his recent article, "Alfred Marshall and the Competitive Firm," [67] he "specifically rules out [oligopoly] from the *Principles*," he often describes business men's behavior in terms which unmistakably involve "mutual dependence recognized." A fine distinction between "theory" and "real life" in Marshall's economics is impossible to draw because Marshall himself did not draw it, and never tired of warning others against drawing it.

As for monopoly and "free competition," we find statements that "they shade into one another by imperceptible degrees"; [68] yet in *Industry and Trade* separate Books are devoted to each; and the *Principles* analyzes the *general* problems of value as a matter of demand and supply, with a *single* chapter on Monopoly, in which the principle changes to maximum net revenue! In this Marshall was typical of his period, indeed in view of his great influence upon it, one would better say that the period was typical of him. But in spite of many passages in which he calls attention to, and even stresses, the particular market of the firm, advertising, etc., is it not fair to say that he himself in his general treatment regarded competition as the fundamental force, and monopoly as a different and *alternative* principle? If so, and *in so far as this is so, Monopolistic Competition* is directed against Marshallian economics (among others), not in terms of the 1926–1933 issues over increasing returns and the representative firm, but on the more general grounds indicated under (2) above.

It is in a little-known passage in the Mathematical Appendix to

[66] *Principles*, p. 368.
[67] *Economic Journal*, LXVIII (Dec. 1958), p. 683.
[68] *Industry and Trade*, p. 397. The identical phrase is used on p. 178 to contrast "open markets" with those "in some degree under monopolistic control." On p. 397, the "shading" is "in practice," whereas the two concepts are said to be "ideally wide apart."

the *Principles* that Marshall, perhaps under pressure from the mathematical formulation of the problem, states his position on monopoly and competition in a way which is comprehensive, and for that very reason among others, seems definitive. It was cited above [69] in connection with marginal revenue, but the real question is the more *general* one of whether or not, with an increase in the amount sold, the diminution in total revenue from the sale of the intramarginal units of a product at a slightly lower price should be taken into account. The passage is too long for quotation, but the answer here is *yes* for monopolies, for a producer with "a limited trade connection" and for many problems "relating to short periods," especially those of depression, etc.; and *no* for the general case.

"When however," he says, "we are studying the action of the individual undertaker with a view of illustrating the *normal action* of the causes which govern the *general demand* for the several agents of production, it seems clear that we should *avoid cases of this kind.* We should leave their *peculiar features* to be analyzed separately in *special discussions.* . . ." In "our normal illustration" the loss on the intramarginal units "may be neglected" and we may speak of "the value of the net product . . . of an agent . . . as the amount of that net product taken at the normal selling value of the product." [70] This is not a "plain and simple" statement "*about* Marshall" which, it was suggested above, would be "necessarily false." It is a statement *by* Marshall, and therefore necessarily — well, perhaps only another piece of evidence. But it seems to be a statement so comprehensive and so clearly to the point, that it might have been Marshall's response if he had been asked point blank to say whether he thought monopoly and monopoly influences had a "normal" role in value theory or whether it was only in the short run and in special cases. It is all there. And so, as evidence, the statement should rank fairly high.

The conclusion would seem to be that, with all his complexity, Marshall did think of the normal long-run problem as one of at least "pure" competition in our terminology. Monopoly on the whole was a special problem or a *short-run* problem. That it continues to be so today in the minds of so many economists must be explained in good part by the persistent strength of the Marshallian tradition.

[69] See above, p. 301 n. 21.

[70] *Principles*, Mathematical Appendix, Note XIV, pp. 849–850. (Italics supplied.) Needless to say, the entire passage should be consulted.

BIBLIOGRAPHY ON
MONOPOLISTIC COMPETITION

A BIBLIOGRAPHY ON MONOPOLISTIC COMPETITION

THIS bibliography lists everything I have been able to find which is specifically related in any important way, constructively or critically, to the theory of monopolistic competition. A few reviews have been included which seemed to have importance, critical or otherwise, for the subject. But it is far from exhaustive in any real sense. On the one hand, it omits at least one large subject falling wholly within its scope. The theory of monopoly, as conventionally defined and treated, is comprehended within the broader theoretical structure of monopolistic competition; yet it would have destroyed the usefulness of this list to bury its few items in the vast literature of that subject. On the other hand, it omits the literature of economic theory in so far as it is more general than monopolistic competition. An example is the technical apparatus of curves of cost and revenue — marginal and average, for individual firms and for "industries" — together with the analysis of the forces lying behind them. Such subjects as these belong as much to the theories of pure competition and of monopoly as to monopolistic competition. To include them would be to confuse issues as well as to expand the list until it covered almost all of economics. Finally, advertising, standards, trade marks, patents, etc., are examples of subjects with large and technical literatures of their own. In these and similar fields, only a few items chosen for their interest have been included, in addition, of course, to those specifically related to our subject by their authors.

With the fourth edition, all items have been listed in alphabetical order. Whatever usefulness the earlier classification may have had, however, is retained by listing below the numbers of the items dealing with various phases of the whole subject.[1]

I. SMALL NUMBERS

1, 4, 8, 10, 11, 13, 21, 33, 43, 55, 57, 58, 59, 60, 64, 66, 69, 73, 76, 77, 78, 84, 85, 87, 89, 90, 96, 97, 99, 104, 107, 108, 113, 124, 125, 126, 130, 132, 133, 140, 144, 149, 150, 154, 166, 168, 176, 177, 178, 179, 180, 183, 185, 186, 187, 188, 190, 194, 197, 198, 204, 211, 212, 219, 220, 221, 223, 225, 227, 229, 231, 238, 242, 244, 251, 252, 258, 260, 262, 263, 266, 267, 272, 274, 275, 278, 279, 281, 283, 287, 288, 289, 296, 297, 298, 299, 300, 301, 303, 304, 305, 307, 314, 319, 320, 330, 337, 340, 349, 350, 351, 353, 354, 360, 361, 365, 377, 380, 381, 382, 384, 389, 390, 391, 393, 397, 400, 401, 407, 409, 413, 414, 415, 418, 420, 421, 428, 431, 435, 439, 443, 444, 445, 446, 447, 448, 449, 450, 452.

[1] The two supplementary bibliographies (nos. 458 ff) are not classified in this way.

II. PRODUCTS AS VARIABLES; PRODUCT COMPETITION, INCLUDING SPATIAL COMPETITION

4, 5, 7, 9, 17, 18, 22, 23, 30, 50, 51, 52, 57, 66, 69, 78, 84, 85, 92, 95, 98, 100, 118, 131, 139, 148, 157, 187, 190, 191, 199, 207, 229, 233, 273, 290, 296, 308, 309, 310, 314, 325, 353, 354, 355, 364, 372, 382, 383, 393, 394, 404, 413, 425, 449, 450, 454.

III. SELLING COSTS

3, 5, 6, 18, 19, 29, 31, 34, 52, 57, 61, 62, 66, 69, 76, 78, 83, 106, 112, 152, 163, 164, 189, 191, 193, 202, 211, 212, 258, 269, 286, 289, 291, 310, 312, 315, 343, 356, 358, 367, 369, 371, 373, 374, 375, 376, 377, 378, 385, 394, 402, 403, 404, 411, 413, 423, 425, 440, 441, 453, 457.

IV. DISTRIBUTION

8, 12, 16, 21, 38, 46, 63, 69, 71, 79, 80, 93, 111, 116, 117, 122, 124, 147, 161, 178, 181, 196, 203, 209, 241, 255, 256, 258, 260, 267, 304, 319, 328, 331, 346, 347, 396, 398, 409, 420, 445.

V. EXCESS CAPACITY AND ALLIED PROBLEMS

75, 76, 78, 145, 146, 160, 207, 208, 231, 294, 295, 315, 318, 334, 408

VI. THE BUSINESS CYCLE AND DYNAMIC PROBLEMS

1, 22, 23, 69, 110, 122, 142, 150, 167, 169, 170, 175, 192, 209, 210, 224, 226, 239, 247, 248, 275, 276, 310, 312, 314, 332, 363, 365, 376, 379, 381, 426, 433, 436.

VII. INTERNATIONAL TRADE

14, 37, 143, 199, 234, 236, 240, 245, 250.

VIII. TAXATION

57, 66, 76, 114, 127, 135, 136, 161, 184, 203, 256, 259, 313, 322, 328, 339.

IX. PUBLIC POLICY

9, 12, 17, 18, 21, 25, 27, 39, 41, 44, 52, 57, 66, 70, 73, 74, 80, 84, 86, 88, 92, 99, 101, 102, 104, 107, 108, 109, 114, 115, 138, 139, 143, 151, 153, 155, 156, 159, 182, 223, 231, 232, 243, 252, 253, 254, 255, 256, 259, 273, 275, 292, 308, 309, 314, 316, 317, 318, 326, 336, 371, 377, 390, 399, 406, 413, 427, 428, 430, 437, 455.

1. Abramovitz, M., "Monopolistic Selling in a Changing Economy," *Quarerly Journal of Economics*, 52: 191 (1938).
2. Abramson, Adolph G., *Theories and Measures of Competition*, unpublished Ph.D. thesis, 1941. Brown University Library.

3. Abramson, A. V., "Advertising and Economic Theory: A Criticism," *American Economic Review*, 21: 685 (1931).

4. Ackley, Gardner, "Spatial Competition in a Discontinuous Market," *Quarterly Journal of Economics*, 56: 212 (1942).

5. Agnew, H. E., "Can Standardization Reduce Advertising Costs?" *Annals of the American Academy of Political and Social Science*, 137: 253 (1928).

6. Allen, R. G. D., "Decreasing Costs: A Mathematical Note," *Economic Journal*, 42: 323 (1932).

7. —— "A Comparison Between Different Definitions of Complementary and Competitive Goods," *Econometrica*, 2: 168 (1934).

8. —— *Mathematical Analysis for Economists*, London, 1938.

9. Alsberg, C. L., "Economic Aspects of Adulteration and Imitation," *Quarterly Journal of Economics*, 46: 1 (1931).

10. Amoroso, Luigi, *Lezioni di Economia Matematica*, Bologna, 1921, pp. 258 ff.

11. —— "La Curva Statica di offerta," *Giornale degli Economisti*, 70: 1, especially 11–20 (1930).

12. —— *Principii di Economica Corporativa*, Bologna, 1938.

13. —— and others, *Cournot nella economia e nella filosofia*, Padua, 1939.

14. Anderson, Karl, "Tariff Protection and Increasing Returns," *Explorations in Economics, Essays in Honor of F. W. Taussig*, New York, 1936.

15. Anderson, Thomas J., Jr., "Note on 'The Rise of Monopoly,'" *American Economic Review*, 30: 118 (1940).

16. —— "Competition and Monopoly in Land Markets," *American Economic Review*, 31: 341 (1941). (Discussion of No. 196.)

17. Annals of the American Academy of Political and Social Science, 137 (May, 1928), *Standards in Industry*.

18. —— 173 (May, 1934), *The Ultimate Consumer* (a collection of articles bearing upon standards, brands, advertising, and other problems arising out of a differentiated product).

19. —— 209 (May, 1940), *Marketing in our American Economy* (a collection of articles bearing upon the motivations, machinery, costs, and social and political aspects of marketing).

20. Aoyama, Hideo, *Dokusen no Keizai-riron* (Economic Theory of Monopoly), Nippon Hyoron-Sha, Tokyo, 1937.

21. Bachi, Riccardo, *Principii di scienza economica*, Torino, 1937.

22. Backman, Jules, "Price Flexibility and Inflexibility," *Contemporary Law Pamphlets*, Law and Business Series, New York University School of Law, Series 4, Number 3 (1940).

23. —— "The Causes of Price Inflexibility," *Quarterly Journal of Economics*, 54: 474 (1940).

24. Bader, Louis, "Imperfect Competition and Its Implications," *The American Marketing Journal*, 2: 179 (1935).

25. —— "Recent Price Legislation and Economic Theory," *Journal of Marketing*, 3: 166 (1938).

26. Bain, Joe S., "The Profit Rate as a Measure of Monopoly Power," *Quarterly Journal of Economics*, 55: 271 (1941).

27. Baird, Enid, *Price Filing Under NRA Codes*, Work Materials No. 76, Vol. 1, Trade Practice Studies Section, Division of Review, National Recovery Administration, March, 1936.

28. Ballande, Laurence, "Entre la concurrence et le monopole: étude sur quelques travaux théoriques récents," *Revue d'Économie Politique*, 52: 65 (1938).

29. Barfod, Børge, *Reklamen i teoretisk-økonomisk Belysning*, Copenhagen, 1937.

30. —— "Forenet Produktion og Kvalitetsaendring," *Nordisk Tidsskrift for Teknisk Økonomi*, Løbe 5: 23 (1936). (Brief summary in English — "Joint Production and Variation of Quality.")

31. —— "The Theory of Advertising" (brief summary in the report of the Elsinore Meeting of the Econometric Society, August 25–26, 1939), *Econometrica*, 8: 279 (1940).

32. Barnard, Chester I., *Concerning the Theory of Modern Price Systems and Related Matters*, South Orange, N. J., 1941. (Privately printed.)

33. Barone, Enrico, *Principi di Economia Politica*, Rome, 1908. (Reprinted as Vol. 2 of *Le opere economiche*, Bologna, 1936–37.)

34. Baster, A. S. J., *Advertising Reconsidered*, London, 1935.

35. Baudin, Louis, *Le mécanisme des prix*, Paris, 1939.

36. Bauer, P. T., "A Note on Monopoly," *Economica*, 8 (new series): 194 (1941).

37. Beach, Edwards, "Some Aspects of International Trade under Monopolistic Competition," *Explorations in Economics, Essays in Honor of F. W. Taussig*, New York, 1936.

38. Beddy, J. P., *Profits, Theoretical and Practical Aspects*, Dublin, 1940.

39. Behling, B. N., "The Competitive Significance of Substitutes for Public Utility Services," *American Economic Review*, 27: 17 (1937). (See also No. 223 for discussion by DeChazeau, M. G.)

40. —— "Note on Monopoly and Competition," *American Economic Review*, 27: 767 (1937). (A comment on No. 242.)

41. —— *Competition and Monopoly in Public Utility Industries*, Urbana, Ill. 1938.

42. Benham, Frederic, *Economics*, London, 1938. (American edition in collaboration with Friedrich A. Lutz, New York, 1941.)

43. Bertrand, J., Review of Cournot, "Recherches," *Journal des Savants*, 1883, p. 503.

44. Bladen, V. W., "The Role of Trade Associations in the Determination of Prices," *Canadian Journal of Economics and Political Science*, 4: 223 (1938).

45. Blodgett, Ralph H., *Principles of Economics*, New York, 1941.

46. Bloom, Gordon, "A Reconsideration of the Theory of Exploitation," *Quarterly Journal of Economics*, 55: 413 (1941).

47. Bloomberg, L. N., *The Investment Value of Goodwill*, Baltimore, 1938.

48. Bober, M. M., "Economic Assumptions and Monopoly," *Explorations in Economics, Essays in Honor of F. W. Taussig*, New York, 1936.

49. —— "Price and Production Policies," *American Economic Review*, 32, No. 2 sup.: 23 (1942).

50. Bolland, Stefan, *Strudjum nad metoda stadystycznego badania terytor-jalnej jednorodnosci rynku. Czasopismo prawnicze* 1935 (Study on the Statistical Method of Examining the Territorial Homogeneity of the Market. Kraków, 1935). Abstract in English appears in *Studia Ekonomiczne* 3: 86. Kraków, 1936. (Polska Akademja Umiejętności).

51. —— "The Problem of Frictions," *Studia Ekonomiczne* 4: 50. Kraków, 1937. (Polska Akademja Umiejętności).

52. Borden, Neil H., *The Economic Effects of Advertising*, Chicago, 1942.

53. Bordin, A., "Un caso di Monopolio Bilaterale," *Rivista Italiana di Scienze Economiche*, 8: 503 (1936).

54. —— "Alcune Generalizzazioni di Un Caso di Monopolio Bilaterale," *Giornale degli Economisti*, Vol. 76, Year 51: 672 (1936).

55. —— "Il Monopolio Bilaterale in Termini di Ofelimità e gli Accordi Intersindacali dell'Economia Corporativa," *Rivista Italiana di Scienze Economiche*, 9: 147 (1937).

56. —— "Nota sulla distribuzione arbitrale," *Rivista Italiana di Scienze Economiche*, 9: (1937).

57. Boulding, Kenneth E., *Economic Analysis*, New York, 1941.

58. Bowley, A. L., *The Mathematical Groundwork of Economics*, Oxford, 1924, p. 38.

59. —— "Bilateral Monopoly," *Economic Journal*, 38: 651 (1928).

60. Braess, P., "Kritisches zur Monopol- und Duopoltheorie," *Archiv für Sozialwissenschaft und Sozialpolitik*, 65: 525 (1931).

61. Braithwaite, Dorothea, "The Economic Effects of Advertisement," *Economic Journal*, 38: 16 (1928). (Reprinted as chapter VII in Braithwaite and Dobbs, *The Distribution of Consumable Goods*.)

62. —— and Dobbs, *The Distribution of Consumable Goods*, London, 1932.

63. Bronfenbrenner, M., "The Economics of Collective Bargaining," *Quarterly Journal of Economics*, 53: 535 (1939).

64. —— "Applications of the Discontinuous Oligopoly Demand Curve," *Journal of Political Economy*, 48: 420 (1940).

65. Broster, E. J., *Cost, Demand and Net Revenue Analysis*, London, 1938.

66. Burns, A. R., *The Decline of Competition*, New York and London, 1936.

67. —— "The Organization of Industry and the Theory of Prices," *Journal of Political Economy*, 45: 662 (1937).

68. Bye, Raymond T., *Principles of Economics*, New York, 1941.

69. Cady, George Johnson, *Entrepreneurial Costs and Price*, Evanston, Ill., 1942.

70. Callman, Rudolph, "Patent License Agreements between Competitors and the Monopoly Issue," *Georgetown Law Journal*, 28: 871 (1940).

71. Carlson, S., *A Study on the Pure Theory of Production*, London, 1939.

72. Carlson, V., "Heterodoxy in Monopolistic Competition," *Journal of Social Philosophy*, 2: 291 (1937).

73. Casper, K., "Zur Preistheorie des Bedarfsdeckungsmonopols — Ein Beitrag zur Theorie des 'Monopoloid,'" *Zeitschrift für National-ökonomie*, 7: 214 (1936).

74. Cassady, Ralph, Jr., "Maintenance of Resale Price by Manufacturers," *Quarterly Journal of Economics*, 53: 454 (1939).

75. Cassels, J. M., "Excess Capacity and Monopolistic Competition," *Quarterly Journal of Economics*, 51: 426 (1937).

76. —— "Monopolistic Competition and Economic Realism," *Canadian Journal of Economics and Political Science*, 3: 376 (1937).

77. Chamberlin, Edward H., "Duopoly: Value Where Sellers are Few," *Quarterly Journal of Economics*, 44: 63 (1929).

78. —— *The Theory of Monopolistic Competition*, 1st edition, Cambridge 1933; 6th edition, 1948. (See Nos. 492, 860.)

79. —— "Monopolistic Competition and the Productivity Theory of Distribution," *Explorations in Economics, Essays in Honor of F. W. Taussig*, New York, 1936. (A revision of a paper read at a meeting of the American Economic Association in Philadelphia, December, 1933, and summarized in the *American Economic Review*, 24 sup.: 23 (1934).) (Reprinted as chapter VIII in *The Theory of Monopolistic Competition*, 3rd ed.)

80. —— "Monopolistic or Imperfect Competition?" *Quarterly Journal of Economics*, 51: 557 (1937). (See also No. 208.)

81. —— Reply to Mr. Kaldor (No. 208), *Quarterly Journal of Economics*, 52: 530 (1938).

82. Chandler, Lester V., "Monopolistic Elements in Commercial Banking," *Journal of Political Economy*, 46: 1 (1938).

83. Clark, F. E., "An Appraisal of Certain Criticisms of Advertising," *American Economic Review*, 15 sup.: 5 (1925).

84. Clark, J. M., "Basing Point Methods of Price Quoting," *Canadian Journal of Economics and Political Science*, 4: 477 (1938).

85. —— "One Form of Price Competition between Geographically Separated Large Producers" (summary of a paper given at the Detroit Meeting of the Econometric Society, December 27–30, 1938), *Econometrica*, 7: 174 (1939).

86. —— "Toward a Concept of Workable Competition," *American Economic Review*, 30: 241 (1940).

87. Clausen, A. R., "Nogle Anvendelser af Begreberne Grænseomsætning og Grænsekost" (Some Applications of the Concepts of Marginal Revenue and Marginal Cost), *Nordisk Tidsskrift for Teknisk Økonomi*, Løbe 3: 177 (1937).

88. Clemens, E. W., "Price Discrimination in Decreasing Cost Industries," *American Economic Review*, 31: 794 (1941).

89. Coase, R. H., "The Problem of Duopoly Reconsidered," *Review of Economic Studies*, 2: 137 (1935).

90. —— "Some Notes on Monopoly Price," *Review of Economic Studies*, 5: 17 (1937).

91. —— "The Nature of the Firm," *Economica*, 4 (new series): 386 (1937).

92. Coles, Jessie V., *Standardization of Consumers' Goods*, New York, 1932.

93. Conrad, Otto, *Die Todsünde der Nationalökonomie*, Vienna, 1934.

94. Copeland, Morris A., "The Theory of Monopolistic Competition", *Journal of Political Economy*, 42: 531 (1934).

95. —— "Competing Products and Monopolistic Competition," *Quarterly Journal of Economics*, 55: 1 (1940).
96. Cournot, A., *Recherches sur les Principes Mathématiques de la Théorie des Richesses*, Paris, 1838, especially chapter VII. English translation: *Researches into the Mathematical Principles of the Theory of Wealth*, by Nathaniel T. Bacon, New York and London, 1897.
97. —— *Revue Sommaire des Doctrines Économiques*, Paris, 1877.
98. Court, A. T., "The Problem of Measuring Automobile Prices and Values" (brief summary in the report of the Detroit Meeting of the Econometric Society, December 27–30, 1938), *Econometrica*, 7: 169 (1939).
99. Cox, Reavis, *Competition in the American Tobacco Industry, 1911–1932*, New York, 1933.
100. Crowder, Walter F., "The Product Concentration of Large Corporations," *Survey of Current Business* (United States Department of Commerce, Bureau of Foreign and Domestic Commerce), May, 1941.
101. Curtis, C. A., "Resale Price Maintenance," *Canadian Journal of Economics and Political Science*, 4: 350 (1938).
102. Custis, V., "Monopolistic Competition and Industrial Control," Summary of a Paper read at a meeting of the American Economic Association at Chicago, December, 1936; *American Economic Review*, 27 sup.: 235 (1937).
103. —— and Murley, J. C., "Monony or Monopsony," *American Economic Review*, 29: 348 (1939).
104. Daugherty, C. R., DeChazeau, M. G., and Stratton, S. S., *The Economics of the Iron and Steel Industry* (Bureau of Business Research Monographs, Number 6, University of Pittsburgh), New York, 1936.
105. Davis, Harold T., *The Theory of Econometrics*, Bloomington, Ind., 1941.
106. Dean, Joel, "Department Store Cost Functions," *Studies in Mathematical Economics and Econometrics*, Lange *et al.*, eds., Chicago, 1942.
107. DeChazeau, Melvin G., "Public Policy and Discriminatory Prices of Steel: A Reply to Professor Fetter" with a Rejoinder by Professor Fetter, *Journal of Political Economy*, 46: 537 (1938).
108. Demaria, G., "Oligopolio e azione corporativa," *Giornale degli Economisti*, 74 (series 4): 714 (1934).
109. Dennison, H. S. and Galbraith, J. K., *Modern Competition and Business Policy*, New York, 1938.
110. De Scitovsky, T., "Prices under Monopoly and Competition," *Journal of Political Economy*, 49: 663 (1941).
111. Deutsch, K. W., "Some Economic Aspects of the Rise of Nationalistic and Racial Pressure Groups," *Canadian Journal of Economics and Political Science*, 8: 109 (1942).
112. Dibblee, G. B., *The Laws of Supply and Demand*, London, 1912.
113. Divisia, F., "À propos du duopole. Fluidité d'un marché et élasticité d'une clientèle" (summary of a paper read at a meeting of the Econometric Society in Leyden, Sept.–Oct. 1933), *Econometrica*, 2: 198 (1934); also in the *Revue d'Économie Politique*, 48: 415 (1934).
114. Döblin, E., *Monopole und Besteuerung*, Berlin, 1933.

115. Dommissee, G. A., *The Regulation of Retail Trade Competition*, New York, 1939.

116. Douglas, Paul H., "The Effect of Wage Increases upon Employment," *American Economic Review*, 29 sup.: 138 (1939).

117. —— "Wage Theory and Wage Policy," *International Labor Review*, 39: 319 (1939).

118. Drewnowski, Jan, "The Classification of Commodities and the Problems of Competition and Monopoly," *Studja Ekonomiczne*, 2: 41. Kraków, 1935. (Polska Akademja Umiejętności).

119. —— "Imperfect Competition and the Consumer," *Studja Ekonomiczne*, 3: 36. Kraków, 1936. (Polska Akademja Umiejętności).

120. Due, J. F., "A Theory of Retail Price Determination," *Southern Economic Journal*, 7: 380 (1941).

121. Duncan, Acheson J., "Monopoly Adjustments to Shifts in Demand," *Econometrica*, 10: 75 (1942).

122. Dunlop, J. T., "The Movement of Real and Money Wages," *Economic Journal*, 48: 413 (1938).

123. —— "Price Flexibility and the 'Degree of Monopoly,'" *Quarterly Journal of Economics*, 53: 522 (1939).

124. —— and Higgins, Benjamin, "'Bargaining Power' and Market Structures," *Journal of Political Economy*, 50: 1 (1942).

125. Edgeworth, F. Y., *Mathematical Psychics*, London, 1881, pp. 20 ff.

126. —— "La Teoria Pura del Monopolio," *Giornale degli Economisti*, 15: 13 (1897). Translated in *Papers Relating to Political Economy*, Vol. I, p. 111. See also *Papers*, Vol. II, p. 313.

127. —— "Professor Seligman on the Mathematical Method in Political Economy," *Economic Journal* 9: 286 (1899). Reprinted in *Papers Relating to Political Economy*, under title of "Professor Seligman on the Theory of Monopoly," Vol. I, p. 143.

128. Edwards, Corwin D., Review of Zeuthen, "Problems of Monopoly and Economic Warfare," *American Economic Review*, 21: 701 (1931).

129. —— Review of Robinson, "The Economics of Imperfect Competition," and Chamberlin, "The Theory of Monopolistic Competition," *American Economic Review*, 23: 683 (1933).

130. da Empoli, Attilio, *The Theory of Economic Equilibrium*, Chicago, 1931.

131. Enke, Stephen, "Profit Maximization under Monopolistic Competition," *American Economic Review*, 31: 317 (1941).

132. Evans, G. C., "A Simple Theory of Competition," *American Mathematical Monthly*, 29: 371 (1922).

133. —— *Mathematical Introduction to Economics*, New York, 1930, especially chapter 3.

134. Ezekiel, Mordecai, "Keynes versus Chamberlin," *Cowles Commission for Research in Economics, Report of Fifth Annual Research Conference on Economics and Statistics* (1939), University of Chicago, p. 54.

135. Fagan, E. D. and Jastram, R. W., "Tax Shifting in the Short-Run," *Quarterly Journal of Economics*, 53: 562 (1939).

136. Fagan, E. D., "Tax Shifting in the Market Period," *American Economic Review*, 32: 72 (1942).

137. Fairchild, Furniss & Buck, *Elementary Economics*, 4th edition (2 vols.), New York, 1939.

138. Fetter, F. A., "Planning for Totalitarian Monopoly," *Journal of Political Economy*, 45: 95 (1937). (Review of No. 66.)

139. —— "The New Plea for Basing-Point Monopoly," *Journal of Political Economy*, 45: 577 (1937). (Review of No. 104.)

140. Fisher, I., "Cournot and Mathematical Economics," *Quarterly Journal of Economics*, 12: 126 (1898).

141. Florence, P. S., "The Problem of Management and the Size of Firms: A Reply," *Economic Journal*, 44: 723 (1934).

142. Fontigny, P., "L'Équilibre économique dans l'hypothèse d'une concurrence imparfaite," *Bulletin de l'Institut des Sciences Économiques* (Louvain), 7: 3 (1935).

143. —— "Note sur certains effets des contingentements et des taxes d'importation," *Bulletin de l'Institut des Sciences Économiques* (Louvain), 7: 367 (1936).

144. Forchheimer, Karl, "Theoretisches zum unvollständigen Monopole," *Jahrbuch für Gesetzgebung, Verwaltung und Volkswirtschaft*, 32: 1 (1908).

145. Ford, P., "Competition and the Number of Retail Shops," *Economic Journal*, 45: 501 (1935).

146. —— "Decentralization and Changes in the Number of Shops, 1901–1931," *Economic Journal*, 46: 359 (1936).

147. Fraser, L. M., *Economic Thought and Language*, London, 1937.

148. Frey, A. W., *Manufacturers' Product, Package and Price Policies*, New York, 1940.

149. Frisch, R., "Monopole — Polypole — la Notion de Force dans l'Économie," *Nationaløkonomisk Tidsskrift*, 71: 241 (1933), (Westergaard Festskrift).

150. Galbraith, J. K., "Monopoly Power and Price Rigidities," *Quarterly Journal of Economics*, 50: 456 (1936).

151. —— "Rational and Irrational Consumer Preference," *Economic Journal*, 48: 336 (1938).

152. Garver & Hansen, *Principles of Economics*, Revised edition, Boston, 1937.

153. Grether, Ewald T., *Price Control Under Fair Trade Legislation*, New York, 1939.

154. Hall, R. L. and Hitch, C. J., "Price Theory and Business Behaviour," *Oxford Economic Papers*, No. 2: 12 (1939).

155. Hamilton, W. H. and Associates, *Price and Price Policies*, New York, 1938.

156. Hamilton, W. H., *The Pattern of Competition*, New York, 1940.

157. Hammersberg, D. O., "Allocation of Milk Supplies Among Contiguous Markets," *Journal of Farm Economics*, 22: 215 (1940).

158. Haney, L. H., *Value and Distribution*, New York, 1939.

159. Harbeson, Robert W., "The Public Interest Concept in Law and in Economics," *Michigan Law Review*, 37: 181 (1938).

160. Harris, S. E., *The Economics of American Defense*, New York, 1941, p. 78.
161. —— *The Economics of Social Security*, New York, 1941, Chapter 19.
162. Harrod, R. F., "Notes on Supply," *Economic Journal*, 40: 232 (1930).
163. —— "The Law of Decreasing Costs," *Economic Journal*, 41: 566 (1931).
164. —— "Decreasing Costs: An Addendum," *Economic Journal*, 42: 490 (1932).
165. —— "A Further Note on Decreasing Costs," *Economic Journal*, 43: 337 (1933).
166. —— Review of Chamberlin, "The Theory of Monopolistic Competition," *Economic Journal*, 43: 661 (1933).
167. —— "Doctrines of Imperfect Competition," *Quarterly Journal of Economics*, 48: 442 (1934).
168. —— "The Equilibrium of Duopoly," *Economic Journal*, 44: 335 (1934).
169. —— "Imperfect Competition and the Trade Cycle," *Review of Economic Statistics*, 18: 84 (1936).
170. —— *The Trade Cycle*, Oxford, 1936.
171. —— "Price and Cost in Entrepreneurs' Policy," *Oxford Economic Papers*, No. 2: 1 (1939).
172. Hawkins, E. R., "Note on Chamberlin's Monopoly Supply Curve," and "Reply" by E. H. Chamberlin, *Quarterly Journal of Economics*, 53: 641 (1939).
173. —— "Marketing and the Theory of Monopolistic Competition," *Journal of Marketing*, 4: 382 (1940).
174. —— *Vertical Price Relations under Conditions of Monopolistic Competition*, unpublished Ph.D. thesis, 1940. University of California Library.
175. Heflebower, R. B., "The Effect of Dynamic Forces on the Elasticity of Revenue Curves," *Quarterly Journal of Economics*, 55: 652 (1941).
176. Henderson, A. M., "A Further Note on the Problem of Bilateral Monopoly," *Journal of Political Economy*, 48: 238 (1940).
177. Heyward, E. J. R., "H. von Stackelberg's Work on Duopoly," *Economic Record*, 17: 99 (1941).
178. Hicks, J. R., "Edgeworth, Marshall, and the Indeterminateness of Wages," *Economic Journal*, 40: 215 (1930).
179. —— "Annual Survey of Economic Theory: The Theory of Monopoly," *Econometrica*, 3: 1 (1935).
180. —— Review of Stackelberg, "Marktform und Gleichgewicht," *Economic Journal*, 45: 334 (1935).
181. —— "Distribution and Economic Progress: A Revised Version," *Review of Economic Studies*, 4: 1 (1936).
182. —— "The Foundations of Welfare Economics," *Economic Journal*, 49: 696 (1939).
183. Higgins, Benjamin, "Indeterminacy in Non-Perfect Competition," *American Economic Review*, 29: 468 (1939). (See No. 237.)
184. —— Jastram, R. W., Due, J. F., and Gilbert, D. W., "The Incidence

of Sales Taxes" (Notes and Discussion), *Quarterly Journal of Economics*, 54: 665 (1940).

185. Hoffman, A. C., "Changing Organization of Agricultural Markets," *Journal of Farm Economics*, 22: 162 (1940).

186. —— *Large Scale Organization in the Food Industries*, unpublished Ph.D. thesis, 1939. Harvard University Archives.

187. Hoover, Edgar M., Jr., "Spatial Price Discrimination," *Review of Economic Studies*, 4: 182 (1937).

188. Horwitz, Arnold, *Preistheorie und Preiseingriff*, Berlin, 1937.

189. Hotchkiss, G. B., "An Economic Defense of Advertising," *American Economic Review*, 15 sup.: 14 (1925).

190. Hotelling, H., "Stability in Competition," *Economic Journal*, 39: 41 (1929).

191. Hoyt, Elizabeth E., *Consumption in our Society*, New York and London, 1938.

192. Humphrey, Don D., "The Nature and Meaning of Rigid Prices 1890–1933," *Journal of Political Economy*, 45: 651 (1937).

193. Hutt, W. H., "Economic Method and the Concept of Competition," *South African Journal of Economics*, 2: 3 (1934).

194. —— "The Nature of Aggressive Selling," *Economica*, New series 2: 298 (1935).

195. —— "Natural and Contrived Scarcities," *South African Journal of Economics*, 3: 345 (1935).

196. Ise, John, "Monopoly Elements in Rent," *American Economic Review*, 30: 33 (1940).

197. Jaffé, William, Summary of a paper read at a meeting of the American Economic Association in Philadelphia, December, 1933; *American Economic Review*, 24 sup.: 27 (1934).

198. Jannaccone, Pasquale, "Questioni Controverse nella Teoria del Baratto," *La Riforma Sociale*, 18: 645 (1907). (Reprinted in his *Prezzie Mercati.*)

199. —— "Il 'dumping' e la discriminazione dei prezzi," *La Riforma Sociale*, 25: 234 (1914). (Reprinted in his *Prezzi e Mercati.*)

200. —— *Prezzi e Mercati*, Torino, 1936.

201. Joseph, M. F. W., "A Discontinuous Cost Curve and the Tendency to Increasing Returns," *Economic Journal*, 43: 390 (1933).

202. Kahn, R. F., "Decreasing Costs: a further Note," *Economic Journal*, 42: 657 (1932).

203. —— "Some Notes on Ideal Output," *Economic Journal*, 45: 1 (1935).

204. —— "The Problem of Duopoly," *Economic Journal*, 47: 1 (1937).

205. Kaldor, N., "The Equilibrium of the Firm," *Economic Journal*, 44: 60 (1934).

206. —— "Mrs. Robinson's 'Economics of Imperfect Competition,'" *Economica*, New series 1: 335 (1934).

207. —— "Market Imperfection and Excess Capacity," *Economica*, New series 2: 33 (1935).

208. —— "Professor Chamberlin on Monopolistic and Imperfect Competition," *Quarterly Journal of Economics*, 52: 513 (1938).
209. Kalecki, M., "The Determinateness of the Distribution of National Income," *Econometrica*, 6: 97 (1938).
210. —— *Essays in the Theory of Economic Fluctuations*, London and New York, 1939.
211. —— "The Supply Curve of an Industry under Imperfect Competition," *Review of Economic Studies*, 7: 91 (1940).
212. —— "A Theory of Long-Run Distribution of the Product of Industry," *Oxford Economic Papers*, No. 5: 31 (1941).
213. —— "'Degree of Monopoly' — A Comment," *Economic Journal*, 52: 121 (1942).
214. Kozlik, A., "Zur Anwendung der Mathematik in der Nationalökonomie," *Zeitschrift für Nationalökonomie*, 9: 86 (1938).
215. —— "Conditions for Demand Curves Whose Curves of Total Revenue, Consumers' Surplus, Total Benefit, and Compromise Benefit are Convex," *Econometrica*, 8: 263 (1940).
216. Kristensen, Thorkil, "Monopol og Konkurrence," *Nationaløkonomisk Tidsskrift*, 74: 266 (1936).
217. —— "Om Udbudet under fri Konkurrence og Monopol" (Supply under Free Competition and Monopoly), *Nordisk Tidsskrift for Teknisk Økonomi*, Løbe 2: 55 (1936).
218. —— "Sammensat og Kollektivt Monopol" (Composite and Collective Monopoly), *Nationaløkonomisk Tidsskrift*, 76: 315 (1938).
219. —— "A Note on Duopoly," *Review of Economic Studies*, 6: 56 (1938).
220. —— "Complex Monopoly" (brief summary of a paper given at the Elsinore meeting of the Econometric Society), *Econometrica*, 8: 284 (1940).
221. Kühne, O., *Die Mathematische Schule in der Nationalökonomie*, Berlin, 1928, Bd. 1, Teil 1, pp. 213–214.
222. Lederer, Emil, "On Imperfect Competition," *Social Research*, 2: 222 (1935).
223. —— "The Theory of Monopolistic Competition and Its Implication for General Theory," Summary of a paper read at a meeting of the American Economic Association at Chicago, December, 1936; Discussion by Machlup, F., Chamberlin, E. H., Higgins, B. H., and De Chazeau, M. G.; *American Economic Review*, 27: 324 (1937).
224. —— "Price Dislocations versus Investments," *Social Research*, 5: 149 (1938).
225. Leduc, G., *La Théorie des Prix de Monopole*, Aix-en-Provence, 1927, pp. 257 ff.
226. Leffson, U., "Die wirtschaftlichen Wirkungen der technischen Fortschritts," *Zeitschrift für Nationalökonomie*, 9: 283 (1938), 9: 414 (1939).
227. Leontief, W., "Stackelberg on Monopolistic Competition" (Review of No. 390), *Journal of Political Economy*, 44: 554 (1936).

228. Lerner, A. P., "The Concept of Monopoly and the Measurement of Monopoly Power," *Review of Economic Studies*, 1: 157 (1934).

229. —— and Singer, H. W., "Some Notes on Duopoly and Spatial Competition," *Journal of Political Economy*, 45: 145 (1937).

230. Levy, M. J., Jr., "Note on Some Chamberlinian Solutions," *American Economic Review*, 30: 344 (1940).

231. Liefmann-Keil, Elizabeth, *Organisierte Konkurrenz-Preisbildung*, Leipzig, 1936.

232. Lohmann, M., "Die Preismeldestellen in der gewerblichen Marktordnung," *Jahrbücher für Nationalökonomie und Statistik*, 146: 513 (1937).

233. Lösch, August, "The Nature of Economic Regions," *Southern Economic Journal*, 5: 71 (1938).

234. Lovasy, Gertrud, "Schutzzölle bei unvollkommener Konkurrenz," *Zeitschrift für Nationalökonomie*, 5: 336 (1934).

235. —— "Preisverbundenheit bei 'Ökonomischer Äquivalenz,'" *Zeitschrift für Nationalökonomie*, 7: 94 (1936).

236. —— "International Trade under Imperfect Competition," *Quarterly Journal of Economics*, 55: 567 (1941).

237. Lynch, E. S., "A Note on Mr. Higgins' 'Indeterminacy in Non-Perfect Competition,'" (No. 183) and "Reply" by B. H. Higgins, *American Economic Review*, 30: 347 (1940)

238. McBurney, R. W., "A Case of Duopoly," *The Commerce Journal* (University of Toronto Commerce Club), 1 (new series): 21 (1941).

239. McCracken, H. L., "Monopolistic Competition and Business Fluctuation," *Southern Economic Journal*, 5: 158 (1938).

240. McDiarmid, O. J., "Imperfect Competition and International Trade Theory," *Essays in Political Economy*, in honor of E. J. Urwick, Toronto, 1938.

241. Machlup, Fritz, "On the Meaning of the Marginal Product," *Explorations in Economics, Essays in Honor of F. W. Taussig*, New York, 1936.

242. —— "Monopoly and Competition: A Classification," *American Economic Review*, 27: 445 (1937).

243. —— "Evaluation of the Practical Significance of the Theory of Monopolistic Competition," *American Economic Review*, 29: 227 (1939).

244. —— "Competition, Pliopoly and Profit, Part I," *Economica*, 9 (new series): 1 (1942).

245. McIntyre, Francis, "Monopolistic Elements in Pricing: The Domestic-Export Spread," *Cowles Commission for Research in Economics, Report of Third Annual Research Conference on Economics and Statistics*, (1937). Colorado Springs, Colo., p. 45.

246. McIsaac, A. M. and Smith, J. G., *Introduction to Economic Analysis*, Boston, 1937.

247. Mahr, Alexander, "Monopolistische Preispolitik in der Depression," *Weltwirtschaftliches Archiv*, 35: 386 (1932).

248. Makower, Helen, "Elasticity of Demand and Stabilization," *Review of Economic Studies*, 6: 25 (1938).
249. —— and Marschak, J., "Assets, Prices and Monetary Theory," *Economica*, 5 (new series): 261 (1938).
250. Marsh, Donald B., "The Scope of the Theory of International Trade under Monopolistic Competition," *Quarterly Journal of Economics*, 56: 475 (1942).
251. Marshall, Alfred, *Principles of Economics*, 1st edition, London, 1890, p. 485 n.; 2nd edition, 1891, p. 457 n.
252. Mason, E. S., "Industrial Concentration and the Decline of Competition," *Explorations in Economics, Essays in Honor of F. W. Taussig*, New York, 1936.
253. —— "Monopoly in Law and Economics," *Yale Law Review*, 47: 34 (1937).
254. —— "Price and Production Policies of Large-Scale Enterprise," *American Economic Review*, 29 sup.: 61 (1939). Discussion, *ibid.*, p. 100.
255. —— "Price Policies and Full Employment," *Public Policy*, edited by C. J. Friedrich and E. S. Mason, Cambridge, 1940.
256. Meade, J. E., *An Introduction to Economic Analysis and Policy*, Oxford, 1936. (American edition edited by C. J. Hitch, New York, 1938.)
257. Meek, H. B., *Hotel Administration: A Theory of Hotel Room Rates*, Ithaca: Cornell University, Department of Hotel Administration, 1938.
258. Meyers, A. L., *Elements of Modern Economics*, New York, 1937.
259. —— *Modern Economic Problems*, New York, 1939.
260. Mikesell, Raymond F., "Oligopoly and the Short-Run Demand for Labor," *Quarterly Journal of Economics*, 55: 161 (1940)
261. Miksch, L., *Wettbewerb als Aufgabe, Die Grundsätze einer Wettbewerbsordnung*, Stuttgart and Berlin, 1937.
262. Millikan, Max F., "Comments on the Duopoly-Oligopoly Problem" (report of the Detroit Meeting of the Econometric Society, December 27–30, 1938), *Econometrica*, 7: 175 (1939).
263. —— *The Equilibrium of the Firm under Conditions of Imperfect Competition*, unpublished Ph.D. thesis, 1941. Yale University Library.
264. Möller, H., "Ordnung der Wirtschaft," *Archiv für mathematische Wirtschafts-und Sozialforschung*, 5: 130 (1939).
265. —— "Die Grenzkosten als Grundlage der Preispolitik der Betriebe," *Zeitschrift für Nationalökonomie*, 9:541 (1939).
266. Monroe, A. E., *Value and Income*, Cambridge, 1931, pp. 24–28.
267. Moore, H. L., "Paradoxes of Competition," *Quarterly Journal of Economics*, 20: 211 (1906).
268. Moore, J. H., Steiner, W. H., Arkin, H., and Colton, R. R., *Modern Economics, Its Principles and Practices*, New York, 1940.
269. Moriarty, W. D., "An Appraisal of the Present Status of Advertising," *American Economic Review*, 15 sup.: 23 (1925).
270. Morrison, L. A. in Spahr and others, *Economic Principles and Problems* 2nd edition, New York, 1934, vol. 1, especially chapter 13.

271. —— Discussion at a meeting of the American Economic Association in Philadelphia, December, 1933. *American Economic Review*, 24 sup.: 30 (1934).

272. Mosak, Jacob L., "Some Theoretical Implications of the Statistical Analysis of Demand and Cost Functions for Steel," *Journal of the American Statistical Association*, 36: 100 (1941).

273. Mulford, H. P., *Information Concerning Commodities — A Study in NRA and Related Experience in Control; Part B: Standards and Labeling*, Work Materials No. 38, Trade Practice Studies Section, Division of Review, National Recovery Administration. February, 1936

274. Mund, V. A., "Prices under Competition and Monopoly," *Quarterly Journal of Economics*, 48: 288 (1934).

275. National Resources Committee, *The Structure of the American Economy, Part I, Basic Characteristics*, Washington, 1939.

276. Neal, Alfred C., "Marginal Cost and Dynamic Equilibrium of the Firm," *Journal of Political Economy*, 50: 45 (1942).

277. Neuling, W., "Die Gestaltungsfähigkeit des Wirtschaftsgeschehens unter den verschiedenen Wirtschaftsordnungen," *Jahrbücher für Nationalökonomie und Statistik*, 148: 19 (1938).

278. Nichol, A. J., *Partial Monopoly and Price Leadership*, Philadelphia, 1930.

279. —— "Professor Chamberlin's Theory of Limited Competition," *Quarterly Journal of Economics*, 48: 317 (1934).

280. —— "The Influence of Marginal Buyers on Monopolistic Competition" ("Comments" by E. H. Chamberlin), *Quarterly Journal of Economics*, 49: 121 (1934). (See also *American Economic Review*, 24 sup.: 30 (1934).

281. —— "A Re-appraisal of Cournot's Theory of Duopoly Price," *Journal of Political Economy*, 42: 80 (1934).

282. —— "Robinson's 'Economics of Imperfect Competition,'" *Journal of Political Economy*, 42: 257 (1934).

283. —— "Edgeworth's Theory of Duopoly Price," *Economic Journal*, 45: 51 (1935).

284. —— "Probability Analysis in the Theory of Demand, Net Revenue and Price," *Journal of Political Economy*, 49: 637 (1941).

285. Nicholls, William H., *Post-War Developments in the Marketing of Cheese*, Research Bulletin 261, Iowa Agricultural Experiment Station, Ames, Iowa, 1939.

286. —— "Post-War Concentration in the Cheese Industry," *Journal of Political Economy*, 47: 823 (1939).

287. —— "Market-Sharing in the Packing Industry," *Journal of Farm Economics*, 22: 225 (1940).

288. —— "Price Flexibility and Concentration in the Agricultural Processing Industries," *Journal of Political Economy*, 48: 883 (1940).

289. —— *Imperfect Competition within Agricultural Industries*, Ames, Iowa, 1941.

290. Nichols, J. R., "The Adulteration of Food," *Science Progress*, 31: 258 (1936).

291. Norris, Ruby Turner, *The Theory of Consumer's Demand*, New Haven, Connecticut, 1941

292. Nourse, E. G. and Drury, H. B., *Industrial Price Policies and Economic Progress*, Washington, 1938.

293. Pabst, W. R., Jr., *Butter and Oleomargarine: An Analysis of Competing Commodities*, New York, 1937.

294. —— "Monopolistic Expectations and Shifting Control in the Anthracite Industry," *Review of Economic Statistics*, 22: 45 (1940).

295. Paine, C. L., "Rationalization and the Theory of Excess Capacity," *Economica*, New series 3: 46 (1936).

296. Palander, Tord, *Beiträge zur Standortstheorie*, Uppsala, 1935, especially chapter 14.

297. —— "Instability in Competition Between Two Sellers," *Abstracts of Papers Presented at the Research Conference on Economics and Statistics Held by the Cowles Commission for Research in Economics, at Colorado College, July 6 to Aug. 8, 1936.* Colorado College Publication, General Series No. 208, p. 53.

298. —— "Konkurrens och marknadsjämvikt vid duopol och oligopol" (Competition and Market Equilibrium under Duopoly and Oligopoly), *Ekonomisk Tidsskrift*, 41: 123, 222 (1939).

299. Pareto, V., *Cours d'Économie Politique*, Lausanne, 1896, p. 68.

300. —— *Manuel d'Économie Politique*, Paris, 1909, pp. 595 ff.

301. —— "Économie Mathématique," *Encyclopédie des Sciences Mathématiques*, 1: 606 (1911).

302. Pedersen, H. Winding, "Omkring den Moderne Pristeori" (Concerning the Modern Price Theory), *Nationaløkonomisk Tidsskrift*, 77: 46, 121, 211 (1939).

303. —— "Problems of Duopoly" (brief summary of a paper given at the Elsinore meeting of the Econometric Society), *Econometrica*, 8: 286 (1940).

304. de Pietri-Tonelli, A., "Teorie economiche e teorie politico-economiche dei cosidetti 'monopoli bilaterali,' specialmente nel caso dei cosidetti 'contratti' collettivi di lavoro," *Rivista Italiana di Scienze Economiche*, 11: 119 (1939).

305. Pigou, A. C., *Economics of Welfare*, 4th edition, London, 1932, chapter 15.

306. —— "A Note on Imperfect Competition," *Economic Journal*, 43: 108 (1933).

307. —— *The Economics of Stationary States*, London, 1935.

308. Plant, A., "The Economic Theory Concerning Patents for Inventions," *Economica*, New series 1: 30 (1934).

309. —— "The Economic Aspects of Copyright in Books," *Economica*, New series 1: 167 (1934).

310. Reder, M., "Inter-temporal Relations of Demand and Supply within the Firm," *Canadian Journal of Economics and Political Science*, 7: 25 (1941).

311. —— "Monopolistic Competition and the Stability Conditions," *Review of Economic Studies*, 8: 122 (1941).

312. Redlich, Fritz, "Reklame und Wechsellagenkreislauf," *Schmollers Jahrbuch*, 59: 43 (1935).
313. Reilly, E. E., "The Use of the Elasticity Concept in Economic Theory with Special Reference to Some Effects of a Commodity Tax," *Canadian Journal of Economics and Political Science*, 6: 39 (1940).
314. *Report of the Royal Commission on Price Spreads*, Ottawa, Canada (J. O. Patenaude), 1935.
315. Reynolds, Lloyd G., "The Canadian Baking Industry: A Study of an Imperfect Market," *Quarterly Journal of Economics*, 52: 659 (1938).
316. —— "Competition in the Rubber-Tire Industry," *American Economic Review*, 28: 459 (1938).
317. —— *The Control of Competition in Canada*, Cambridge, 1940.
318. —— "Cutthroat Competition," *American Economic Review*, 30: 736 (1940).
319. —— "Relations between Wage Rates, Costs, and Prices," *American Economic Review*, 32, No. 1 sup.: 275 (1942). Discussion by Montgomery, Royal E., 303.
320. Ricci, S., *Dal protezionismo al sindacato*, Bari, Laterza, 1926, pp. 131, 165. (Mentioned by Schneider, *Reine Theorie*, p. 132.)
321. Ricci, Umberto, "On the Demand for Rival (or Substitute) Commodities," *Econometrica*, 1: 181 (1933).
322. —— "Die Verteuerung einer monopolisierten Ware durch ein Verbrauchssteuer," *Archiv für mathematische Wirtschafts- und Sozialforschung*, 5: 11 (1939).
323. Robinson, E. A(ustin) G., "The Problem of Management and the Size of Firms," *Economic Journal*, 44: 242 (1934).
324. —— "Monopoly and Imperfect Competition," *Economic Journal*, 47: 169 (1937).
325. —— "A Problem in the Theory of Industrial Location," *Economic Journal*, 51: 270 (1941).
326. —— *Monopoly*, London, 1941.
327. Robinson, Joan, "Imperfect Competition and Falling Supply Price," *Economic Journal*, 42: 544 (1932).
328. —— *The Economics of Imperfect Competition*, London, 1933.
329. —— "Decreasing Costs: A Reply to Mr. Harrod," *Economic Journal*, 43: 531 (1933).
330. —— "What is Perfect Competition?" *Quarterly Journal of Economics*, 49: 104 (1934).
331. —— "Euler's Theorem and the Problem of Distribution," *Economic Journal*, 44: 398 (1934).
332. —— Review of Harrod "The Trade Cycle," *Economic Journal*, 46: 691 (1936).
333. —— "Rising Supply Price," *Economica*, 8 (new series): 1 (1941).
334. Rockefeller, David, *Unused Resources and Economic Waste*, Chicago, 1941.
335. Roll, Erich, *Elements of Economic Theory*, London and New York, 1938.
336. —— "The Social Significance of Recent Trends in Economic Theory," *Canadian Journal of Economics and Political Science*, 6: 448 (1940).

338   BIBLIOGRAPHY

337. Roos, C. F., "A Mathematical Theory of Competition," *American Journal of Mathematics*, 47: 163 (1925).
338. Rossi, Lionello, "Il monopolio dell' intermediario," *Giornale degli Economisti*, 71 (series 4): 697 (1931).
339. —— "L'elasticità della domanda e la traslazione dell' imposta in régime di monopolio," *Giornale degli Economisti*, 72(series 4): 601 (1932).
340. —— "Polipolio e Sindacato, orizzontali e verticali," *Giornale degli Economisti*, Vol. 76, Year 51: 82 (1936).
341. —— "L'unità del processo economico," *Rivista Italiana di Scienze Economiche*, 11: 549 (1939).
342. Rothschild, K. W., "The Degree of Monopoly," *Economica*, 9 (new series): 24 (1942).
343. —— "A Note on Advertising," *Economic Journal*, 52: 112 (1942).
344. Rowe, Harold B., "Economic Significance of Changes in Market Organization," *Journal of Farm Economics*, 22: 173 (1940).
345. Samuelson, Paul A., "A Restatement of the Theory of Cost and Production with Emphasis on Its Operational Aspects" (brief summary of a paper presented at the meeting of the American Economic Association at Detroit, December, 1938), *American Economic Review*, 29 sup.: 120 (1939).
346. Saxton, C. Clive, *The Economics of Price Determination*, London, 1942.
347. Schimmel, Jerzy, *Miejska renta gruntowa* (Urban ground rent) Poznan, 1933. Abstract in English appears in *Studia Ekonomiczne* 2: 90. Kraków, 1935. (Polska Akademja Umiejętności).
348. Schneider, Erich, "Über den Einfluss von Änderungen der Nachfrage auf die Monopolpreisbildung," *Archiv für Sozialwissenschaft und Sozialpolitik*, 64: 281 (1930).
349. —— "Zur Theorie des mehrfachen Monopols, insbesondere der des Duopols," *Archiv für Sozialwissenschaft und Sozialpolitik*, 63: 539 (1930); also 64: 380 (1930).
350. —— "Drei Probleme der Monopoltheorie," *Zeitschrift für Nationalökonomie*, 2: 376 (1931).
351. —— *Reine Theorie monopolistischer Wirtschaftsformen*, Tübingen, 1932.
352. —— *Theorie der Produktion*, Vienna, 1934.
353. —— "Preisbildung und Preispolitik unter Berücksichtigung der geographischen Verteilung von Erzeugern und Verbrauchern," *Schmollers Jahrbuch*, 58: 257 (1934).
354. —— "Bemerkungen zu einer Theorie der Raumwirtschaft," *Econometrica*, 3: 79 (1935).
355. —— "Bemerkungen zum Kalkulationsproblem bei Verbundener Produktion," *Nordisk Tidsskrift for Teknisk Økonomi*, Løbe 11: 21 (1938).
356. —— "Reklamen i teoretiskøkonomisk Belysning. Bemaerkninger til Børge Barfod's Bog med samme Titel," *Nordisk Tidsskrift for Teknisk Økonomi*, Løbe 12: 79 (1938).
357. —— "Zur Konkurrenz und Preisbildung auf vollkommenen und unvollkommenen Märkten," *Weltwirtschaftliches Archiv*, 48: 399 (1938). (English summary.)

358. —— "Eine Theorie der Reklame," *Zeitschrift für Nationalökonomie*, 9: 450 (1939).

359. Schultz, T. W., "Needed Additions to the Theoretical Equipment of an Agricultural Economist," *Journal of Farm Economics*, 22: 60 (1940).

360. Schumpeter, J. A., "Zur Einführung der folgenden Arbeit Knut Wicksells," *Archiv für Sozialwissenschaft und Sozialpolitik*, 58: 238 (1927).

361. —— "The Instability of Capitalism," *Economic Journal*, 38: 369 n. (1928).

362. —— "Robinson's 'Economics of Imperfect Competition,'" *Journal of Political Economy*, 42: 249 (1934).

363. —— *Business Cycles* (2 vols.), New York, 1939.

364. Seidler, Gustav, "Geographical Price Relations and Competition," *Journal of Marketing*, 1: 198 (1937).

365. Shepherd, Geoffrey S., "Competition and Oligopoly," *Journal of Farm Economics*, 17: 575 (1935).

366. —— *Agricultural Price Analysis*, Ames, Iowa, 1941.

367. Shone, R. M., "Selling Costs," *Review of Economic Studies*, 2: 225 (1935).

368. Shove, G. F., "The Representative Firm and Increasing Returns," *Economic Journal*, 40: 94 (1930).

369. —— "The Imperfection of the Market: A Further Note," *Economic Journal*, 43: 113 (1933).

370. —— Review of Robinson, "The Economics of Imperfect Competition," *Economic Journal*, 43: 657 (1933).

371. Silcock, T. H., "Some Problems of Price Maintenance," *Economic Journal*, 48: 42 (1938).

372. Singer, H. W., "A Note on Spatial Price Discrimination," *Review of Economic Studies*, 5: 75 (1937).

373. Smith, Henry, "Advertising Costs and Equilibrium," *Review of Economic Studies*, 2: 62 (1934). (See Nos. 491, 1364, 852.)

374. —— "Discontinuous Demand Curves and Monopolistic Competition: A Special Case," *Quarterly Journal of Economics*, 49: 542 (1935).

375. —— "The Imputation of Advertising Costs," *Economic Journal*, 45: 682 (1935).

376. —— "Imperfect Competition and Trade Depression," *The Manchester School*, 7: 38 (1936).

377. —— *Retail Distribution*, New York, 1937.

378. Smithies, A., "The Theory of Value Applied to Retail Selling," *Review of Economic Studies*, 6: 215 (1939).

379. —— "The Maximization of Profits over Time with Changing Cost and Demand Functions," *Econometrica*, 7: 312 (1939).

380. —— "Equilibrium in Monopolistic Competition," *Quarterly Journal of Economics*, 55: 95 (1940).

381. —— and Savage, L. J., "A Dynamic Problem in Duopoly," *Econometrica*, 8: 130 (1940).

382. —— "Monopolistic Price Policy in a Spatial Market," *Econometrica*, 9: 63 (1941).

383. —— "Optimum Location in Spatial Competition," *Journal of Political Economy*, 49: 423 (1941).

384. —— "Equilibrium in Monopolistic Competition: an addendum," *Quarterly Journal of Economics*, 56: 332 (1942).

385. Soucey, R. D., "Group Equilibrium with Selling Costs Variable," *Review of Economic Studies*, 6: 222 (1939).

386. Spahr, W. E., editor, *Economic Principles and Problems* (2 vols.), New York, 1940.

387. Sraffa, P., "The Laws of Returns Under Competitive Conditions," *Economic Journal*, 36: 535 (1926).

388. von Stackelberg, H., *Grundlagen einer reinen Kostentheorie*, Vienna, 1932.

389. —— "Sulla teoria del duopolio e del polipolio," *Rivista italiana di statistica, economia e finanza*; 5: 275 (1933).

390. —— *Marktform und Gleichgewicht*, Vienna and Berlin, 1934.

391. —— "Neues Schrifttum über unvollständigen Wettbewerb," *Schmollers Jahrbuch*, 59: 641 (1935).

392. —— "Probleme der unvolkommenen Konkurrenz," *Weltwirtschaftliches Archiv*, 48: 95 (1938). (English summary.)

393. —— "Das Brechungsgesetz des Verkehrs," *Jahrbücher für Nationalökonomie und Statistik*, 148: 680 (1938).

394. —— "Theorie der Vertriebspolitik und der Qualitätsvariation," *Schmollers Jahrbuch*, 63: 43 (1939).

395. Stigler, George J., "A Generalization of the Theory of Imperfect Competition," *Journal of Farm Economics*, 19: 707 (1937).

396. —— "Production and Distribution in the Short Run," *Journal of Political Economy*, 47: 305 (1939).

397. —— "Notes on the Theory of Duopoly," *Journal of Political Economy*, 48: 521 (1940).

398. —— *Production and Distribution Theories*, New York, 1941.

399. —— "The Extent and Bases of Monopoly," *American Economic Review*, 32, No. 2 sup.: 1 (1942).

400. Sting, K., "Die polypolitische Preisbildung," *Jahrbücher für Nationalökonomie und Statistik*, 134: 761 (1931).

401. —— "Über Gründungstypen und Gründungsreihen," *Jahrbücher für Nationalökonomie und Statistik*, 136: 42 (1932).

402. Stocking, C. A., "Advertising and Economic Theory," *American Economic Review*, 21: 43 (1931).

403. Stocking, Samuel B., "The Value and Significance of Advertising," *The Commerce Journal* (University of Toronto Commerce Club), 1 (new series): 63 (1941).

404. Stolper, Wolfgang F., "The Possibility of Equilibrium under Monopolistic Competition," *Quarterly Journal of Economics*, 54: 519 (1940).

405. von Strigl, Richard, *Einführung in die Grundlagen der Nationalökonomie*, Vienna, 1937.

406. Sumner, John D., "The Effects of the War on Price Policies and Price Making," *American Economic Review*, 32, No. 1 sup.: 404 (1942).

407. Sweezy, Paul M., "On the Definition of Monopoly," *Quarterly Journal of Economics*, 51: 362 (1937).

408. —— *Monopoly and Competition in the English Coal Trade, 1550–1850*, Cambridge, 1938.

409. —— "Demand under Conditions of Oligopoly," *Journal of Political Economy*, 47: 568 (1939).

410. Taussig, F. W., *Principles of Economics*, 4th edition (2 vols.), New York, 1939.

411. Taylor, F. W., *The Economics of Advertising*, London, 1934.

412. Teixeira Ribeiro, J. J., *Teoria Econômica dos Monopólios*, Coimbra, 1934.

413. Temporary National Economic Committee, Investigation of Concentration of Economic Power, Monographs and Hearings before the Committee, especially Monographs No. 1, *Price Behavior and Business Policy*, and No. 21, *Competition and Monopoly in American Industry*, Washington, 1939–41.

414. Tinbergen, J., "Bestimmung und Deutung von Angebotskurven. Ein Beispiel," *Zeitschrift für Nationalökonomie*, 1: 669 (1930).

415. —— "Annual Survey of Significant Developments in General Economic Theory," *Econometrica*, 2: 13 (1934).

416. Tintner, Gerhard, Review of Schneider, "Reine Theorie monopolistischer Wirtschaftsformen," *Schmollers Jahrbuch*, 57: 747 (1933).

417. —— "Monopoly over Time," *Econometrica*, 5: 160 (1937).

418. —— "Note on the Problem of Bilateral Monopoly," *Journal of Political Economy*, 47: 263 (1939).

419. Travaglini, Volrico, *Punti Controversi della Teoria del Costo Crescente*, Rome, 1933.

420. Triffin, Robert, *Monopolistic Competition and General Equilibrium Theory*, Cambridge, 1940.

421. —— "Monopoly in Particular-Equilibrium and in General-Equilibrium Economics," *Econometrica*, 9: 121 (1941).

422. Tucker, Rufus S., "The Degree of Monopoly," *Quarterly Journal of Economics*, 55: 167 (1940).

423. Veblen, T., *The Theory of Business Enterprise*, New York, 1904, especially chapter 3.

424. Waite, W. C. and Cassady, Ralph, *The Consumer and the Economic Order*, New York, 1939.

425. Walker, E. R., "Limited Competition," *Economic Record*, 10: 195 (1934).

426. Wallace, D. H., "Monopoly Prices and Depression," *Explorations in Economics, Essays in Honor of F. W. Taussig*, New York, 1936.

427. —— "Monopolistic Competition and Public Policy," *American Economic Review*, 26 sup.: 77 (1936).

428. —— *Market Control in the Aluminum Industry*, Cambridge, 1937.

429. —— "Monopolistic Competition at Work: A Review" (Review of No. 66), *Quarterly Journal of Economics*, 51: 374 (1937).

430. —— "Industrial Markets and Public Policy," *Public Policy*, edited by C. J. Friedrich and E. S. Mason, Cambridge, 1940.

431. Weinberger, Otto, "Einige Bemerkungen zur deutschen Ausgabe der 'Untersuchungen über die mathematischen Grundlagen der Theorie des Reichtums' Augustin Cournot's," *Jahrbücher für Nationalökonomie und Statistik*, 125: 153–154 (1926).

432. White, Horace G., "A Review of Monopolistic and Imperfect Competition Theories," *American Economic Review*, 26: 637 (1936).

433. Whitman, R. H., "A Note on the Concept of 'Degree of Monopoly,'" *Economic Journal*, 51: 261 (1941).

434. Whittaker, Edmund, *A History of Economic Ideas*, New York, 1940.

435. Wicksell, K., "Mathematische Nationalökonomie," *Archiv für Sozialwissenschaft und Sozialpolitik*, 58: 252 (1927).

436. deWolff, P., "The Demand for Passenger Cars in the United States," *Econometrica*, 6: 113 (1938). Reply by Solo, Robert, and Rejoinder, *Ibid.*, 7: 271 (1939).

437. Wolff, Reinhold P., "Monopolistic Competition in Distribution," *Governmental Marketing Barriers* (Spring 1941 issue of *Law and Contemporary Problems*, Duke University Law School), p. 303.

438. Wood, Ralph C., "Dr. Tucker's 'Reasons' for Price Rigidity," *American Economic Review*, 28: 663 (1938).

439. Wood, Ramsay, *Conditions of Oligopoly and Oligopsony*, Ph.D. thesis announced for 1942, Columbia University.

440. Yntema, T. O., Summary of a paper on "Selling Costs" read at a meeting of the American Economic Association in Philadelphia, December, 1933; *American Economic Review*, 24 sup.: 21 (1934).

441. —— "The Measurement of Incremental Revenue and Cost," *Cowles Commission for Research in Economics, Report of Fourth Annual Research Conference on Economics and Statistics* (1938), Colorado Springs, Colo., p. 62.

442. —— (chairman), Clark, J. M., Dean, Joel, Whitman, R. H. and Stigler, G. J., "Round Table on Cost Functions and their Relation to Imperfect Competition," *American Economic Review*, 30 sup.: 400 (1940).

443. Young, A. A., Review of Bowley's "Mathematical Groundwork of Economics," *Journal of the American Statistical Association*, 20: 134 (1925).

444. Zawadski, W., *Les Mathématiques Appliquées à l'Économie Politique*, Paris, 1914, pp. 68–75.

445. Zeuthen, F., *Den Økonomiske Fordeling* (The Economic Distribution), Copenhagen, 1928.

446. —— "Mellem Konkurrence og Monopol," *Nationaløkonomisk Tidsskrift*, 67: 265 (1929).

447. —— *Problems of Monopoly and Economic Warfare*, London, 1930.

448. —— "Du Monopole Bilatéral," *Revue d'Économie Politique* 47: 1651 (1933).

449. —— "Theoretical Remarks on Price Policy — Hotelling's Case with Variations," *Quarterly Journal of Economics*, 47: 231 (1933).

450. —— "Afstanden Mellem Bedriftscellerne og det Prispolitiske Sammenspil," *Nationaløkonomisk Tidsskrift*, 71: 209 (1933), (Wester-

gaard Festskrift). (A summary is given in English: "The Distance between the Sellers and the Interplay of Price-Policy").

451. —— Review of Robinson, "The Economics of Imperfect Competition," and Chamberlin, "The Theory of Monopolistic Competition," *Nationaløkonomisk Tidsskrift*, 72: 200 (1934).

452. —— Review of Stackelberg, "Marktform und Gleichgewicht," *Zeitschrift für Nationalökonomie*, 6: 548 (1935).

453. —— "Effect and Cost of Advertisement from a Theoretic Aspect," *Nordisk Tidsskrift for Teknisk Økonomi*, 1: 62 (1935). The same article appears in German in the *Archiv für mathematische Wirtschafts- und Sozialforschung*, 1: 159 (1935); and in French in the *Revue des Sciences Economiques*, 9: 251 (1935).

454. —— "Monopolistic Competition and the Homogeneity of the Market," *Econometrica*, 4: 193 (1936).

455. —— "Nogle økonomiske og sociale Udviklingstendenser og deres politiske Konsekvenser," *Statsøkonomisk Tidsskrift*, Oslo, Hefte 3, 1938, p. 115.

456. —— "The Theory of Prices" (brief summary of a paper given at the Elsinore meeting of the Econometric Society), *Econometrica*, 8: 284 (1940).

457. Zingler, E. K., "Advertising and the Maximization of Profit," *Economica*, 7 (new series): 318 (1940).

SUPPLEMENT: MAY 1948

458. Abramovitz, Moses, *Price Theory for a Changing Economy*, New York, 1939.

459. Abramson, A. G., "Price Policies," *Southern Economic Journal*, 12: 39 (1945).

460. Adelman, M. A., *The Dominant Firm, with Special Reference to the A & P Tea Company*, Harvard Ph.D. Thesis, 1948.

461. Aizsilnieks, Arnold P., "Price Theory and the Price Policy of Consumers' Cooperatives," *Ekonomisk Tidskrift*, September 1947.

462. Åkerman, J., "Wages and Full Employment," *Ekonomisk Tidskrift*, March 1946.

463. Arnold, Sam, "Forward Shifting of a Payroll Tax under Monopolistic Competition," *Quarterly Journal of Economics*, 61: 267 (1947).

464. Ashton, Herbert, *Economic Analysis of the Element of Speed in Transportation*, Harvard Ph.D. thesis, 1936.

465. Aubert, Jane, *La Courbe d'Offre*, Paris, 1949.

466. Bain, Joe S., "Market Classifications in Modern Price Theory," *Quarterly Journal of Economics*, 56: 560 (1942).

467. —— "Measurements of the Degree of Monopoly: a note," *Economica*, 10 (new series); 66 (1943). (Based on No. 342). Added comment by Rothschild, p. 69.

468. —— *The Economics of the Pacific Coast Petroleum Industry*, Berkeley and Los Angeles, 1945.

469. —— *Pricing, Distribution, and Employment*, New York, 1948.
470. —— and Moore, Frederick T., *Literature on Price Policy and Related Topics, 1933–47* (Bibliography), Berkeley and Los Angeles, University of California Press, 1947.
471. Balakrishna, R., "Monopolistic Influences in Capitalistic Economy," *Indian Journal of Economics*, 24: 368 (1944).
472. Ballaine, Wesley C., "How Government Purchasing Procedures Strengthen Monopoly Elements," *Journal of Political Economy*, 51: 538 (1943).
473. Barfod, B., "Priskalculation ved Forenet Produktion, etc.," *Nordisk Tidsskrift for Teknisk Økonomi*, 1944–45, No. 2–4.
474. Barna, T., *Profits during and after the war*, Fabian Publications, Ltd., Research Series No. 105, London, 1945.
475. Beach, E. F., "Triffin's Classification of Market Positions," *Canadian Journal of Economics and Political Science*, 9: 69 (1943).
476. Behling, Burton N., "The Nature and Control of the Transport Market," in *Transportation and National Policy*, p. 238. National Resources Planning Board, Washington, 1942.
477. Bellamy, R., "The Changing Pattern of Retail Distribution," "Size and Success of Retail Distribution," "The Cost of Retail Distribution," *Bulletin of the Oxford Institute of Statistics*, vol. 8, numbers 8, 10, 11.
478. Bilimovič, A., "Der Preis bei beiderseitigem Monopol," *Weltwirtschaftliches Archiv*, 57: 312 (1943).
479. Bishop, F. P., *The Economics of Advertising*, London, 1944.
480. Black, Duncan, "On the Rationale of Group Decision Making," *Journal of Political Economy*, 56: 23 (1948).
481. Bloom, Gordon, and Belfer, Nathan, "Unions and Real Labor Income," *Southern Economic Journal*, 14: 290 (1948).
482. Boulding, K. E., "The Theory of the Firm in the Last Ten Years," *American Economic Review*, 32: 791 (1942).
483. —— "In Defense of Monopoly," *Quarterly Journal of Economics*, 59:524 (1945). Comments by Holben, Ralph E., and Rothschild, K. W., 60: 612 (1946).
484. Bowman, Mary J., and Bach, George L., *Economic Analysis and Public Policy*, Second edition, New York, 1948.
485. Brems, Hans, "The Interdependence of Quality Variations, Selling Effort and Price," *Quarterly Journal of Economics*, 62: 418 (1948).
486. Bronfenbrenner, M., "Price Control under Imperfect Competition," *American Economic Review*, 37: 107 (1947).
487. Buchanan, Norman S., "Advertising Expenditures: a Suggested Treatment," *Journal of Political Economy*, 50: 537 (1942).
488. Carlson, Valdemar, *An Introduction to Modern Economics*, Philadelphia, 1946.
489. Cassady, Ralph, Jr., "Some Economic Aspects of Price Discrimination under Non-Perfect Market Conditions," *Journal of Marketing*, 11: 7 (1946).

490. —— "Techniques and Purposes of Price Discrimination," *Journal of Marketing*, 11: 135 (1946).

491. Chamberlin, Edward H., "Advertising Costs and Equilibrium — A Correction" (see 373), *Review of Economic Studies*, 12: 116 (1944-45). (See also Nos. 1364, 852.)

492. —— *Teoria de la Competencia Monopolica*, (Spanish translation of the 5th ed. of *The Theory of Monopolistic Competition* by Cristóbal Lara Beautell and Victor L. Urquidi) Mexico, 1946.

493. —— Review of Stigler, "The Theory of Price," *American Economic Review*, 37: 414 (1947).

494. —— "Proportionality, Divisibility and Economies of Scale," *Quarterly Journal of Economics*, 62: 229 (1948).

495. —— "An Experimental Imperfect Market," *Journal of Political Economy*, 56: 95 (1948).

496. Chamley, Paul, *L'Oligopole*, Paris, 1944.

497. —— "Remarques sur la théorie de l'oligopole," *Revue d'Economie Politique*, 56: 110 (1946).

498. Clark, J. M., "Imperfect Competition Theory and Basing-Point Problems," *American Economic Review*, 33: 283 (1943). Reply by Mund, Vernon A., 33: 612.

499. —— "Realism and Relevance in the Theory of Demand," *Journal of Political Economy*, 54: 347 (1946).

500. Coase, R. H., "The Marginal Cost Controversy," *Economica*, 13 (new series): 169 (1946).

501. —— "Monopoly Pricing with Interrelated Costs and Demands," *Economica*, 13 (new series): 278 (1946).

502. —— "The Marginal Cost Controversy: Some Further Comments," *Economica*, 14 (new series): 150 (1947).

503. —— "The Economics of Uniform Pricing Systems," *The Manchester School*, 15: 139 (1947).

504. Cochran, T. C., Marburg, T. F., Clark, T. D., and Dennison, H. S., "Historical Aspects of Imperfect Competition," *Journal of Economic History*, 3 sup.:27 (December 1943).

505. Cole, A. H., and Williamson, H. F., *The American Carpet Manufacture*, Cambridge, Mass., 1942.

506. Comer, George P., "The Outlook for Effective Competition," *American Economic Review*, 36 (no. 2):154 (1946).

507. Cornejo, Benjamin, *La Competencia Imperfecta y la Teoria Tradicional*, Córdoba, Argentina, 1945.

508. —— "La 'Competencia Monopólica' de Chamberlin," *El Trimestre Económico* (Mexico), 14:55 (1947).

509. Cowden, Dudley J. and Connor, William S., "Quality Control in Industry by Statistical Methods," *Southern Economic Journal*, 12: 115 (1945).

510. Cox, Reavis, "Non-Price Competition and the Measurement of Prices," *Journal of Marketing*, 10:370 (1946).

511. —— "The Meaning and Measurement of Productivity in Distribution," *Journal of Marketing*, 12: 433 (1948).
512. Cronin, John F., *Economic Analysis and Problems*, New York, 1945.
513. Crum, W. L., *Advertising Fluctuations, Seasonal and Cyclical*, Chicago & New York, 1927.
514. Dean, Joel, *The Relation of Cost to Output for a Leather Belt Shop*, with a Memorandum on Empirical Cost Studies by C. Reinold Noyes, New York, National Bureau of Economic Research, Technical Paper No. 2, 1941.
515. Denis, Henri, *Le Monopole Bilatéral*, Paris, 1943.
516. Dickson, H., and Östlind, A., "Prisstabiliserande Egenskaper hos en Säljares Efterfrågeförestallningar," (Price-stabilizing Factors in a Seller's Expectation of Demand), *Ekonomisk Tidskrift*, 45:215 (1943).
517. Dingwall, J., "Equilibrium and Process Analysis in the Traditional Theory of the Firm," *Canadian Journal of Economics and Political Science*, 10: 448 (1944).
518. Domarchi, J., "Le Monopole Bilatéral," *Revue de l'Économie Contemporaine*, 1943.
519. Due, John F., *Intermediate Economic Analysis*, Chicago, 1947.
520. Dunlop, John T., "Wage Policies of Trade Unions," *American Economic Review*, 32 (No. 1, sup.): 290 (1942).
521. —— *Wage Determination under Trade Unions*, New York, 1944.
522. Efroymson, C. W., "A Note on Kinked Demand Curves," *American Economic Review*, 33: 98 (1943).
523. Eiteman, Wilford J., "The Equilibrium of the Firm in Multi-Process Industries," *Quarterly Journal of Economics*, 59: 280 (1945). Comments by Adelman, M. A., 60: 464.
524. —— "Factors Determining the Location of the Least Cost Point," *American Economic Review*, 37: 910 (1947). (See No. 946.)
525. Ellmers, G., "Produktionslenkung und Preisbildung in der Marktform des Kollektivmonopols," *Zeitschrift für Nationalökonomie*, 10: 62 (1942).
526. Enke, Stephen, "Space and Value," *Quarterly Journal of Economics*, 56: 627 (1942).
527. —— *Monopolistic Competition and the General Welfare*, Harvard Ph.D. thesis, 1943.
528. —— "The Monopsony Case for Tariffs," *Quarterly Journal of Economics*, 58: 229 (1944).
529. —— "Consumer Coöperatives and Economic Efficiency," *American Economic Review*, 35: 148 (1945).
530. —— "Monopolistic Output and International Trade," *Quarterly Journal of Economics*, 60: 233 (1946).
531. Eucken, W., *Die Grundlagen der Nationalökonomi*, Jena, 1940. Third edition, 1943.

532. Evans, G. C. and May, Kenneth, "Stability of Limited Competition and Cooperation," *Reports of a Mathematical Colloquium*, 2nd. series, No. 1, p. 3. Notre Dame University.

533. Fellner, William, "Prices and Wages under Bilateral Monopoly," *Quarterly Journal of Economics*, 61: 503 (1947).

534. Friedman, Milton, and Kuznets, Simon, *Income from Independent Professional Practice*, New York, National Bureau of Economic Research, 1945.

535. Galbraith, J. K., "Price Control: Some Lessons from the First Phase," *American Economic Review*, 33 No. 1 Sup.: 253 (1943).

536. —— "Reflections on Price Control," *Quarterly Journal of Economics*, 60: 475 (1946).

537. Gallahue, Edward E., *Some Factors in the Development of Market Standards*, Washington, 1942.

538. Gaumnitz, E. W., and Reed, O. M., *Some Problems Involved in Establishing Milk Prices*, U. S. Dep't of Agric., Ag. Adj. Adm., Division of Marketing and Marketing Agreements — Dairy Section, September 1937.

539. Gregory, Paul M., "Imperfect Competition in the Mortgage Market," *Southern Economic Journal*, 10: 275 (1944).

540. —— "An Economic Interpretation of Women's Fashions," *Southern Economic Journal*, 14: 148 (1947).

541. —— "Fashion and Monopolistic Competition," *Journal of Political Economy*, 56: 69 (1948).

542. Hahn, F. H., "A Note on Profit and Uncertainty," *Economica*, 14 (new series): 211 (1947).

543. Hall, Oswald, "The Informal Organization of the Medical Profession," *Canadian Journal of Economics and Political Science*, 12: 30 (1946).

544. Hansen, Alvin H., "Cost Functions and Full Employment," *American Economic Review*, 37: 552 (1947).

545. Hawtrey, R. G., "Competition from Newcomers," *Economica*, 10 (new series): 219 (1943).

546. Hayes, J. P., "A Note on Selling Costs and the Equilibrium of the Firm," *Review of Economic Studies*, 12: 106 (1944–45).

547. Hayes, Samuel P., Jr., "Potash Prices and Competition," *Quarterly Journal of Economics*, 57: 31 (1942).

548. Healey, Kent T., "Workable Competition in Air Transport," *American Economic Review*, 35 (No. 2): 229 (1945).

549. Heflebower, Richard B., "The Effects of the War on the Structure of Commodity and Labor Markets," *American Economic Review*, 36 (No. 2): 52 (1946).

550. Heimann, Eduard, *History of Economic Doctrines*, New York, 1945.

551. Henderson, A. M., "The Pricing of Public Utility Undertakings," *The Manchester School*, 15: 223 (1947).

552. Hennipman, P., "Afzetpolitiek en prijsvorming," *De Economist*, 93: 147 (1944). (Review article of No. 600.)

553. Hochwald, Werner, "Collective Bargaining and Economic Theory," *Southern Economic Journal*, 13: 228 (1947).

554. Holleran, O. C., *Check Sheet — Introduction of New Industrial Products*, Market Research Series No. 6; *Check Sheet — Introduction of New Consumer Products*, Market Research Series No. 7. Washington, U. S. Government Printing Office, 1935. (The introduction of additional products by existing firms.)

555. Hotchkiss, G. B., "Some Fundamental Objections to Mandatory A B C Grades," *Journal of Marketing*, 10: 128 (1945).

556. Houghton, Harrison F., "The Growth of Big Business," *American Economic Review*, 38 No. 2: 72 (1948). Discussion by Tucker, R. S.; Stocking, G. W.; Gray, H. M.; and Mund, V. A.

557. Hurwicz, Leonid, "The Theory of Economic Behavior," (Review of No. 611), *American Economic Review*, 35: 909 (1945).

558. —— "The Theory of the Firm and of Investment," *Econometrica*, 14: 109 (1946).

559. Hutchison, T. W., "Expectation and Rational Conduct," *Zeitschrift für Nationalökonomie*, 8: 636 (1937).

560. Jervis, F. R., "Gas and Electricity in Britain: A Study in Duopoly," *Land Economics*, 24: 31 (1948).

561. Jöhr, Walter A., *Theoretische Grundlagen der Wirtschaftspolitik*, Band 1, St. Gallen, Switzerland, 1943.

562. Kalecki, Michal, *Studies in Economic Dynamics*. London, 1943.

563. Kaysen, C., "A Revolution in Economic Theory?" (review of No. 611), *Review of Economic Studies*, 14: 1 (1946–7).

564. Keirstead, B. S., *Essentials of Price Theory*, Toronto, 1942.

565. —— and Coore, D. H., "Dynamic Theory of Rents," *Canadian Journal of Economics and Political Science*, 12: 168 (1946).

566. Keynes, J. M., "Relative Movements of Real Wages and Output," *Economic Journal*, 49: 34 (1939).

567. Keyes, Lucille Sheppard, *Federal Control of Entry into Air Transportation*, Radcliffe Ph.D. thesis, 1948.

568. Klebs, F., *Kartellform und Preisbildung*, Stuttgart and Berlin, 1939.

569. Knight, Frank H., "Immutable Law in Economics: Its Reality and Limitations," *American Economic Review*, 36 (No. 2): 93 (1946). Discussion by Chamberlin, E. H., page 139.

570. Kozlik, Adolph, "Monopol oder monopolistische Konkurrenz?" *Zeitschrift für Schweizerische Statistik und Volkswirtschaft*, 77: 341 (1941).

571. Kristensson, Folke, *Studier i Svenska Textila Industriers Struktur*, Stockholm, 1946.

572. Kristensen, Thorkil, *Faste og variable Omkostninger*, Copenhagen, 1939.

573. Küng, Emil, "Zur Lehre von den Marktformen und Marktbeziehungen," in: Amonn, Alfred, *et al*, *Konkurrenz und Planwirtschaft*, Bern, 1946.

574. Lange, Oscar, "A Note on Innovations," *Review of Economic Statistics*, 25: 19 (1943).

575. —— *Price Flexibility and Employment*, Bloomington, Indiana, 1944.

576. Leontief, W., "Multiple Plant Firms: Comment" (see No. 626), *Quarterly Journal of Economics*, 61: 650 (1947). "Note on the Allocation of Output," by Patinkin, Don, 61: 651.

577. Lester, Richard A., "Reflections on the 'Labor Monopoly' Issue," *Journal of Political Economy*, 45: 513 (1947).

578. —— "Absence of Elasticity Considerations in Demand to the Firm," *Southern Economic Journal*, 14: 285 (1948).

579. —— and Shister, Joseph (editors), *Insights into Labor Issues*, New York, 1948.

580. Lever, E. A., *Advertising and Economic Theory*, London, 1947.

581. Lewis, H. Gregg, "Some Observations on Duopoly Theory," *American Economic Review*, 38 No. 2: 1 (1948). Discussion by Jaffé, W.; Bronfenbrenner, M.; McCracken, H. L.; and Wright, D. McC.

582. Lewis, W. Arthur, "Notes on the Economics of Loyalty," *Economica*, 9 (new series): 333 (1942).

583. —— "Competition in Retail Trade," *Economica*, 12 (new series): 202 (1945).

584. —— "Fixed Costs," *Economica*, 13 (new series): 231 (1946).

585. Lindblom, Charles E., " 'Bargaining Power' in Price and Wage Determination," *Quarterly Journal of Economics*, 62: 396 (1948).

586. Lynch, D., *The Concentration of Economic Power*, New York, 1946.

587. Machlup, Fritz, "Competition, Pliopoly and Profit, Part II," *Economica*, 9 (new series): 153 (1942).

588. —— "Marginal Analysis and Empirical Research," *American Economic Review*, 36: 519 (1946).

589. —— "Monopolistic Wage Determination as a Part of the General Problem of Monopoly," in *Wage Determination and the Economics of Liberalism*, Chamber of Commerce of the United States, Washington, D. C., 1947.

590. Marchal, Jean, *Le Mécanisme des Prix et la Structure de l'Économie*, Paris, 1946.

591. Maroni, Yves, *International Trade under Monopolistic Competition*, Harvard Ph.D. thesis, 1946.

592. —— Maroni, Yves, "Discrimination under Market Interdependence," *Quarterly Journal of Economics*, 62: 95 (1947).

593. Marschak, J., "Neumann's and Morgenstern's New Approach to Static Economics," *Journal of Political Economy*, 54: 97 (1946).

594. McIsaac, A. M., and Smith, J. G., *Essential Economic Principles*, Boston, 1941.

595. Mehta, J. K., "The Conception of a Market in Economic Theory," *Indian Journal of Economics*, 23: 364 (1943).

596. von Mering, Otto, *The Shifting and Incidence of Taxation*, Philadelphia, 1942.

597. Mirkowich, M., "Grenzen der Theorie der monopolistischen Konkur-

renz," *Jahrbücher für Nationalökonomie und Statistik,* 154: 362 (1941).

598. Moffat, James E., Christenson, C. L., and associates, *Economics, Principles and Problems,* New York, 1947.

599. Moïsseev, Moïse, "La Réclame, Ses Aspects, Son Rôle," *Revue des Sciences Économiques,* 11: 92 (1937).

600. Möller, H., *Kalkulation, Absatzpolitik und Preisbildung. Die Lehre von der Absatzpolitik der Betriebe auf preistheoretischer und betriebswirtschaftlicher Grundlage,* Vienna, 1941.

601. —— "Die Formen der regionalen Preisdifferenzierung," *Weltwirtschaftliches Archiv,* 57: 81 (1943).

602. —— "Grundlagen einer Theorie der regionalen Preisdifferenzierung," *Weltwirtschaftliches Archiv,* 58: 335 (1943).

603. —— "Das Konkurrenzsystem im Versicherungswesen," *Jahrbücher für Nationalökonomie und Statistik,* 159: 1 (1944).

604. Moos, S., "Statistics of Advertising," *Bulletin of the Oxford Institute of Statistics,* 5: 181 (1943).

605. Morgan, Theodore, "A Measure of Monopoly in Selling," *Quarterly Journal of Economics,* 60: 461 (1946).

606. Morgenstern, Oskar, "Vollkommene Voraussicht und wirtschaftliches Gleichgewicht," *Zeitschrift für Nationalökonomie,* 6: 337 (1935).

607. —— "Oligopoly, Monopolistic Competition, and the Theory of Games," *American Economic Review,* 38 No. 2: 10 (1948). Discussion by Jaffé, W.; Bronfenbrenner, M.; McCracken, H. L.; and Wright, D. McC.

608. —— "Demand Theory Reconsidered," *Quarterly Journal of Economics,* 62: 165 (1948).

609. Mund, V. A., "Monopolistic Competition Theory and Public Price Policy," *American Economic Review,* 32: 727 (1942).

610. National Bureau of Economic Research, Committee on Price Determination, *Cost Behavior and Price Policy,* New York, 1943.

611. Neumann, J., and Morgenstern, O., *Theory of Games and Economic Behavior,* Princeton, 1944.

612. Nichol, A. J., "Production and the Probabilities of Cost," *Quarterly Journal of Economics,* 57: 69 (1942).

613. —— "Monopoly Supply and Monopsony Demand," *Journal of Political Economy,* 50: 861 (1942).

614. Nicholls, W. H., "Social Biases and Recent Theories of Competition," *Quarterly Journal of Economics,* 58: 1 (1943).

615. —— "Imperfect Competition in Agricultural Processing and Distributing Industries," *Canadian Journal of Economics and Political Science,* 10: 150 (1944).

616. —— "Some Economic Aspects of the Margarine Industry," *Journal of Political Economy,* 54: 221 (1946).

617. —— "Reorientation of Agricultural Marketing and Price Research," *Journal of Farm Economics,* 30: 43 (1948).

618. Nicols, Alfred, *Cyclical Adjustments under Oligopoly*. Harvard Ph.D. thesis, 1946.

619. —— "The Rehabilitation of Pure Competition," *Quarterly Journal of Economics*, 62: 31 (1947).

620. Nordin, J. A., "The Marginal Cost Controversy: A Reply" (see No. 500), *Economica*, 14 (new series): 134 (1947).

621. Norris, Harry, "State Enterprise Price and Output Policy and the Problem of Cost Imputation" (see No. 501), *Economica*, 14 (new series): 54 (1947).

622. Nourse, Edwin G., *Price Making in a Democracy*, Washington, 1944.

623. Oliver, Henry M., Jr., "Average Cost and Long-Run Elasticity of Demand," *Journal of Political Economy*, 45: 212 (1947).

624. Oxenfeldt, Alfred R., *New Firms and Free Enterprise*, Washington, D. C., 1943.

625. Pabst, William R., Jr., "Unstable Conditions of Competition and Monopoly in Exhaustible Resource Industries," *Journal of Political Economy*, 50: 739 (1942).

626. Patinkin, Don, "Multiple-Plant Firms, Cartels, and Imperfect Competition," *Quarterly Journal of Economics*, 61: 173 (1947).

627. Paulson, W. E., "Diagrammatic Economics," *Journal of Farm Economics*, 28: 687 (1946).

628. Pedersen, H. Winding, "Konkurrencens Tilbagegang," *Nordisk Tidsskrift for Teknisk Økonomi*, 6: 119 (1936).

629. Phelps, Clyde W., "Monopolistic and Imperfect Competition in Consumer Loans," *Journal of Marketing*, 8: 382 (1944).

630. Phelps, Dudley M., *Planning the Product*, Chicago, 1947.

631. Pigon, A. C., "Some Considerations on Stability Conditions, Employment and Real Wage Rates," *Economic Journal*, 55: 346 (1945). (Answer to No. 671.)

632. Pritchard, L. J., "The Effects of Specific and *Ad Valorem* Taxes," *Quarterly Journal of Economics*, 58: 149 (1943) (Comment on No. 135).

633. Rangnekar, S. B., *Imperfect Competition in International Trade*, Bombay, Oxford University Press, 1947.

634. Reder, Melvin W., *Studies in the Theory of Welfare Economics*, New York, 1947.

635. —— "A Reconsideration of the Marginal Productivity Theory," *Journal of Political Economy*, 55: 450 (1947).

636. Reynolds, Lloyd G., "Wage Differences in Local Labor Markets," *American Economic Review*, 36: 366 (1946).

637. —— "The Supply of Labor to the Firm," *Quarterly Journal of Economics*, 60: 390 (1946).

638. Ricardo, Rita, "Annual Wage Guarantee Plans," *American Economic Review*, 35: 870 (1945).

639. Robinson, Joan, *An Essay in Marxian Economics*, London, 1942.

640. Roll, Erich, *A History of Economic Thought*, revised and enlarged. New York, 1946.

641. Ross, A. M , "Trade Unions as Wage-Fixing Institutions," *American Economic Review*, 37: 566 (1947).

642. Rothschild, K. W., "Advertising in War-Time," *Bulletin of the Oxford Institute of Statistics*, 4: 169 (1942).

643. —— "Monopsony, Buying Costs, and Welfare Expenditures," *Review of Economic Studies*, 10: 62 (1942–43).

644. —— "Price Theory and Oligopoly," *Economic Journal*, 57: 299 (1947).

645. Samuelson, Paul A., *Economics, An Introductory Analysis*, New York, 1948.

646. Scheibli, H. P., *Marktformen und Marktinterventionismus in der schweizerischen Tabakwirtschaft*, Bern, 1947.

647. Schneider, Erich, "Absatz, Produktion und Lagerhaltung bei einfacher Produktion," *Archiv für mathematische Wirtschafts- und Sozialforschung*, 4: 99 (1938).

648. —— "Wirklichkeitsnahe Theorie der Absatzpolitik," *Weltwirtschaftliches Archiv*, 56: 92 (1942) (Review article of No. 600).

649. —— "Ziehsetzung, Verhaltensweise und Preisbildung," *Jahrbücher für Nationalökonomie und Statistik*, 157: 405 (1943).

650. Schumpeter, Joseph A., chairman, Round Table on Cost and Demand Functions of the Individual Firm. (Abstracts of papers by Staehle, Hans; Dean, Joel; Tintner, Gerhard; and of discussion by Lange, Oscar; Smithies, A.; Metzler, Lloyd A.; and Döblin, E.), *American Economic Review*, 32 (No. 1, sup.): 349 (1942).

651. de Scitovsky, T., "Some Consequences of the Habit of Judging Quality by Price," *Review of Economic Studies*, 12: 100 (1944–45).

652. Seelye, Alfred L., "The Importance of Economic Theory in Marketing Courses," *Journal of Marketing*, 11: 223 (1947).

653. Shister, Joseph, "The Theory of Union Wage Rigidity," *Quarterly Journal of Economics*, 57: 522 (1943).

654. Smith, Victor E., "The Statistical Production Function," *Quarterly Journal of Economics*, 59: 543 (1945).

655. Smithies, Arthur, "The Stability of Competitive Equilibrium," *Econometrica*, 10: 258 (1942).

656. —— "Aspects of the Basing Point System," *American Economic Review*, 32: 705 (1942). Comment by Salera, Virgil, 33: 900 (1943).

657. Snijders, W. L., *Beschouwingen over de Theorie der Monopolistische Concurrentie*, Utrecht, 1945. (Reviewed in *American Economic Reveiw*, December 1946.)

658. Spengler, Joseph J., "Monopolistic Competition and the Use and Price of Urban Land Service," *Journal of Political Economy*, 54: 385 (1946).

659. von Stackelberg, H., "Die Grundlagen der Nationalökonomie," *Weltwirtschaftliches Archiv*, 51: 245 (1940). (Review article of No. 531.)

660. —— *Grundzüge der theoretischen Volkswirtschaftslehre*, Stuttgart and Berlin, 1943.

661. —— *Grundlagen der theoretischen Volkswirtschaftslehre*, Bern, 1948.
662. Stauss, James H., "The Entrepreneur: The Firm," *Journal of Political Economy*, 52: 112 (1944).
663. Steindl, J., *Small and Big Business, Economic Problems of the Size of Firms*, Institute of Statistics, Monograph No. 1, Oxford, 1945.
664. —— "Capitalist Enterprise and Risk," *Oxford Economic Papers*, No. 7: 21 (1945).
665. Stigler, George J., *The Theory of Price*, New York, 1946.
666. —— "The Kinky Oligopoly Demand Curve and Rigid Prices," *Journal of Political Economy*, 55: 432 (1947). (See No. 945.)
667. Sufrin, Sidney C., "Monopolies and Labor Regulation," *American Economic Review*, 29: 551 (1939).
668. Sundbom, I., "Market Forms and the Conditions for Monopolistic Coöperation among Producers," *Ekonomisk Tidskrift*, March 1944.
669. Thirlby, G. F., "The Marginal Cost Controversy: A Note on Mr. Coase's Model" (see No. 500), *Economica*, 14 (new series): 48 (1947).
670. Tinbergen, J., *Beperkte Concurrentie*, Leiden, 1946. (Reviewed in *American Economic Review*, December 1946.)
671. Tsiang, S. C., "Professor Pigou on the Relative Movements of Real Wages and Employment," *Economic Journal*, 54: 352 (1944).
672. Wald, A., "Über einige Gleichungssysteme der Mathematischen Ökonomie," *Zeitschrift für Nationalökonomie*, 7: 637 (1936).
673. Walker, E. R., *From Economic Theory to Policy*, Chicago, 1943.
674. Weintraub, Sidney, "The Foundations of the Demand Curve," *American Economic Review*, 32: 538 (1942).
675. —— "Monopoly Equilibrium and Anticipated Demand," *Journal of Political Economy*, 50: 427 (1942).
676. —— "The Classification of Market Positions: Comment," *Quarterly Journal of Economics*, 56: 666 (1942). Reply by Robert Triffin.
677. —— "Price Cutting and Economic Warfare," *Southern Economic Journal*, 8: 309 (1942).
678. —— "Monopoly Pricing and Unemployment," *Quarterly Journal of Economics*, 61: 108 (1946).
679. Whitman, Roswell H., "Demand Functions for Merchandise at Retail," in *Studies in Mathematical Economics and Econometrics*, Lange, *et al.*, eds., Chicago, 1942.
680. Williams, Faith, and Hoover, Ethel D., "Measuring Price and Quality of Consumers' Goods," *Journal of Marketing*, 10: 354 (1946).
681. Wolfe, A. B., "Price Making in a Democracy" (Review of No. 622), *Journal of Economics*, 53: 73 (1945).
682. Woolley, Herbert B., "The Anomalous Case of the Shifting Cost Curve," *Quarterly Journal of Economics*, 57: 646 (1943).
683. —— *The Theory of Administered Price*, Harvard Ph.D. thesis, 1947.
684. —— "The General Elasticity of Demand," *Econometrica*, 15: 226 (1947).
685. Yntema, T. O., "The Market for Consumer Credit: A Case in 'Im-

perfect Competition' ", *Annals of the American Academy of Political and Social Science*, March 1938, p. 79.

686. Yoder, Dale, "The Structure of the Demand for Labor," *American Economic Review*, 32 (No. 1, sup.): 261 (1942). Discussion by W. Rupert Maclaurin, p. 302.

687. Zeuthen, F., *Økonomisk Teori og Metode*, Copenhagen 1942. (Reviewed in *American Economic Review*, December 1946).

688. —— "Der wirtschaftliche Zusammenhang — ein Netz von Teilzusammenhangen," *Weltwirtschaftliches Archiv*, 58: 175 (1943).

689. —— "Paa Vej til en forenklet og realistik Teori om Virksomhedernes Prispolitik?" *Nordisk Tidsskrift for Teknisk Økonomi*, 1944–45, No. 1.

690. Zijlstra, J., "Marktvorm, kostenverloop en structuur van de handel," *De Economist*, April–May 1947.

691. Zolotas, X. E., Θεωρητιχη Οιχονομιχη, Athens, 1944.

SUPPLEMENT: MAY 1956

Abbreviations Used in this Supplement

A.E.R.	*American Economic Review*
C.J.	*Canadian Journal of Economics and Political Science*
E.A.	*Économie Appliquée*
Eca	*Economica*
Ecta	*Econometrica*
E.I.	*Economia Internazionale*
E.J.	*Economic Journal*
E.R.	*Economic Record*
E.T.	*Ekonomisk Tidsskrift*
G.E.	*Giornale degli Economisti e Annali di Economia*
H.B.R.	*Harvard Business Review*
J.B.U.C.	*Journal of Business of the University of Chicago*
J.I.E.	*Journal of Industrial Economics*
J.M.	*Journal of Marketing*
J.N.S.	*Jahrbücher für Nationalökonomie und Statistik*
J.P.E.	*Journal of Political Economy*
N.T.	*Nationaløkonomisk Tidsskrift*
N.T.T.O.	*Nordisk Tidsskrift for Teknisk Økonomie*
O.E.P.	*Oxford Economic Papers*
Q.J.E.	*Quarterly Journal of Economics*
R.E.	*Revue Économique*
R.E.P.	*Revue d'Économie Politique*
R.E.Stat.	*Review of Economics and Statistics* (also *Review of Economic Statistics*)
R.E.Stud.	*Review of Economic Studies*
R.I.S.S.	*Revista Internazionale di Scienze Sociali*
S.A.J.E.	*South African Journal of Economics*
S.E.J.	*Southern Economic Journal*
S.J.	*Schmollers Jahrbuch*
S.Z.	*Schweizerische Zeitschrift für Volkswirtschaft und Statistik*
W.A.	*Weltwirtschaftliches Archiv*

692. Aaronovitch, S., *Monopoly. A Study of British Monopoly Capitalism*, London, 1955.

693. Abbott, Lawrence, "Vertical Equilibrium under Pure Quality Competition," *A.E.R.*, 43:826 (1953).

694. —— *Quality and Competition*, New York, 1955.

695. Abrams, Mark, "Statistics of Advertising," *Journal of the Royal Statistical Society*, 115:258 (1952).

696. Adams, Robert W. and Wheeler, John T., "External Economies and the Supply Curve," *R.E.Stud.*, 20:24 (1952–53).

697. Adams, Walter (ed.), *The Structure of American Industry*, New York and London, 1950.

698. —— "The Aluminum Case: Legal Victory — Economic Defeat," *A.E.R.*, 41:915 (1951). Discussion, 42:893 (1952).

699. —— "Competition, Monopoly and Countervailing Power," *Q.J.E.*, 67:469 (1953). See also 68:481 (1954).

700. —— "The 'Rule of Reason': Workable Competition or Workable Monopoly," *Yale Law Journal*, 63:348 (1954).

701. Adelman, Morris A., "Effective Competition and the Antitrust Laws," *Harvard Law Review*, 61:1289 (1948).

702. —— "Integration and Antitrust Policy," *Harvard Law Review*, 63:27 (1949).

703. —— "The A & P Case: A Study in Applied Economic Theory," *Q.J.E.*, 63:238 (1949).

704. —— "The Large Firm and Its Suppliers," *R.E.Stat.*, 31:113 (1949).

705. —— "The A & P Case," *A.E.R.*, 39:280 (May, 1949). Discussion, p. 311.

706. —— "Business Size and Public Policy," *J.B.U.C.*, 24:269 (1951).

707. —— "The Measurement of Industrial Concentration," *R.E.Stat.*, 33:269 (1951). Discussion, 34:156 (1952).

708. —— "Dirlam and Kahn on the A & P Case," *J.P.E.*, 61:436 (1953).

709. Alderson, Wroe, "A Functionalist Approach to Competition," in *The Role and Nature of Competition in our Marketing Economy*, Harvey W. Huegy, ed., University of Illinois Bulletin, Vol. 51, No. 76, June 1954.

710. Alderson, Wroe and Cox, Reavis, "Towards a Theory of Marketing," *J.M.*, 13:137 (1948).

711. Alderson, Wroe and Sessions, Robert E., *"Unjustly Discriminatory or Promotive of Monopoly" Defined and Applied to Tire Distribution* (privately printed), Philadelphia, 1950.

712. Alexander, R. S. and Snitzler, James, "Wholesale Buying and Merchandising," *J.M.*, 14:178 (1949).

713. Alhadeff, David, "The Market Structure of Commercial Banking in the United States," *Q.J.E.*, 65:62 (1951).

714. —— *Monopoly and Competition in Banking*, London, 1955.

715. Allen, Clark L., Morgner, Aurelius and Strotz, Robert H., *Problems in the Theory of Price*, New York, 1954.

716. Allen, G. R., "The Size of the Factory," *E.J.*, 63:915 (1953). Reply by Florence, P. Sargent, 64:625 (1954).

717. Allen, Layman E., "Games Bargaining: A Proposed Application of the Theory of Games to Collective Bargaining," *Yale Law Journal*, 65:660 (1956).

718. Allin, Bushrod W., "Is Group Choice a Part of Economics?" *Q.J.E.*, 67:362 (1953). Comments by Knight, Frank H. and Ellis, Howard S. and Reply, 67:605 (1953).

719. Alt, Richard M., "Competition Among Types of Retailers in Selling the Same Commodity," *J.M.*, 14:441 (1949).

720. —— "The Internal Organization of the Firm and Price Formation: an Illustrative Case," *Q.J.E.*, 63:92 (1949).

721. Andrews, K. R., "Product Diversification and the Public Interest," *H.B.R.*, 29, No. 4:91 (1951).

722. Andrews, P. W. S., *Manufacturing Business*, London, 1949.

723. —— "A Reconsideration of the Theory of the Individual Business," *O.E.P.*, 1 (new series:54 (1949).

724. —— "Some Aspects of Competition in Retail Trade," *O.E.P.*, 2:137 (1950).

725. —— "Industrial Economics as a Specialist Subject," *J.I.E.*, 1:72 (1952).

726. Andrews, P. W. S. and Elizabeth Brunner, "Productivity and the Business Man," *O.E.P.*, 2:197 (1950).

727. Angehrn, Otto, "Markttransparenz und Marktforschung," *S.Z.*, 86:158 (1950).

728. Angiolini, V., "Alcune osservazzioni su un vecchio tema," *G.E.*, 9:372 (1950).

729. Apel, Hans, "Marginal Cost Constancy and Its Implications," *A.E.R.*, 38:870 (1948).

730. Arant, Willard, "Competition of the Few Among the Many," *Q.J.E.*, 70:327 (1956).

731. Arndt, Helmut, "Konkurrenz und Monopol in Wirklichkeit," *J.N.S.*, 161:222 (1949).

732. —— "Wettbewerbsprozesse und Arbeitslosigkeit," *W.A.*, 66:70 (1951).

733. —— *Schöpferischer Wettbewerb und klassenlose Gesellschaft*, Volkswirtschaftliche Schriften, Heft 2, Berlin, 1952.

734. Arrasate, J. A., "Analisis de la Competencia en la Economia Neoclasica" (Parts I, II, III), *Boletin de Estudios Economicos* (Bilbao), 4:119, 215 (1950); and 5:43 (1951).

735. *Attorney General's National Committee to Study the Antitrust Laws, Report of*, Washington, 1954.

736. Aubert, Jane, "Note Analytique sur les Sources du Profit," *Analyses et Discussions Théoriques*, Paris, Librairie Marcel Rivière et Cie, 1948.

737. Aubert-Krier, Jane, "Le Comportement des Entreprises Commerciales et leur Influence sur le Marché," *R.E.*, May 1954, p. 422.

738. —— "Une Réformulation de la Théorie de la Concurrence Pure," *R.E.P.*, 64:447 (1954).

739. —— "La Théorie de la Concurrence Monopolistique du Professeur E. H. Chamberlin," *E.A.*, 8:399 (1955).

740. —— "Les schémas théoriques de la croissance de la firme," *E.A.*, 8:437 (1955).

741. Aubert-Krier, Jane and Krier, Henri, "Éléments pour une Théorie de la Distribution," *R.E.*, May 1954, p. 342.

742. Austin, Robert W., "Looking Around (Perspective on Regulation of Competition)" *H.B.R.*, 30, No. 2:19 (1952).

743. Backman, Jules, "Price Inflexibility — War and Postwar," *J.P.E.*, 56:428 (1948).
744. —— *Price Practices and Price Policies*, New York, 1953.
745. Bailey, M. J., "Price and Output Determination by a Firm Selling Related Products," *A.E.R.*, 44:82 (1954).
746. Bain, Joe S., "Price and Production Policies," in *A Survey of Contemporary Economics*, Howard S. Ellis, ed., for the American Economic Association, Philadelphia and Toronto, 1948.
747. —— "Output Quotas in Imperfect Cartels," *Q.J.E.*, 62:617 (1948). (Discussion of No. 626).
748. —— "Pricing in Monopoly and Oligopoly," *A.E.R.*, 39:448 (1949).
749. —— "Workable Competition in Oligopoly: Theoretical Considerations and Some Empirical Evidence," *A.E.R.*, 40 (no. 2):35, 64 (May 1950).
750. —— "Relation of Profit-Rate to Industry Concentration: American Manufacturing, 1936–40," *Q.J.E.*, 65:293 (1951).
751. —— *Price Theory*, New York, 1952.
752. —— "Economies of Scale, Concentration, and the Conditions of Entry in Twenty Manufacturing Industries," *A.E.R.*, 44:15 (1954).
753. —— "Advantages of the Large Firm: Production, Distribution and Sales Promotion," *J.M.*, 20:336 (1956).
754. Baldamus, W., "Mechanization, Utilization, and Size of Plant," *E.J.*, 63:50 (1953).
755. Balderston, F. E., "Scale of Output and Internal Organization of the Firm," *Q.J.E.*, 69:45 (1955).
756. Banks, Seymour, "The Measurement of the Effect of a New Packaging Material upon Preference and Sales," *J.B.U.C.*, 23:71 (1950).
757. —— "The Relationships between Preference and Purchase of Brands," *J.M.*, 15:145 (1950).
758. Barfod, Børge, "Polysony — Polypoly," *N.T.T.O.*, 12:31 (1948).
759. Basmann, Robert L., "A Theory of Demand with Consumer's Preferences Variable," *Ecta*, 24:47 (1956).
760. Bauchet, Pierre, "La Structure d'une branche d'industrie: l'automobile," *E.A.*, 5:359 (1952).
761. Baudin, L., Director, et al., *Traité d'Économic Politique*, Paris, 1952–3.
762. Bauer, P. T., *The Rubber Industry. A Study in Competition and Monopoly*, London, 1948.
763. —— "Concentration in Tropical Trade: Some Aspects and Implications of Oligopoly," *Eca*, 20:302 (1953).
764. —— *West African Trade. A Study of Competition, Monopoly and Oligopoly in a Changing Economy*, London, 1954.
765. Bauer, P. T. and Yamey, B. S., "Competition and Prices: A Study of Groundnut Buying in Nigeria," *Eca*, 19:31 (1952).
766. —— "The Economics of Marketing Reform," *J.P.E.*, 62:210 (1954).
767. Baumol, W. J. and Chandler, L. V., *Economic Processes and Policies*, New York, 1954.

768. Baykov, Alexander, *The Development of the Soviet Economic System*, New York, 1948.
769. Becker, Arthur P., "Psychological Production and Conservation," *Q.J.E.*, 63:577 (1949).
770. Beckmann, Martin J., "A Continuous Model of Transportation," *Ecta*, 20:643 (1952).
771. —— "The Partial Equilibrium of a Continuous Space Market," *W.A.*, 71:73 (1953).
772. Beckmann, Martin J. and Marschak, Thomas, *An Activity Analysis Approach to Location Theory*, Cowles Foundation Paper No. 99, New Haven, Conn., 1956.
773. Beckwith, B. P., *Marginal-Cost Price-Output Control*, New York, 1956.
774. Beem, Eugene R. and Ewing, John S., "Business Appraises Consumer Testing Agencies," *H.B.R.*, 32, No. 2:113 (1954).
775. Behrman, J. N., "Distributive Effects of an Excise Tax on a Monopolist," *J.P.E.*, 58:546 (1950).
776. Bell, J. F., *A History of Economic Thought*, New York, 1953.
777. Bernstein, Peter L., "Profit Theory — Where Do We Go from Here?", *Q.J.E.*, 67:407 (1953).
778. Biet, Bernard, *Théories Contemporaines du Profit*, Paris, 1956.
779. Bingham, Robert H., "The Uniform Delivered Pricing Method in the Grocery Manufacturing Industry," *J.M.*, 14:594 (1950).
780. Birch, Cecil M., "Papendreou's Coefficients of Penetration and Insulation," *A.E.R.*, 40:407 (1950).
781. —— "A Revised Classification of Forms of Competition," *C.J.*, 20:157 (1954).
782. Bishop, R. L., "Elasticities, Cross-Elasticities, and Market Relationships," *A.E.R.*, 42:779 (1952). Discussion by Fellner, William and Chamberlin, E. H. and Reply, 43:898 (1953). Comment by Hieser, R., 45:373 and Reply, 45:382 (1955).
783. Black, Guy, "Product Differentiation and Demand for Marketing Services," *J.M.*, 16:73 (1951).
784. Blackwell, Richard, "The Pricing of Books," *J.I.E.*, 2:174 (1954).
785. Blair, J. M., "Economic Concentration and Depression Price Rigidity," *A.E.R.*, 45 (no. 2):566 (May 1955). Discussion.
786. Blank, David M. and Winnick, Louis, "The Structure of the Housing Market," *Q.J.E.*, 67:181 (1953). Discussion, 70:314 (1956).
787. Bliss, Perry, "Price Determination at the Department Store Level," *J.M.*, 17:37 (1952).
788. —— "Non-Price Competition at the Department Store Level," *J.M.*, 17:357 (1953).
789. Bliumin, I. G., "The Bourgeois Economists of the United States as Apologists for Capitalist Monopoly" (in Russian), *Kommunist*, Vol. 4 (1955).
790. —— *Kritika sovremennoi politicheskoi economii Anglii* (Critique of Contemporary English Bourgeois Economics), Moscow, 1953.

791. Bober, M. M., *Intermediate Price and Income Theory*, New York, 1955.

792. Böhler, E., "Die Konkurrenz als Organisationsprinzip der Wirtschaft," *S.Z.*, 86:381 (1950).

793. Böhm, Franz, "Das Kartellproblem," *S.Z.*, 87:193 (1951).

794. Borden, Neil H., *Advertising in Our Economy*, Chicago, 1945.

795. Boulding, Kenneth E., "Implications for General Economics of More Realistic Theories of the Firm," *A.E.R.*, 42:35 (May, 1952).

796. Bouquerel, F., *L'Étude des Marchés au Services des Entreprises*, Paris, 1954.

797. Bowman, Raymond T. and Phillips, Almarin, "The Capacity Concept and Individual Investment," *C.J.*, 21:190 (1955).

798. Bowman, Ward S., Jr., "Resale Price Maintenance — A Monopoly Problem," *J.B.U.C.*, 25:141 (1952).

799. —— "The Report of the Attorney General's National Committee to Study the Antitrust Laws," *J.I.E.*, 4:81 (1956).

800. Brems, Hans, "Some Notes on the Structure of the Duopoly Problem," *N.T.T.O.*, 12:41 (1948).

801. —— "Antitrust i U. S. A.," *N.T.*, 87:295 (1949).

802. —— "Karteller og konkurrence," *N.T.*, 87:347 (1949).

803. —— "Er den frie konkurrence død?", *Det Danske Marked*, 9:216 (1950).

804. —— "En ny fremstilling af oligopolteorien," *N.T.*, 88:216 (1950).

805. —— *Reklame, købelyst og købeevne*, Copenhagen, 1950.

806. —— *Some Problems of Monopolistic Competition*, mimeographed, Einar Munksgaard. Copenhagen, 1950. (Danish summary). Discussed by H. Winding Pedersen and F. Zeuthen, *N.T.*, 88:139 (1950).

807. —— *"Gränserne for fastsättelsen af Kartelpriser,"* *E.T.*, 53:90 (1951).

808. —— *Product Equilibrium under Monopolistic Competition*, Cambridge, Mass., 1951.

809. —— "On the Theory of Price Agreements," *Q.J.E.*, 65:252 (1951).

810. —— "Cartels and Competition," *W.A.*, 66:51 (1951).

811. —— "A Discontinuous Cost Function," *A.E.R.*, 42:577 (1952).

812. —— "En samenligning mellem den gaengse og den jantzen'ske omkostningsteori," *N.T.*, 90:193 (1952).

813. —— "Employment, Prices, and Monopolistic Competition," *R.E.Stat.*, 34:314 (1952).

814. —— "Foreign Exchange Rates and Monopolistic Competition," *E.J.*, 63:289 (1953). Comment by R. F. Harrod.

815. —— "Konkurrentreaktion, pris og kvalitet," *Det Danske Marked*, 15:1 (1956).

816. Bresciani-Turroni, C., *Corso di Economia Politica* (Vol. II), Milano, 1951.

817. Brewster, Kingman, "Enforceable Competition: Unruly Reason or Reasonable Rules?", *A.E.R.*, 46 (no. 2):482 (May 1956). Discussion.

818. Brinkmann, Carl, "Der Ertrag der neueren Wirtschaftstheorie für die Orientierung der Wirtschaftspolitik," *J.N.S.*, 162:421 (1950).

819. Brochier, Hubert, "Autofinancement des entreprises et théorie économique," *R.E.*, Sept., 1952, p. 609.

820. Brockie, Melvin D., "Rent Concepts and the Theory of Opportunity Cost," *W.A.*, 72:239 (1954).

821. Brodsky, Michel and Rocher, Pierre, *L'Économie Politique Mathématique*, Paris, 1949.

822. Bronfenbrenner, Martin, "Price Control under Imperfect Competition: The Joint Production Problem," *C.J.*, 15:210 (1949).

823. —— "Imperfect Competition on a Long-Run Basis," *J.B.U.C.*, 23:81 (1950).

824. —— "Wages in Excess of Marginal Revenue Product," *S.E.J.*, 16:297 (1950).

825. —— "Contemporary Economics Resurveyed," *J.P.E.*, 61:160 (1953).

826. Brown, George H., "Measuring Consumer Attitudes Towards Products," *J.M.*, 14:691 (1950).

827. —— "What Economists Should Know about Marketing," *J.M.*, 16:60 (1951).

828. Brown, Theodore H., "Quality Control," *H.B.R.*, 29, No. 6:69 (1951).

829. Brown, William F., "The Determination of Factors Influencing Brand Choice," *J.M.*, 14:699 (1950).

830. Browning, H. E. and Sorrell, A. A., "Cinemas and Cinema-Going in Great Britain," *Journal of the Royal Statistical Society*, 117:133 (1954).

831. Bruce, Colin, "Some Comments on the Current State of Price Theory," *S.A.J.E.*, 21:327 (1953).

832. Brunner, E., "Competition and the Theory of the Firm," Parts I and II, *E.I.*, 5:509, 727 (1952).

833. Buchanan, James M., "The Theory of Monopolistic Quantity Discounts," *R.E.Stud.*, 20:199 (1952–53).

834. Büchner, R., *Grundfragen der Wirtschaftspolitik*, Berlin, 1951.

835. Burrows, H. R., ed., *Monopoly and Public Welfare*, Pietermaritzburg, 1952.

836. Bursk, Edward C., "Selling the Idea of Free Enterprise," *H.B.R.*, 26:372 (1948).

837. Business Advisory Council, *Effective Competition*, Report to the Secretary of Commerce, Washington, Dec. 18, 1952.

838. Butt, D. B., "Some Elementary Theory about Accumulation," *O.E.P.*, 6:306 (1954).

839. Cady, George J., "An Approach to the Theory of Multiple Production," *S.E.J.*, 16:326 (1949–50).

840. —— *Economics of Business Enterprise*, New York, 1950.

841. Capet, Marcel F., *L'Interaction des Marchés: La Liaison Horizontale*, Paris, 1952.

842. —— "Le pliopole et le développement économique," *E.A.*, 8:335 (1955).

843. Carell, Erich, *Grundlagen der Preisbildung*, Volkswirtschaftliche Schriften, Heft 1, Berlin, 1952.

844. Carlin, Edward A., "Intangible Property as a Tool for Analyzing the Relationships between Government and Private Enterprise," *Q.J.E.*, 67:112 (1953).

845. Cartwright, Philip W., "Marginalism and Price Theory Reconsidered," *C.J.*, 17:543 (1951).

846. Chacón, Enrique, "Monopolio y Competencia Monopolistica," *Anales de Economia*, Jan.–March 1944, p. 6.

847. Chalom, G., *La Détermination Fiscale des Bénéfices Commerciaux et Industriels en Égypte et les Recours Contentieux*, Cairo, 1949.

848. Chamber of Commerce of the U. S., *Delivered Pricing and the Law*, Washington, D. C., 1948.

849. —— *The Hidden Payroll, Non-Wage Labor Costs of Doing Business*, Washington, D. C., 1949.

850. Chamberlin, Edward H., "Some Final Comments" on a Symposium on the Monopoly Problem, *R.E.Stat.*, 31:123 (1949). (Discusses especially No. 1242.)

851. —— (Discussion of No. 494: Comments by McLeod, A. N. and Hahn, F. H. and Reply), *Q.J.E.*, 63:128 (1949).

852. —— "Advertising Costs and Equilibrium: a Rejoinder," *R.E.Stud.*, 17:226 (1949–50). (See Nos. 373, 491, and 1364.)

853. —— "Product Heterogeneity and Public Policy," *A.E.R.*, 40 (no. 2): 85, 101 (May 1950). Translation into Danish, *Det Danske Marked*, 9:193 (1950).

854. —— "The Monopoly Power of Labor," in *The Impact of the Union*, David McC. Wright, ed., New York, 1951.

855. —— "Monopolistic Competition Revisited," *Eca*, 18:343 (1951).

856. —— "The Impact of Recent Monopoly Theory on the Schumpeterian System," *R.E.Stat.*, 33:133 (1951). (Also in *Schumpeter, Social Scientist*, Harris, S. E., ed., Cambridge, Mass., 1951.)

857. —— "Une Formulation Nouvelle de la Théorie de la Concurrence Monopolistique," *E.A.*, 5:169 (1952). Translation into Italian, *R.I.S.S.*, 25:1 (1954).

858. —— " 'Full Cost' and Monopolistic Competition," *E.J.*, 62:318 (1952). Comment by Joan Robinson.

859. —— "The Product as an Economic Variable," *Q.J.E.*, 67:1 (1953).

860. —— *La Théorie de la Concurrence Monopolistique* (French translation of the 6th ed. of the *Theory of Monopolistic Competition* by Guy Trancart, with Preface by François Perroux), Paris, 1953.

861. —— ed., *Monopoly and Competition and their Regulation. Papers and Proceedings of a Conference held by the International Economic Association*, London, 1954. Papers by: Allen, G. C.; Aubert-

Krier, Jane; Bain, J. S.; Bladen, V. W.; Boehm, F.; Brems, H.; Chamberlin, E. H.; Clark, J. M.; Edwards, Corwin; Goetz-Girey, R.; Heflebower, R. B.; Hennipman, P.; Jeanneney, J. M.; Jöhr, W. A.; Lewis, W. A.; Lombardini, S.; Machlup, F.; McGregor, F. A.; Robinson, Joan; Rothschild, K.; Schneider, E.; Steenkamp, W. F. J.; Svennilson, I.; Vito, F.

862. —— "Some Aspects of Nonprice Competition," in *The Role and Nature of Competition in our Marketing Economy*, Harvey W. Huegy, ed. University of Illinois Bulletin, Vol. 51, no. 76, June 1954.

863. Chang, P. K., *"Agriculture and Industrialization,"* Cambridge, Mass., 1949.

864. Charnes, A., Cooper, W. W. and Mellon, B., "A Model for Optimizing Production by Reference to Cost Surrogates," *Ecta*, 23:307 (1955).

865. Chenery, Hollis B., "Overcapacity and the Acceleration Principle," *Ecta*, 20:1 (1952).

866. Chipman, John S., "Returns to Scale and Substitution," *C.J.*, 16:215 (1950).

867. Clark, J. M., "Law and Economics of Basing Points," *A.E.R.*, 39:430 (1949).

868. —— "Machlup on the Basing Point System," *Q.J.E.*, 63:315 (1949). (Review article on No. 1168.)

869. —— "The Orientation of Antitrust Policy," *A.E.R.*, 40, No. 2:93, 103 (May 1950).

870. —— "Competition: Static Models and Dynamic Aspects," *A.E.R.*, 45:450 (May 1955).

871. Clark, L. H., ed., *Consumer Behavior*, New York, 1955.

872. Clarke, G. C., "Determining the Advertising Budget," *Quarterly Journal of Commerce*, 14:79 (1949–50).

873. Clemens, E. W., "The Marginal Revenue Curve Under Price Discrimination," *A.E.R.*, 38:388 (1948).

874. —— "Price Discrimination and the Multiple Product Firm," *R.E.Stud.*, 19:1 (1950–51).

875. Clover, Vernon T., "Price Influence of Unbranded Gasoline," *J.M.*, 17:388 (1953).

876. Coase, R. H., "Wire Broadcasting in Great Britain," *Eca*, 15:194 (1948).

877. —— *British Broadcasting: a Study in Monopoly*, London, 1950.

878. Coen, E., "Decreasing Costs and the Gains from Trade," *Eca*, 18:285 (1951).

879. Conant, Michael, "Competition in the Farm-Machinery Industry," *J.B.U.C.*, 26:26 (1953).

880. Cook, Arnold and Jones, Edwin, "Full Cost Pricing in Western Australia," *E.R.*, 30:272 (1954).

881. Cooke, C. A., "English Law and Monopolistic Practices," *J.I.E.*, 2:1 (1953).

882. Cooper, W. W., "Revisions to the Theory of the Firm," *A.E.R.*, 39:1204 (1949).

883. —— "A Proposal for Extending the Theory of the Firm," *Q.J.E.*, 65:87 (1951).

884. Cooper, W. W. and Charnes, A., "Silhouette Functions of Short-Run Cost Behavior," *Q.J.E.*, 68:131 (1954).

885. Corden, W. M., "The Maximization of Profit by a Newspaper," *R.E.Stud.*, 20:181 (1952–53).

886. Cowen, D. U., "A Survey of the Law Relating to the Control of Monopoly in South Africa," *S.A.J.E.*, 18:124 (1950).

887. Cox, Reavis and Alderson, Wroe, eds., *Theory in Marketing*, Chicago, 1950.

888. Cruz, Salviano, *Competição Monopolística Nos Minérios do Brasil e a Previdência Social*, Lisbon, 1953.

889. Cunningham, Ross M., "Brand Loyalty — What, Where, How Much?", *H.B.R.*, 34, No. 1:116 (1956).

890. Curtis, Clayton C., and Gillies, James M., "The Academic Economist and the Businessman," *Business Quarterly*, 16:150 (1951–52).

891. Cyert, R. M., "Oligopoly Price Behaviour and the Business Cycle," *J.P.E.*, 63:41 (1955).

892. Cyert, R. M. and March, J. G., "Organizational Structure and Pricing Behaviour in an Oligopolistic Market," *A.E.R.*, 45:129 (1955).

893. Dahmén, Erik, *Svensk Industriell Förelagarverksamnet: Kausalanalys av den industriella utvecklingen 1919–39*, Stockholm, 1950.

894. D'Alauro, O., "Commercio internazionale e concorrenza monopolistica," *E.I.*, 2:876 (1949).

895. Davis, Richard M., "The Current State of Profit Theory," *A.E.R.*, 42:245 (1952).

896. Dayre, Jean, "Considerations Nouvelles sur l'Imperfection de la Concurrence Envisagée dans ses Relations avec le Gaspillage et le Chomage," *Nouvelle Revue de l'Économie Contemporaine*, 14:9 (Jan. 1955).

897. Dean, Joel, "Determination of Pricing Policy under Competitive Conditions," *American Management Association*, Marketing Series No. 75, 1949. (11 pages.)

898. —— "Cost Forecasting and Price Policy," *J.M.*, 13:279 (1949).

899. —— "Pricing Policies for New Products," *H.B.R.*, 28, No. 6:45 (1950).

900. —— "Product-Line Policy," *J.B.U.C.*, 23:248 (1950).

901. —— "Problems of Product-Line Pricing," *J.M.*, 14:518 (1950).

902. —— "How Much to Spend on Advertising," *H.B.R.*, 29, No. 1:65 (1951).

903. —— "Cyclical Policy on the Advertising Appropriation," *J.M.*, 15:265 (1951).

904. —— "Competition as Seen by the Business Man and by the Economist," in *The Role and Nature of Competition in our Marketing*

Economy, Harvey W. Huegy, ed., University of Illinois Bulletin, Vol. 51, No. 76, June 1954.

905. —— "Competition — Inside and Out," *H.B.R.*, 32, No. 6:63 (1954).

906. De Bruyn, G., "Concentratie van Eigendom in de Dagbladpers," *De Economist*, Sept. 1951, p. 561.

907. De Jong, F. J., "De Economische Terminologie in het Nederlands," *De Economist*, July–Aug. 1950, p. 481.

908. —— "Het Systeem van de Marktvormen, Leiden, 1951.

909. —— "Een mogelijk beginpunt van een weg uit de prijstheoretische impasse," *De Economist*, Dec. 1951, p. 801.

910. —— "Zimmermans Proeve van een Dynamische Theorie van de Marktvormen," *De Economist*, June 1954, p. 401.

911. De Luca, Mario, "Il monopolio temporaneo nella sua esplicazione e rispetto alla ricostruzione," *Revista di Politica Economica*, 39:22 (1949).

912. —— "Oligopolio, concorrenza monopolistica ed avvicendamento di forme del progresso tecnico," *R.I.S.S.*, 24:120 (1953).

913. Demaria, G., "Sulla Misura del Grado di Monopolio Economico di Una Collettività Nazionale," *G.E.*, 8:302 (1949).

914. Denis, Henri, "Théorie et réalité dans l'analyse de l'équilibre de la firme," *R.E.*, Nov. 1951, p. 705.

915. —— "Oligopole et progrès technique," *E.A.*, 8:411 (1955).

916. DeVries, F., "Honderd Jaar Theoretische Economie," *De Economist*, Jubileumnummer 1852–1952, p. 828.

917. Dewey, Donald, "Romance and Realism in Antitrust Policy," *J.P.E.*, 63:93 (1955).

918. —— "A Reappraisal of F.O.B. Pricing and Freight Absorption," *S.E.J.*, 22:48 (1955).

919. Dick, John Reid, *The Engineer's Approach to the Economics of Production*, London, 1952.

920. Dieterlen, Pierre, "Schumpeter, Analyste du profit," *E.A.*, 3:497 (1950).

921. Dirlam, Joel B. and Kahn, Alfred E., "Antitrust Law and the Big Buyer: Another Look at the A. & P. Case," *J.P.E.*, 60:118 (1952). Comment by Adelman, M. A., 61:436 (1953).

922. —— *Fair Competition. The Law and Economics of Antitrust Policy*, Ithaca, N. Y., 1954.

923. Dobb, Maurice, "The Problem of Marginal-Cost Pricing Reconsidered," *Indian Economic Review*, 1:1 (1952).

924. Donnahoe, Alan S., "Can Advertising Markets be Defined or Measured as Geographical Areas?", *J.M.*, 18:113 (1953).

925. Dorfman, Robert, *The Application of Linear Programming to the Theory of the Firm: Including an Analysis of Monopolistic Firms by Non-Linear Programming*, Berkeley and Los Angeles, 1951.

926. Dorfman, Robert and Steiner, P. O., "Optimal Advertising and Optimal Quality," *A.E.R.*, 44:826 (1954).

927. Dow, Louis A., "Marketing Costs and Economic Theory," *J.M.*, 19:346 (1955).
928. Dowdell, E. G., "The Concerted Regulation of Price and Output," *E.J.*, 58:210 (1948).
929. —— "Oligopoly and Imperfect Competition," *O.E.P.*, 1 (new series): 217 (1949).
930. Dreyfuss, Henry, "The Industrial Designer and the Business Man," *H.B.R.*, 28, No. 6:77 (1950).
931. Earley, James S., "Recent Developments in Cost Accounting and the 'Marginal Analysis,'" *J.P.E.*, 63:227 (1955).
932. —— "Marginal Policies of 'Excellently Managed' Companies," *A.E.R.*, 46:44 (1956).
933. Edwards, Corwin D., "Basing Point Decisions and Business Practices," *A.E.R.*, 38:828 (1948).
934. —— *Maintaining Competition, Requisites of a Governmental Policy*, New York, 1949.
935. —— "Trends in Enforcement of the Antimonopoly Laws," *J.M.*, 14:657 (1950).
936. —— "Further Comments on Bigness and the Regulation of Marketing," *J.M.*, 15:190 (1950).
937. —— "Public Policy and Business Size," *J.B.U.C.*, 24:280 (1951).
938. —— "Antimonopoly Policy During Rearmament," *A.E.R.*, 42:404 (May, 1952). Discussion.
939. —— "Vertical Integration and the Monopoly Problem," *J.M.*, 17:404 (1953).
940. Edwards, Edgar O., "The Analysis of Output under Discrimination," *Ecta*, 18:163 (1950).
941. Edwards, H. R., "Goodwill and the Normal Cost Theory of Price," *E.R.*, 28:52 (1952).
942. —— "Mr. Wiles and the Normal Cost Theory of Price," *E.J.*, 62:666 (1952). See also 65:348 (1955).
943. —— "Price Formation in Manufacturing Industry and Excess Capacity," *O.E.P.*, 7:94 (1955).
944. Edwards, Ronald S., "The Pricing of Manufactured Products," *Eca*, 19:298 (1952).
945. Efroymson, C. W., "The Kinked Oligopoly Curve Reconsidered," *Q.J.E.*, 69:119 (1955).
946. Eiteman, Wilford J., (Discussion of No. 524 by Bishop, R. L., and Haines, W. W.), *A.E.R.*, 38:607 (1948). Continued, 38:899. Also 39:1287 (1949).
947. —— *Price Determination: Business Practice vs. Economic Theory*, Bureau of Business Research, University of Michigan, Jan. 1949.
948. Eiteman, Wilford J., and Guthrie, G. E., "The Shape of the Average Cost Curve," *A.E.R.*, 42:832 (1952). Discussion, 43:621 (1953).
949. Elliott, G. A., "On Some Fashions in Economic Theory," *C.J.*, 20:478 (1954).

950. Enke, Stephen, "Resource Malallocation within Firms," *Q.J.E.*, 63:572 (1949).

951. —— "On Maximizing Profits: A Distinction between Chamberlin and Robinson," *A.E.R.*, 41:566 (1951).

952. —— "Equilibrium among Spatially Separated Markets: Solution by Electric Analogue," *Ecta*, 19:40 (1951).

953. Farrell, M. J., "The Case against the Imperfect Competition Theories," *E.J.*, 61:423 (1951).

954. —— "An Application of Activity Analysis to the Theory of the Firm," *Ecta*, 22:291 (1954). Discussion by Champernowne, D. G.

955. Federal Trade Commission, *Report on Corporate Mergers and Acquisitions*, May, 1955.

956. Fein, Rashi, "Price Discrimination and the A. & P. Case," *Q.J.E.*, 65:271 (1951). Comment by M. A. Adelman.

957. Fellner, William, "Average-cost Pricing and the Theory of Uncertainty," *J.P.E.*, 56:249 (1948).

958. —— *Competition among the Few*, New York, 1949.

959. —— "Collusion and Its Limits under Oligopoly," *A.E.R.*, 40 (no. 2):54 (May 1950).

960. —— "Une Théorie de l'Oligopole," *E.A.*, 5:197 (1952).

961. —— "The Influence of Market Structure on Technological Progress," *Q.J.E.*, 65:556 (1951). See also 66:297 (1952).

962. Fetter, F. A., "Exit Basing Point Pricing," *A.E.R.*, 38:815 (1948).

963. Fischer, Curt Eduard, "Die Marktform des unvollständigen Wettbewerbs und ihre wirtschaftsrechtliche Behandlung," *S.J.*, 74:23 (1954).

964. Fleming, Harold, "Business and the Antitrust Laws," *H.B.R.*, 28, No. 3:97 (1950).

965. Fleming, Marcus, "Production and Price Policy in Public Enterprise," *Eca*, 17:1 (1950).

966. —— "External Economies and the Doctrine of Balanced Growth," *E.J.*, 65:241 (1955).

967. Florence, P. Sargent, *Investment, Location and the Size of Plant*, Cambridge, England, 1948.

968. —— *The Logic of British and American Industry*, London, 1953.

969. Fog, Bjarke D., "Price Theory and Reality," *N.T.T.O.*, 12:89 (1948).

970. —— "Bilateralt Monopol i den internationale handel," *N.T.*, 91:211 (1953).

971. —— "Priskalkulation og Prispolitik i den Danske Industri," *N.T.*, 92:51 (1954).

972. Forstmann, S., *Neue Wirtschaftlehren, Theorien, und Hypothesen*, Berlin, 1954.

973. Fouraker, L. E. and Lee, W. A., "Competition and Kinked Functions in the Marketing of Perishables," *S.E.J.*, 22:367 (1956).

974. Fox, Karl A. and Taeuber, Richard C., "Spatial Equilibrium Models of the Livestock-Feed Economy," *A.E.R.*, 45:584 (1955).

975. Fredens, Svend, "Nogle bemaerkninger om en virksomheds prispolitik

over for købere i et geografisk markedsområde," *N.T.*, 87:317 (1949).

976. Friedman, Milton, "The Methodology of Positive Economics," in *Essays in Positive Economics*, Chicago, 1953.

977. Friedmann, John R. P., "The Concept of a Planning Region," *Land Economics*, 32:1 (1956).

978. Friedmann, Wolfgang, "Monopoly, Reasonableness and Public Interest in the Canadian Anti-Combines Law," *Canadian Bar Review*, 33:133 (1955).

979. —— ed., *Antitrust Law: A Comparative Symposium*, Toronto, 1956. A collection of articles on the monopoly problem, including "Combines Policy and the Public Interest: An Economist's Evaluation," by V. W. Bladen and S. Stykolt.

980. Gabor, André and Pearce, I. F., "A New Approach to the Theory of the Firm," *O.E.P.*, 4:252 (1952).

981. Galbraith, J. K., "Monopoly and the Concentration of Economic Power," in *A Survey of Contemporary Economics*, Howard S. Ellis, ed., for the American Economic Association, Philadelphia and Toronto, 1948.

982. —— *American Capitalism: The Concept of Countervailing Power*, Boston, 1952.

983. —— "Countervailing Power" *A.E.R.*, 44 (no. 2):1 (May 1954).

984. Ghosh, M. K. and Prakash, O., *Principles and Problems of Industrial Organization*, Allahabad (The Indian Press), 1953.

985. Gill, F. W. and Bates, G. L., *Airline Competition*, Boston, 1949.

986. Gillman, Leonard, "Operations Analysis and the Theory of Games: An Advertising Example," *Journal of the American Statistical Association*, 45:541 (1950).

987. Glover, J. D., *The Attack on Big Business*, Boston, 1954.

988. Goldner, William, "Spatial and Locational Aspects of Metropolitan Labor Markets," *A.E.R.*, 45:113 (1955).

989. Gordon, R. A., "Short Period Price Determination," *A.E.R.*, 38:265 (1948).

990. Gornall, Eric, "Some Aspects of the Retail Greengrocery Trade in an Industrial Working-Class District," *J.I.E.*, 2:207 (1954).

991. Graaff, J. de V., "Income Effects and the Theory of the Firm," *R.E.Stud.*, 18:79 (1950–51).

992. Green, L. P., "The Nature of Economic Principles," *S.A.J.E.*, 19:331 (1951).

993. Greenhut, Melvin L., "Integrating the Leading Theories of Plant Location," *S.E.J.*, 18:526 (1951–52).

994. —— "The Size and Shape of the Market Areas of a Firm," *S.E.J.*, 19:37 (1952–53).

995. —— "A General Theory of Plant Location," *Metroeconomica*, 7:59 (1955).

996. —— *Plant Location in Theory and in Practice: The Economics of Space*, Chapel Hill, N. C., 1956.

997. Grether, Ewald T., "External Product and Enterprise Differentiation and Consumer Behavior," *Consumer Behavior and Motivation*, University of Illinois Bulletin, October 1955, p. 82.

998. Griffin, Clare E., *Enterprise in a Free Society*, Chicago, 1949.

999. —— *An Economic Approach to Antitrust Problems*, American Enterprise Association, Washington, D. C., 1951.

1000. Groes, Lis, "Er detailhandelen rationel — og for hvem?" *N.T.*, 91:36 (1953).

1001. Guiheneuf, R., "Quelques aspects de la théorie de la firme; incertitude, autonomie, calculs forfaitaires," *R.E.*, Sept. 1954, p. 673.

1002. Guilbaud, Geoges Th., "La théorie des jeux," *E.A.*, 2:275 (1949).

1003. —— "La théorie des jeux," *R.E.P.*, 65:153 (1955).

1004. Gurzynski, Z. S., "Variable Costing: An Aid to Management" (Parts I & II), *S.A.J.E.*, 19:62 and 149 (1951).

1005. Gustafson, E., "Stordriftens Problem," *E.T.*, 54:21 (1952).

1006. Guthrie, J. A., "Impact of Geographical Price Discrimination on the Buyer," *J.M.*, 14:538 (1950).

1007. Haffner, Karl, *Ein Schweizerisches Kartellgesetz auf privatrechtlicher Grundlage*, Veröffentlichungen der Handels-Hochschule St. Gallen, Heft 37, Zurich and St. Gallen, 1953.

1008. Hague, D. C., "Economic Theory and Business Behaviour," *R.E.Stud.*, 16:144 (1949–50).

1009. Hahn, F. H., "Excess Capacity and Imperfect Competition," *O.E.P.*, 7:229 (1953).

1010. Hale, G. E., "Diversification: Impact of Monopoly Policy upon Multi-Product Firms," *University of Pennsylvania Law Review*, Feb. 1950.

1011. Haley, Bernard F., "Value and Distribution," in *A Survey of Contemporary Economics*, Howard S. Ellis, ed., for the American Economic Association, Philadelphia and Toronto, 1948.

1012. Hall, F. G., *The Inadequacy of Irish Commercial Profits*, Dublin, 1954.

1013. Hall, Margaret, "Some Aspects of Competition in Retail Trade," *O.E.P.*, 3:240 (1951). Comments by Efroymson, C. W. and Reply, 3:246 (1951).

1014. Hall, Margaret and Knapp, John, "Number of Shops and Productivity in Retail Distribution in Great Britain, the United States and Canada," *E.J.*, 65:72 (1955).

1015. —— "Gross Margins and Efficiency Measurement in Retail Trade," *O.E.P.*, 7:312 (1955).

1016. Haller, Heinz, "Der Erkenntniswert der Oligopoltheorien," *J.N.S.*, 162:81 (1950).

1017. Haney, Lewis H., *History of Economic Thought*, 4th ed., New York, 1949.

1018. Hansen, Harry L. and Powell, Niland, "Esso Standard: A Case Study in Pricing," *H.B.R.*, 30, No. 3:114 (1952).

1019. Hansen, Harry L. and Smith, Marcell N., "The Champion Case: What is Competition?" *H.B.R.*, 29, No. 3:89 (1951).

1020. Harberger, Arnold C., "Monopoly and Resource Allocation," *A.E.R.*, 44 (no. 2):77 (May 1954). Discussion by Mack, Ruth P.

1021. Harrod, R. F., *Economic Essays*, New York, 1952.

1022. Harsanyi, John C., "Welfare Economics of Variable Tastes," *R.E.Stud.*, 21:204 (1953–54).

1023. Hawkins, E. K., "Competition Between the Nationalized Electricity and Gas Industries," *J.I.E.*, 1:55 (1953).

1024. Hawkins, Edward R., "Price Policies and Theory," *J.M.*, 18:233 (1954).

1025. Hawtrey, R. G., "The Nature of Profit," *E.J.*, 61:489 (1951).

1026. Hayes, William A., *An Economic Analysis of the American Hotel Industry*, Catholic University of America Studies in Economics, No. 4 (1952).

1027. Hazari, R. K., "Monopolistic Competition and Welfare in Underdeveloped Countries," *Indian Journal of Economics*, 33:425 (1953).

1028. Heflebower, Richard B., "An Economic Appraisal of Price Measures," *Journal of the American Statistical Association*, 46:461 (1951).

1029. —— "Economics of Size," *J.B.U.C.*, 24:253 (1951).

1030. —— "Some Observations on Industrial Prices," *J.B.U.C.*, 27:187 (1954).

1031. Henderson, Alexander, "The Theory of Duopoly," *Q.J.E.*, 68:565 (1954).

1032. Henderson, Alexander and Schlaifer, Robert, "Mathematical Programming," *H.B.R.*, 32, No. 3:73 (1954).

1033. Henell, Olof, *Marketing Aspects of Housewives' Knowledge of Goods*, Institutet för distributionsekonomisk och administrativ forskning, Göteborg, 1953.

1034. Hession, Charles Henry, *Competition in the Metal Food Container Industry, 1916–1946*, Brooklyn, N. Y. (privately printed), 1948.

1035. —— "The Economics of Mandatory Fair Trade," *J.M.*, 14:707 (1950).

1036. Heuss, E., *Wirtschaftssysteme und Internationaler Handel*, Zurich, 1955.

1037. Hickman, C. Addison, "Managerial Motivation and the Theory of the Firm," *A.E.R.*, 45 (no. 2):544 (May 1955). Discussion.

1038. Hicks, J. R., "The Process of Imperfect Competition," *O.E.P.*, 6:41 (1954).

1039. Hieser, R., "The Degree of Monopoly Power," *E.R.*, 28:1 (1952).

1040. —— "A Kinked Demand Curve for Monopolistic Competition," *E.R.*, 39:19 (1953).

1041. Hildebrand, Karl-Gustaf, "Monopolistisk Konkurrens som Ekonomisk-Historiskt Problem," *E.T.*, 53:27 (1951).

1042. Hines, Howard, "Effectiveness of Entry by Established Firms," *Q.J.E.*, 71: (Feb. 1957).

1043. Hirsch, Werner Z. and Votaw, Dow, "Giant Grocery Retailing and the Antitrust Laws," *J.B.U.C.*, 25:1 (1952).

1044. Hirschleifer, Jack, "The Exchange between Quantity and Quality," *Q.J.E.*, 69:596 (1955).

1045. Hoelen, H., "Belangrijke Factoren Betreffende Vraag en Aanbod op de Biermarkt," *De Economist*, Nov. 1951, p. 736; and Dec. 1951, p. 832.

1046. Hofsten, Erland v., *Price Indexes and Quality Changes*, Stockholm and London, 1952.

1047. Hollander, Sidney, Jr., "A Rationale for Advertising Costs," *H.B.R.*, 27:79 (1949).

1048. Holton, Richard H., "Marketing Structure and Economic Development," *Q.J.E.*, 67:344 (1953).

1049. —— *The Supply and Demand Structure of Food Retailing Services*, Harvard Studies in Marketing of Farm Products, No. 10–H, Cambridge, Mass., 1954.

1050. Hood, Julia and Yamey, B. S., "Imperfect Competition in Retail Trades," *Eca*, 18:119 (1951). Discussion by Hall, Margaret and Smith, Henry, 19:19 (1952).

1051. Hood, William C., "Linear Programming and the Firm," *C.J.*, 18:208 (1952).

1052. Hoover, Calvin B., "The Relevance of the Competitive Laissez-Faire Economic Model to Modern Capitalistic National Economies," *Kyklos*, 8:40 (1955).

1053. Hoover, E. M., *The Location of Economic Activity*, New York, 1948.

1054. Horwood, O. P. F., "Product Pricing Policy," *S.A.J.E.*, 21:131 (1953).

1055. Houthakker, H. S., "The Econometrics of Family Budgets," *Journal of the Royal Statistical Society, Series A*, 1952, p. 1 (especially Section 4).

1056. —— "Compensated Changes in Quantities and Qualities Consumed," *R.E.Stud.*, 19:155 (1952–53).

1057. Houthakker, H. S. and Prais, S. J., "Les Variations de Qualité dans les Budgets de Famille," *E.A.*, 5:65 (1952).

1058. Howard, John A., "Collusive Behavior," *J.B.U.C.*, 27:196 (1954).

1059. —— "British Monopoly Policy: A Current Analysis," *J.P.E.*, 62:296 (1954).

1060. Howard, Marshall C., "Interfirm Relations in Oil Products Markets," *J.M.*, 20:356 (1956).

1061. Howell, Paul L., "Competition in the Capital Markets," *H.B.R.*, 31, No. 3:83 (1953).

1062. Howrey, Edward F., "Economic Evidence in Antitrust Cases," *J.M.* 19:119 (1954).

1063. Hung, Chia-Chun, *A Classification of Market Structures: Theory and Empirical Implications*, unpublished doctoral dissertation, University of Washington, 1955.

1064. Hunter, Alex, "The Monopolies Commission and Economic Welfare," *The Manchester School*, 23:22 (1955).

1065. —— "Product Differentiation and Welfare Economics," *Q.J.E.*, 69:533 (1955).

1066. Hurwicz, Leonid, "What Has Happened to the Theory of Games?", *A.E.R.*, 43 (no. 2):398 (May 1953).

1067. Innis, H. A., *The Press, A Neglected Factor in the Economic History of the Twentieth Century*, London, 1949.

1068. Isard, Walter, "The General Theory of Location and Space-Economy," *Q.J.E.*, 63:476 (1949).

1069. —— "Distance Inputs and the Space Economy, Part I: The Conceptual Framework; Part II: The Locational Equilibrium of the Firm," *Q.J.E.*, 65:181 and 373 (1951).

1070. —— "Interregional and Regional Input-Output Analysis: A Model of a Space-Economy," *R.E.Stat.*, 33:318 (1951).

1071. —— "A General Location Principle of an Optimum Space-Economy," *Ecta*, 20:406 (1952).

1072. —— "Some Remarks on the Marginal Rate of Substitution Between Distance Inputs and Location Theory," *Metroeconomica*, 5:11 (1953).

1073. Ischboldin, Boris, "Die Theorie der Quasirente und des Profits," *S.J.*, 72:291 (1952).

1074. Jacoby, Neil H., "Antitrust Policy Re-examined," *J.P.E.*, 58:61 (1950). (Review article of No. 934.)

1075. —— "Perspective on Monopoly," *J.P.E.*, 59:514 (1951).

1076. James, Émile, *Histoire des Théories Économiques*, Paris, 1950.

1077. —— *Histoire de la Pensée Économique au XXe Siècle*, 2 vols. Paris, 1955.

1078. —— *Histoire Sommaire de la Pensée Économique*, Paris, 1956.

1079. Jannaconne, P., *Prezzi e mercati*, Turin, 1951.

1080. Jantzen, Ivar, "Increasing Return in Industrial Production," *N.T.T.O.*, 5:1 (1939).

1081. —— "Laws of Production and Costs," *Ecta*, 17 sup.:58 (July 1949).

1082. Jastram, Roy W., "Advertising Ratios Planned by Large-Scale Advertisers," *J.M.*, 14:13 (1949).

1083. —— "Advertising Outlays under Oligopoly," *R.E.Stat.*, 31:106 (1949).

1084. —— "The Development of Advertising Appropriation Policy," *J.B.U.C.*, 23:154 (1950).

1085. —— "A Treatment of Disputed Lags in the Theory of Advertising Expenditure," *J.M.*, 20:36 (1955).

1086. Jefferys, James B., *The Distribution of Consumable Goods*, London, 1950.

1087. Jewkes, J., "The Size of the Factory," *E.J.*, 62:237 (1952).

1088. —— "Monopoly and Economic Progress," *Eca*, 20:197 (1953). Comment by Allen, G. C., 20:359 (1953).

1089. Johnson, Harry G., "The Economics of Undertaking," ("a long-neglected industry"), *The Cambridge Journal*, 4:240; Bowes and Bowes, Cambridge, England, January, 1951.

1090. Jöhr, Walter A., "Die Leistungen des Konkurrenzsystems und seine Bedeutung für die Wirtschaft unserer Zeit," *S.Z.*, 86:398 (1950).

1091. —— "Die verschiedenen Varianten des Kollektivmonopols," *S.Z.*, 87:281 (1951).

1092. Justman, E., "La Théorie des Jeux," *R.E.P.*, 59:616 (1949).

1093. Kahn, Alfred E., "Standards for Antitrust Policy," *Harvard Law Review*, 67:28 (1953).

1094. Kahn, R. F., "Oxford Studies in the Price Mechanism," *E.J.*, 62:119 (1952).

1095. Kaldor, Nicholas, "The Economic Aspects of Advertising," *R.E.Stud.*, 18:1 (1949–50).

1096. —— "Alternative Theories of Distribution," *R.E.Stud.*, 23:83 (1955–56).

1097. Kaldor, N. and Silverman, R., *A Statistical Analysis of Advertising Expenditure and of the Revenue of the Press*, London, 1948.

1098. Kamerman, Michael, *Resale Price Maintenance: An Example of Vertical Market Coordination*, Publications of the Graduate Economics Seminar of Syracuse University, No. 15 (1955). (20 pages.) Discussion.

1099. Kaplan, A. D. H., "The Influence of Size of Firms on the Functioning of the Economy," *A.E.R.*, 40 (no. 2):74 (May 1950).

1100. —— *Big Business in a Competitive System, Washington*, D. C., 1954.

1101. Kapp, K. W., *The Social Costs of Private Enterprise*, Cambridge, Mass., 1950.

1102. Katona, T., *Psychological Analysis of Economic Behaviour*, New York, 1951.

1103. Kaysen, Carl, "Basing Point Pricing and Public Policy," *Q.J.E.*, 63:289 (1949).

1104. —— "A Dynamic Aspect of the Monopoly Problem," *R.E.Stat.*, 31:109 (1949).

1105. —— "Dynamic Aspects of Oligopoly Price Theory," *A.E.R.*, 42 (no. 2):198 (May 1950).

1106. —— "Looking Around (Old and new doctrines of competition)," *H.B.R.*, 32, No. 3:137 (1954).

1107. Keezer, Dexter M., ed., "The Antitrust Laws: A Symposium," *A.E.R.*, 39:689 (1949).

1108. —— and Associates, *Making Capitalism Work*, New York and London, 1950.

1109. Keirstead, B. S., *The Theory of Economic Change*, Toronto, 1948.

1110. —— "Note sur les mobiles de l'entrepreneur et la distribution des profits," *E.A.*, 5:35 (1952).

1111. —— *An Essay in the Theory of Profits and Income Distribution*, Oxford, 1953.

1112. Keirstead, B. S. and Weldon, J. C., "Note sur les conjectures des oligopoleurs," *E.A.*, 8:425 (1955).

1113. Kemp, Murray C., "The Efficiency of Competition as an Allocator of Resources," *C.J.*, 21:30, 217 (1955).

1114. Kennedy, William F., "The Optimum Geographic Unit in Electric Rate Making," *A.E.R.*, 42 (no. 2):654 (May 1952).

1115. Keyes, Lucile S., *Federal Control of Entry into Air Transportation*, Cambridge, Mass., 1951.

1116. —— "Monopolistic Market Structures and Stabilization," *Q.J.E.*, 66:436 (1952).

1117. —— "The Shoe Machinery Case and the Problem of the Good Trust," *Q.J.E.*, 63:287 (1954).

1118. —— "A Reconsideration of Federal Control of Entry into Air Transportation," *Journal of Air Law and Commerce*, 22:192 (1955).

1119. Kilroy, Dame Alix, "The Task and Methods of the Monopolies Commission," *The Manchester School*, 22:37 (1954).

1120. Klarman, Herbert E., "The Economics of Hospital Service," *H.B.R.*, 29, No. 5:71 (1951).

1121. Kline, Charles H., "The Strategy of Product Policy," *H.B.R.*, 33, No. 4:91 (1955).

1122. Klingender, F. D., *Art and the Industrial Revolution*, London, 1947.

1123. Knauth, Oswald, "Considerations in the Setting of Retail Prices," *J.M.*, 14:1 (1949).

1124. Kolms, Heinz, "Zum Optimumproblem in der neueren Wirtschaftstheorie," *S.J.*, 72:163 (1952).

1125. Kreukniet, P. B., *Aanvaardbare Mededinging* (Acceptable Competition), Haarlem, 1951.

1126. —— "Aanvaardbare Mededinging," *De Economist*, Jan. 1951, p. 1.

1127. Kristensson, Folke, "Metodfrågor vid Analys av Produktions och Distributionsstrukturen inom en Industri," *E.T.*, 49:135 (1947).

1128. Krutilla, John V., "Aluminum — A Dilemma for Antitrust Aims," *S.E.J.*, 22:164 (1955).

1129. Kuipers, J. D., *Resale Price Maintenance in Great Britain*, Wageningen, 1950.

1130. Kutish, L. John, "A Theory of Production in the Short Run," *J.P.E.*, 61:25 (1953).

1131. Labini, Paolo Sylos, "Qualche Osservazione sul monopolio e sul monopsonio," *R.I.S.S.*, 61:1 (1953).

1132. Lacey, K., *Profit Measurement and Price Changes*, London, 1953.

1133. Lachmann, L. M., "Some Notes on Economic Thought, 1933–1953," *S.A.J.E.*, 22:22 (1954).

1134. Lacroix, J., "Essai de généralisation de la théorie du monopole bilatéral," *R.E.*, April, 1951, p. 219.

1135. Laffer, Kingsley, "A Note on Some Marginalist and Other Explanations of Full Cost Price Theory," *E.R.*, 29:51 (1953).
1136. Lagache, M., "L'analyse structurale en économie: la théorie des jeux," *R.E.P.*, 60:399 (1950).
1137. Lambers, H. W., "Marktstrategie en Mededinging," *De Economist*, Dec. 1950, p. 801.
1138. Lanzillotti, Robert F., "Multiple Products and Oligopoly Strategy: A Development of Chamberlin's Theory of Products," *Q.J.E.*, 68:461 (1954).
1139. Learned, Edmund P., "Pricing of Gasoline: A Case Study," *H.B.R.*, 26:723 (1948).
1140. Leavitt, Harold J., "A Note on Some Experimental Findings about the Meanings of Price," *J.B.U.C.*, 27:205 (1954).
1141. Lecaillon, Jacques, "Les coûts et les prix en courte période," *R.E.*, Jan. 1952, p. 36.
1142. Leftwich, Richard H., *The Price System and Resource Allocation*, New York, 1955.
1143. Leibenstein, Harvey, "The Proportionality Controversy and the Theory of Production," *Q.J.E.*, 69:619 (1955).
1144. Leiter, Robert D., "Advertising, Resource Allocation and Employment," *J.M.*, 15:158 (1950).
1145. Lerner, Joseph, "Constant Proportions, Fixed Plant and the Optimum Conditions of Production," *Q.J.E.*, 63:361 (1949).
1146. Lester, R. A., "Equilibrium of the Firm," *A.E.R.*, 39:478 (1949).
1147. Leunbach, G., "The Theory of Games and Economic Behaviour," *N.T.T.O.*, 12:175 (1948).
1148. Levin, Harvey J., "Standards of Welfare in Economic Thought," *Q.J.E.*, 70:117 (1956).
1149. Levitt, Theodore, "Law, Economics, and Antitrust Revision," *S.E.J.*, 21:405 (1954–55).
1150. Lewis, H. Gregg, "The Labor-Monopoly Problem: A Positive Program," *J.P.E.*, 59:277 (1951).
1151. Lewis, W. Arthur, "The British Monopolies Act," *The Manchester School*, 17:208 (1949).
1152. —— *Overhead Costs*, New York, 1949.
1153. Leyland, N. H., "A Note on Price and Quality," *O.E.P.*, 1 (new series):269 (1949).
1154. Liebhafsky, H. H., "A Curious Case of Neglect: Marshall's Industry and Trade," *C.J.*, 21:339 (1955).
1155. Lindblom, Charles E., "The Union as a Monopoly," *Q.J.E.*, 62:671 (1948).
1156. —— *Unions and Capitalism*, New Haven, 1949.
1157. Loescher, Samuel M., "Geographic Pricing Policies and the Law," *J.B.U.C.*, 27:211 (1954).
1158. —— "Inert Antitrust Administration: Formula Pricing and the Cement Industry," *Yale Law Journal*, 65:1 (1955).

1159. Lombardini, Siro, "Osservazioni sulla teoria della concorrenza monopolistica," *R.I.S.S.*, 21:29 (1949).
1160. —— "Discussioni su Concorrenza e Monopolio," *R.I.S.S.*, 22:483 (1951).
1161. —— *Il Monopolio nella Teoria Economica*, Milan, 1953.
1162. Long, Erven J., "Returns to Scale in Family Farming: Is the Case Overstated?", *J.P.E.*, 57:543 (1949).
1163. Lösch, August, "Beiträge zur Standortstheorie," *S.J.*, 63:329 (1938).
1164. —— *Die Räumliche Ordnung der Wirtschaft; eine Untersuchung über Standort, Wirtschaftsgebiete und internationalen Handel,* Jena, 1940. Translated by William H. Woglom with assistance of Wolfgang F. Stolper, *The Economics of Location*, New Haven, 1954. (Reviewed, Nos. 1396, 1428.)
1165. Lydall, H. F., "Conditions of New Entry and the Theory of Price," *O.E.P.*, 7:300 (1955).
1166. MacAllen, Douglas H., "Should Businessmen Utilize Theory in Pricing?" *The Business Quarterly*, 16:114 (1951–52).
1167. Macdonald, David, "Product Competition in the Relevant Market under the Sherman Act," *University of Michigan Law Review*, 53:69 (1954).
1168. Machlup, Fritz, *The Basing Point System*, Philadelphia, 1949.
1169. —— "The Characteristics and Classifications of Oligopoly," *Kyklos*, 5:145 (1952).
1170. —— *The Economics of Sellers Competition*, Baltimore, 1952.
1171. —— *The Political Economy of Monopoly. Business, Labor, and Government Policies.*, Baltimore, 1952.
1172. —— "Oligopolistic Indeterminacy," *W.A.*, 68:1 (1952).
1173. Macintosh, R. M., "The Price Mechanism in the Market for Mortgage Loans," *C.J.*, 19:151 (1953).
1174. Mahr, Alexander, "Monopolistiche Preispolitik im Konjunkturzyklus," *Metroeconomica*, 1:105 (1949).
1175. Marbach, Fritz, "Das Kartellproblem in schweizerischer Sicht," *S.Z.*, 87:214 (1951).
1176. Marchal, Jean, "Les Facteurs qui determinent les taux des salaires dans le monde moderne: du prix du travail au revenu du travailleur," *R.E.*, July 1950, p. 129.
1177. —— "The Construction of a New Theory of Profit," *A.E.R.*, 41:549 (1951).
1178. Marengo, Louis, "The Basing Point Decisions and the Steel Industry," *A.E.R.*, 45 (no. 2):509 (May 1955). Discussion.
1179. Markham, Jesse W., "The Concept of Workable Competition," *A.E.R.*, 40:349 (1950).
1180. —— "Public Policy and Monopoly: A Dilemma in Remedial Action," *S.E.J.*, 16:413 (1949–50).
1181. —— "Integration in the Textile Industry," *H.B.R.*, 28, No. 1:74 (1950).
1182. —— *Competition in the Rayon Industry*, Cambridge, Mass., 1952.

1183. —— "The Nature and Significance of Price Leadership," *A.E.R.*, 41:891 (1951). Discussion by Oxenfeldt, *A.R.*, 42:380 (1952). Reply, 43:152 (1953).

1184. —— "Economic Analysis and the Antitrust Laws," *Proceedings of the American Bar Association*, 1954, p. 145.

1185. —— "The Per Se Doctrine and the New Rule of Reason," *S.E.J.*, 22:22 (1955).

1186. —— "The Report of the Attorney General's Committee on Antitrust Laws," *Q.J.E.*, 70:193 (1956).

1187. Mason, Edward S., "The Current Status of the Monopoly Problem in the United States," *Harvard Law Review*, 62:1265 (1949).

1188. —— "Schumpeter on Monopoly and the Large Firm," *R.E.Stat.*, 33:139 (1951). (Also in *Schumpeter, Social Scientist*, Harris, S.E., ed., Cambridge, Mass., 1951).

1189. —— "The New Competition," *Yale Review, Autumn*, 1953.

1190. —— "Labor Monopoly and All That," *Proceedings of Industrial Relations Research Association*, Vol. 8 (1955).

1191. —— "Market Power and Business Conduct," *A.E.R.*, 46, No. 2: 471 (May 1956). Discussion.

1192. May, Kenneth, "The Structure of the Production Function of the Firm," *Ecta*, 17:186 (1949).

1193. Mayberry, J. P., Nash, J. F., and Shubik, M., "A Comparison of Treatments of a Duopoly Situation," *Ecta*, 21:141 (1953).

1194. McConnell, C. R., "Trouble Spots in Collective Bargaining Theory," *American Journal of Economics and Sociology*, 15:13 (1955).

1195. McDonald, John, *Strategy in Poker, Business, and War*, New York, 1950.

1196. McGarry, Edmund D., "The Contactual Function in Marketing," *J.B.U.C.*, 24:96 (1951).

1197. McGhee, John S., "Cross Hauling — A Sympton of Incomplete Collusion Under Basing-Point Systems," *S.E.J.*, 20:369 (1953–54).

1198. McKenzie, Lionel, "Ideal Output and the Interdependence of Firms," *E.J.*, 61:785 (1951).

1199. McKie, J. W., "The Decline of Monopoly in the Metal Container Industry," *A.E.R.*, 45 (no. 2):499 (May 1955).

1200. McMillan, S. S., *Individual Firm Adjustments under O.P.A.*, Bloomington, Ind., 1949.

1201. McNair, Malcolm P., "Policies for Making Competition Socially Effective in Marketing," in *The Role and Nature of Competition in our Marketing Economy*, Harvey W. Huegy, ed., University of Illinois Bulletin, Vol. 51, No. 76, June 1954.

1202. Mehta, M. M., *Structure of Cotton-Mill Industry of India*, Allahabad, 1949.

1203. Meij, J. L., "Some Critical Remarks on the Significance and Use of the Break-Even Point," *J.I.E.*, 1:132 (1953).

1204. —— "Some Fundamental Principles of a General Theory of Management," *J.I.E.*, 4:16 (1955).

1205. Meinhardt, P., *Inventions, Patents, and Monopoly*, London, 1950.

1206. Mercillon, Henri,*Cinéma et Monopoles: Le Cinéma aux États-Unis: Étude Économique*, Paris, 1953.

1207. Meriam R. S., "Bigness and the Economic Analysis of Competition," *H.B.R.*, 28, No. 2:109 (1950).

1208. Mesaki, Kenji, "Anti-Monopoly Law and Elimination of Excessive Concentration of Economic Power Law in Japan — Comparison Between Anti-Trust Laws of Japan and Those of the United States," *Osaka Economic Papers*, 2:18 (1954).

1209. Meyer-Lindemann, Hans Ulrich, *Typologie der Theorien des Industriestandortes*, Bremen-Horn, 1951.

1210. Meyers, Samuel, *Textile and Apparel Testing and Labeling*, Harvard University Studies in Marketing of Farm Products, No. 5–H, Cambridge, Mass., 1954.

1211. Mickwitz, Gösta, "Några Synpunkter på Prisbildning, Konkurrens, och Konkurrens-begränsning," ("Some Points of View on Price Determination, Competition and the Limitation of Competition"), *Ekonomiska Samfundets Tidsskrift* (Helsingfors), 8:140 (1955).

1212. Miller, John Perry, "Competition and Countervailing Power," *A.E.R.*, 44 (no. 2):15 (May 1954). Discussion.

1213. Miller, Merton H., "Decreasing Average Cost and the Theory of Railroad Rates," *S.E.J.*, 21:390 (1954–55).

1214. Millican, Richard D. and Rogers, Ramona J., "Price Variability of Non-Branded Food Items Among Food Stores in Champaign-Urbana," *J.M.*, 18:282 (1954).

1215. Misch, Leonard, "Zur Theorie des Räumlichen Gleichgewichts," *W.A.*, 66:5 (1951).

1216. Mishan, E. J., "Toward a General Theory of Price, Income, and Money," *J.P.E.*, 60:487 (1952).

1217. Mitchell, Wesley C., *Lecture Notes on Types of Economic Theory*, New York, 1949.

1218. *Monopoly Power, Hearings before Subcommittee of the House Committee of the Judiciary on Study of*, 81st Congress, 1st Session, (1949).

1219. Moore, John R. and Levy, Lester S., "Price Flexibility and Industrial Concentration," *S.E.J.*, 21:435 (1954–55).

1220. Morgan, James N., "Bilateral Monopoly and the Competitive Output," *Q.J.E.*, 63:371 (1949). Discussion, 64:648 (1950).

1221. Morgan, Theodore, *Introduction to Economics*, Englewood Cliffs, N. J., 2nd, ed., 1956.

1222. Morgenstern, Oscar, "Economics and the Theory of Games," *Kyklos*, 3:294 (1949).

1223. —— ed., *Economic Activity Analysis*, New York, 1954.

1224. Mouly, J., "De la Firme et de ses Comportements," *R.E.P.*, 64:984 (1954).

1225. Muhs, Karl, "Zur Fortbildung der Preistheorie," *S.J.*, 69:695 (1949).
1226. Mullen, Wadsworth H., "Measurement of National Advertising," *H.B.R.*, 27:622 (1949).
1227. Mund, Vernon A., *Open Markets*, New York and London, 1948.
1228. —— "Ethical Concepts Implicit in Monopolistic and Competitive Price Analysis," *Review of Social Economy*, 13:20 (1955).
1229. Myrvoll, Ole, "The Profit Motive and the Theory of Partial Equilibrium of the Firm," *N.T.T.O.*, 12:179 (1948).
1230. Nash, John F., "The Bargaining Problem," *Ecta*, 18:155 (1950).
1231. —— "Two-Person Coöperative Games," *Ecta*, 21:128 (1953).
1232. National Bureau of Economic Research, *Business Concentration and Price Policy*, Princeton, 1955. Report of a Conference of the Universities — National Bureau Committee for Economic Research. Papers by: Adelman, M. A.; Butters, J. Keith; Conklin, M. R.; Edwards, Corwin D.; Goldstein, H. T.; Heflebower, R. B.; Lintner, John; Machlup, Fritz; Markham, Jesse W.; Miller, J. P.; Rosenbluth, G.; Ruggles, R.; Scitovsky, T.; Smith, Caleb; Stigler, G. J.
1233. National Industrial Conference Board, *New Product Development*, Studies in Business Policy, No. 69, New York, 1954.
1234. Neisser, Hans, "L'Oligopole, les anticipations et la théorie des jeux," *E.A.*, 5:225 (1952).
1235. —— "The Strategy of Expecting the Worst," *Social Research*, 19:346 (1952).
1236. Nerlove, S. H., "Professor Machlup on Monopoly," *J.B.U.C.*, 26:200 (1953).
1237. Nervik, Ottar and Black, John D., *Research in Selling and Buying with Special Reference to Goods Sold or Bought by Farm People*, Harvard Studies in Marketing Farm Products, No. 2–H, Cambridge, Mass., 1951.
1238. de Neumann, A. M., "Real Economies and the Balance of Industry," *E.J.*, 58:373 (1948).
1239. Nicholls, William H., "The Tobacco Case of 1946," *A.E.R.*, 39 (no. 2):284 (May 1949). Discussion, 39:311.
1240. —— *Price Policies in the Cigarette Industry*, Nashville, 1951.
1241. Nicols, Alfred, "The Cement Case," *A.E.R.*, 39:297 (May, 1949). Discussion, 39:311.
1242. —— "The Development of Monopolistic Competition and the Monopoly Problem," *R.E.Stat.*, 31:118 (1949). Discussed, No. 850.
1243. North, Douglass C., "Location Theory and Regional Economic Growth," *J.P.E.*, 63:243 (1955).
1244. Nutter, G. Warren, "Competition: Direct and Devious," *A.E.R.*, 44 (no. 2):69 (May 1954). Discussion by Mack, Ruth P.
1245. —— "The Plateau Demand Curve and Utility Theory," *J.P.E.*, 63:512 (1955).

1246. Nyblén, Göran, "Atomistisk och Holistisk Ekonomisk Teori," *E.T.*, 51:258 (1949).
1247. Oger, Eric, "Le cinéma français et l'oligopole des rentiers," *E.A.*, 8:525 (1955).
1248. Oliver, Henry M. and Strotz, Robert H., "Long-run Marginal Cost and Fluctuating Output," *S.E.J.*, 18:160 (1951).
1249. Oppenheim, S. Chesterfield, "Federal Antitrust Legislation: Guideposts to a Revised National Antitrust Policy," *Michigan Law Review*, 50:1139 (1952).
1250. Osborn, Richards C., "Efficiency and Profitability in Relation to Size," *H.B.R.*, 29, No. 2:82 (1951).
1251. Östlind, A., "Sysselsättnings-problemet vid monopolistisk prispolitik," *E.T.*, 54.87 (1952). Discussion by Ralph Turvey and Lars Lindberger, 54:147 (1952).
1252. Ott, Alfred E., "Zur dynamischen Theorie der Marktformen," *J.N.S.*, 167:1 (1955).
1253. Oxenfeldt, Alfred R., "Consumer Knowledge: Its Measurement and Extent," *R.E.Stat.*, 32:300 (1950).
1254. —— *Industrial Pricing and Market Practices*, New York, 1951.
1255. Ozga, S. A., "Pearce's General Equilibrium Model," *R.E.Stud.*, 23:145 (1955–56). Reply by Pearce, I. F.
1256. Palamountain, Joseph C., *The Politics of Distribution*, Cambridge, Mass., 1955.
1257. Papendreou, Andreas G., "Market Structure and Monopoly Power," *A.E.R.*, 39:883 (1949). Discussion by Birch, C. M., 40:407 (1950).
1258. —— "Some Basic Problems in the Theory of the Firm," in *A Survey of Contemporary Economics*, Vol. II, Bernard S. Haley, ed., for the American Economic Association, Homewood, Ill., 1952.
1259. Papendreou, Andreas G. and Wheeler, John T., *Competition and Its Regulation*, New York, 1954.
1260. Passer, H. C., *The Electrical Manufacturers, 1875–1900*, Cambridge, Mass., 1953.
1261. Paton, William A., *Shirtsleeve Economics*, New York, 1952.
1262. Paul, M. E., "Notes on Excess Capacity," *O.E.P.*, 6:33 (1954).
1263. Pearce, I. F., "Total Demand Curves and General Equilibrium," *R.E.Stud.*, 20:216 (1952–53).
1264. Pegrum, Dudley F., "The Present Status of Geographic Pricing," *J.M.*, 15:425 (1951).
1265. Pen, J., "De Voorkeursintensiteit en het Tweezijdige Monopolie," *De Economist*, Feb. 1949, p. 145.
1266. —— "Oligopolistische Agressie," *De Economist*, June 1951, p. 417.
1267. —— "A General Theory of Bargaining," *A.E.R.*, 42:24 (1952).
1268. Pennance, F. G. and Yamey, B. S., "Competition in the Retail Grocery Trade," *Eca*, 22:303 (1955).
1269. Penrose, Edith T., "Biological Analogies in the Theory of the Firm," *A.E.R.*, 42:804 (1952). Discussion, 43:600 (1953).

469. —— *Pricing, Distribution, and Employment*, New York, 1948.
470. —— and Moore, Frederick T., *Literature on Price Policy and Related Topics, 1933–47* (Bibliography), Berkeley and Los Angeles, University of California Press, 1947.
471. Balakrishna, R., "Monopolistic Influences in Capitalistic Economy," *Indian Journal of Economics*, 24: 368 (1944).
472. Ballaine, Wesley C., "How Government Purchasing Procedures Strengthen Monopoly Elements," *Journal of Political Economy*, 51: 538 (1943).
473. Barfod, B., "Priskalculation ved Forenet Produktion, etc.," *Nordisk Tidsskrift for Teknisk Økonomi*, 1944–45, No. 2–4.
474. Barna, T., *Profits during and after the war*, Fabian Publications, Ltd., Research Series No. 105, London, 1945.
475. Beach, E. F., "Triffin's Classification of Market Positions," *Canadian Journal of Economics and Political Science*, 9: 69 (1943).
476. Behling, Burton N., "The Nature and Control of the Transport Market," in *Transportation and National Policy*, p. 238. National Resources Planning Board, Washington, 1942.
477. Bellamy, R., "The Changing Pattern of Retail Distribution," "Size and Success of Retail Distribution," "The Cost of Retail Distribution," *Bulletin of the Oxford Institute of Statistics*, vol. 8, numbers 8, 10, 11.
478. Bilimovič, A., "Der Preis bei beiderseitigem Monopol," *Weltwirtschaftliches Archiv*, 57: 312 (1943).
479. Bishop, F. P., *The Economics of Advertising*, London, 1944.
480. Black, Duncan, "On the Rationale of Group Decision Making," *Journal of Political Economy*, 56: 23 (1948).
481. Bloom, Gordon, and Belfer, Nathan, "Unions and Real Labor Income," *Southern Economic Journal*, 14: 290 (1948).
482. Boulding, K. E., "The Theory of the Firm in the Last Ten Years," *American Economic Review*, 32: 791 (1942).
483. —— "In Defense of Monopoly," *Quarterly Journal of Economics*, 59:524 (1945). Comments by Holben, Ralph E., and Rothschild, K. W., 60: 612 (1946).
484. Bowman, Mary J., and Bach, George L., *Economic Analysis and Public Policy*, Second edition, New York, 1948.
485. Brems, Hans, "The Interdependence of Quality Variations, Selling Effort and Price," *Quarterly Journal of Economics*, 62: 418 (1948).
486. Bronfenbrenner, M., "Price Control under Imperfect Competition," *American Economic Review*, 37: 107 (1947).
487. Buchanan, Norman S., "Advertising Expenditures: a Suggested Treatment," *Journal of Political Economy*, 50: 537 (1942).
488. Carlson, Valdemar, *An Introduction to Modern Economics*, Philadelphia, 1946.
489. Cassady, Ralph, Jr., "Some Economic Aspects of Price Discrimination under Non-Perfect Market Conditions," *Journal of Marketing*, 11: 7 (1946).

gaard Festskrift). (A summary is given in English: "The Distance between the Sellers and the Interplay of Price-Policy").

451. —— Review of Robinson, "The Economics of Imperfect Competition," and Chamberlin, "The Theory of Monopolistic Competition," *Nationaløkonomisk Tidsskrift*, 72: 200 (1934).

452. —— Review of Stackelberg, "Marktform und Gleichgewicht," *Zeitschrift für Nationalökonomie*, 6: 548 (1935).

453. —— "Effect and Cost of Advertisement from a Theoretic Aspect," *Nordisk Tidsskrift for Teknisk Økonomi*, 1: 62 (1935). The same article appears in German in the *Archiv für mathematische Wirtschafts- und Sozialforschung*, 1: 159 (1935); and in French in the *Revue des Sciences Economiques*, 9: 251 (1935).

454. —— "Monopolistic Competition and the Homogeneity of the Market," *Econometrica*, 4: 193 (1936).

455. —— "Nogle økonomiske og sociale Udviklingstendenser og deres politiske Konsekvenser," *Statsøkonomisk Tidsskrift*, Oslo, Hefte 3, 1938, p. 115.

456. —— "The Theory of Prices" (brief summary of a paper given at the Elsinore meeting of the Econometric Society), *Econometrica*, 8: 284 (1940).

457. Zingler, E. K., "Advertising and the Maximization of Profit," *Economica*, 7 (new series): 318 (1940).

SUPPLEMENT: MAY 1948

458. Abramovitz, Moses, *Price Theory for a Changing Economy*, New York, 1939.

459. Abramson, A. G., "Price Policies," *Southern Economic Journal*, 12: 39 (1945).

460. Adelman, M. A., *The Dominant Firm, with Special Reference to the A & P Tea Company*, Harvard Ph.D. Thesis, 1948.

461. Aizsilnieks, Arnold P., "Price Theory and the Price Policy of Consumers' Cooperatives," *Ekonomisk Tidskrift*, September 1947.

462. Åkerman, J., "Wages and Full Employment," *Ekonomisk Tidskrift*, March 1946.

463. Arnold, Sam, "Forward Shifting of a Payroll Tax under Monopolistic Competition," *Quarterly Journal of Economics*, 61: 267 (1947).

464. Ashton, Herbert, *Economic Analysis of the Element of Speed in Transportation*, Harvard Ph.D. thesis, 1936.

465. Aubert, Jane, *La Courbe d'Offre*, Paris, 1949.

466. Bain, Joe S., "Market Classifications in Modern Price Theory," *Quarterly Journal of Economics*, 56: 560 (1942).

467. —— "Measurements of the Degree of Monopoly: a note," *Economica*, 10 (new series); 66 (1943). (Based on No. 342). Added comment by Rothschild, p. 69.

468. —— *The Economics of the Pacific Coast Petroleum Industry*, Berkeley and Los Angeles, 1945.

1270. —— "Limits to the Growth and Size of Firms," *A.E.R.*, 45 (no. 2):531 (May 1955). Discussion.

1271. Perroux, François, "L'effet de domination dans les relations économiques," *Hommes et Techniques*, 5:9 (Jan. 1949).

1272. —— "Economic Space: Theory and Applications," *Q.J.E.*, 64:89 (1950). French Text, "Les Espàces Économiques," *E.A.*, 3:225 (1950).

1273. —— "Note sur le dynamisme de la domination," *E.A.*, 3:245 (1950).

1274. —— "Esquisse d'une théorie de l'économie dominante," *E.A.*, 1:243 (1948). Translated into German, *Zeitschrift für Nationalökonomie*, 13:1 (1950).

1275. —— "Concurrence et Effet de Domination," *Banque*, May 1952, p. 265.

1276. Picton, G., *Commercial Agreements. The Form and Content of some Agreements between Firms.* Cambridge, England, 1952. (Product Agreements).

1277. Pigou, A. C., "A Comment on Duopoly," *Eca*, 15:254 (1948).

1278. Pirou, G., *La Valeur et les Prix*, Paris, 1948.

1279. Pollard, S. and Hughes, J. D., "Retailing Costs: Some Comments on the Census of Distribution, 1950," *O.E.P.*, 7:71 (1955).

1280. Ponsard, C., *Économie et Espace: essai d'integration du facteur spatial dans l'analyse économique*, Paris, 1955.

1281. Pool, A. G. and Llewellyn, G., *The British Hosiery Industry: A Study in Competition, First Report*, University College, Leicester.

1282. Predöhl, Andreas, "Le plein emploi dans la perspective spatiale," *E.A.*, 4:369 (1951).

1283. Preiser, Erich, "Besitz und Macht in der Distributionstheorie," in *Synopsis, Festgabe für Alfred Weber*, Heidelberg, 1949. Translation into English in *International Economic Papers*, No. 2, 1952.

1284. Rasch, Harold, "Der Begriff des Oligopols im Kartellgesetzenwurf," *Wirtschaft und Wettbewerb*, 6:3 (1956).

1285. Rasmussen, Arne, "The Determination of Advertising Expenditure," *J.M.*, 16:439 (1952). Discussion, 17:277 (1953).

1286. —— *Pristeori eller Parameterteori*, Copenhagen, 1953.

1287. Ratcliff, R. U., *Urban Land Economics*, London, 1949.

1288. Ray, Royal H., *Analysis of Some Economic Causes and Consequences of Daily Newspaper Integration*, Publications of the Graduate Economics Seminar of Syracuse University, No. 4 (1951) (20 pages.) Discussion.

1289. —— "Competition in the Newspaper Industry," *J.M.*, 15:444 (1951).

1290. Reck, Dickson, "The Effect of Buying Policies on Products and Prices," *J.M.*, 16:257, 409 (1952).

1291. Recktenwald, Horst C., "Zur Lehre von den Marktformen," *W.A.*, 67:298 (1951).

1292. Reder, Melvin W., "Rehabilitation of Partial Equilibrium Theory," *A.E.R.*, 42 (no. 2):182 (May 1952).

1293. —— "The Theory of Union Wage Policy," *R.E.Stat.*, 34:34 (1952).
1294. Rees, Albert, "Labor Unions and the Price System," *J.P.E.*, 58:254 (1950). (Review article of No. 1156).
1295. Renwick, C., "The Equilibrium of the Firm in Monopolistic and Imperfect Competition Theories," *E.R.*, 24:32 (1948).
1296. Reynolds, Clifton, *A Simple Guide to Big Business*, London, 1948.
1297. Reynolds, Lloyd G., "Towards a Short-Run Theory of Wages," *A.E.R.*, 38:289 (1948).
1298. Richardson, G. B., "Imperfect Knowledge and Economic Efficiency," *O.E.P.*, 5:136 (1953).
1299. Richter, Rudolph, *Das Konkurrenzproblem im Oligopol*, Volkswirtschaftliche Schriften, Heft 12, Berlin, 1954.
1300. Riedle, H., *Ein Wegbereiter der modernen ökonomischen Theorie*, Winterthur, 1953.
1301. Ritschl, Hans, "Aufgabe und Methode der Standortslehre," *W.A.*, 53:115 (1941).
1302. —— "Wirtschaftsordnung und Wirtschaftspolitik," *W.A.*, 65:218 (1950).
1303. Riviere, A., "Coordinaçion entre la Publicidad y la Venta," *Boletin de Estudios Economicos* (Bilbao), May, 1947, p. 133.
1304. Robertson, D. H., "A Revolutionist's Handbook," *Q.J.E.*, 64:1 (1950).
1305. Robinson, E. A. G., "The Pricing of Manufactured Products," *E.J.*, 55:771 (1950) (Review article on No. 722); "The Pricing of Manufactured Products and the Case against Imperfect Competition: A Rejoinder," 61:429 (1951).
1306. Robinson, Joan, Review of No. 982, *E.J.*, 62:925 (1952).
1307. —— "Imperfect Competition Revisited," *E.J.*, 63:579 (1953).
1308. Rodgers, Raymond and Luedicke, H. E., "Dynamic Competition," *H.B.R.*, 27:237 (1949).
1309. Ronimois, H. E., "The Cost-Profit-Output Relationship in a Soviet Industrial Firm," *C.J.*, 18:173 (1952). Discussion, 19:523 (1953).
1310. Röper, Burkhardt, "Ansätze zu einer Marktformlehre bei J. J. Becher," *S.J.*, 69:591 (1949).
1311. —— "Ansätze zu einer wirklichkeitsnahen und dynamischen Theorie der Monopole und Oligopole," *W.A.*, 67:218 (1951).
1312. —— *Die Konkurrenz und ihre Fehlentwicklungen*, Volkswirtschaftliche Schriften, Heft 6, Berlin, 1952.
1313. Rose, Stanley D., "Your Right to Lower Your Prices," *H.B.R.*, 29, No. 5:90 (1951).
1314. Rosenbluth, G., "Industrial Concentration in Canada and the United States," *C.J.*, 20:332 (1954).
1315. Ross, N. S., "Management and the Size of the Firm," *R.E.Stud.*, 19:148 (1952–53).
1316. Rossi, L., "A proposito di monopolio bilaterale," *R.I.S.S.*, 25:164 (1954).

1317. Rostas, L. *Productivity, Prices, and Distribution in Selected British Industries*, Cambridge, England, 1948.

1318. Rostow, Eugene, "The New Sherman Act: A Positive Instrument of Progress," *University of Chicago Law Review*, 14:567 (1947).

1319. Rothenberg, Jerome, "Welfare Comparisons and Changes in Tastes," *A.E.R.*, 43:885 (1953).

1320. Rothschild, K. W. "Fellner on Competition Among the Few," *Q.J.E.*, 66:128 (1952). (Review article on No. 958.)

1321. —— *The Theory of Wages*, Oxford, 1954.

1322. Rottier, Georges, "Notes sur le maximation du profit," *E.A.*, 4:67 (1951).

1323. —— *Salaires et Prix: Étude de Modèles Statiques*, No. 4 of Cahiers Series B, I.S.E.A., Paris, 1951.

1324. Ruggles, Nancy, "The Welfare Basis of the Marginal Cost Pricing Principle," *R.E.Stud.*, 17:29 (1949–50).

1325. —— "Recent Developments in the Theory of Marginal Cost Pricing," *R.E.Stud.*, 17:107 (1949–50).

1326. Samuelson, Paul A., "Spatial Price Equilibrium and Linear Programming," *A.E.R.*, 42:283 (1952).

1327. Sarda, J., *Una Introducción a la Economía*, Barcelona, 1950.

1328. Sargan, J. D., "A New Approach to the General Distribution Problem," *Metroeconomica*, 3:108 (1951).

1329. Saville, Lloyd, "A Problem in the Economics of Price Control," *S.E.J.*, 18:179 (1951).

1330. Schmidt, Detlef, *Das Quantenproblem: Eine Annäherung des Modells der Vollkommenen Konkurrenz an die Wirklichkeit*, Hamburg, 1949. (Dissertation).

1331. Schmookler, Jacob, "Invention, Innovation, and Competition," *S.E.J.*, 20:380 (1953–54).

1332. Schneider, Erich, "Les tâches actuelles de la recherche sur les oligopoles," *E.A.*, 5:401 (1952).

1333. —— *Pricing and Equilibrium*, New York, 1952. (Translation by T. W. Hutchison of *Einführung in die Wirtschaftstheorie, II. Teil, Wirtschaftspläne und Wirtschaftsliches Gleichgewicht in der Verkehrswirtschaft*.)

1334. —— "Grundlagen der Betriebswirtschaftslehre," *W.A.*, 70:79 (1953).

1335. —— "Der Realismus der Marginalanalyse in der Preistheorie," *W.A.*, 73:38 (1954).

1336. Schumpeter, Joseph A., *History of Economic Analysis*, New York, 1954.

1337. Schwartzman, D., "Mutliple-Company Mergers and the Theory of the Firm," *O.E.P.*, 7:197 (1955).

1338. Schweitzer, Arthur, "A Critique of Countervailing Power," *Social Research*, 21:253 (1954).

1339. Schweizerischen Gessellschaft für Statistik und Volkswirtschaft, Report of meeting at Locarno, Sept. 22–3, 1950, *S.Z.*, 86:427 (1950).

1340. Scitovsky, Tibor, "A New Approach to the Theory of the Firm" (abstract of a paper), *Ecta*, 16:214 (1948).

1341. —— "Ignorance as a Source of Oligopoly Power," *A.E.R.*, 40 (no. 2):48 (May 1950).

1342. —— *Welfare and Competition*, Chicago, 1951.

1343. —— "Two Concepts of External Economies," *J.P.E.*, 62:143 (1954). Discussion, 63:446 (1955).

1344. —— "Monopoly and Competition in Europe and America," *Q.J.E.*, 69:607 (1955). (Review article on No. 861.)

1345. Serrano, J. L., "La Discriminacion de Precios," *Boletin de Estudios Economicos* (Bilbao), May 1947, p. 115.

1346. Shackle, G. L. S., "Professor Keirstead's Theory of Profit," *E.J.*, 64:116 (1954).

1347. Shephard, R. W., *Cost and Production Functions*, Princeton, 1953.

1348. Sherrard, Alfred, "Advertising, Product Variation and the Limits of Economics," *J.P.E.*, 59:126 (1951).

1349. Shubik, Martin, "Information, Theories of Competition, and the Theory of Games," *J.P.E.*, 60:145 (1952).

1350. —— "A Comparison of Treatments of a Duopoly Problem," *Ecta*, 23:417 (1955).

1351. Shillinglaw, Gordon, "The Effects of Requirements Contracts on Competition," *J.I.E.*, 2:147 (1954).

1352. Sieber, Hugo, "Über das Ziel der staatlichen Monopol-, Kartell- und Trustpolitik," *S.Z.*, 88:132 (1952).

1353. Silberston, A., "A Note on Plant Mechanisation and Utilisation," *E.J.*, 63:844 (1953).

1354. —— "The Pricing of Manufactured Products: A Comment," *E.J.*, 61:426 (1951). (See No. 1305.)

1355. Silcock, T. H., "Professor Chamberlin and Mr. Smith on Advertising," *R.E.Stud.*, 15:34 (1947–48).

1356. —— "Advertising Costs in Monopolistic Competition," in *Dundee Economic Essays*, J. K. Eastham, ed., London, Economists' Bookshop, 1955.

1357. Silverman, R., *Advertising Expenditure in 1948*, London, 1951.

1358. Simkin, C. G. F., "Some Aspects and Generalisations of the Theory of Discrimination," *R.E.Stud.*, 15:1 (1947–48).

1359. Simon, Herbert A., "Invention and Cost Reduction in Technological Change," *Ecta*, 17:173 (1949).

1360. —— "A Comparison of Organisation Theories," R. E. Stud., 20:40 (1952–53).

1361. Skeoch, L. A., "The Combines Investigation Act: Its Intent and Application," *C.J.*, 22:17 (1956).

1362. Sloan, Douglas, "A Note on Market Types," *S.A.J.E.*, 20:389 (1952).

1363. Smith, Blackwell, "Effective Competition: Hypothesis for Modernizing the Antitrust Laws," *New York University Law Review*, 26:405 (1951).

1364. Smith, Henry, "Advertising Costs and Equilibrium: A Reply," *R.E.Stud.*, 15:40 (1947–48). (See Nos. 491, 852.)

1365. Smith, Victor E., "Note on the Kinky Oligopoly Demand Curve," *S.E.J.*, 15:205 (1948).

1366. Smithies, Arthur, "Economic Consequences of the Basing Point Decisions," *Harvard Law Review*, 63:308 (1949).

1367. —— "Devaluation with Imperfect Markets and Economic Controls," *R.E.Stat.*, 32:21 (1950).

1368. Sobotka, Stephen P., "Union Influence on Wages: The Construction Industry," *J.P.E.*, 61:127 (1953).

1369. Solo, Carolyn S., "Innovation in the Capitalist Process: A Critique of the Schumpeterian Theory," *Q.J.E.*, 65:417 (1951).

1370. Solomons, David, *Studies in Costing*, London, 1952.

1371. Spengler, Joseph J., "Vertical Integration and Antitrust Policy," *J.P.E.*, 58:347 (1950).

1372. Spraos, J., "Imperfect Competition and the Elasticity of Demand for Imports: A Note," *E.J.*, 66:171 (1956).

1373. von Stackleberg, Heinrich, *The Theory of the Market Economy*, Edinburgh, 1952. Translation by Alan T. Peacock of *Grundlagen der Theoretischen Volkswirtschaftslehre*, 1948. (Also published in Spanish.)

1374. Staudt, Thomas A., "Program for Product Diversification," *H.B.R.*, 32, No. 6:121 (1954).

1375. Steenkamp, W. F. J., "Restrictive Practices and Their Regulation," *S.A.J.E.*, 22:52 (1954).

1376. Steinbrück, K., *Vom Unvollkommenen Markt zur heterogenen Konkurrenz*, Mannheimer Schriftenreihe, Heft 2, Frankfurt am Main, 1951. Also Mainz, 1954.

1377. Steindl, J., *Maturity and Stagnation in American Capitalism*, Oxford, 1952.

1378. Steiner, Peter O., "Program Patterns and Preferences, and the Workability of Competition in Radio Broadcasting," *Q.J.E.*, 66:194 (1952).

1379. Steinkraus, H. W., *Measuring Monopoly: A New Approach*, Statement of Policy of the National Chamber of Commerce on Concentration of Economic Power, 1949.

1380. Stevens, Carl M., "Regarding the Determinants of Union Wage Policy," *R.E.Stat.*, 35:221 (1953).

1381. Stigler, George J., "A Theory of Delivered Price Systems," *A.E.R.*, 39:1143 (1949).

1382. —— *Five Lectures on Economic Problems*, London, 1949. No. 2 on "Monopolistic Competition in Retrospect," and No. 5 on "Competition in the United States."

1383. —— "Monopoly and Oligopoly by Merger," *A.E.R.*, 40 (no. 2): 23, 63 (May 1950).

1384. —— "The Economist Plays with Blocs," *A.E.R.*, 44, (no. 2):7 (May 1954). Discussion.

1385. —— "The Statistics of Monopoly and Merger," *J.P.E.*, 64:33 (1956).

1386. Stocking, George W., "The Economics of Basing Point Pricing," *Law and Contemporary Problems*, Duke University School of Law, Durham, N. C., Spring 1950, p. 159.

1387. —— *Basing Point Pricing and Regional Development*, Chapel Hill, 1954.

1388. —— "Saving Free Enterprise from Its Friends," *S.E.J.*, 19:431 (1953).

1389. —— "The Attorney General's Committee's Report: The Business Man's Guide through Antitrust," *Georgetown Law Journal*, 44:1 (1955).

1390. —— "The Law on Basing Point Pricing: Confusion or Competition," *Journal of Public Law*, Emory University Law School, Georgia, 2:1 (1953).

1391. —— "The Rule of Reason, Workable Competition and Monopoly," *Yale Law Journal*, 64:1107 (1955).

1392. —— "The Rule of Reason, Workable Competition, and the Legality of Trade Association Activities," *University of Chicago Law Review*, 21:527 (1954).

1393. Stocking, G. W. and Mueller, W. F., "The Cellophane Case and the New Competition," *A.E.R.*, 45:29 (1955).

1394. Stocking, G. W. and Watkins, M. W., *Cartels or Competition?*, New York, 1948.

1395. —— *Monopoly and Free Enterprise*, New York, 1951.

1396. Stolper, W. F., Review of Lösch, No. 1164, *A.E.R.*, 33:626 (1943).

1397. Stone, J. R. N., "The Theory of Games," *E.J.*, 58:185 (1948).

1398. Stonier, Alfred W. and Hague, Douglas C., *A Textbook of Economic Theory*, London, New York and Toronto, 1953.

1399. Streeten, Paul, "The Theory of Pricing," *J.N.S.*, 161:161 (1949).

1400. —— "Reserve Cacapity and the Kinked Demand Curve," *R.E.Stud.*, 18:103 (1950–51).

1401. —— "Two Comments on the Articles by Mrs. Paul and Professor Hicks," *O.E.P.*, 7:259 (1955). (See Nos. 1262, 1038.)

1402. Stykolt, Stefan, "Combines Policy: An Economist's Evaluation," *C.J.*, 22:38 (1956).

1403. —— "A Curious Case of Neglect: Marshall on the 'Tangency Solution,'" *C.J.*, 22:251 (1956).

1404. Swerling, Boris C., "Some Limitations of Competitive Equilibrium," *S.E.J.*, 17:33 (1950–51).

1405. Sykes, J., "Diversification of Industry," *E.J.*, 60:697 (1950).

1406. Sznahovich, Josef, "Zur Entwicklung der Preistheorie in Deutschland," *Zeitschrift für Nationalökonomie*, 14:104 (1954).

1407. Takata, Yasuma, "Power and Stagnation," *Osaka Economic Papers*, 4:1 (1955). "Reply" by Fritz Machlup.

1408. Taylor, Horace and Barger, Harold, *The American Economy in Operation*, New York, 1949.

1409. Tennant, R. B., *The American Cigarette Industry*, New Haven, 1950.
1410. Theil, H., "Qualities, Prices and Budget Enquiries," *R.E.Stud.*, 19: 129 (1952–53).
1411. Thirlby, G. F., "Notes on the Maximization Process in Company Administration," *Eca*, 17:266 (1950).
1412. —— "The Economist's Description of Business Behaviour," *Eca*, 19:148 (1952).
1413. Thurlings, L. M., "Enige Toepassingen van de Leer van de Marktvormen," *De Economist*, May, 1950, p. 21.
1414. Tintner, Gerhard, "Homogeneous Systems in Mathematical Economics," *Ecta*, 16:273 (1948). Discussion, 18:60 (1950).
1415. —— "Complementarity and Shifts in Demand," *Metroeconomica*, 4:1 (1951).
1416. Townsend, Harry, "Economic Theory and the Cutlery Trades," *Eca*, 21:224 (1954).
1417. Trieb, Rudolph, "Die Bestimmung des Monopolpunktes beim kollektiven Angebotsmonopol," *S.Z.*, 86:249 (1950).
1418. Triffin, R., "National Central Banking and the International Economy," *R.E.Stud.*, 14:53 (1946–47). (Oligopoly in International Trade.)
1419. Troxel, Emery, "Cost Behaviour and the Accounting Pattern of Public Utility Regulation," *J.P.E.*, 57:413 (1949).
1420. Turner, H. S., "How Much Should a Company Spend on Research?" *H.B.R.*, 32, No. 3:101 (1954).
1421. Ulman, Lloyd, "Union Wage Policy and the Supply of Labor," *Q.J.E.*, 65:237 (1951).
1422. —— "Marshall and Friedman on Union Strength," *R.E.Stat.*, 37: 384 (1955). Comment by Milton Friedman.
1423. Umbreit, M. H., Hunt, E. F. and Kintner, C. U., *Fundamentals of Economics*, New York and London, 1948.
1424. United Nations Economic and Social Council, *Restrictive Business Practices*, New York, 1953.
1425. Uri, P., "Deux Études Récentes de théories économique," *R.E.P.*, 55:71 (1945).
1426. Urquidi, V. L., Review of No. 507, *El Trimestre Economico*, 13: 374 (1946–47). Discussion by Cornejo, Benjamin, and Reply, 13:533 (1946–47).
1427. Vaile, Roland S., "Science Applied to Advertising," *J.M.*, 20:48 (1955).
1428. Valavanis, Stefan, "Lösch on Location," *A.E.R.*, 45:637 (1955). (Review article of No. 1164.)
1429. van Rees, J., "Over de Terminologie in het Marktonderzoek," *De Economist*, June 1950, p. 430.
1430. Vatter, Harold G., "The Closure of Entry in the American Automobile Industry," *O.E.P.*, 4:213 (1952).
1431. Verdoorn, P. J., *Grondslagen en Technisk van de Marktanalyse*, Leiden, 1950.

1432. —— "Marketing from the Producer's Point of View," *J.M.*, 20:221 (1956).

1433. Verhulst, Michel, *Les Industries d'utilité publique: Bases théoriques et statistiques d'une étude rationelle*, Paris, 1952.

1434. Vickrey, William, "Some Objections to Marginal-Cost Pricing," *J.P.E.*, 56:218 (1948).

1435. Vinci, Felicé, "Monopoli e Concorrenze nel Pensiero di Pareto," *G.E.*, 7:689 (1948).

1436. —— *I Fondamenti dell'Economia*, Milano, 1952.

1437. Vining, Rutledge, "Delimitation of Economic Areas: Statistical Conceptions of the Spatial Structure of an Economic System," *Journal of the American Statistical Association*, March 1953, p. 44.

1438. —— "A Description of Certain Spatial Aspects of an Economic System," *Economic Development and Cultural Change*, Jan. 1955, p. 160.

1439. Vito, F., ed., *Gli aggruppamenti di imprese nelle economia corporativa*, Universita Cattolica del Sacro Cuore, Milano, 1939.

1440. Voss-Lytton, Annie, "Étude concrète de l'effet de domination," *E.A.*, 8:485 (1955).

1441. Vuillemin, Jules, "Les syndicats ouvriers et les salaires," *E.A.*, 5: 261 (1952).

1442. Wadsworth, H. E., "Utility Cloth and Clothing Scheme," *R.E.Stud.*, 16:82 (1949–50).

1443. Wald, Abraham, "On Some Systems of Equations of Mathematical Economics," *Ecta*, 19:368 (1951).

1444. Walker, Q. Forrest, "Some Principles of Department Store Pricing," *J.M.*, 14:529 (1950).

1445. Wedding, Nugent, "Advertising and Public Relations," *J.B.U.C.*, 23:173 (1950).

1446. Weintraub, Sidney, *Price Theory*, New York, 1949.

1447. —— "The Theory of Consumer Monopsony," *R.E.Stud.*, 17:168 (1949–50).

1448. —— "Note on the Limitations of Planning Curves," *S.E.J.*, 17:187 (1950–51).

1449. —— "The Theory of the Consumer Price Level," *C.J.*, 18:163 (1952).

1450. —— "Revised Doctrines of Competition," *A.E.R.*, 45 (no. 2):463 (May 1955). Discussion.

1451. Weldon, J. C., "The Multi-Product Firm," *C.J.*, 14:176 (1948).

1452. Wells, H. A., *Monopoly and Social Control*, Washington, D. C., 1952.

1453. Welsh, Edward C., "Government Aid to Business Expansion," *A.E.R.*, 42 (no. 2):418 (May 1952). Discussion.

1454. Westfield, Fred M., "Marginal Analysis, Multi-Plant Firms, and Business Practice: an Example," *Q.J.E.*, 69:253 (1955).

1455. Weston, J. Fred, "Enterprise and Profit," *J.B.U.C.*, 22:141 (1949).

1456. —— *The Role of Mergers in the Growth of Large Firms*, Berkeley, 1953.

1457. —— "The Profit Concept and Theory: A Restatement," *J.P.E.*, 62:152 (1954).

1458. Weststrate, C. *Theorie van drie Stelsels van Sociaaleconomisch Leven*, Leiden, 1948.

1459. Whitin, T. M. and Peston, M. H., "Random Variations, Risk, and Returns to Scale," *Q.J.E.*, 68:603 (1954).

1460. Whitney, Simon N., "Errors in the Concept of Countervailing Power," *J.B.U.C.*, 26:238 (1953).

1461. —— "Vertical Disintegration in the Motion Picture Industry," *A.E.R.*, 45 (no. 2):491 (May 1955). Discussion.

1462. Wickham, Sylvain, "Observations sur l'Intégration et la diversification des entreprises," *R.E.*, July 1953, p. 485.

1463. —— "Note sur l'étude et la politique du développement des firmes," *E.A.*, 7:545 (1954).

1464. Wilcox, Clair, "On the Alleged Ubiquity of Oligopoly," *A.E.R.*, 40 (no. 2):67, 100 (May 1950). Discussion.

1465. —— "Concentration of Power in the American Economy," *H.B.R.*, 28, No. 6:54 (1950).

1466. —— "The Verdict on Antitrust and Its Significance," *A.E.R.*, 46 (no. 2):490 (May 1956). Discussion.

1467. Wiles, P. "Empirical Research and the Marginal Analysis," *E.J.*, 60:515 (1950). See also 64:350 (1954); 65:351 (1955).

1468. Willeke, Franz-Ulrich, "Betrachtungen zur Unvollkommenheit des Kreditmarktes," *J.N.S.*, 167:241 (1955).

1469. Williams, B. R., "Types of Competition and the Theory of Employment," *O.E.P.*, 1 (new series): 121 (1949).

1470. Wilson, J. R., "Maximization and Business Behaviour," *E.R.*, 28:29 (1952).

1471. Wilson, T., "Private Enterprise and the Theory of Value," *The Manchester School*, 16:165 (1948).

1472. —— "The Inadequacy of the Theory of the Firm as a Branch of Welfare Economics," *O.E.P.*, 4:18 (1952).

1473. Wilson, T. and Andrews, P. W. S., eds., *Oxford Studies in the Price Mechanism*, Oxford, 1951. Contains a reprint of No. 154 and a new essay, "Industrial Analysis in Economics," by P. W. S. Andrews.

1474. Winding Pederson, H., "Konkurrence-begraensning og monopolkontrol," *N.T.*, 91:299 (1953).

1475. Wolfe, J. N., "The Problem of Oligopoly," *R.E.Stud.*, 21:181 (1953–54). Comment by J. H. Davies, 22:228 (1954–55). Reply by J. N. Wolfe, 23:163 (1955–56).

1476. —— "The Representative Firm," *E.J.*, 64:337 (1954). Comment by J. H. Davies and rejoinder by J. N. Wolfe, 65:710 (1955).

1477. Wolman, L., *Industry-Wide Bargaining*, New York, 1948.

1478. Woodruff, W., "Early Entrepreneurial Behaviour in Relation to Costs and Prices," *O.E.P.*, 5:41 (1953).

1479. Worcester, D. A., Jr., "Justifiable Price 'Discrimination' under Conditions of Natural Monopoly," *A.E.R.*, 38:382 (1948).
1480. —— *Fundamentals of Political Economy*, New York, 1953.
1481. Wright, David McCord, "Towards Coherent Antitrust," *Virginia Law Review*, 35:665 (1949).
1482. —— *A Key to Modern Economics*, New York, 1954.
1483. Yamey, B. S., "The Price Policy of Co-operative Societies," *Eca*, 17:23 (1950).
1484. —— "Notes on Resale Price Maintenance," *Eca*, 17:254 (1950).
1485. Yolande, Sister Mary, "Some Economic and Ethical Considerations for Legislation Protecting the Consumer," *Review of Social Economy*, March, 1949.
1486. Zamora, Francisco, "Monopolio y Monopsonio," *El Trimestre Economico* (Mexico), 20:1 (1953).
1487. Zellner, Arnold, "An Interesting General Form for a Production Function," *Ecta*, 19:188 (1951).
1488. Zeuthen, F., "Nogle Bidrag til Teorien om de Store Virksomheders Priser," *N.T.T.O.*, 6:15 (1940).
1489. —— "Betrachtungsweisen und Massstäbe in der Ökonomie," *Zeitschrift für Ökonometrie*, 1:14 (1950).
1490. —— "Note sur le Developpement de la Théorie de l'Oligopole après vingt-cinq ans," *E.A.*, 8:327 (1955).
1491. —— "La Théorie du Monopole Bilatéral et Multilatéral toujours à l'ordre du jour," *E.A.*, 8:331 (1955).
1492. —— *Economic Theory and Method*, Cambridge, Mass., 1955. (A translation, revision and enlargement of No. 687.)
1493. Zimmerman, L. J., *Geschiedenis van het economisch denken*, The Hague, 1950.
1494. —— "Die Bedeutung der Nachfrage- und Angebotselastizität für die Marktform; Versuch einer dynamischen Theorie der Marktformen, *Zeitschrift für Ökonometrie*, 1:63 (June, 1950).
1495. —— *The Propensity to Monopolize*, Amsterdam, 1952.
1496. Zipf, George K., "A Note on Brand-names and Related Economic Phenomena," *Ecta*, 18:260 (1950).
1497. —— "Quantitative Analysis of Sears, Roebuck and Company's Catalogue," *J.M.*, 15:1 (1950).

INDEX